About Previous Books in the Series

"One of the best books on programming I have come across."
—**Philip Rezk, Ridgefield, CT**

"I like the easy-to-follow progression from basic to complex topics with thorough explanation of each topic."
—**Michael Mills, Boca Raton, FL**

"Gave me everything I needed to know..."
—**Steve Dehues, Killeen, TX**

"An excellent book for anyone trying to learn C in a few days."
—**Mohammad Zamad, Norman, OK**

"It is wonderful that you can use the hands-on approach to learning."
—**Neil Laporte, Gatineau, Quebec**

"An easy-to-understand programming book with many helpful hints."
—**Ronald White, Newtown, PA**

"I liked the author's exceptional, readable writing style."
—**Jason Lee, Canada**

"I liked the author's experience and the fact that it's an IDG book... I knew right away I was buying a great book!"
—**Paul Joseph Walker, Greenville, RI**

"Simple, comprehensive... everybody can understand..."
—**Ural Gunaydin, Australia**

"Brilliant approach to teaching."
—**Paul Dugas, Richford, VT**

"[This book] explains stuff in a few paragraphs what others couldn't do in a whole book."
—**Robert Doucet, Toronto, Ontario**

About Tom Swan, Series Editor

"Everything that's done by Tom Swan is satisfaction guaranteed."
— **Albert Lee, Indonesia**

"Tom's writing style makes even dense programming issues crystal clear."
—**Brett Salter, President, The Periscope Company**

"Tom Swan makes learning C simple and easy."
—**Brian Mayfield, Silverdale, CT**

What I like most about this book: "It's by Tom Swan."
—**David Peng, La Jolla, CA**

Learn C++ Today!

by Martin L. Rinehart

A Division of IDG Books Worldwide, Inc.

Foster City, CA • Chicago, IL • Indianapolis, IN • Braintree, MA • Dallas, TX

Learn C++ Today!

Published by

IDG Books Worldwide, Inc.

An International Data Group Company

919 East Hillsdale Boulevard, Suite 400

Foster City, CA 94404

Library of Congress Catalog Card No.: 95-75058

ISBN 1-56884-310-0

Printed in the United States of America

First Printing, August, 1995

10 9 8 7 6 5 4 3 2 1

Distributed in the United States by IDG Books Worldwide, Inc.

is a registered trademark of IDG Books Worldwide, Inc.

Welcome to the world of IDG Books Worldwide.

IDG Books Worldwide, Inc. is a subsidiary of International Data Group, the world's largest publisher of computer-related information and the leading global provider of information services on information technology. IDG was founded more than 25 years ago and now employs more than 7,500 people worldwide. IDG publishes more than 235 computer publications in 67 countries (see listing below). More than fifty million people read one or more IDG publications each month.

Launched in 1990, IDG Books Worldwide is today the #1 publisher of best-selling computer books in the United States. We are proud to have received 3 awards from the Computer Press Association in recognition of editorial excellence, and our best-selling ...*For Dummies*™ series has more than 18 million copies in print with translations in 24 languages. IDG Books, through a recent joint venture with IDG's Hi-Tech Beijing, became the first U.S. publisher to publish a computer book in the People's Republic of China. In record time, IDG Books has become the first choice for millions of readers around the world who want to learn how to better manage their businesses.

Our mission is simple: Every IDG book is designed to bring extra value and skill-building instructions to the reader. Our books are written by experts who understand and care about our readers. The knowledge base of our editorial staff comes from years of experience in publishing, education, and journalism — experience which we use to produce books for the '90s. In short, we care about books, so we attract the best people. We devote special attention to details such as audience, interior design, use of icons, and illustrations. And because we use an efficient process of authoring, editing, and desktop publishing our books electronically, we can spend more time ensuring superior content and spend less time on the technicalities of making books.

You can count on our commitment to deliver high-quality books at competitive prices on topics consumers want to read about. At IDG, we value quality, and we have been delivering quality for more than 25 years. You'll find no better book on a subject than an IDG book

John J. Kilcullen

John Kilcullen
President and CEO
IDG Books Worldwide, Inc.

From the Publisher

Learn C++ Today! is part of the *Learn Today!* book series, brought to you by Programmers Press. The designers of the *Learn Today!* series understand that there are numerous obstacles to learning how to program. So we worked with one of the industry's finest authors, Tom Swan, to develop a learning method for you, the beginner programmer. *Learn Today!* is the result of extensive research and testing on the part of Tom Swan and IDG Books Worldwide.

The formula for the book is simple: Learn by doing. It's been proven that a hands-on approach not only speeds learning, but also helps you to remember what you learn. When you can perform an action and see the results, you'll remember what you did *and* why you did it.

Professional programmers often say that reading about programming is nice, but writing code is better. The fact is it's fundamental to your success. That's why each book includes a disk with software. This software is not casual filler; it is strategically linked to the content and topic of a book so you can begin programming immediately.

We believe that the author has the experience to teach programming as well as the skill to present complex topics to beginner programmers. We know that you will benefit from the informal, hands-on approach. When you finish this book, you will not only understand how a program works, but you'll have written several programs, and you'll be prepared to move onto the next programming level. So, turn the page and begin learning today!

Chris Williams

Chris Williams
Publisher, IDG Books

For More Information...

For general information on IDG Books in the U.S., including information on discounts and premiums, contact IDG Books at 800-434-3422.

For information on where to purchase IDG's books outside the U.S., contact Christina Turner at 415-655-3022.

For information on translations, contact Marc Jeffrey Mikulich, Foreign Rights Manager, at IDG Books Worldwide; fax number: 415-655-3295.

For sales inquiries and special prices for bulk quantities, contact Tony Real at 800-434-3422 or 415-655-3048.

For information on using IDG's books in the classroom and ordering examination copies, contact Jim Kelly at 800-434-2086.

Learn C++ Today! is distributed in Canada by Macmillan of Canada, a Division of Canada Publishing Corporation; by Computer and Technical Books in Miami, Florida, for South America and the Caribbean; by Longman Singapore in Singapore, Malaysia, Thailand, and Korea; by Toppan Co. Ltd. in Japan; by Asia Computerworld in Hong Kong; by Woodslane Pty. Ltd. in Australia and New Zealand; and by Transword Publishers Ltd. in the U.K. and Europe.

About the Author

This is Martin L. Rinehart's sixth book. He's lost count of the articles he's published.

Marty, as he's known among friends, learned BASIC from its co-inventer, Professor John Kemeny, at Dartmouth College in 1965. He's been programming ever since.

Languages he's used professionally include BASIC, PL/I, Fortran, APL, Xbase, C, PC assembler and C++.

He's worked as a freelance programmer, manager of the Quantitative Analysis group at a major investment bank, Product Marketing Manager at a timesharing company, founder and CEO of a PC software company and, most recently, as an independent author and consultant specializing in object-oriented, client/server applications.

When Marty is not at the computer keyboard you can find him at his piano's keyboard or out on a local soccer field. If you can't find him around home—and it's warm out—he's probably backpacking in the mountains, and when it snows, he'll be skiing down them.

Dedication

This book is dedicated to Robert Rinehart, known to his friends as Bob, and, to a lucky few of us, as Dad.

Acknowledgments

A book is a big project and a team effort, not just the work of the author. These are some of the people who deserve some of the credit.

Series Editor Tom Swan pioneered the concepts and created the series. Amy Pedersen (senior acquisitions editor at IDG Books) and Matt Wagner (my agent) put this project and author together. They're the book's fathers.

In addition to your author, the book's mothers are Bob Campbell, manuscript editor, Ellie Moradeshaghi, technical editor, and Denise Peters and Jim Markham, project editors. I was lucky to have such a fine team. The book's mid-wives are listed on the Credits page.

One extra word about Ellie: If you call Borland for technical support on C++, Ellie may be the person who helps you. I doubt she found every bug I wrote, but she certainly reduced the critter count. We all owe her.

Special thanks too are due to my personal support team here on Conklin Road. Thanks guys, I couldn't have done it without you.

The publisher would like to give special thanks to Patrick McGovern, without whom this book would not have been possible.

Credits

Group Publisher and Vice President
Christopher J. Williams

Publishing Director
John Osborn

Senior Acquisitions Manager
Amorette Pedersen

Editorial Director
Anne Marie Walker

Production Director
Beth A. Roberts

Project Editors
Jim Markham
Denise Peters

Manuscript Editor
Robert Campbell

Technical Editor
Ellie Moradeshaghi

Composition and Layout
Benchmark Productions, Inc.

Indexer
Elizabeth Cunningham

Book Design
Benchmark Productions, Inc.

Cover Design
Cynthia Busch

Contents at a Glance

Table of Contents

Introduction

Since many people don't read introductions, the bulk of the introductory material (which covers, for instance, installing and using the accompanying C++ development system) is included in Chapter 1. You can skip straight past there without missing too much.

I want to comment on how you can get the most out of this book. And, I want to provide a small hint to reward your perseverence. First, this book is all about hitting the keyboard, since I don't know any other way to master a programming language—especially a large, powerful, sophisticated one like C++.

I'm sure you know that you can't really learn C++ in one day, since it's a nontrivial language. What you can do—and do *Today!*—is make a plan.

Today! you can follow through Chapter 1, get installed, and get ready. Tomorrow you can work through Chapter 2, working out your initial "Hello, World!" program. Then you can plan on perhaps 10 pages an hour. If you can give this book two hours each evening . . .

You get the idea. Make a plan, set a personal schedule, and stick to it. By the way, you'll make faster headway if you measure your progress in pages per hour, at least in the early parts, where there's more reading and less programming. Later on, your learning may speed up, but your progress through the book will slow down. You'll be doing lots of programming and very little reading. But you'll actually be programming in C++, which is the point, isn't it?

Now that hint: A recent weekend guest taught us a nice game of solitaire, played with two decks. It takes a lot more thinking than the normal kind. It was the sort of game I wished I had on my computer.

Really, shuffling two decks at once is a nuisance with physical cards. You never get a really random selection. And computers are so good about things like keeping the face-up cards neatly in rows. So guess what I did over the next week? That's right. I wrote a program, and it worked out well. It wasn't the best code I ever wrote, but it's sure been used a lot in our family. If I can ever talk my wife into doing the artwork for a deck of cards, I'll make it a Windows game.

Since we finish our book's main project in Chapter 14, can you figure out what the code is I sneaked in as the Chapter 15 listings? The code's relevant to Chapter 15, since it shows a completely worked-out version of the mouse routines that are sketched there. It's also a lot of fun. You'll need to know how to use the multifile project building capability of TCLite to turn the source into a complete program. That comes in Chapter 6, so you don't have to wait too long.

When you finish Chapter 6, take a short break to explore CHP15.ZIP. Tell your boss you're working on the details of the mouse interrupts. And if you're having fun while you're at it, that's my way of saying "Thanks" to you, too.

Welcome!

This chapter is your introduction to this book and your roadmap to learning C++. Every chapter in this book starts with a brief statement of what we're going to do and ends with a summary of what we've done. This is what we're going to do in Chapter 1:

▶ We'll list our goals and the prerequisites so you'll know if this book is for you.

▶ I'll discuss how I learned C++.

▶ We'll consider how this book will help you avoid the mistakes I made.

▶ You'll install TCLite.

▶ We'll learn a little about the history of C and C++.

These bullet points give you a roadmap for the trip just ahead. Use them to plan your journey. (If your friend Sue just told you all about how she's used this book to learn C++, and then she helped you install TCLite, you can skip right ahead to the history.)

Let's get started.

chapter

1

Learning C++

I think I know why you're here. You want to learn C++. You already know some programming, perhaps some BASIC, COBOL, Fortran, or Xbase, but you've decided that C++ is for you.

You know that the compilers and interpreters for the other languages you've used were written in C++. You know that C++ systems, such as the TCLite system that comes with this book, are also written in C++. In fact, there's very little major PC, Macintosh, or UNIX software written in any other language these days.

GOALS AND PREREQUISITES

C++ grew from C, a language invented for system programming. While C++ added many detailed improvements to C, its biggest improvement was the addition of support for object-oriented programming (OOP). Today, objects are considered a key part of all major programming efforts, and for good reasons.

You've decided that you want to become one of the people who know C++ and OOP for professional reasons (C++ programmers make more money!) or for personal reasons (C++ programs run fast!).

If you want to learn C++, this is what you'll need:

▶ A '386 or better PC

▶ Two or three megabytes of spare disk space

▶ A background in any sort of programming

▶ A serious desire to learn C++

And it helps if you like playing around with computers.

This is an equal opportunity book, of course. Persons of all ages, races, sexes, and nationalities are equally welcome. The privileged upper-computing class with 90 MHz Pentiums is welcome. Impoverished college students who had to scrounge to get their hands on a 25MHz '386 are welcome, too. (TCLite runs nicely on a '386.) Desire and a sense of fun are what's important.

Programming should be fun. It's not for everyone, but then again, this isn't a book for everyone. It's a book for people who want to learn C++. It's even a book for people who think C++ is difficult.

HOW HARD IS IT?

I tried to learn C++ three times, with little success. And I've learned and worked professionally in dozens of programming languages. Alphabetically, they include APL, assembler, BASIC, C, dBASE. . . . Well, you get the idea.

Each time I tried C++, I bought a different book and diligently worked through all the sample code and read all the text. It didn't work. By the time I was learning the syntax for inheritance, I was forgetting the syntax for operator overloading.

At the end of each book, I went back to Borland C++ or Microsoft's Visual C++ and tried to do some useful work. I couldn't.

Then I figured out what I was doing wrong. Using Borland C++ or Visual C++, you have to deal with C++, with a powerful but daunting set of visual programming tools, with the Windows API, and with a class library (OWL or MFC) that is a whole subject in itself. It's too much at once.

Finally, I realized the obvious: I needed to learn one thing at a time. I downgraded to Turbo C++ for DOS so that I could write simple programs, worrying about C++ alone. Then I picked a project that I had been fiddling with for a while, one that worked better in text mode than it would in Windows, and I set out to complete it in C++.

The Turbo C++ integrated development environment (IDE) didn't take a lot of learning. It did a lot more to help than to hinder my work, even on a first project. Working one step at a time, I got my project running. By the time I got to the end of it, I had learned enough about C++ and OOP to rewrite it, but that's about what you'd expect for a first project.

So I rewrote it using what I'd learned, and then I was off to the races. All the strange concepts were becoming part of my working vocabulary. Most important, I was enjoying my work.

I had discovered two things, both completely obvious after the fact. First, if you're learning C++, you shouldn't try to learn the Windows API and several other complex things at the same time. Second, OOP and C++ are two sides to one coin. OOP is tough to explain, but it's obvious when you see it in action in a real project. At that point, you won't need anyone to explain the theory.

LEARN C++ TODAY!

The *Learn . . . Today!* series was originally christened *Type & Learn.* Tom Swan, Series Editor, developed the method: Type Once, Learn Forever.

> You've probably done this. At the grocery store, you reach into your pocket and discover that you left your carefully prepared list on the kitchen table. You don't have time to return home, so you complete your shopping from memory. To your amazement, you manage to purchase nearly every item on the list. How is that possible?

> The answer is obvious: Just writing things down improves your ability to learn and remember. (Tom Swan, *Type & Learn C,* [Boston: IDG Programmers Press, 1994], p.4.)

To implement that simple concept, Tom didn't put full listings on disk, as nearly everyone else does. He put listings on disk minus key parts. These parts were highlighted in the text so you would enter them yourself. Entering the code is like writing your grocery list, of course.

Almost as important as getting the code right are the mistakes you make. When you don't quite understand, you get things wrong, and the compiler gives you error messages. You look at the message; you look at what you entered; you look at the listing in the book; you learn from your mistakes.

I've taken Tom's concept one step further. After our very first step, writing a "Hello, world!" program, we'll get to work on a programming project, a Tiny Editor. I'll explain what you need to know about C++ to implement this project. That way we won't need to spend any time on the theory of, for example, function overloading.

Instead of reading about the theory, you'll implement an overloaded function and put it to work. By the second or third time you've used overloading, it won't be a strange concept at all—it will be a technique you use to get your work done.

Each disk listing will have the complete program file, excluding the part you're adding at the current step. You'll add the new code, compile, and run. (Or maybe compile, fix, compile, fix, compile, and run.)

You can cheat, too. Sneak a look at Listing 6 when you're on step 5, and you'll find all the step 5 code already entered. Complete source files are on disk for the end of every chapter, too, in case you get lost along the way.

Late in the book you'll find some longer listings for when you may want to save yourself the trouble of entering the code. Go ahead and cheat if you're confident that you understand the points we're working on. Most of the listings you enter are short enough that typing all the new code will be faster than working with the disk copies, though. Entering most of the code yourself is the fastest way to learn C++, of course.

Another benefit of working a real project is that we'll use the most common parts of C++ repeatedly and we'll use the less common parts rarely, if at all. The work you'll do will be naturally focused on the important parts of the language, because it's the work you need to do to complete a project.

No project will make use of every bit of C++, of course, but don't worry about that. In the last chapter I'll give you a short review of the topics we've missed. Once you start doing productive work in a language, it's easy to pick up the small points.

Although it's not the main point, there's an additional advantage to this project. Your Tiny Editor will be a reasonably well-featured, multiwindowing, multifile editor, not just a toy. Unlike any other text editor, since it's your own work, it will behave exactly as you've always wanted a text editor to behave.

We programmers all take our text editors seriously. We all want one that works exactly the way we want. This time, you won't need to make a single compromise with the way someone else thinks a text editor should work. It's yours, so you'll do it your way.

This is the book that I wish I'd had when I first tried to learn C++.

INSTALLING TCLITE

Beginning in this section, I'll use four icons to set off material that I want you to notice.

WARNING

Warnings, like this one, should be taken seriously. Your disk *is* backed up, isn't it?

NOTE

Notes such as this add further technical details. You can skip them entirely or stop and mull them over slowly.

T I P

Tips like this are for saving time. You'll want to know that Ctrl+F9 can be quicker than clicking on the menus.

H I N T

Hints are like tips, but they focus on subtle points you might miss or not realize if you didn't think about a topic.

In addition to these icons, we'll use step-by-step lists, such as the one that follows, when a cookbook approach is appropriate.

To install TCLite, do the following:

S T E P   B Y   S T E P

1. Make a backup copy of the disk in the back of this book.

2. Log on to a hard drive (C:, D:, or your choice) where you'll be working. You'll need about three megabytes of available space.

3. Plug the disk at the back of this book into a drive. If it's not your A: drive, substitute your choice in what follows.

4. Type "A:INSTALL" at the DOS prompt and read on while your computer does the rest.

W A R N I N G

You must be logged onto a hard drive to run INSTALL. Don't log onto A: (or another 3.5" drive) and type "install." Follow the steps as given and you'll have no problem.

Is your computer working hard? Good. Here's what it's doing. First, it makes a directory, \TCLITE. Then it makes three subdirectories, \TCLITE\BIN, \TCLITE\INCLUDE, and \TCLITE\LIB.

The BIN subdirectory will hold the executables (as in BINaries) and the online help. These will be PKUNZIPped from BIN.ZIP.

The INCLUDE subdirectory is populated from INCLUDE.ZIP. It will hold all the standard .H files. If you don't know what a .H (as in Header) file does, rest assured that by the end of this book they'll be your friends.

The LIB subdirectory, built from LIB.ZIP, holds library code. Nothing in C++ runs without library startup code, math, and so on. If your installation goes correctly, TCLite will never again bother you about these libraries, however. You can forget them, but you can't work without them.

It's Not All Installed

All the listings are still on the floppy disk. CHP02.ZIP has all the listings from Chapter 2, and so on. If you've got lots of hard disk space, make a directory (don't use \TCLITE) and copy CHP*.ZIP from the floppy. If you've got lots of disk space, you can even unzip all the listings right now.

All the files for Chapter 2 start with 02, and so on. The second listing in Chapter 5, Listing 5-2, is 05-02.CPP. (Listing 5-15 is a header file, so it's 05-15.H.) Listing 05TEWIN.CPP is TEWIN.CPP as it stands at the end of Chapter 5.

Another thing you can do with these files is forget they exist. Put the floppy away and do all your work from the listings printed in the book. That's what I'd do if I were you.

Checking TCLite's Installation

Change to the TCLite directory and create a batch file that looks like this:

```
:TC.BAT          ←——— File name
```

```
@echo off
\TCLITE\BIN\TC %1 %2 %3 %4 %5
```

file content →

Then run the batch file with *TC* (no command line parameters, yet). Click Options|Environment, and your screen should look like the one shown in Figure 1-1.

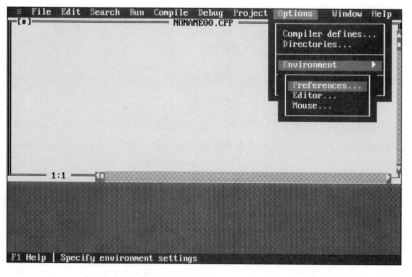

Figure 1-1: Setting options in TCLite.

Click Preferences, and you'll get the dialog window shown in Figure 1-2. Set up yours exactly as you see in Figure 1-2.

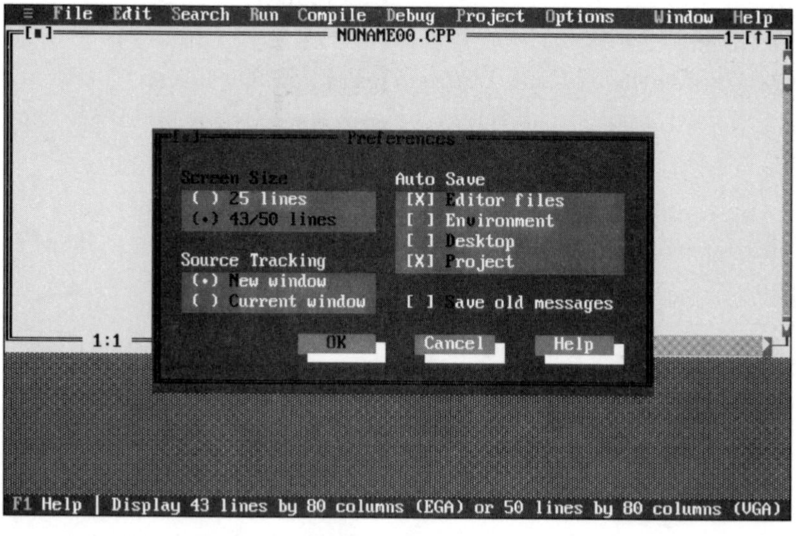

Figure 1-2: Selecting preferences for your TCLite work.

Once you are set up this way, click OK. Then click Options|Save to make this selection permanent.

N O T E

In this book all the figures will show TCLite in 25-line mode. This makes them more readable on the printed page. In programming work, 50-line mode is preferable unless you have a very poor video setup (such as an old laptop).

Before you go on, check your directories, as set in Options|Directories. They should be set as shown in Figure 1-3.

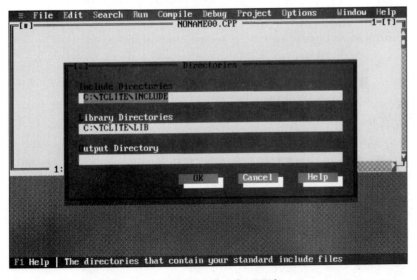

Figure 1-3: Setting your directories in TCLite.

If they aren't set this way, change them, click OK, and then click Options|Save again.

You should be ready to run at this point. Before you go on, spend some time looking through the menus. Then press F1 and Shift+F1 to tour the extensive online help. TCLite's a lot more than you'd have any reason to expect from a product bound with a book.

W A R N I N G

There's one limitation to TCLite: You can't run TCLite .EXEs without first loading TCLite. This is no problem when you're learning C++, but you'll want a full C++ environment by the time you finish this book.

When you've got a good idea what's in TCLite, exit (choose File | Quit or press Alt+X) and go on to the next section.

THE GENESIS OF C++

A little bit of historical perspective is a good thing. Since I know that you're itching to get into actual programming, I'll keep this brief. We'll start with Series Editor Tom Swan's history of C++'s predecessor language, C.

A BRIEF HISTORY OF C

▶ Knowing some of C's history will give you a better appreciation of the language and why it has evolved into its present form as explained in this book. C was originally designed as a symbolic code that formalized programming practices in use at that time. In other words, C was created to do what was needed and a little bit more. Today, C remains true to its origins. It is a language written by programmers for programmers, and its terse design is still one of its key strengths.

In 1978, C blossomed into what was to become the most popular computer programming language ever. That year saw the publication of *The C Programming Language*, written by Brian W. Kernighan and Dennis M. Ritchie, a book that established the standard by which all C compilers were judged for almost a decade.

That version of C, known today as *K&R C*, was the direct descendant of a C dialect written by Dennis Ritchie for the UNIX operating system running on DEC PDP-11 computer. Actually, UNIX, its tools, and C were developed more or less simultaneously, with each part in the system inspiring changes to the others. C literally grew up with UNIX, but the C language has since left the nest and is now available on just about every computer system around.

K&R C traces its ancestry back even further to another language called BCPL (Basic Combined Programming Language) written by Martin Richards in 1969 at Cambridge University. As computer languages go, BCPL was extremely low level—that is, its elements corresponded directly to the computer's architecture. In 1970, Ken Thompson wrote a BCPL-like language for an early UNIX operating system running on a DEC PDP-7 computer. In the spirit of the times, when small memory cores forced programmers to jealously conserve RAM, Thompson named the language B, "saving" three letters.

BCPL and B were *typeless* languages in which variables were simply words in memory. The languages served the needs of their times, and were still in heavy use ten years after their creation. As software tasks grew more demanding, however, it became clear that something better had to be invented. Programmers needed a *structural programming language* with *data types* that would enable them to use integers (whole numbers like 100 and -99), floating-point values (fractional values like 3.14159 and -0.5), and characters (letters, digits, and punctuation), in relatively safe ways.

That language was K&R C, which added functions, integers, floating-point values, characters, dozens of operators, and other components to B. As the story goes, the name C was borrowed from the second letter in BCPL. Others say C's name arose because C is alphabetically "higher" than B, raising the question among trivia buffs of whether C's next incarnation will be named *D* or *P*. (C's authors won't say.)

Whatever the source of its name, K&R C was a smash hit. Soon after the publication of *The C Programming Language*, C compilers began to pop up like buds in a flower show. Possibly due to the book's existence, most of these implementations were largely compatible, meaning that a program written for one computer required only minor changes to be transferred, or *ported*, to another system. C's widespread use and its relative compatibility among implementations led directly to the language's next and more formal stage.

In recognition of C's growing use—and, probably, in fear of losing control over the de facto standard that had evolved independently among C compiler authors—in 1983, the American National Standards Institute charged the Programming Language Committee X3J11 to adopt a rigorous standard for C implementors to follow. In five years of grueling work and dueling egos, the committee accomplished the impossible: they cleaned C's house of quirks, conflicts, and ambiguities, and they added a few carefully selected features, resisting attempts to bloat the language with capabilities from countless proposals received during the evaluation period.

The result was ANSI C, a standard that remains virtually unchanged since its adoption in 1988. The publication of the ANSI C standard also marked the end of K&R C, which quickly faded from the scene and is rarely used today. Nevertheless, many compilers continue to support the older K&R syntax and ANSI C, among them the version of Turbo C++ packed with this book. If you run across older K&R code, you can use it with Turbo C++. New programs, however, should be written to conform to the ANSI C standard as are all programs in this book. ◀

The C language and its companion operating system UNIX spread from their home in Bell Labs to find use around the world on a huge variety of computers. It was easy to bring up a subset of C on a new computer. With a subset you could compile a full-featured C implementation, and with full C you could compile the UNIX operating system. The combination was immensely popular.

Of course, C wasn't a perfect language. One reason is that there's no such thing as a perfect language. COBOL is good in business, and Fortran is good in engineering; languages that try to do everything, such as PL/I, haven't really succeeded.

But there were specific problems with C that were discovered in use. Some were minor annoyances. For instance, the syntax for a comment in C was a nuisance to type.

And there was a big problem that appeared as software evolved—C didn't support object-oriented programming. This brings us up to the work of Bjarne Stroustrup.

Bjarne Stroustrup, a computer scientist programming in C at Bell Labs, was working on problems he thought might be better handled using the techniques of object-oriented programming. He made a simple decision that proved wildly successful—he decided to add OOP features to the C language. In 1980 he published a paper on a language he called "C with Classes."

By 1984 that language was extended and named C++. It was a simple language to adopt if you already knew the underlying C language. The quality of Stroustrup's C++ extensions was matched by the intelligence of his implementation.

Stroustrup used C to write a compiler, which he called CFRONT. The CFRONT compiler read C++ and wrote C. This implementation meant that anyone with a C compiler could compile using CFRONT. Since CFRONT wrote C, not machine code, it was available everywhere C was running. It also guaranteed that the resultant code was no less efficient than C code.

The rest, as the saying goes, is history. C++ caught on everywhere C was in use, since OOP is one of those advances that people are never be able to live without once they try them. It's easier to write object-oriented code than it is to explain the theory.

I'd be remiss if I didn't add that Stroustrup made many very intelligent choices when it came to fixing minor details. The new C++ comments, for example, are very easy to type.

SUMMARY

C++ is an excellent language for professional programming and for serious hobbyists. This book is written for people who want to learn C++.

We won't repeat the mistakes I made, trying to learn C++ along with Windows programming and a huge class library. We'll work in DOS and in text mode so we can focus on learning to write object-oriented programs in C++.

We'll be using Series Editor Tom Swan's approach, which gives you listings with critical parts omitted. You enter the omitted parts and then compile and run your code. You learn through writing good C++, and through the mistakes you make.

We'll be working on a project called Tiny Editor, which we'll follow throughout the book. By working on a project, you'll see how the concepts of OOP are implemented in C++, and how they work in a real system. You'll see how C++ works in practice, not in theory.

You'll also finish the book with a very nice, reasonably full-featured text editor that is very small, is very fast, and works exactly as you always wanted a text editor to work.

To get ready to begin programming, which is our job in Chapter 2, we installed TCLite, a complete C++ programming system.

Finally, we paused for a brief history of C++ and its predecessor language, C. If you hate ads, turn right to Chapter 2 and dive in.

If you've got a moment, I want to plug a product for Borland. They didn't ask me to say this, by the way.

I've used Borland's products for many years. The DOS version of Turbo C++ is one of my favorites. TCLite is a modified version of Turbo C++ version 1.01. There is a coupon at the back of this book that gives you a super deal on your own copy of TC++—it saves you more than the price of this book. If you sent it in today, you'd have a full TC++, in the latest version, by the time you finished this book.

I've got other, bigger C++ products. But DOS TC++ is still my favorite for any work that doesn't absolutely require a Windows front end. TC++ is fast on a 25 MHz '386. It flies on a Pentium. If you like programming, you'll love TC++. Go get it.

Enjoy your C++ programming!

In this chapter you're going to write your first program, one that displays "Hello, World!" on your screen. As we planned from the beginning, this will complete our preliminary work. We'll go one step at a time, and I'll explain everything.

Along the way, you'll learn to:

▶ Write a C++ function

▶ Write a block statement

▶ Write a return statement

▶ Use function calls as statements

▶ Use character string constants

▶ Use the #include preprocessor directive

▶ Compile and run your own programs

Say "Hello, World!"

Many of you already have a beginning grasp of the fundamentals of C or C++. If you do, you'll find this chapter a bit slow. If you're in that category, skim the material, type and run the examples in the last part, and get on to Chapter 3, where the real work gets going. Don't worry—I'm not going to sneak in anything sophisticated here.

Now, the rest of you are new to C++, I assume. This chapter is not short, but all the material is fundamental. Our progress will be dead slow, since absolutely everything is new.

I'll explain each concept and point out how it fits into the code. Later on in the book, we'll be doing about 99 percent coding and 1 percent studying concepts. At this point, sorry to say, that ratio is reversed.

Relax and take it slow. Remember, if you want to build a fine house, you start by digging the foundation.

F U N C T I O N S

We're going to start by writing a C++ *function*. Why will we start with a function? Because all C++ code is written in functions. If you look at C++ code, you are looking at functions. (Actually, definitions of objects and other data structures are also things you write in C++, but whether these are correctly called code is a matter of definition.)

With one exception, you can give your C++ functions any name you like. The exception is that you must have one function named "main" so that C++ knows where to start. The simplest possible programs (such as the one we're about to write) have a function named "main" and no others.

These are the parts of a function definition:

```
<function type> <function name> <parameters>
<code>
```

We'll look at each one, in turn, beginning with the function type.

The Function Type

The *function type* refers to the value that a function returns. In DOS, for instance, the value that a program returns is available to batch files as the ERRORLEVEL value. The main () function (I'll explain those parentheses in a minute) returns an integer value to DOS. If a DOS program works correctly, it returns a zero value. Higher integers are used to signal errors. Here's a typical batch file fragment:

```
:SOMEFILE.BAT—a sample batch file
...


FIXUP %1.CPP %1.LST
IF ERRORLEVEL 1 GOTO screwup


... (continue work here)


:screwup ECHO Something went wrong—not fixed up!
```

Assume that FIXUP is a program that reads a source file (.CPP) and, after doing some fixups, writes a file (.LST) ready for printing. FIXUP normally returns zero to DOS, but if something went wrong (it couldn't open one of the files, for example) it will return a 1. This behavior provides a very primitive but useful communication between the program and the batch file that is running the program.

If FIXUP is a C++ program, its main() function will return zero when everything works, or it will return 1 on any sort of error. The main() function is an integer function, since it returns integers.

As we write more programs, we'll write functions that return lots of different values. Some of these values, such as integers, will be built-in C++ data types. Many of them will be objects and other data types that we create. One of the most popular types is "void," which means that the function doesn't return anything at all. For the moment, we'll use the "int" type for main().

A function returning an integer is written this way:

```
int <function name> <parameters>
<code>
```

What's in a Name?

The main() function is named "main," of course. You don't have any choice about this one. You have a huge range of choices for naming all your other functions, however.

The only restriction on names is that the name of a function must be a combination of the 52 letters, the 10 digits, and the underscore character.

That's right: 52 letters. In C++ uppercase letters are distinct from lowercase letters. An "A" is not even related to an "a" except in our human minds.

The function name is one type of *identifier*. We'll use identifiers to name lots of other things as we go along. They all share the same rules. You start an identifier with one of the 52 letters and then continue with more letters, digits, or underscore characters until you think you've got enough.

Modern C++ compilers generally let you pick your upper limit on the number of characters in an identifier. It's been years since I've actually run into the limit in practice. Make your names meaningful by using a sensible number of characters. Here are two program fragments that might do the same thing:

```
invoice_total = invoice_subtotal + taxes + shipping

x3 = zx1 + f33 + a_j_1_9_q
```

In the first example, you can see exactly what the line of code is doing. It's calculating the invoice total by adding taxes and shipping to the subtotal. The second example doesn't give you a clue what it's up to.

H I N T

It's hard to tell the numeral "1" from the letter "l" in many screen fonts. Don't use these characters unless they are clear from the context, as is the "l" in "total."

It's a good rule to be sparing with your use of digits in your identifiers. Most of the time, they just obscure the actual meaning of the identifier. The next example shows a good use of digits, in the control logic of a program that prepares a three-part report:

```
calculate( part1 )
print( part1 )

calculate( part2 )
print( part2 )

calculate( part3 )
print( part3 )
```

Of course, if your report's parts have more meaningful names than "part1," "part2," and "part3," you should use those, instead:

```
calculate( introduction )
print( introduction )

calculate( report_body )
print( report_body )

calculate( summary )
print( summary )
```

By the way, you can use the underscore character as the first letter in an identifier, but don't do it. Most C++ systems, including Borland's, add leading underscore characters to your names to create internal function names. They also use leading underscore characters for their own internal functions and other identifiers.

Don't use leading underscore characters until you are writing your own C++ compiler. Then always use them so that your names aren't like any used by the programmers who use your compiler.

Some programmers use underscore characters, as I do, to separate words that are part of an identifier:

```
invoice_subtotal
report_body
```

An older but still common style is to use capital letters for a similar effect:

```
InvoiceSubtotal
ReportBody
```

T I P

Some people avoid the underscore character because it's a bit of a nuisance to type. I cheat. When I write a program, I'll use quick but otherwise awful variable names, such as "is" instead of "invoice_subtotal." As soon as I've entered the program, I ask my editor to find all the occurrences of "is" and replace them with a good name, like "invoice_subtotal." This approach makes the typing quick but still gives you an excellent program.

Enough on names. Our function now looks like this:

```
int main <parameters>
<     code>
```

The Parameters

Parameters are not as complicated as our terminology makes them. The distinction between parameters and function *arguments*, which we'll get to in due course, is both subtle and profoundly silly. Sometimes I think it was invented to confuse beginning programmers.

For now, we'll consider the parameters to the main() function. In the simple case, a main() function has no parameters. Since the parameters are always enclosed in parentheses, you can write the first line of the main() function this way:

```
int main()
```

You could also write it this way, although I never do:

```
int main(void)
```

The word "void" specifies that there are no parameters. Putting nothing at all between the parentheses also specifies this and saves some typing. Without parameters, our program now looks like this:

```
int main()
<code>
```

If there were parameters, they would appear inside the parentheses. Here's a common example, so you can see where parameters go:

```
int main( int argc, char* argv [/])
```

Don't worry about those parameters—we'll get to them in time. For now, recognize that they go inside the parentheses.

There's no rule about leaving space between the parentheses and the parameters. I use space to help make the code easy to read.

The next example works just as well as the one above, from the computer's point of view:

```
int main(int argc, char* argv)
```

When I write a function name in the text, I always put parentheses after it so that you recognize it as a function, not some other identifier. You've already seen main(), for example. That's a shorthand notation that saves you from always reading "the function main" or "the main function." I just call it main().

Okay? Now we're ready to get on to the <code> portion of our program.

BLOCK STATEMENTS

There are several types of statements in C++. Any group of them can be combined inside curly braces—{}—to form a *block statement*. The syntax for a block statement is:

```
{
    <statements>
}
```

The statements inside the braces can be any C++ statements you like, including other block statements. (Actually, that's not entirely true. However, the exceptions, as you'll see when we get to them, are sensible enough that you don't even need to think about them.)

The only statement that can follow the parameters of a function definition is a block statement, so now our code looks like this:

```
int main()
{
    <statements>
}
```

As you'll see when we get to other statements, C++ lets you be quite free about how you enter your code. The way I've suggested here is the way that I use. It's commonly considered good C++ programming style. There are a few other ways to write code in good style and lots of other ways that will work correctly.

Here's one example:

```
int main() {
    <statements>
}
```

If you're trying to save paper when you print your code, here's another example:

```
int main() { <statements> }
```

The indentation that I've shown helps make your programs more readable—a virtue you'll appreciate the first time you go back to one after a few days working on something else. You could skip the indentation altogether:

```
int main()
{
<statements>
}
```

That's bad style. On the other hand, some people prefer to have the braces indented to match the statements. Here's an alternative that could be a good style:

```
int main()
    {
    <statements>
    }
```

I said "could be," not "is," a good style. No style is good if you don't stick to it completely. You won't go wrong if you adopt my style for your work in this book. When you're done, think about it and make any changes that suit your own needs. But be consistent—one of your main goals is to write readable programs.

A block statement doesn't really do anything. It just holds a bunch of other statements together. As we'll see, this is a very useful thing to do, but for now, let's get to statements that actually do something. The first one we'll look at is the return statement.

THE RETURN STATEMENT

The *return statement* sends a value back to the routine that called the current function. It also terminates the current function, letting processing pick up where it left off in a previous function.

HINT

Actually, the return statement doesn't quite terminate the current function. When we get to objects you'll see that some cleanup work may happen before a function terminates. But for now, you can ignore that complication.

While most of our functions are run by other functions, main() is called by the operating system or from a program shell, such as DOS's COMMAND or Windows' Program Manager. A return statement in main() returns control to the program that called it and returns a value. Here's the common way to exit from main() when all has gone well:

```
return 0;
```

What's that semicolon? In C++, the semicolon terminates a statement other than a block statement. As you learn C++ you'll get in the habit of typing semicolons at the end of every statement.

Until you develop the habit of typing semicolons at the end of every statement, you'll be in the less pleasant habit of reading all the error messages that your compiler gives you telling you about the semicolons it can't find.

Almost the first thing an experienced C++ programmer looks for when the compiler flags an error is the semicolon missing from the line *before* the error. Without the semicolon, the compiler thinks that the following line is still part of the current statement.

With that background, here's a complete program that does nothing at all useful. Since it does nothing, it confidently signals to DOS that it did it successfully:

```
int main()
{
    return 0;
}
```

At last! We've gone this far into the chapter, and we've finally got a complete program. If you're in a good mood, you won't mind too much that it does absolutely nothing except return to the operating system reporting success.

More precisely, it reports no errors. More precisely still, TCLite, like all C++ environments, adds standard startup and termination code to the code you write. This code creates an invisible sandwich around your program. The operating system really calls the startup code, and your return statement really transfers control to the exit code.

H I N T

What does startup code do? For one example, when DOS loads a program, it assigns it all available memory. The first thing a well-mannered DOS program does is return any excess memory to DOS. This is one example of the sort of thing that you don't have to worry about, because TCLite, or any other good C++ system, takes care of it for you.

C O M M E N T S

Before we dive into writing our own program, let's add some comments. Comments are explanatory lines that tell you what your program is doing. Without comments, most programs make no sense at all. Add comments so that you will not have to puzzle through your code a few weeks (or months) after you write it.

C++ Comments

In C++, *comments* can be written in either of two styles. The newer style starts with a double slash and continues to the end of the line. Here are some examples:

```
int main()      // our first complete program
{               // (it's just for learning)

    return 0;   // reports NO ERRORS to the OS
}
```

The compiler doesn't read anything after the // up to the end of the line. On the next line, it starts reading again. What you put after the // is for us humans.

These comments are sometimes called C++ comments, to distinguish them from the older style of comment that was, for many years, the only type available in the C language.

C-Style Comments

The C-style comment starts with a slash-star combination—/*—and ends with a star-slash combination—*/. It is more of a nuisance to type these four characters than just the two in the newer style, but it also gives you more choices, so it has been retained in C++.

First, the C style is more convenient for typing multiline commentary in your program, such as the following:

```
/*
    This is a programming example from Chapter 2 of
    _Learn C++ Today_,
    Martin L. Rinehart, IDG Books, 1995.

    We're working up to the Hello, World! program, here.
*/

int main()      // our first complete program
{               // (it's just for learning)

    return 0;   // reports NO ERRORS to the OS
}
```

You can use it instead of the newer style, but no one does, since it's an extra nuisance to type:

```
{
     return 0;   /* this is more trouble to type */
               // this is easier
}
```

You can also sneak comments into the middle of your lines of code, but that's generally bad practice:

```
{
     return /* NO ERRORS */ 0; // bad style!
}
```

T I P

In 30 years of programming, I've never picked up a piece of old code and complained that it had too many comments. On the other hand, I've often picked up a piece and had the opposite problem.

It would generally be more helpful to have a good set of comments without code than to have good code without comments. With good comments, it's easy enough to write code. Without comments, you often have to throw out the code and start over, if you need to fix or improve anything.

Here's the code the we've been looking at, with reasonable comments:

```
/*
     This is a programming example from Chapter 2 of
     _Learn C++ Today_,
     Martin L. Rinehart, IDG Books, 1995.

     We're working up to the Hello, World! program, here.
*/

int main()      // our first complete program
{
     return 0;   // reports NO ERRORS to the OS
}
```

You may be thinking that the comments identifying this book are a little silly, considering that it's printed here. That's true, but consider why you add comments.

Presumably, this is going to be entered into a program file and run. That file will be on some computer. Someone without this book is going to encounter the file and wonder why it's there. In that context, the comments here are exactly what the next reader would like to know.

Always use lots of comments!

INCLUDING LIBRARY CODE

At the beginning of this chapter, I promised you that we'd be writing a program to say "Hello, World!" and I meant it. What I didn't mention was that C++, like C, has no commands that do either input or output.

There's no command to read the keyboard or mouse. There's no command to write to the screen. There are no commands to read or write to the disks or other storage devices. We need some help here.

The help comes in the form of functions. The designers of C deliberately avoided all hardware-related tasks, such as input and output, when they designed the language. This approach makes the core language much simpler and cleaner than it would otherwise be.

On the other hand, it means that you have to provide a bunch of functions that handle the complexities of hardware. Thanks largely to our friends on X3J11, the committee that developed the ANSI standard for C, the basic input and output functions have been standardized and are available in a standard form for all implementations of C and C++.

The compiled code for these functions is included in *library* (.LIB) files provided here with TCLite and similarly provided with other C++ environments. To use the code in these libraries, you have to tell the C++ compiler about these functions. That's a job for a header (.H) file.

We'll get to the header files in just a bit. First, let's take a look at a function we can use to write to the screen.

Using printf()

To display the message "Hello, World!" on our screen, the most common output function, printf(), is a good choice. It prints data, with optional formatting. Its first argument can be a *character string constant*.

The simplest form of a character string constant is some characters enclosed in double quotes:

```
"character constant"
```

The quotes are delimiters, marking the start and end of the character string. They are not part of the string itself. For now, we'll not be using quotes inside a character constant, since that would conflict with their use as delimiters.

To print a character string constant with printf(), you can write a statement like this:

```
printf( "character string" );
```

The statement that will write our "Hello, World!" message is this one:

```
printf( "Hello, World!" );
```

C++ provides other output mechanisms, including a class called *streams*. Streams are often covered in beginning C++ books, but I don't use them, so I don't teach them. For small programs, the overhead (40 to 50K added to the .EXE file) compares very unfavorably with that of older C routines, such as printf(). For large programs, output will go through an interface library, such as Borland's Object Windows Library, also bypassing streams.

H I N T

A function on a line by itself is another type of C++ statement. The printf() shown here is a good example of a function that does some work but doesn't return a value. Its type is void.

We're almost ready to write our complete program, but the compiler won't know where printf() comes from or if we're using it correctly.

Including STDIO.H

There are several header files installed in the \TCLITE\INCLUDE directory. Some of the ones you'll use regularly are:

▶ STDIO.H—Standard input/output functions

▶ STRING.H—String manipulation functions

▶ CONIO.H—Console (screen and keyboard) I/O

▶ STDLIB.H—Standard library routines

You could copy any of these files directly into your source file, but this would be a nuisance at best. After you had copied one of them into dozens or hundreds of individual source files, it would be worse than a nuisance. Imagine the trouble if you found something in the .H file that you wanted to change!

C++ uses a standard "preprocessor" technique to incorporate these and other files into your programs. There are several preprocessor commands, called directives, that you can place in your source files. These are interpreted by C++ before your code is actually sent to the compiler.

The most common preprocessor directive is #include. It is used when you want to include a file, such as a header file, in your source file without actually physically making a copy. Its syntax is:

```
#include file_to_include
```

The file_to_include can come from the standard include file directory. For TCLite, that's \TCLITE\INCLUDE. To include a file in this directory, such as STDIO.H, you use angle bracket delimiters around the filename:

```
#include <STDIO.H>
```

The filename inside the angle brackets follows the operating system conventions. For DOS, you can use either uppercase or lowercase. I use uppercase, since that's consistent with my use of other preprocessor directives. Lowercase will work just as well.

Use upper- or lowercase filenames in the #include directive, but be consistent.

N O T E

The <> delimiters are used for files in the standard header directory. You will write project-specific header files, too. These are delimited with double quotes if you have them in your source code directory.

Putting It Together

We've now seen everything you need to write the full "Hello, World!" program, and you've read about every bit of it. Here's the full program that we'll be using in the next section, when we get on to actually compiling and running our program:

```
/*
        This is a programming example from Chapter 2 of
        _Learn C++ Today!_,
        Martin L. Rinehart, IDG Books, 1995.

        We're working up to the Hello, World! program, here.
*/


#include <STDIO.H>

int main()        // our first complete program
{
    printf( "Hello, World!" );
    return 0;    // reports NO ERRORS to the OS
}
```

We've covered a lot of ground, even though we haven't achieved too much. C++ does not make it easy to write trivial programs. There are better languages for beginners. As we go further, you'll see that C++ repays your investment in time when you get to more sophisticated programming, which we'll begin in the next chapter.

Our last section in this chapter is about entering, compiling, linking, and running this program.

COMPILING, LINKING, AND RUNNING

Before you can compile, link, and run your code, you have to enter it into your computer, of course. Since this is our first program, we'll approach the task a little differently now than we will later.

Generally, you'll start with an example on disk and type in some additions or changes. Since this is our first program, there is nothing on disk. It's all new, so you have to type it all.

Typing your own code is the key to learning C++ using this book. When you type, you are reinforcing what you have read. You'll also make mistakes, of course. When the compiler reports errors, you'll know that you haven't got everything perfect. Fixing your errors may be the biggest part of the learning experience.

Editors

TCLite comes with a built-in multifile editor. It's a good small programming editor. If you remember Borland's Sidekick product, or the earlier WordStar word processor, you already know most of the keystrokes. If you don't know either of these, using the arrow keys, the menus, and the mouse will produce results that you've learned to expect in most contemporary editors.

You may, of course, have your own favorite editor that you know and love. As long as it can write an ASCII file, you can use it in addition to the built-in editor.

If you use the File|DOS Shell menu-choice to get to DOS from within TCLite, you'll have no problem using your own editor. You use your editor and save the file in the normal way. When you return to TCLite, you'll be able to load the latest version of your file.

Better still, if you have the file open in TCLite, it will sense that you have made changes using another editor and ask you if you want it to reload the file from disk. The default choice is Yes, so this makes your life very simple.

Of course, faster than shelling to DOS from within TCLite is using a multitasking operating system. OS/2 is ideal. Even a simple multitasking system such as Windows 3.x can handle running TCLite in one DOS session and your favorite editor in another DOS session.

W A R N I N G

If you use multiple, simultaneous DOS sessions, TCLite will be outsmarted. It won't know that the file it has open was changed in another DOS session while it wasn't looking.

Remember that if you edit in one DOS session and run TCLite in another, TCLite has no way of knowing about the second session. This is the fastest way to work, but you have to close the file in TCLite (without saving!) and reload it. This is very easy to do, but it's also very easy to forget.

Probably the best idea is to do any bulk typing, such as your first entry of our HELLO.CPP program, using your favorite editor. Then switch to TCLite's built-in editor to correct mistakes, do any debugging, and make any other minor changes.

Entering the Program

To enter the program in Listing 2-1, follow these steps:

STEP   BY   STEP

1. If you are not in DOS, switch to DOS or launch a DOS session.

2. Change to the disk drive with the \TCLITE directory.

3. Change to the \TCLITE directory.

4. [Optional] Using your favorite editor, type a copy of Listing 2-1 and save it in a file named HELLO.CPP.

5. Launch TCLite's IDE by running TC.EXE.

6. Choose File|Open and open HELLO.CPP. If you did step 4, this will be ready to use. If not, type the file in now.

Listing 2-1: HELLO.CPP

```
// HELLO.CPP–Sample Hello, World! program
// Copyright 1995, Martin L. Rinehart

/*

    This is a programming example from Chapter 2 of
    _Learn C++ Today_,
    Martin L. Rinehart, IDG Books, 1995.

    We're working up to the Hello, World! program, here.

*/
```

```
#include <STDIO.H>

int main()       // our first complete program
{
    printf( "Hello, World!" );
    return 0;    // reports NO ERRORS to the OS
}


// end of HELLO.CPP
```

H I N T

Pressing F2 in the TCLite IDE will save the current file. TCLite automatically saves for you when you compile and run, so this is seldom necessary, however.

At this point, your TCLite session should look something like the one in Figure 2-1.

```
≡  File  Edit  Search  Run  Compile  Debug  Project  Options     Window  Help
┌─[■]═══════════════ \CPPBK1\HELLO.CPP ═════════════1═[↑]─┐
// HELLO.CPP -- Sample Hello, World! program               ▲
// Copyright 1995, Martin L. Rinehart

/*
    This is a programming example from Chapter 2 of
    _Learn C++ Today!_, Martin L. Rinehart,
    IDG Books, 1995.

    We're working up to the Hello, World! program, here.
*/

#include <STDIO.H>

int main()       // our first complete program
{
    printf( "Hello, World!" );
    return 0;    // reports NO ERRORS to the OS
}

// end of HELLO.CPP                                         ▼
└─── 1:1 ──────◄─□                                    ◄□─────┘
 F1 Help  F2 Save  F3 Open  Alt-F9 Compile  F9 Make  F10 Menu
```

Figure 2-1: HELLO.CPP is ready to compile.

Once you have the file available, make a small change (change one of the comments) and press F2 to save the file. Press Alt+F3 to close the window and the file. Now use F3 again to reopen the file. Your change should still be in place.

Make another small change in one of the comments, only this time just press Alt+F3 to close the file and the window. You'll be prompted with a message box dialog that asks you if you want to save your work. You can press Esc or click on Cancel to exit from this dialog and to skip the Alt+F3 command.

Now we're ready to turn our code into a running program.

Compiling, Linking, and Running

If you've used other compilers, you know that compiling and linking can take a fair amount of work. This is *not* the case with TCLite, or with Borland's other C++ products. With your HELLO.CPP file still open, choose the Run option from the Run menu. (Clicking the menu and option or Alt+R followed by Enter will work.)

This menu choice starts an involved process, which will result in a complete compilation, linking, and execution for your program. The process is quite complex from the point of view of TCLite. However, from your point of view you have only a moment or two to wait, and the job is done.

With HELLO.CPP, your screen will blink, and you'll be back where you started. The program has run to completion. During the blink, TCLite saved its own screen and reloaded the DOS screen. Then it ran the program. Finally, it reloaded its own screen.

If you press Alt+F5, you'll switch from the TCLite screen to the DOS screen. Mine looks like the one in Figure 2-2. As you can see, the "Hello, World!" message was written to the next DOS output line, which is just what we had in mind.

T I P

If you work so slowly and meticulously that you never get a compile error, you're spending entirely too much of your own time checking your work. Let TCLite do the checking—it's much faster than you are!

If you got error messages from the compiler, you're working well. Fix your typos and press Ctrl+F9 (the same as choosing Run|Run) and try again. Repeat this until it works.

Got it? Good! Your first C++ program is now alive and well.

```
HotDIR 2.1
Path: C:\CPPBK1\SCREEN\*.*

.      <dir>  ..      <dir>  LC02-01   IGF    4294

        3 files totaling 4294 bytes consuming 8192 bytes of disk space.
 11055104 bytes available on Drive C:     Volume label: MS-DOS_5
 C:\CPPBK1\SCREEN>ch tclite.d
 C:\TCLITE.D>exit

Type EXIT to return to Turbo C++. . .

Microsoft(R) MS-DOS(R) Version 5.00
         (C)Copyright Microsoft Corp 1981-1991.

 C:\TCLITE.D>q chp02.bk
 C:\TCLITE.D>copy con e.bat
 q \cppbk1\bk\chp02.bk^Z
        1 file(s) copied

 C:\TCLITE.D>e

 C:\TCLITE.D>q \cppbk1\bk\chp02.bk
 C:\TCLITE.D>exit
Hello, World!
```

Figure 2-2: Hello, World! appears on your DOS screen.

Making Changes

With the program running, it's time to make some changes. The first change that I want is to have the program pause after it displays the "Hello, World!" message.

One way to do this is to ask for a character from the keyboard. The getch() function, one of the console input/output functions listed in CONIO.H, does this job. This is a function that returns a char, or character, datum. For our present use, we'll ignore the return value, using the function as if it were type void.

Listing 2-2 shows the improved code. You can delete your existing code and read 02-02.CPP from the SAMPLES subdirectory, or you can use your HELLO.CPP as is.

T I P

Use your existing program, instead of the SAMPLES code, whenever you can. It will save time, and it will preserve all the changes you've made on your own. Use SAMPLES when you get stuck.

As with all our improvements, from now on you'll be typing the lines shown in boldface. Our listing is complete in this case, but we'll be showing only enough of the existing code to allow you to see where the changes and additions go.

Listing 2-2: HELLO.CPP

```
// HELLO.CPP—Sample Hello, World! program
// Copyright 1995, Martin L. Rinehart

/*

    This is a programming example from Chapter 2 of
    _Learn C++ Today_,
    Martin L. Rinehart, IDG Books, 1995.

    We're working up to the Hello, World! program, here.
*/

#include <STDIO.H>
#include <CONIO.H>

int main()      // our first complete program
{
    printf( "Hello, World!" );
    getch();

    return 0;    // reports NO ERRORS to the OS
}

// end of HELLO.CPP
```

Once you make those two additions, press Ctrl+F9 and see what happens. If all is well, your program now pauses, showing you the DOS screen. Press any key, and it returns to TCLite, which is exactly what you want.

What happens if you forget to #include the proper header files? Put two slashes in front of the #include <CONIO.H> line to comment it out. Then try running the program again.

You'll get a message box that tells you you've got errors. Specifically, it will say that getch() should have a *prototype*. The prototype, which we'll get to in detail later, tells the compiler what type of function getch() is, including what arguments it needs and what value it returns. The prototype is found, of course, in CONIO.H.

Remove the two slashes from in front of the #include <CONIO.H> line and press Ctrl+F9 again. Your program should run correctly.

As you'll see on the DOS screen, the second "Hello, World!" message starts right at the end of the first one. C++ doesn't add a carriage return or a linefeed unless you tell it too. We'll learn more about that later on.

Before you go to the summary, try various combinations of what you've learned. Change the message and press Ctrl+F9. Add a second printf() and getch() pair, with an additional message.

Make some mistakes. Drop a parenthesis and try to compile. Delete the closing curly brace and see what happens. Spend a little time here to get comfortable with doing everything you've learned this far, and with doing it wrong and fixing your mistakes.

SUMMARY

Well, congratulations. You've entered and run your first C++ program. In the process, you learned a lot about the C++ language and a little more about the TCLite IDE.

You learned that all C++ code is placed in functions. Every C++ program has a function named "main()," which is where C++ starts.

You've learned that functions have types, and that the integer type, called "int," is the right one for main(). We saw that functions can include parameters in parentheses and that the parentheses themselves always get included, even if there are no parameters.

You've seen that block statements follow the parentheses when you define a function. The block statement is a pair of braces delimiting a set of other statements.

You used a return statement to return a zero value to the DOS operating system. That's the value that can be tested as the ERRORLEVEL return in DOS batch programs.

You also used other function calls as statements. The functions you called were printf(), which writes to the screen, and getch(), which gets a character from the keyboard.

You used standard header files, STDIO.H and CONIO.H, to identify these functions to the compiler.

You used the #include preprocessor directive to include these standard header files.

You learned that the semicolon ends C++ statements, and that the compiler insists on getting its semicolons. On the other hand, the compiler is very flexible about your spacing.

Finally, you've added enough comments, using both the C style and the new C++ style, so that a sensible person can read your program and understand it without your help.

This brings you to the end of the preliminaries. Beginning in Chapter 3, we're going to start right in programming our editor. We'll go slowly at first, but you'll be bringing real, professional C++ code to life as we go along.

As we build our C++ skills, we'll also be building TEd, our Tiny Editor. By the time you get to the end of this book, you'll have a working text editor, as well as a working knowledge of C++ programming. Starting with this chapter, our programming will be woven together with learning and building TEd.

In this chapter we'll build a routine that draws boxes. While we're building it, you'll learn to:

▶ Clear the screen

▶ Assign colors, or text attributes

▶ Display individual characters

▶ Position the screen cursor

▶ Use defined constants

▶ Write and call your own functions

▶ Loop with while statements

▶ Use character arrays

▶ Declare and initialize variables

▶ Manipulate null-terminated strings

▶ Initialize character arrays

▶ Use global variables

▶ Use the if statement

Now let's get into the programming.

Let's Draw Boxes

Numerous studies of programmer productivity have revealed that professional programmers average about ten lines of finished code per working day. Just ten.

On the other hand, the same studies show that the best programmers average over 100 lines. Of course, part of the difference is experience. At this point in your C++ knowledge, no one would expect you to set productivity records.

But a month or two from now, you'll know C++ well enough to be reasonably productive. You'll be one of a large number of C++ programmers with a good grasp of the language. You can be one of the hundred-line-per-day aces, or one of the ten-line-per-day average programmers.

The difference is technique. Slow programmers write a lot of code very fast. Then they test it. It has bugs, of course. All code starts buggy. During debugging, as one bug is fixed, another bug appears. Getting all the bugs out is slow, exacting work. Most programmers, as you know from using most systems, never get all the bugs out.

That is not how fast programmers succeed. Fast programmers don't work nearly as hard as the slow ones, except in one respect, which I'll get to. Fast programmers never write more than a handful of lines of code at once.

To program quickly means to program very little. As we work through this book, you'll be entering a few lines at a time and testing those lines. Sometimes, you'll enter and test just one or two lines at a single step.

This is not just because this book is a tutorial, teaching a language. This is because writing and testing little bits of code is the fastest way to get a program written. Fastest by a factor of ten or more.

The one thing fast programmers do slowly that slow programmers skip right past is designing for debugging. The slow programmer thinks, "How can I code this?" The fast programmer thinks, "How can I code a little bit of this at a time so I can test it?"

As we work through this project, we'll be working the fast way, one small step at a time. You'll be slowed down by the need to learn all about the various parts of C++, of course. Still, you'll find that TEd will come together more quickly and easily than you would guess.

That's because the work has been thought out and broken down for you into very small, easily tested steps. When you do it right, it's effortless. When you start to do your own work on TEd, don't write a single line until you have broken your task down just this way. It will become second nature, and you'll be one of the heroes who writes over 100 lines per day.

Let's get started.

GETTING SET

There are two main ways to add code to a project: Add the code directly into the project, or write a standalone test program. We'll start with a standalone program, and later we'll figure out how it can be integrated into the project.

To begin, let's build T.CPP, a simple test program. I use T (as in Temporary) whenever I write throwaway code. When I start a day's work, I can always DEL T.[*] and know that no harm will come of it. Listing 3-1 shows a simple, do-nothing mainline program.

Listing 3-1: T.CPP

```
// T.CPP—test routine

int main()
{
    return 0;
}


// end of T.CPP
```

Listing 3-1 is all new code, so there's no disk listing. To prepare yours:

S T E P   B Y   S T E P

1. Press F3 to open a new file.

2. Name the file T. If you omit the extension, .CPP is supplied for you.

3. Enter Listing 3-1.

4. Compile to check your work.

To eliminate your worst typos, you can compile without running. Choose Compile | Compile (Alt+C and then Enter to accept the default) from the menus, or press Alt+F9. Either way, you'll get the Compiling dialog box, and after you correct any errors, it will report Success, as shown in Figure 3-1.

T I P

If you get the "Success" report on your first try, you ought to consider working faster. Perfection requires either meticulous work or frequent presses of Alt+F9 to see what dumb mistakes we've made. Alt+F9 is much faster, and the end result is just as good. Save your concentration for serious problems.

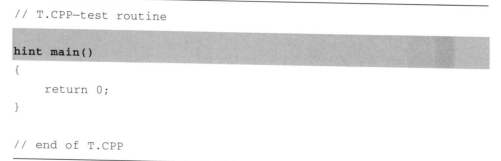

Figure 3-1: A successful compilation.

Just for practice, let's introduce an error and track it down. Change the correct word "int" to an erroneous "hint" as shown in Listing 3-2 (not on disk—use your own code).

Listing 3-2: T.CPP

```
// T.CPP—test routine

hint main()
{
    return 0;
}


// end of T.CPP
```

With the function type deliberately wrong, press Alt+F9 again to compile. When you do, you'll get an error message in the Message window, as shown in Figure 3-2.

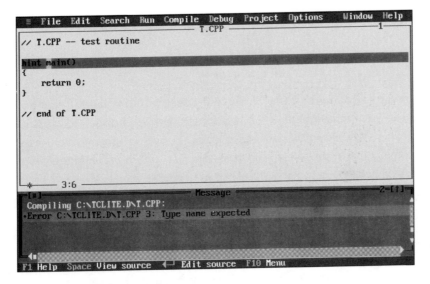

```
≡  File  Edit  Search  Run  Compile  Debug  Project  Options   Window  Help
┌──────────────────────────────── T.CPP ────────────────────────────1──┐
│ // T.CPP -- test routine                                              │
│                                                                       │
│ hint main()                                                           │
│ {                                                                     │
│     return 0;                                                         │
│ }                                                                     │
│                                                                       │
│ // end of T.CPP                                                       │
│                                                                       │
│                                                                       │
│                                                                       │
│                                                                       │
│─── 3:6 ──────                                                         │
┌─[ ]──────────────────────────── Message ───────────────────2─[↑]─┐
│ Compiling C:\TCLITE.D\T.CPP:                                         ▲│
│•Error C:\TCLITE.D\T.CPP 3: Type name expected                        │
│                                                                      ▼│
│◀                                                                    ▶│
└──────────────────────────────────────────────────────────────────────┘
 F1 Help  Space View source   ◀┘ Edit source  F10 Menu
```

Figure 3-2: A compilation error.

The message "Type name expected" tells us that the compiler did not find a type name where it thought one should be. In this case, it read "hint," but there is no "hint" data type that a function could return, so it didn't recognize this as a possible type.

The error message in the Message window also names the file and line number where the error was found. Right now we're working with code in just one file, but later on we'll work across multiple code files, so the filename will become important. Knowing the line number is interesting, but more helpful is the fact that if you press Enter with an error highlighted in the Message window, the problem file's window is activated with the cursor on the line where the compiler found the error.

Remember that the line where the compiler finds an error may come after the actual error. To try an example, delete the semicolon after the return statement and see where the compiler flags the error.

With the error message in the Message window, press Enter; you go right to the line in the T.CPP window. At this line, correct the mistake and press Alt+F9 again to recompile. This time your Compile dialog should report Success.

H I N T

We're not running this code with Ctrl+F9, since it doesn't do anything. If you try Ctrl+F9, you'll see your screen blink if the two screen rewrites happen to cross a screen refresh cycle. You may not even see a blink if your computer is very fast or you hit the timing just right. Alt+F9 ensures that you get the Compile dialog and its "Success" message.

At this point, we're ready to start programming.

MORE CONIO.H FUNCTIONS

In this chapter, we'll be doing procedural programming, drawing boxes on the screen. In the next chapter, we'll use the procedure we develop here when we create a box class. This procedure will become one of the methods of that class.

A *method* is one of the things that an object knows how to do when we ask it. Our box objects, for example, will know how to draw themselves on the screen. You'll find that it's common to develop standalone procedural code and then use that code as a method for a class.

To develop the box drawing procedure, we'll need to use some more functions from the console input/output library.

Clearing the Screen

Let's start by clearing the screen. The header file CONIO.H defines a clrscr() function that does this job. Listing 3-3 shows three additions to T.CPP. Make these additions in this way:

S T E P   B Y   S T E P
---

1. Use your existing T.CPP, or open a new T.CPP window and read in 03-03.CPP from the SAMPLES\ subdirectory.

2. Add the #include <CONIO.H> line.

3. Add the clrscr() line.

4. Add the getch() line.

5. Compile, link, and run with Ctrl+F9.

Listing 3-3: T.CPP

```
// T.CPP-test routine

#include <CONIO.H>

int main()
{
    clrscr();
    getch();

    return 0;
}

// end of T.CPP
```

When you have this routine running, your program will clear the screen and then wait for a keypress, giving you a chance to see the clear screen.

Are you wondering how you know that the clrscr() function in the CONIO.H header does the job you need done? Try pressing F1 when you are in a program window. You get a nice help window listing the editor commands.

This is helpful but not what we were after. Press Esc to exit from that help window and then try pressing Shift+F1 to go to the help index. You'll get the window shown in Figure 3-3.

If your help window doesn't fill the screen, try pressing F5 to toggle between partial and full-screen views.

In the Turbo Help Index, press the first few letters of CONIO.H, slowly, and watch your search home in on this topic. Once CONIO.H is highlighted in the index, press Enter, and you will go immediately to the right page of the help documentation. Figure 3-4 shows the CONIO.H documentation.

On the CONIO.H page, all the functions in this header file are listed in an array near the top of the page. They are highlighted in yellow, which means that you can get additional help on them.

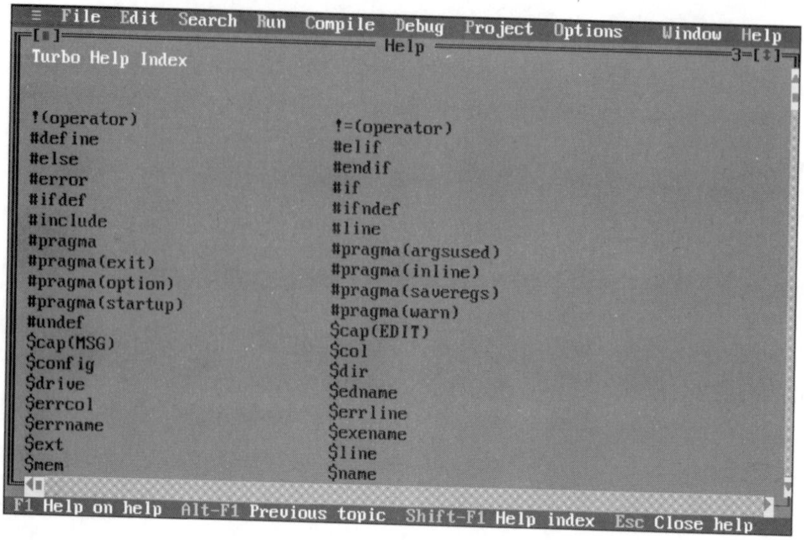

Figure 3-3: Use the Turbo Help Index for help on a specific topic.

To check the clrscr() function, for example, you can double-click "clrscr" with your mouse, or you can use Tab, Shift+Tab, or the up- and down-arrow keys to highlight your choice and then press Enter.

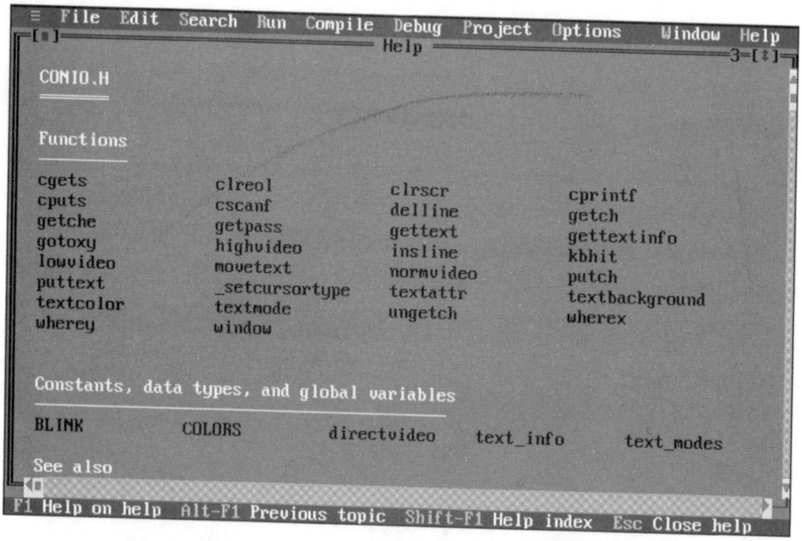

Figure 3-4: CONIO.H in the Help file.

Now, to answer the question, if you want to do something with the screen, such as clearing it, CONIO.H is a likely place to look. Once you see the list of functions, pick a likely looking one and check its documentation. Of course, this technique gets more useful as you learn more about the contents of the various header files, which you'll do as we move along here.

Let's go on to using some more of the CONIO.H functions.

Choosing Colors

White text on a black screen is not the most fascinating color combination you can use. In the default text mode for TCLite programs, you can use one of 256 color combinations that you can select individually for each character on the screen.

N O T E

TCLite will let you address your hardware directly, so your color choices are limited only by the capabilities of your video adapter. For portability in a project such as TEd, you want to avoid this sort of custom work and stick to the simpler defaults.

Actually, speaking about the color choices is a little loose. More correctly, we want to speak about the text attributes. In the default text mode, the text attributes include color, foreground intensity, and blink. To see all 256 choices, run the program COLORS.COM that is in your SAMPLES\ subdirectory.

Move COLORS.COM into \DOS or whatever directory in your path includes your commonly used utilities. You'll be running COLORS.COM frequently. (Don't worry about space—it's an assembly language program I wrote with a 1K space budget.)

When you run COLORS, you'll see the 256 possibilities organized into 16 rows and 16 columns. Each row is a separate background color specification, with the decimal number of the combination written in the foreground color. For example, you can see that attribute 26 is high-intensity green written on a blue background.

Attributes 128 through 255 duplicate 0 through 127, except that they set the blink attribute on. Unless your intent is to drive users crazy, use blink sparingly, if at all. It's appropriate for serious warnings: Leave the premises—this computer is about to explode! For anything else, blink is overkill.

Let's say you've decided that white (I mean low-intensity white, if I don't say otherwise) letters on a blue background are what you want. Running COLORS.COM, you see that this is attribute 23.

To use attribute 23, or any other, simply set the text attribute byte, using textattr(). Listing 3-4 shows the line to type into your current T.CPP (or into 03-04.CPP from SAMPLES\) to choose this attribute.

Listing 3-4: T.CPP

```
// T.CPP—test routine

#include <CONIO.H>

int main()
{
    textattr( 23 );
    clrscr();
    getch();

    return 0;
}


// end of T.CPP
```

The textattr() function sets the current text attribute byte. Everything that you write to the screen from that point on is written with that attribute until you use textattr() again to set a different attribute.

When you use Ctrl+F9 to compile, link, and run this version, your screen clears to a blue background color. If you look in the upper-left corner, you'll see the cursor blinking in your selected white foreground color.

The attribute byte uses its four high bits to set the background. The highest bit sets the blink attribute, and the next three control the red, green, and blue color guns, respectively. Similarly, bits 3 through 0 set the intensity (high, if bit 3 is on) and the color guns (red, green, and blue for bits 2, 1, and 0). You can use C++ operators to set these bits separately, or you can use the textbackground() and textcolor() functions to set background and foreground separately. The textattr() function seems simpler, to me.

You can try other colors if you like.

Writing Characters

We've already used printf(), from STDIO.H, to write character string constants to the screen. You can also use putch(), from CONIO.H, to write individual characters. You'll see when we start drawing boxes that this ability can be very handy.

There are two things I want to point out about the putch() function. First, the value we supply inside the parentheses is called the *argument* to the function. I don't know why we've settled on that word—nobody's having an argument. Arguments are the values you supply when you call a function.

Second, the putch() function's argument is a single character. A character constant is written by enclosing a character inside apostrophes, or single quotes. Listing 3-5 shows a sample.

Listing 3-5: T.CPP

```
// T.CPP—test routine

#include <CONIO.H>

int main()
{
    textattr( 23 );
    clrscr();

    putch( 'a' );
    putch( 'b' );
    putch( 'c' );

    getch();
```

```
        return 0

    }

    // end of T.(
```

Add the three p   k lines that separate them from   -5. (I'm going to
stop saying that   1PLES\ subdirectory gets the fil   nber how this
works when in 1   `a file that's far
too long for you

N O T E

You've now used single quotes to surround a character constant such as 'a'—and double quotes to surround a string constant such as "Hello, world!" You can test a common mistake by substituting double quotes for the single quotes in one of the putch() lines. The error message is interesting.

When you run (Ctrl+F9) this program, your screen should say "abc" in the upper-left corner. Much more specifically, clrscr() sends the cursor to column 1, row 1—the upper-left corner of the screen. Each putch() call sends a character to the screen at the current cursor position and advances the cursor to the next screen position.

The screen position following column 1, row 1 is column 2, row 1. Screen positions march across the screen until you get to column 80, row 1. The next position is then column 1, row 2.

Finally, if you checked the documentation for putch(), you'd see that it accepts an integer argument. We've been giving it characters, which are definitely not the same thing as integers. To the computer, though, a character is simply a one-byte number. An integer in TCLite is a two-byte number. C++ will automatically adjust a smaller number to a larger size when it needs to.

Now let's control the screen position without having to putch() individual characters to move the cursor.

Positioning the Cursor

The clrscr() function also sets the cursor to the upper-left corner of the screen. To get it moved to another location, you can use the gotoxy() function. This function takes two integer arguments. As its name suggests, the first argument sets the x coordinate (viewing the screen as an x-y graph), and the second sets the y coordinate.

In standard text modes, the x coordinate can be column 1 through column 80. The y coordinate can be line numbers 1 through 25, or 1 through 50 for VGA-compatible monitors. (The older EGA standard supported 43 rows, not 50—we'll use this fact in a couple of minutes.)

Listing 3-6 shows three gotoxy() calls woven in with the putch() statements.

Listing 3-6: T.CPP

```
// T.CPP—test routine

#include <CONIO.H>

int main()
{
    textattr( 23 );
    clrscr();

    gotoxy( 10, 5 );
    putch( 'a' );
    gotoxy( 20, 10 );
    putch( 'b' );
    gotoxy( 30, 15 );
    putch( 'c' );

    getch();

    return 0;
}

// end of T.CPP
```

Add these three gotoxy() lines in your T.CPP file and press Ctrl+F9 to see the result. You should have your three letters marching diagonally down the screen.

Setting the Number of Rows

So far, we've been working with the default screen, which, unless you've changed it, is 25 rows tall. I like to work in 50 rows when I'm doing text editing. It's not quite as easy to read, but being able to see more lines of code more than makes up for that negative, for me.

I'm going to build TEd in 50-line mode. If you have a contemporary desktop computer, this should probably suit your needs, too. On the other hand, if you will be doing a lot of work on a laptop with a small screen, you may want to stick with 25 lines. If that's you, pay attention here and make the appropriate adjustments for your situation.

The call to set the number of lines is actually a call to select a video mode. A handful of the video modes are reasonably standard, and almost all programming is done in this small subset. In fact, you'll probably use only two for all your text work.

The function that we'll use is textmode(). It takes an integer parameter. The integer parameter that we'll use is one of these two funny-looking numbers:

▶ C80—80-column, 23-row, color mode

▶ C4350—80-column, 50-row, color mode

Is C80 unlike any integer you've ever seen? It's actually a form of *defined constant*. Defined constants are used to make programs more readable. C80 happens to be mode 3. C4350 happens to be mode 64. These two calls are equivalent:

```
textmode( C4350 );   // switch to 43/50 row mode

textmode( 64 );      // ditto
```

The first version is going to be a lot more help some weeks from now when you look at this bit of code again.

N O T E

C80 distinguishes the normal video mode from C40, which displays only 40 columns. C40 resolution lets you use a PC with a standard television set as a monitor—a practice that dates to the very early days of personal computing when hobbyists were building homebrew machines in the late 1970s. C4350 switches EGA monitors to 43 lines per screen or current VGA monitors to 50 lines per screen.

With that preamble, Listing 3-7 will run our test program in 50-line mode.

Listing 3-7: T.CPP

```cpp
// T.CPP—test routine

#include <CONIO.H>

int main()
{
    textmode( C4350 );

    textattr( 23 );
    clrscr();

    gotoxy( 10, 5 );
    putch( 'a' );
    gotoxy( 20, 10 );
    putch( 'b' );
    gotoxy( 30, 15 );
    putch( 'c' );

    getch();
```

```
    return 0;
}


// end of T.CPP
```

Add this line to T.CPP and run the program with Ctrl+F9. (Actually, you know by now that Ctrl+F9 does a save, compile, link, and run. Saying "run the program with Ctrl+F9" is very sloppy. On the other hand, you get the idea and it saves us time, so I'm going to use the sloppy form and trust that you'll know what I mean.)

Your letters will now be smaller and march down the screen at a shallower angle than they did before. If you were in 50-row mode, experiment with C80 instead of C4350 to see the result in 25-row mode.

Well, now you've got a small repertoire of console I/O commands that are adequate to draw a box on the screen. What we want to do is write a function that will draw a box, in the colors and location we choose, for any purpose we may conceive.

WRITING MULTIPLE FUNCTIONS

So far, we've used just main() to do all our work. We haven't broken our code down into smaller modules. Before we can write a box-drawing function, we have to know how to construct and call our own functions. Fortunately, there's not much to learn to do that.

Let's start by writing a startup function. Over time we can add to it, but for now, let's have it clear the screen to white on blue and set us in 50-line mode.

Writing Startup

In Listing 3-8, I've moved the three function calls that we need out of main() and into a function named startup(). In main(), I've replaced those lines with a line that calls the startup() function.

As you see in the listing, startup() is of type void, since it doesn't return a value. Also, when you write yours, make sure that it appears before main(), as you see in the listing.

Listing 3-8: T.CPP

```cpp
// T.CPP—test routine

#include <CONIO.H>

void startup()
{
    textmode( C4350 );

    textattr( 23 );
    clrscr();
}

int main()
{
    startup();

    gotoxy( 10, 5 );
    putch( 'a' );
    gotoxy( 20, 10 );
    putch( 'b' );
    gotoxy( 30, 15 );
    putch( 'c' );

    getch();

    return 0;
}

// end of T.CPP
```

If you are new to the Borland editor, you can mark text by dragging the mouse over it or by holding a Shift key down while you move the cursor with the arrow keys. You can cut marked text to the clipboard (a clipboard internal to the Borland IDE) by pressing Shift+Del. Shift+Ins copies text from the clipboard back into your file at the current cursor location.

T I P

The quick way to build your own copy of Listing 3-8 is to cut the three working lines out of main() and paste them in above main(). Then add the call to startup() in main() and add the rest of the details to startup() to make it a complete function.

When you are done, press Ctrl+F9 to test your work. You should get the same result you had before.

If you know the Pascal language, you'll be used to putting your subroutines first in the file, followed by your mainline. C programmers find that to be annoying. When I read a program, I want to see the main things first and then work down into the details.

Using a Function Declaration

To keep the compiler happy and at the same time to make humans like me happy, C++ lets you declare functions prior to defining them. So far we've just worked with function definitions.

A function *definition* explains to the compiler what type of function you have, what parameters it uses, and what code it has that does its work. A function *declaration* doesn't include the code; it just defines the function's type and parameters.

After reading a function declaration, the compiler can see uses for your function written in the code and decide whether you have supplied sensible parameters and returned a reasonable value, for example. This type checking is one of the big advantages of C++ over older C programs—a lot of stupid mistakes can be caught by the compiler.

The price for this convenience is a little duplication of effort. Begin by moving the startup() function definition from its current location above main() to a new location below main(), as you see in Listing 3-9. This code won't work, but go ahead and try to run it anyway.

Listing 3-9: T.CPP

```
// T.CPP—test routine

#include <CONIO.H>

int main()
{
    startup();

    gotoxy( 10, 5 );
    putch( 'a' );
    gotoxy( 20, 10 );
    putch( 'b' );
    gotoxy( 30, 15 );
    putch( 'c' );

    getch();

    return 0;
}

void startup()
{
    textmode( C4350 );

    textattr( 23 );
    clrscr();
}
```

```
// end of T.CPP
```

T I P

The new lines in Listing 3-9 aren't really new. They're moved from above main().
Select them and move them with Shift+Del followed by Shift+Ins.

When you try Ctrl+F9 on this version, the compiler stops at the call to startup() in main() and tells you that "'startup' should have a prototype." *Prototype* is another term for declaration.

A function declaration is just the first line (in the style I've been using here) terminated by a semicolon. When the compiler sees a semicolon following the parameter list's closing parenthesis, it doesn't expect (or accept) code to follow, defining the function. It registers the declaration in its lists of functions, assuming that you'll define the function when it's convenient.

In this case, the full listing with a declaration for startup() is in Listing 3-10.

Listing 3-10: T.CPP

```
// T.CPP—test routine

#include <CONIO.H>

void startup();

int main()
{
    startup();

    gotoxy( 10, 5 );
    putch( 'a' );
    gotoxy( 20, 10 );
    putch( 'b' );
    gotoxy( 30, 15 );
    putch( 'c' );

    getch();

    return 0;
}

void startup()
{
    textmode( C4350 );
```

```
    textattr( 23 );
    clrscr();
}
```

```
// end of T.CPP
```

Enter the function declaration line and press Ctrl+F9 again. This time, you will be back in business.

Now you know the technique for writing your own functions that can be called from main(). The first function we'll write is one that draws a box on the screen.

WRITING A BOX

The first step in designing any subroutine is to decide what data it should act on. For a general-purpose box-drawing routine, these are the items I want to use:

▶ The location (left, top, right, and bottom)

▶ The border (single line, double, or whatever)

▶ The colors (main color and border color)

These values will be the arguments that we pass to the box-drawing function. Looked at another way, they will be the parameters that the box-drawing function receives. Now we are ready to specify them more precisely.

N O T E

When you provide values in a function call, those values are called arguments. When the function receives these values, they're called parameters. That's a lot like calling the football one thing when it's thrown and another when it's caught. In this game, the quarterback throws arguments and the receiver catches parameters. It helps to have a sense of humor.

The location can be specified with four integer numbers. I always keep to the x-y scheme used in gotoxy()—left and top first (column before row), right and bottom second.

The border characters can be specified as individual characters, but that scheme will make for a very long list of parameters. A more compact way will be to specify a string of characters. I'll use an eight-character string, starting with the character for the top-left corner and proceeding clockwise around the box:

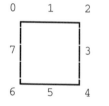

Finally, two more integers will do for the two colors. I write the color for the border before the color for the rest of the box, which I call the contents color. I do it this way because that's the order in which you use the colors, as you'll see when we get to writing the function.

Here's a sample call of the function, which we can call box_draw():

```
// 62 is yellow on cyan, 23 is white on blue
box_draw( 5, 5, 45, 15, "┌─┐│┘─└│", 62, 23 );
```

Of course the comment doesn't mean anything to the C++ compiler, but I consider it an integral part of a function call when you use values that would be meaningless without it.

N O T E

In SAMPLES\ I've provided another program, CHARS.EXE, that you can run to view all the characters in the IBM-extended ASCII set used by the PC. You can find all the box-drawing characters in this set in the rows labeled A through D.

The parameters that catch all those arguments can be written this way:

```
void box_draw( int lft, int top, int rgt, int btm,
      char* border, int outline_clr, int contents_clr );
```

What does char* mean? It means the type of parameter is a pointer to a set of characters. (Without the "*" it would be just a single character.) A character string in C++ is an array of characters. Square brackets are used for array subscripts, and the first element of an array is numbered 0. Here's the array of characters:

```
/* char* border == an array of 8 characters

border[0] == left-top corner
border[1] == top center
border[2] == right-top corner
border[3] == right side
border[4] == right-bottom corner
border[5] == bottom center
border[6] == left-bottom corner
border[7] == left side

*/
```

(In C++, the double equal sign means "is equal to.") The parameter border is specified as a pointer to characters. It can be used in your function either as a pointer or as an array. In this code, we'll use it as an array, since that's more convenient.

Before we begin writing, let's get organized. First, replace the existing gotoxy() and putch() lines of T.CPP with the new lines in Listing 3-11.

Don't overlook the added #include directive. You need the STDIO.H header file to use printf().

Listing 3-11: T.CPP

```
// T.CPP—test routine

#include <STDIO.H>
#include <CONIO.H>

void startup();

int main()
{
    startup();

    gotoxy( 1, 1 );
```

```
    printf( "write the top line" );
    gotoxy( 1, 2 );
    printf( "write the center" );
    gotoxy( 1, 3 );
    printf( "write the bottom" );

    getch();

    return 0;
}

void startup()
{
    textmode( C4350 );

    textattr( 23 );
    clrscr();
}


// end of T.CPP
```

You'll see when we get to the coding that the printf() comments correspond to our actual activities. This is a form of pseudocode that I often use before diving into a long routine.

Write the Top Line

Set to begin work on our new routine? Good. Start by building the framework that it will live in. First, we'll move the gotoxy()s and printf()s out of main() into a box_draw() function. Listing 3-12 shows this step completed.

Listing 3-12: T.CPP

```
#include <STDIO.H>
#include <CONIO.H>

void box_draw();
void startup();

int main()
{
    startup();
```

```
    box_draw();

    getch();

    return 0;
}

void box_draw()
{
    gotoxy( 1, 1 );
    printf( "write the top line" );
    gotoxy( 1, 2 );
    printf( "write the center" );
    gotoxy( 1, 3 );
    printf( "write the bottom" );
}

void startup()
{
    textmode( C4350 );

    textattr( 23 );
    clrscr();
}

// end of T.CPP
```

When you hit Ctrl+F9 in this version, you should see a neat list of the steps we need in the upper-left corner of an otherwise empty screen. Next, let's add the arguments and parameters we'll be using.

T I P

To be sure your function declaration matches your function definition, type the definition first. Then copy the top line of the definition to the clipboard with Ctrl+Ins. Use Shift+Ins to paste it into position at the top of the file and add a semicolon to terminate the declaration.

Listing 3-13 shows the parameters added to the function declaration and to the function definition. It also shows the arguments added to the line in main() that calls the box_draw() function.

Listing 3-13: T.CPP

```
// T.CPP—test routine

#include <STDIO.H>
#include <CONIO.H>

void box_draw( int lft, int top, int rgt, int btm,
    char* border, int outline_clr, int contents_clr );
void startup();

int main()
{
    startup();
    box_draw( 5, 5, 45, 15, "┌┐│┘─└│", 62, 23 );

    getch();

    return 0;
}

void box_draw( int lft, int top, int rgt, int btm,
    char* border, int outline_clr, int contents_clr )
{
    gotoxy( 1, 1 );
    printf( "write the top line" );
    gotoxy( 1, 2 );
    printf( "write the center" );
    gotoxy( 1, 3 );
    printf( "write the bottom" );
}

void startup()
{
    textmode( C4350 );
```

```
    textattr( 23 );
    clrscr();
}


// end of T.CPP
```

Make these changes and try Ctrl+F9 again. You should get the same result as before—three neat comments in the upper-left. However, if you press Alt+F9 to just compile, you'll get a different result.

Instead of reporting "Success" the Message dialog tells you that there are warnings. Each of the warnings tells you that a parameter to box_draw() has not been used. If you thought you were done with a routine, this dialog would probably uncover a mistake. Right now, it's just uncovering the fact that we're about to get to work with these parameters.

The Left-Top Corner

The first thing we can do is to position and display the left-top corner character. This is the first character in the border array, border[0]. Before we display it, we should set the color (text attribute) to the outline color. Listing 3-14 shows these additions.

Listing 3-14: T.CPP

```
void box_draw( int lft, int top, int rgt, int btm,
    char* border, int outline_clr, int contents_clr )
{
    // set the outline color
        textattr( outline_clr );

    // write the top line
        gotoxy( lft, top );
        putch( border[0] );

    gotoxy( 1, 2 );
    printf( "write the center" );
    gotoxy( 1, 3 );
    printf( "write the bottom" );
}
```

Up to now, we've been looking at the complete listing. Listing 3-14 shows only box_draw(). As you can imagine, showing complete listings will get less and less practical as our listings grow longer. From now on, I'll be giving you just the portion of the listing that has the new or changed code, along with enough of the surrounding context that you can make the change in your own copy.

H I N T

As you see in the new code, I've written a comment first and then indented the code that implements the comment directly underneath the comment. This style makes it easy to read the code. You read the comments to find out what is going on, and you look at the actual code if you need to see the details.

When you hit Ctrl+F9 with this version, you will have a single box-corner character underneath the comments, as Figure 3-5 shows.

Figure 3-5: The left-top corner appears.

The Top Center

Now we're ready to draw a line from the left-top corner to the right-top corner. If you remember that putch() advances the cursor, you can see that all we have to do is to putch() enough top-line characters to draw the line. The character is border[1], of course.

There are two main program loops, for and while, that you can use to repeatedly putch() the line character. For this one, the while loop works nicely. Its syntax is:

```
while ( <some condition> )
        <some statement>;
```

As always, the statement can be any valid C++ statement, including a block statement. This is a common way to write a while loop:

```
while ( <some condition> )
{
    do this;
    that;
    and the other;
}
```

In pseudocode, this is what we want to do:

```
while ( we're not at the right )
{
    putch( border[1] );
}
```

To determine our position, we can create a variable, tell it where we started, and increment it every time we putch() another character. To create a variable, you just provide a type and a name. This statement creates an integer variable, called i:

```
int i;
```

N O T E

For most variables, longer descriptive names are preferred. For little integer counters, single letters (such as i, j, k) are traditional. This practice goes back to the 1950s when the first compilers, for the Fortran language, were written. The Fortran default was that the letters "i" through "n" stood for integer variables. Go ahead and use these one-letter names if the variable does its whole job in one or two code lines.

In C, you had to declare all your variables at the beginning of your functions. One of the nicest C++ improvements is that you can declare a variable anywhere you like. It's good practice to declare your variables where you use them.

You can also provide an initial value when you declare your variable, like this:

```
int i = lft + 1;
```

In this case, we put the cursor at lft, top and then used putch() to write the first character. So our cursor is now at lft + 1.

C++ gets its name from C's increment operator, ++. This operator adds 1 to a variable. These two lines are equivalent:

```
i++;         // adds one to i
i = i + 1; // ditto
```

The ++ form may compile to a more efficient operation, so you should use it when it's appropriate.

Now that we have that information, Listing 3-15 writes the middle part of the top line.

Listing 3-15: T.CPP

```
void box_draw( int lft, int top, int rgt, int btm,
    char* border, int outline_clr, int contents_clr )
{
    // set the outline color
        textattr( outline_clr );
```

```
// write the top line
    gotoxy( lft, top );
    putch( border[0] );

    int i = lft+1;
    while( i < rgt )
    {
        putch( border[1] );
        i++;
    }

gotoxy( 1, 2 );
printf( "write the center" );
gotoxy( 1, 3 );
printf( "write the bottom" );
}
```

Enter those additions and run the program with Ctrl+F9. Your top line now lacks only the far right corner, as you see in Figure 3-6.

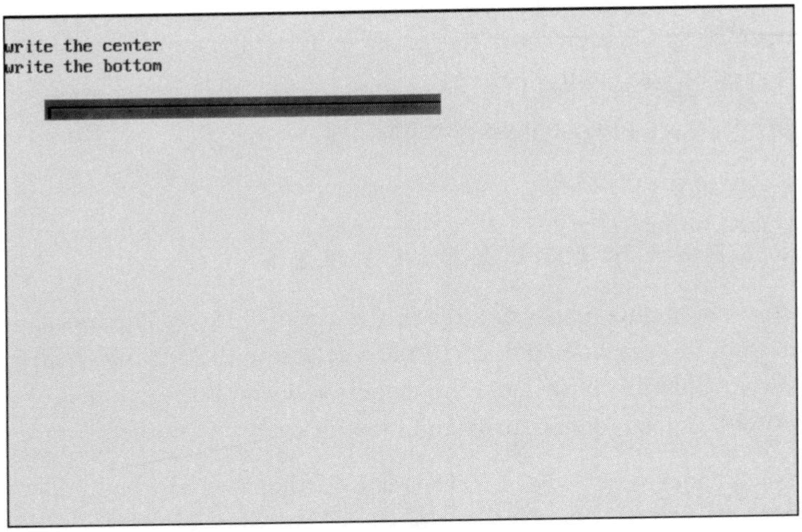

Figure 3-6: The top line nears completion.

The Right-Top Corner

The nice thing about the far corner is that you already know how to do it. You may want to add it yourself, before you look at the listing.

Listing 3-16: T.CPP

```
// write the top line
    gotoxy( lft, top );
    putch( border[0] );

    int i = lft+1;
    while( i < rgt )
    {
        putch( border[1] );
        i++;
    }

        putch( border[2] );

    gotoxy( 1, 2 );
    printf( "write the center" );
```

As you see in Listing 3-16, you need only one more putch() and your top line is complete. Figure 3-7 shows my completed top line.

Now you are ready to get on to the center of the routine.

WRITE THE MIDDLE LINES

One way to write the middle lines would be to use a pair of loops. The outside loop could run from the row after the top to the row before the bottom. Within this loop, each row could be constructed the same way we built the top line, writing the corner characters individually and looping over the middle distance.

But there's a much better way to do it. If we create a string that has the middle part preassembled, we can use printf() to write it once for each middle line. To do this, we'll have to take a closer look at strings.

Strings Are Null-Terminated

When you write a string constant—such as "abcde"—C++ puts one extra character at the end of the string. It's the character zero, or null. C++, like C before

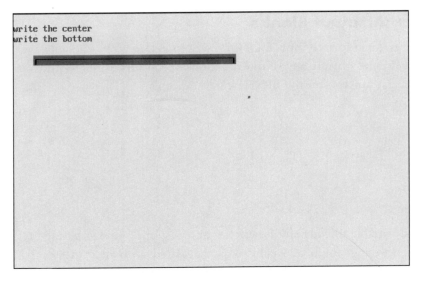

Figure 3-7: The top line is completed.

---

it, uses the null-terminated string format in its string manipulation work. For example, printf() writes characters until it comes to a null.

If we started with a string of blanks, or spaces, we could get printf() to print just the right number of blanks by inserting a null character at the right spot. Here's an example:

```
// blanks is a long string of blank characters

blanks[5] = 0;     // put a null in character 6
printf( blanks ); // prints 5 blanks
```

If you were bothered by that counting, you probably forgot that the first element of an array is numbered zero. In this example, blanks[0] through blanks[4] (that's five of them) are written by the printf() function. Blanks[5] is a null character.

N O T E

You can assign a char value with single quotes—as in 'a'—or with a number. An 'a' is also character 97. A char that has the value 97 will display an 'a'—whereas in the computer, of course, it's neither a 97 nor an 'a'—it's 01100001. Either 97 or 'a' is just a human-oriented way of looking at 01100001.

Building an Array of Blanks

What we need is a handy array of blanks. One way to get an array of blanks is to make a global array, outside any of our functions. To do this, you declare your data above the first function in the file. Here's an example:

```
// start of file

char blanks[80];

int main()
...
```

Positioning the variable outside any function makes it global—it can be used by every function. In the example above, blanks[] is declared as an array of 80 values of type char. The compiler will make sure that you have at least 80 bytes available for the blanks[] variable.

Initializing Character Arrays

An easy way to initialize character arrays is to assign a string constant to them. If you omit the length, the compiler will count the amount of space you need based on the length of the string that you assign to it. For example:

```
char sample[] = "abc";
```

In this case, you've told the compiler that you want sample[] to be an array of characters, and that you want it assigned the string "abc." Remember that the compiler adds a trailing null character to the end of a string constant, so "abc" is really four characters long.

If you specify multiple strings, one after another, the compiler puts them together as a single string:

```
char test[] = "abc" "def"; // same as "abcdef"
```

Of course, splitting a string like that on a single line doesn't make much sense. Remember that C++ statements don't end at the end of a line—they end with the semicolon. Here's a use for that feature that should make more sense:

```
char test[] = "This is a very long string that "
    "is written on two lines.";
```

What we want is 80 blanks, because the widest window we could have would be 80 columns. That will work this way:

```
char blanks[] =
    "                                                        "
    "                                                        ";
```

Building a Middle Line

To build a middle line, we can put the left-side border character, border[7], into the first position in the blanks array, blanks[0]. Then we can put the right-side border character, border[3], into an appropriate spot in blanks[] and follow it immediately with a zero. Then when we pass blanks to printf(), printf() will think the string ends at the zero, which is just what we want.

There's a minor problem that you'll find when we try this, but it will be easy to fix, so go right ahead.

Enter the additions in Listing 3-17. The gotoxy() and printf() calls are for testing. They replace the existing gotoxy() and printf() calls for the middle.

Listing 3-17: T.CPP

```
void startup();

char blanks[] =   // 80 space chars
    "                                   "
    "                                   ";

int main()
...

void box_draw( int lft, int top, int rgt, int btm,
    char* border, int outline_clr, int contents_clr )
{
    // set the outline color
        textattr( outline_clr );

    // write the top line
        gotoxy( lft, top );
        putch( border[0] );

        int i = lft+1;
        while( i < rgt )
        {
```

```
            putch( border[1] );
            i++;
        }

        putch( border[2] );
```

```
// build the center line
    blanks[0] = border[7];
    i = rgt - lft;
    blanks[ i ] = border[3];
    blanks[ i+1 ] = 0;

// write the center lines
    gotoxy( lft, top+1 );
    printf( blanks );
```

```
    gotoxy( 1, 3 );
    printf( "write the bottom" );
}
```

When you enter this, be sure that you initialize blanks[] above main(). The other changes replace the gotoxy() and printf() that were dummies holding a place for the center section code.

When you hit Ctrl+F9, you'll see that there's a problem. A center line is displayed in the right place, but it ignores the text attribute we've set. That's because printf() is a general-purpose output routine, not one written specifically for the DOS screen.

Fortunately, the fix is trivial. There's not even a listing on disk for this one. You have to switch from printf() to a console-specific version, cprintf(). That means adding the letter "c" to the printf() line, as shown in Listing 3-18.

Listing 3-18: T.CPP

```
// write the center lines
    gotoxy( lft, top+1 );
    cprintf( blanks );

    gotoxy( 1, 3 );
```

With that change, when you press Ctrl+F9, your box's center line is printed in the color you've specified. The center, as well as the border, is in that color, but we'll take care of that before we're done.

Now we want to replace that gotoxy() and that cprintf() we put in for testing with a loop that writes enough center lines for the size box we're dealing with.

Listing 3-19 shows a loop that will do just what we want. Enter this code and press Ctrl+F9. You now need just the bottom line to have a passable box.

Listing 3-19: T.CPP

```
// build the center line
    blanks[0] = border[7];
    i = rgt - lft;
    blanks[ i ] = border[3];
    blanks[ i+1 ] = 0;


// write the center lines
    i = top + 1;
    while ( i < btm )
    {
        gotoxy( lft, i );
        cprintf( blanks );
        i++;
    }

gotoxy( 1, 3 );
printf( "write the bottom" );
```

If you remembered that the new code in 3-19 replaces the gotoxy() and cprintf() we put in for testing, you should have most of a box. Figure 3-8 shows the box to this point.

Let's go right on to putting the bottom line on.

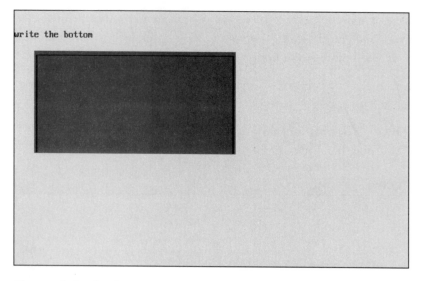

Figure 3-8: The box gets a top and sides.

Write the Bottom Line

Before you even look at the next listing, see if you can add the bottom line, yourself. Do it in three steps:

S T E P   B Y   S T E P

1. Position the lower-left corner and draw the lower-left border character.

2. Fill in the bottom line's center.

3. Finish with the lower-right corner.

If I were doing this, I'd copy freely from the group of lines that created the top line. The process is identical—you just have to make some small adjustments in exactly where you gotoxy() and in which border characters you use.

If you copied the code intact, your compiler will complain about the second time you declare i:

```
int i = ...
```

Even though i is an int, the compiler won't let you declare it a second time. Just take off the word "int" and you are in business.

Listing 3-20 shows my version, which should be very similar to yours.

Listing 3-20: T.CPP

```
// write the center lines
    i = top + 1;
    while ( i < btm )
    {
        gotoxy( lft, i );
        cprintf( blanks );
        i++;
    }

    // write the bottom line
    gotoxy( lft, btm );
    putch( border[6] );

    i = lft+1;
    while( i < rgt )
    {
        putch( border[5] );
        i++;
    }

    putch( border[4] );

}

void startup()
```

Figure 3-9 shows the box with the complete outline we've drawn.

Now if only our box's center had respected the contents color that we supplied as a parameter. That's our last job in building a completed box.

Figure 3-9: The box outline is complete.

Clear the Center

To begin, our box already has a center that matches the color of the border. If the contents_clr parameter matches the outline_clr parameter, we're done. Bear this in mind when I make the next observation.

One of the possible border strings would be a string of blanks. If you passed an all-blank border string to box_draw(), it would draw a colored rectangle, with no visible border. With these two observations in mind, we can color in the box's center portion just by calling box_draw() again, when the two colors don't match.

We'll use an if statement to color the center when the two colors don't match. The form of an if statement is:

```
if ( <condition> )
    <statement>
```

As always, one possible statement is a block statement, which I write this way:

```
if ( <condition> )
{
    this;
    that;
    and the other;
}
```

The <condition> is any expression resulting in a logical value. For our while statements, we used expressions that looked like they did just what we wanted, and they worked. Another logical expression uses the == ("is equal to") operator to compare two values for equality. The opposite of == is the !=, or "is not equal to," operator. We'll use that operator this way:

```
if ( outline_clr != contents_clr )
    color in the center;
```

(Of course, we'll have to substitute a real C++ statement for "color in the center.") Listing 3-21 combines this if statement with a second call to box_draw() to get the effect we want.

Listing 3-21: T.CPP

```
    // write the bottom line
        gotoxy( lft, btm );
        putch( border[6] );


        i = lft+1;
        while( i < rgt )
        {
            putch( border[5] );
            i++;
        }


        putch( border[4] );


    // repaint the center
        if ( outline_clr != contents_clr )
            box_draw( lft+1, top+1, rgt-1, btm-1,
                "            ", contents_clr, contents_clr);


}


void startup()
```

All we need to do is paint a second box inside the first, adjusting the coordinates by one and using just the contents color. This is *not* the most efficient way to paint the interior of the box, but it is the fastest to code. Feel free to experiment with better ways if you think the time savings will be useful.

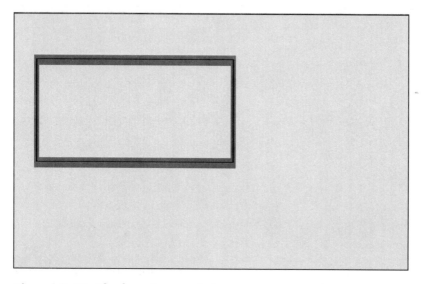

N O T E

A recursive program is one that calls itself. Our use of box_draw() to color the contents of a box is recursive. When you write recursively, make sure that the program will not just go on calling itself forever. In this case, the second call has the two colors equal, so there won't be a third call.

When you enter this addition and press Ctrl+F9, you'll get a complete, two-color box. You can see my box in Figure 3-10.

Figure 3-10: The box is complete.

You're entitled to pat yourself on the back at this point. You've created your first useful C++ function.

C L E A N U P

Before we move on, there are some items that we haven't handled. It's always good practice to take a critical look at your work after it seems complete, looking for the loose ends.

Testing

First, we've created exactly one box. That doesn't prove that our routine will work in all cases. Don't start in calling your routine with a handful, or even a heapful, of different input values. Start thinking!

First, how is our test case inadequate? There are two problems that jump out at me. One is that we've used values for lft and top that don't distinguish one from the other. We might have inadvertently switched those two in the code and we'd never know it. We've also used a contents color that matches our screen background, which is another potential problem.

Run another test, but this time be sure that you can check each of your four coordinates and both colors. With that test, you can be sure that your routine correctly handles the inputs you give it.

Now what about other inputs? Think about errors and extremes.

When I write code for my own use, I don't bog down my code with a lot of error checking. I insist that the routines that call others, such as box_draw(), pass sensible arguments. I don't add code to functions like box_draw() to check that all coordinates fall within the screen, that lft is actually to the left of rgt, and so on. In the next section we'll note the restrictions that do apply to this function.

Now what about extremes? We've used integers for our coordinates, so certainly upper bounds should be no problem (at least, not until our physical screens can display 32K rows or columns). Lower bounds, though, could be a problem. Our code assumes that we always want to draw all the border characters—which means our boxes must be at least three characters tall and wide.

Of course, using our two-tone boxes, we draw a box within a box, and the inner box also wants to be at least 3 × 3. Try testing a box that is only 3 × 3 and see what happens.

At 3 × 3, my inner box wipes out the right center border character of the outline. Testing at 4 × 3 (columns by rows) shows that these dimensions work fine. You could call the 3 × 3 behavior a bug and fix it. I'm just going to call it a restriction and document it. (Really, what useful purpose does a 3 × 3 box serve?)

Another interesting limit to test is boxes drawn at the borders of the screen. Try the top, left, bottom, and right edges. Any problems?

I found that I can draw either to the right edge or to the bottom edge, but not both. Again, that's peculiar, but I'm just going to document the restriction and move on.

Restrictions

Our testing showed that our boxes must be at least four columns wide and three rows tall, and that they can go to either the far right or the bottom of the screen, but not both. Let's make sure that nobody who looks at this code (probably you or me, a few weeks from now!) misses these restrictions. Listing 3-22 shows how I've achieved this goal.

Listing 3-22: T.CPP

```
void box_draw( int lft, int top, int rgt, int btm,
    char* border, int outline_clr, int contents_clr )
{
/*

COORDINATES MUST BE WITHIN SCREEN.  MINIMUM BOX IS 4 COLS
BY 3 ROWS.  DRAWING FAILS IF YOU GO TO BOTH SCREEN RIGHT AND
SCREEN BOTTOM.

Border chars are top-left corner, top-center, etc.,
clockwise to left-center.  Valid colors are from 0 to 255.

*/
        // set the outline color
        textattr( outline_clr );
```

In higher-level languages, you don't write as many (or any) very fundamental routines, such as box_draw(), as you do in C++. Making sure that these routines either work or have their restrictions documented is very important.

Repairing Blanks

One item that we haven't considered is our use of blanks[] to draw the box. This technique has worked fine so far because we haven't drawn multiple boxes. (Running repeated tests, pressing Ctrl+F9 each time, reloads a fresh copy of the program every time.)

The use we made works only if blanks[] is all blank, as we initialized it. To make sure that it works the second, and every other, time we call box_draw(), we'll need to repair the damage we do to this array. Listing 3-23 shows how you can replace the three characters you changed.

Listing 3-23: T.CPP

```
    // repaint the center
        if ( outline_clr != contents_clr )
            box_draw( lft+1, top+1, rgt-1, btm-1,
            "         ", contents_clr, contents_clr);

    // repairing blanks[]
        i = rgt-lft;
        blanks[0] = blanks[i] = blanks[i+1] = ' ';
}


void startup()
```

If you want to see the problem, add a second call to box_draw() in main(). Just copy the first one, and then make sure that the second one draws a box that is slightly wider than the first. You'll see problems at the right side.

N O T E

In C++ the = operator returns a value, just as the + operator does. The value it returns is the value being assigned. Among other conveniences, this fact lets you write multiple assignments such as "a = b = c = 0;", assigning zero to all three variables on one line.

When you enter the repair shown in Listing 3-23, you'll see that the problem is solved.

This code is not *reentrant*—it can't be called while another copy of itself is being used. Whenever a routine modifies global data, it is not reentrant. The fully general version would make a local copy of the blanks array and then make changes to this local copy.

The way we've done it here is smaller and faster than a true reentrant routine, but you can't use this method as part of an operating system or a library that is called by multiple running programs.

A Permanent Name

Before we call this chapter complete, you need to assign a permanent name to the code you've written. As we go along, we'll take code out of a test context, such as T.CPP, and put it into a permanent file that is part of our system. For this chapter, we haven't got a permanent system, so we'll have to use an expedient.

Just rename T.CPP to BOX_DRAW.CPP. You can choose File|DOS shell from the menus and rename the file in DOS. Alternatively, you can choose File|Save as... to save the file under the new name, without leaving the TCLite IDE.

When you save the file under the new name, be sure to change the comments at the top and bottom of the file to correspond to your new name.

After you give your file a permanent name, make sure you include it in whatever backup system you use, and get this file properly backed up.

SUMMARY

If you've followed to this point, you've earned some praise. Your first non-trivial C++ programming is complete. You've got a box-drawing routine that will become part of lots of other larger routines. In TEd, for example, we'll use it to create windows for files and dialog boxes.

While you've built a box-drawing routine you've looked at many things in C++. You've learned a lot more C++.

We started with console input/output functions. You used clrscr() to clear the screen, textattr() to set the text attribute (or colors), putch() to send individual characters to the screen, and gotoxy() to position the cursor.

While you were using these functions we took a look at defined constants, such as C4350, that let you call textmode() with values that are more readable than meaningless numeric constants.

Then you went on to write and call your own functions from main(). You started with a startup() function and then implemented the box_draw() function.

You used the while statement to control looping and the if statement for conditional processing. With both you used logical expressions, including a *relational operator*, <, and a *comparison operator*, !=.

You learned a lot about character strings. You used array notation to manipulate individual characters, and you saw how the zero character is used to terminate a string.

You also learned to use character string constants to initialize a null-terminated string.

Finally, you used a global character array, initialized with consecutive string constants.

While you learned all this, you were busily programming the box_draw() logic that we'll be using in the next chapter. While we've concentrated on the procedures for drawing a box up to now, in the next chapter we'll be putting this logic into an object-oriented framework.

In the last chapter we created a box-drawing function. That was a good example of old-fashioned procedural programming. In this chapter we're going to convert that procedural code into contemporary object-oriented code.

Along the way you'll:

▶ Use C-style structures

▶ Use C++ structures and classes

▶ Write class and structure definitions

▶ Create, initialize, and use structure and object variables

▶ Create and use pointers to structures

▶ Use the scope resolution operator

▶ Use public and private members

▶ Create member functions, or methods

▶ Use member operators

▶ Use the *new* and *delete* operators

▶ Write and use constructor and destructor member functions

▶ Learn about variable scoping

▶ Use for loops

▶ Use the #define preprocessor directive

▶ Step, trace, and set watches in the debugger

chapter

4

Creating a Box Object

As we work through this chapter, we'll create a box class from which you can launch as many box objects as you like. Each box object will have methods that it can perform. The first method we'll implement will be draw(), which, as you can probably guess, draws the box object on the screen.

You'll see that the code lying underneath the object is, in fact, procedural. But the concepts and the packaging are very different and offer, in many cases, a far better organization than procedural code normally supplies.

In C++, *structures* and *classes* are nearly identical. The only difference is in the default access protection, which is a topic that we will meet in a while. On the other hand, C had structures long before C++ and its classes were invented.

The structures that C provides are a relatively simple, but still highly useful, subset of the classes and structures that C++ provides. When a programmer speaks about structures in C or C++, the implication is a C-style structure. We'll look at this subset of C++'s capabilities first.

STRUCTURES GET YOU ORGANIZED

In C++, both structures and classes can have data and code as part of them. In C, classes don't exist and structures can have only data, not code.

In common parlance, a structure is still a creation that has data but not code, although as we will see, C++ certainly imposes no such limitation. However, these old-fashioned structures are a good place to begin.

A Data Organization

A structure gives you a way to create new, often complex, types of data. So far we've looked at char and int data, two built-in types in C++. With structures, you can define any sort of data organization that meets your needs.

Let's begin by defining a structure for boxes. The elements of the data structure are the same items that we used as arguments to the box_draw() routine:

▶ Ints for left, top, right, and bottom

▶ Chars for the border characters

▶ Ints for the outline and contents colors

You can use a structure to put all these items together as a single named parameter or variable, just as using an int variable holds a bundle of bits together in a sensible way.

One syntax for defining a structure is:

```
struct <type_name>
{
    <data members>
};
```

The <type_name> is any name that you want, following the normal rules for an identifier (one of the 52 letters, followed by zero or more letters, digits, and underscore characters). The <data members> are any number of declarations of variables. Here's an example for a box structure:

```
struct box
{
    int lft;
```

```
       int top;
       int rgt;
       int btm;

       char* border;

       int outline_clr;
       int contents_clr;
  };
```

You can also declare several variables following a single type specification. Here's an alternate form of the above structure definition:

```
struct box
{
    int lft, top, rgt, btm;

    char* border;

    int outline_clr, contents_clr;
};
```

This structure definition is a reasonable one. It doesn't waste a lot of lines, but it uses enough space to show you clearly what you've got. Dating back to the early days of C, the pointer form has been preferred over the array form. In this case, I'll replace the char* border with this:

```
       char border[8];
```

In general, the other form is preferred, but in this case you want an array of exactly eight characters. Another way to provide for these characters is this:

```
       char l_t_corner;
       char top_line;
       char r_t_corner;
       char rgt_side;
       char r_b_corner;
       char btm_line;
       char l_b_corner;
       char lft_side;
```

You can even spell out "left_top_corner," if you prefer. These eight chars have no terminating null such as a string has.

Now let's fire up TCLite and enter our first listing. (It's all new, so it's not on disk.) Listing 4-1 shows a correctly defined box structure. After you enter it, use Alt+F9 (not Ctrl+F9) to check for errors.

Listing 4-1: T.CPP

```
// T.CPP-test routine

struct box
{
    int lft, top, rgt, btm;

    char border[8];

    int outline_clr, contents_clr;
};

// end of T.CPP
```

Did you notice that you need a semicolon after the closing curly brace? If you haven't already made this mistake, take that semicolon off and press Alt+F9 again.

Without the closing semicolon, the Message dialog reports an error:

```
Declaration missing ;
```

When you press Enter in response to this message, you are returned to the scene of the crime. Add the semicolon and you are back in business. Before you go on, remove the semicolon from the line above the closing brace and press Alt+F9 again. What do you think will happen?

You get the identical error message, and the compiler thinks it's in the identical spot. Press Enter and you are returned to the line of the closing brace. This is a typical missing semicolon report, which the compiler almost always finds on the line after the actual mistake. Go ahead and fix the problem, returning your code to syntactic correctness.

Let's go on to write a short routine to create a structure and then to assign and access the members of that structure.

Member Operators

Once you define a class or structure, the name you choose becomes another type that the compiler will use just like any of the built-in types, such as int or char. Once you define a box structure, for example, you can declare a variable of type box with the standard declaration syntax:

```
box my_box;
```

You use the name of your structure type as if it were "char" or "int" and assign any name you like to the individual structure. Once you have declared a box variable, for example, you can access its members using the *dot* operator (the period character) this way:

```
my_box.lft = 5;
my_box.rgt = 45;

int width;
width = my_box.rgt - my_box.lft + 1;
```

Listing 4-2 shows a box variable declared with the coordinates assigned. Use Alt+F9 after you have entered the new lines.

Listing 4-2: T.CPP

```cpp
// T.CPP—test routine

struct box
{
    int lft, top, rgt, btm;

    char border[8];

    int outline_clr, contents_clr;
};

int main()
{
    box b;

    b.lft = 1;
    b.top = 5;
    b.rgt = 45;
```

```
    b.btm = 15;


    return 0;
}
```

// end of T.CPP

This program doesn't do anything yet. This is often the case as you develop a program—your first work creates an object or structure that you will be using later. A powerful feature of the IDE is the built-in debugger that lets you examine work in progress, such as this.

Using the Debugger

The debugger has many capabilities that let you run a portion of a program and stop the run where you like. When you stop a run, you can use the debugger to examine the internals of any variable or parameter, such as a structure.

To start, press F7. The IDE will compile and link your program if it needs to. (If you've changed the source code since you last compiled and linked, you'll get the warning message, "Source modified, rebuild?") Then it begins running the program, advancing to the first line of main().

The current location of the program (the line that is about to run) is shown by a highlight bar. Press F7 again, and the highlight bar will move down to the next line, ready to create b, your box variable.

Go ahead and use F7 to step through each line of the program. After you reach the end, pressing F7 will start your program again. Stop stepping when you get back to the starting line, "int main()."

H I N T

Pressing F7 works only when your cursor is in a program file window. If you are in another window, press Alt+the number of a file window, as shown in the upper-right corner of the window. You can also use F6 to step from one window to the next or press Alt+0 (zero) to get a list of all windows, from which you can choose your program window.

With "int main()" highlighted, let's open a *watch* window. Press Ctrl+F7 and you get the Add Watch dialog box. In this box, type "b.lft" and press Enter. As you see in Figure 4-1, the Watch window is opened, and b.lft is shown as your first watch variable.

```
≡  File  Edit  Search  Run  Compile  Debug  Project  Options    Window  Help
┌─────────────────────────────── T.CPP ──────────────────────────1─┐
│// T.CPP -- test routine                                          │
│                                                                  │
│struct box                                                        │
│{                                                                 │
│    int lft, top, rgt, btm;                                       │
│                                                                  │
│    char border[8];                                               │
│                                                                  │
│    int outline_clr, contents_clr;                                │
│};                                                                │
│int main()                                                        │
│{                                                                 │
│    box b;                                                        │
│─── 12:1 ─────────────────────────────────────────────────────── │
├─[■]──────────────────────── Watch ═════════════════════════3═[↑]═┤
│  b.lft: Undefined symbol 'b'                                   ▲ │
│                                                                  │
│                                                                ■ │
│                                                                ▼ │
│◄■                                                             ► │
└──────────────────────────────────────────────────────────────────┘
 F1 Help  F7 Trace  F8 Step  ←┘ Edit  Ins Add  Del Delete  F10 Menu
```

Figure 4-1: Watching b.lft in the debugger.

The window says "b.lft: Undefined symbol 'b'" because at this point in the program, there is no variable b. Press F7 to step to the next line, and you will see a random value reported for b.lft.

Remember that as you step through a program, the highlight bar shows the line that is about to be executed. Your assignment, b.lft = 1, has yet to be executed when the highlight is on this line. Press F7 again, and you will see the value 1 reported for b.lft.

You can add additional watches to examine the other members of your box structure. As you press F7, you'll see them assigned as your program directs.

Pointers to Structures

Another way to create a structure is to use a variable that points to the structure. When you use a box variable, your program actually reserves the space needed for all the members of a box structure, as you have defined it.

When you use a pointer to a structure, the compiler reserves enough space in your program for the pointer (two or four bytes, depending on the memory model, which we'll discuss later). At runtime, the *new* operator gathers the needed space from the heap, an area of available data storage.

When a function ends, all its variable space is discarded. If you use the *new* operator to allocate heap space, it is up to you to return the allocated space when you no longer need it. The *delete* operator returns unused space to the heap. This is how the pair should be used:

```
box* b = new box;

... // use the box

delete b;
```

N O T E

If you use the *new* operator, get in the habit of writing the corresponding *delete* immediately. Forgetting to free some variable's space could be relatively harmless, but in other cases it could quickly run into hundreds of thousands of bytes lost.

Listing 4-3 shows a program equivalent to the one in Listing 4-2, but using the "pointer to structure" form. Make the changes and run your own program again, using F7 to step through the code.

Listing 4-3: T.CPP

```
// T.CPP—test routine

struct box
{
    int lft, top, rgt, btm;

    char border[8];

    int outline_clr, contents_clr;
```

```
};

int main()
{
    box* b = new box;

    b->lft = 1;
    b->top = 5;
    b->rgt = 45;
    b->btm = 15;

    delete b;

    return 0;
}

// end of T.CPP
```

The dot member access operator is replaced by the arrow member access operator (hyphen followed by greater-than sign). The *new* operator is used to allocate the space you need, and the *delete* operator is used after you are done with the space.

When you step through the code, your Watch window will report "left side must be a structure" when it attempts to evaluate b.lft. Figure 4-2 shows my Watch window raising this complaint.

Replace b.lft with b->lft, and the statement will function as planned.

W A R N I N G

Failing to delete allocated structures, even small ones such as our sample box, can quickly lead to loss of serious amounts of space. It will eventually lead to failure of your system. Always write *new* and *delete* in pairs.

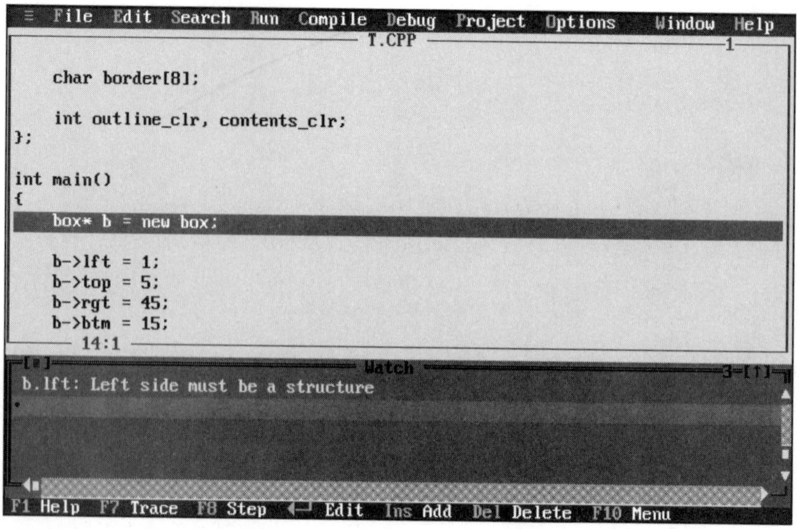

```
≡  File  Edit  Search  Run  Compile  Debug  Project  Options        Window  Help
┌──────────────────────────── T.CPP ────────────────────────────1─┐
│      char border[8];                                              │
│                                                                   │
│      int outline_clr, contents_clr;                               │
│ };                                                                │
│                                                                   │
│ int main()                                                        │
│ {                                                                 │
│      box* b = new box;                                            │
│                                                                   │
│      b->lft = 1;                                                  │
│      b->top = 5;                                                  │
│      b->rgt = 45;                                                 │
│      b->btm = 15;                                                 │
│ ── 14:1 ──                                                        │
├─[■]──────────────────────── Watch ───────────────────────3─[↑]─┤
│   b.lft: Left side must be a structure                        ▲ │
│ •                                                              ▒ │
│                                                               ▒ │
│                                                               ▒ │
│                                                               ▒ │
│ ◄■                                                          ►  ▼ │
└──────────────────────────────────────────────────────────────────┘
 F1 Help  F7 Trace  F8 Step  ⏎ Edit  Ins Add  Del Delete  F10 Menu
```

Figure 4-2: The Watch window insists on a structure.

More Debugging

Before we leave the structure and go on to the class, let's do some simple member arithmetic and use the debugger to check our results.

Add the statement in Listing 4-4 to your program.

Listing 4-4: T.CPP

```
int main()
{
    box* b = new box;

    b->lft = 1;
    b->top = 5;
    b->rgt = 45;
    b->btm = 15;

    int width;
    width = b->rgt - b->lft + 1;

    delete b;
```

```
        return 0;
}


// end of T.CPP
```

Instead of using F7 to step all the way through the program, position your cursor at the line with the width formula and press F4. The F4 key tells the debugger to run until it comes to the line with the cursor and then to stop. Use Ctrl+F7 to add a watch on width and then use F7 to step over the width line. That will show you the value of width—it's 45 using the data I've given.

Another way to stop at a particular line is to set a *breakpoint* on that line. Pressing Ctrl+F8 toggles breakpoints at the cursor line. Again, set your cursor on the width assignment statement and press Ctrl+F8. You'll see a red highlight band appear on the line, showing that a breakpoint is set. Figure 4-3 shows a breakpoint set this way.

```
≡  File  Edit  Search  Run  Compile  Debug  Project  Options      Window  Help
┌─[■]──────────────────────── T.CPP ──────────────────────1=[↑]─┐
│};                                                              │
│int main()                                                      │
│{                                                               │
│    box* b = new box;                                           │
│                                                                │
│    b->lft = 1;                                                 │
│    b->top = 5;                                                 │
│    b->rgt = 45;                                                │
│    b->btm = 15;                                                │
│                                                                │
│    int width;                                                  │
│    width = b->rgt - b->lft + 1;                                │
│                                                                │
│═══ 22:1 ═══◄□                                               ►  │
│──────────────────────────── Watch ──────────────────── 3 ─────│
│•b->lft: Undefined symbol 'b'                                   │
│                                                                │
│                                                                │
└────────────────────────────────────────────────────────────────┘
 F1 Help  Alt-F8 Next Msg  Alt-F7 Prev Msg  Alt-F9 Compile  F9 Make  F10 Menu
```

Figure 4-3: Setting a breakpoint.

After you set the breakpoint, our old friend Ctrl+F9 will run the program until it reaches the breakpoint, where execution will halt.

TIP

Pressing F4 is a quicker way to stop at a line than setting a breakpoint (Ctrl+F8) and running (Ctrl+F9). A breakpoint will stop the program at the same point if you run it again, however. The breakpoint will stay in force until you toggle it off with another Ctrl+F8.

Now that you've added some structures, we'll go on to the general form, the *class*.

CLASSES ARE POWERFUL STRUCTURES

Again, I'm using the terms structure and class to signify the older C-style structures and the newer C++-style classes, respectively. In C++ the two are almost identical. Structures and classes are interchangeable, except for one detail of member access, which we'll get to later. For now, remember that the distinction between structures and classes is one that most programmers understand, but it is not part of the C++ language.

To start our exploration, let's convert our structure to a class. You do this by simply replacing the struct keyword with the class keyword. This is a correct class definition:

```
class box
{
    int lft, top, rgt, btm;

    char border[8];

    int outline_clr, contents_clr;
};
```

We now have a box class, instead of a box structure. When you define a structure, the word "structure" is used to refer both to the definition and to individual structures. The program syntax is the same for classes, but the terminology is different.

When you have defined a class, you refer to an *instance* of that class as an *object*. As with the structure, you can create a box variable this way:

```
box my_box;
```

However, this time you refer to my_box as a box object, or as an instance of the box class. Go ahead and change the struct keyword in your T.CPP to "class" and try Alt+F9 again. What happens?

I get a number of error messages like this one:

```
'box::lft' is not accessible in function main()
```

That brings us to the one difference between structures and classes that is part of the C++ language.

Member Access Privileges

By default, all members of a structure are *public* members. That means that any function that has access to a structure variable or a pointer to a structure also has access to the members of that structure. If lft is a member of the box structure, any function can access b.lft if b is a box variable, or b->lft if b is a pointer to a box.

This is not true for classes. By default, all members of a class are *private* members. That means that only *member functions* of the class can access the data members. (We're coming to member functions in just a minute.) Other functions, such as main(), cannot access these members directly. They depend on member functions to grant them access if it is needed.

You can control the access type with one of three keywords, two of which are *private* and *public*, as in this example:

```
struct my_struct
{
public:
    type1 memb1;
    type2 memb2;
    ...
};

class my_class
{
```

```
    private:
        type1 memb1;
        type2 memb2;
        ...
    };
```

These keywords specify the access allowed for members of the structure or class. In the examples above, the access keywords are redundant, since they are the default access types. In the next example, a class is given the same access permission as a struct:

```
class my_class
{
public:
    type1 memb1;
    type2 memb2;
    ...
};
```

You can use both these keywords within a single class or struct:

```
class my_class
{
private:
    type1 priv_memb1;
    type2 priv_memb2;
    ...
public:
    type3 pub_memb3;
    type4 pub_memb4;
    ...
};
```

In Listing 4-5, I have converted the struct of Listing 4-4 into an entirely equivalent class. To do this, you just change the keyword from struct to class and then add the public: access qualifier at the beginning of the list of members.

Listing 4-5: T.CPP

```
// T.CPP—test routine


class box
{
```

```
public:
    int lft, top, rgt, btm;

    char border[8];

    int outline_clr, contents_clr;
};

int main()
{
    box* b = new box;

    b->lft = 1;
    b->top = 5;
    b->rgt = 45;
    b->btm = 15;

    int width;
    width = b->rgt - b->lft + 1;

    delete b;

    return 0;
}

// end of T.CPP
```

As with a struct, you could declare a box variable and use the dot operator to access the members, or you could, as we do in this example, create a box pointer variable and use the arrow operator to access data members.

N O T E

If you don't like suspense, the third access type is *protected*, which is the same as private except when a class is used as a base class for another class that inherits its members. This topic will become important, but for now it's far ahead of our current needs.

This discussion has shown you the formal differences between structures and classes in the C++ language. However, there's a much more common difference in their typical uses. Classes are assumed to have member functions.

Member Functions

In C, the only members of a structure are the data members, such as the ones we have used. C++ adds member functions. A function can be a member of either a class or a structure in C++. In common usage, a class has member functions, and a structure (going back to its roots in C) does not.

A member function is also called a *method*. A method is something that an object knows how to do, when asked. We'll be converting our box_draw() into a draw() method before the end of this chapter, for one example.

This is where you declare member functions:

```
class <class name>
{
    <data members>
    <function members>
};
```

Actually, the declaration of data and function members can be jumbled in as disorganized a fashion as you like. By tradition (and I think it's a wise tradition) the data members are declared first, and the functions are declared afterward.

This is the form of a member function declaration:

```
class <class name>
{
    <data members>

    <type> <func_name>( <parameters> );
};
```

Assume that you can draw(), resize(), and move() boxes. This is a class with those methods (omitting the details of the parameters):

```
class box
{
    ... <data members>
```

```
        void draw( params );
        void resize( params );
        void move( params );
    };
```

You access these member functions as you do the data members, but you use parens following the function names, enclosing any required parameters. Here are two examples:

```
    main()
    {
        box   b;
        box* bp = new box;


        . . .


        b.draw();
        bp->move();


        . . .


        delete bp;
    }
```

Of course, the draw() method may require the same parameters that our box_draw() used. Alternatively, it may depend on those values already being assigned as the data members of the box object. It's very likely that the move() method would require an x distance and a y distance to move. Here's one possible way of moving a box to the right:

```
        . . .
        bp->move( 3, 0 );   // 3 columns to the right
        . . .
```

The declaration of a function in a class (or structure) definition is analogous to the function declaration in plain procedural code, such as the code we wrote in the last chapter. It tells the compiler that the function exists, what type (if any) it will return, and what arguments should be passed. Like a procedural function declaration, it depends on the definition of the function being found elsewhere.

Defining Member Functions

The definition of a member function is placed in your code listing anywhere that would be sensible for a procedural function definition. I like to group all the member functions for a single class together, following any definitions for procedural functions.

There are two differences between a member function and a nonmember function. The first is that the member function is assigned to its class (or structure) with the *scope resolution* operator (::). The second is that, in the body of the member function, data and function members of the class are not preceded with an object variable or pointer.

For example, let's write a very simple version of a box::move() method:

```
void box::move( int xdist, int ydist )
{
    lft = lft + xdist;
    rgt = rgt + xdist;

    top = top + ydist;
    btm = btm + ydist;

    draw();
}
```

The syntax "box::move()" shows the scope resolution operator. We could have other objects, such as a menu cursor, that also have a move() method. The respective functions could be defined as box::move() and cursor::move(), so the compiler will know which function applies to which class.

Inside the member function, there is no prefix to members, such as lft or draw(). Outside a member function you would refer to b.lft or bp->draw(), for example. Inside, this is not done since the calling object specifies the object for which these are members:

```
    . . .
    box b;
    box c;
    . . .
    b.draw(); // uses box b's members
    c.draw(); // uses box c's members
```

Two special member functions are an exception to the syntax above. Neither the constructor nor the destructor function can be given a type.

Constructor and Destructor Functions

Most classes have a *constructor* function, and many classes have a *destructor* function. The constructor is called when a new object is created, and the destructor is called when it is deleted.

Two jobs are typical of the constructor function. First, the constructor will assign initial values to the data members of the object. Second, it will allocate space for any members that need a variable amount of space.

The destructor has one common job. It frees any space allocated by the constructor. (The fixed space needed for members, such as top and lft in our box example, is automatically allocated and freed by the compiler.)

N O T E

The constructor and destructor functions are not in any way restricted in what they can do. The jobs described here are typical, but your code can do anything at all.

The name of the constructor function is the name of the class (or structure). It cannot be given a type when it is declared or defined, and it cannot return a value. Here's a portion of a typical constructor for a box object:

```
// declaration in class definition
class box
{
private:
    int top, lft, ... ;
    ...

public:
    box( int lf, int tp, ... );
    ...
};
```

```
...
// definition of box constructor function
box::box( int lf, int tp, ... )
{
    lft = lf;
    top = tp;
    ...
}
```

The box class we have defined doesn't have any variable-length data to create, so simply assigning values to the box object's data members is the typical job for this constructor.

The sample shows a typical arrangement where the object's data members are private and its member functions are public. The constructor and destructor must be public to be of any use (except in base functions in the case of inheritance, which we'll come to later).

If our code is going to refer frequently to the width of a box, it may make sense to calculate and store this value when we create the box.

```
// declaration in class definition
class box
{
private:
    int top, lft, ... ;
    ...
    int width, length;

public:
    box( int lf, int tp, ... );
    ...
};


...
// definition of box constructor function
box::box( int lf, int tp, ... )
{
    lft = lf;
    top = tp;
```

```
     . . .
     width = rgt-lft+1;
     . . .

}
```

This constructor creates a calculated data member, width, that we can use whenever we may otherwise need to calculate the width of the box.

The destructor function's name is the same as that of the constructor except that it is prefixed with a tilde character:

```
public:
     box( int lf, int tp, ... ); // constructor
     ~box();                      // destructor
```

This name is also used in the definition. A typical style places the definition of the destructor function just after the definition of the constructor. Here is an example:

```
// declaration in class definition
class box
{
private:
     int top, lft, ... ;
     . . .
     int width, length;

public:
     box( int lf, int tp, ... );
     ~box();
     . . .
};


. . .
// definition of box constructor function
box::box( int lf, int tp, ... )
{
     lft = lf;
     top = tp;
     . . .
     width = rgt-lft+1;
```

```
        . . .
    }


    box::~box()
    {
        . . . // cleanup when a box is deleted
    }
```

In our example, there is no real need for a box destructor function, since there is no data space allocated in the constructor. A typical case that would need a destructor would be if we assigned a title to the box.

The title would be a string (a character array). We could allocate space to fit whatever title was assigned in the constructor and then copy the title into the allocated space. The destructor would then be responsible for deleting that space. The following example shows the general idea, omitting the details:

```
    class box
    {
    private:
        . . .
        char* title;

    public:
        box( ..., char* ttl, ... );
        ~box();
        . . .
    };


    box::box( ..., char* ttl, ... )
    {
        . . .
        title = new string( ttl );   // allocates space for title
        . . .
    }


    box::~box()
    {
        delete title;
    }
```

Calling the Constructor and Destructor

Are you getting itchy to put some of these concepts into practice? Hang on just a minute and we'll start preparing a box class to do just that. This is that last topic we have to cover before you can start writing code.

The *new* and *delete* operators, as you might expect, call the constructor and destructor functions, respectively. The *new* operator returns a pointer to the space where it created the new object (or structure). The *delete* operator is called with that pointer.

Here's an example:

```
box* bp = new box; // calls box::box()

... // box used

delete bp;          // calls box::~box()
```

There is another way to create a box, of course. That's by using a box variable, instead of a pointer to a box. When you use a box (or other class or structure) variable, you also call the constructor and destructor functions. The constructor is called when your variable is created, and the destructor is called when it goes out of scope.

We haven't considered scope, yet. One type of scope for a variable is the range of a function in which the variable exists. A variable exists in the function that declares the variable, except for global variables declared outside functions. Here's an example:

```
main()
{
    ...
    my_func();
    ...
}

void my_func()
{
    int i;
        // i exists here
    ...
```

```
}          // i is gone here
```

In this example, the variable i is declared in my_func(), so it exists from the point where it is declared until the end of my_func(). Object and structure variables have the same lifespan:

```
void my_func()
{
    box b;  // b exists here

    ... // box b is used

}          // b is gone here
```

You can guess from this example when the constructor and destructor are called. The constructor is called when the object variable (or structure variable) is declared. The destructor is called at the end of the function. Here's the same example, with more explicit comments:

```
void my_func()
{
    box b;  // calls box::box()
    ...         // box used
}          // calls box::~box()
```

N O T E

To be more technically correct, functions are one example of the use of a block statement, enclosing other statements in {} delimiters. Variables created within a block go out of scope at the end of that block. You can create variables, including object and structure variables, inside a while block, or an if block, or any other block you create. Exiting the block in which you declare the variable triggers the call of the destructor function.

With all that said, it's time to start working on our first class. Don't worry about having good notes or forgetting some of the details we've just gone over. We'll be using all these principles constantly throughout the rest of this book, so they will become second nature to you.

WE WRITE A BOX CLASS

To create box objects, we need a box class. The box is basic to any contemporary user interface work. Boxes surround dialog boxes, file editor windows, help messages, and nearly every other feature that we'll show on the screen.

I haven't used the word *window* because that implies more than a box. A window would know how to draw itself, how to maximize and minimize itself, how to have a title, and so on. A box, on the other hand, has a minor subset of a window's capabilities. As you'll see in the next chapter, we can use our box as the base class from which we start building windows.

For now, let's get on to the box class, beginning with the basics. Our first decision is fundamental to the design: Should the constructor function just record the basic characteristics of a box, or should it draw the box?

My first box class constructor drew the box. That was a mistake. One of the basic things that your user interface will need to do is to redraw itself. Consider Borland's TCLite as one example of a typical text-mode interface.

When you open a file, a new window pops up over any other windows on the screen. When you close the top window, the other windows get repainted. Popping up the Watch window, for another example, may obscure a portion of your file window. When you close the Watch window, the user interface (UI) repaints the file window.

So drawing itself has to be a capability of a box, if boxes are to be the basis for windows. You don't want the draw() method to be part of the constructor.

T I P

When you face a decision about what to put in the constructor, always err on the side of creating multiple methods. The constructor can call draw(), for example. In this way, the drawing will be done when the box is created, but the draw() method will be available whenever else you need it.

Let's get on to actually building a constructor function.

The Constructor

First, we'll need a framework. I'll call the files that I use TE*xxx*. The TE stands for Tiny Editor. The *xxx* will describe whatever capabilities are in the particular file. I'll put all the windowing-related classes into TEWIN.CPP, for example.

Start with a new file, TEWIN.CPP. It's all new, so there's no sample on disk. Listing 4-6 shows the starting skeleton.

Listing 4-6: TEWIN.CPP

```
// TEWIN.CPP—Tiny Editor windowing capabilities
// Copyright 1995, Martin L. Rinehart

// mainline for testing only
   int main()
   {
       return 0;
   }

// end of TEWIN.CPP
```

Eventually, we'll have our Tiny Editor mainline in TE.CPP. For the moment, it's convenient to have it here in our first TE file.

Next, we'll need a class definition. We can borrow the parameters from our box_draw() code. By reusing the names of those parameters, we'll be able to recycle the code, too. Listing 4-7 adds the class definition.

Listing 4-7: TEWIN.CPP

```
// TEWIN.CPP—Tiny Editor windowing capabilities
// Copyright 1995, Martin L. Rinehart


class box
{
private:
    int lft, top, rgt, btm;

    char border[8];
```

```
      int outline_clr, contents_clr;

public:
    box( int lf, int tp, int rt, int bt,
        char* brdr,
        int out_clr, int con_clr );
    ~box();

    void draw();
};
```

```
// mainline for testing only
    int main()
    {
        return 0;
    }
```

```
// end of TEWIN.CPP
```

Enter this class definition and check your work with Alt+F9. The line private: is redundant—class members are private by default. I still like to put this line into my class definitions. It doesn't cost anything in the compiled code.

I've allowed exactly eight characters for the border character array. That will work out in the constructor, but you'll need to remember that there is no trailing null on this array.

The public members are the constructor, the destructor, and the draw() method. As you can see, the names of the parameters are shortened versions of the names of the data members. This convention lets us write lines like:

```
lft = lf; // data member = parameter value
```

To write the constructor, we could write eight separate assignment statements, such as:

```
border[0] = brdr[0];
    border[1] = brdr[1];
        . . .
    border[7] = brdr[7];
```

A loop will take care of these assignments more succinctly, however. The for loop is perfect for this use. Its syntax is:

```
for ( <init>; <condition>; <end action> )
    <statement>
```

Like the while loop and the if statement, the typical for statement is a block statement, so the for loop often looks like this:

```
for ( <init>; <condition>; <end action> )
{
    <statements>
}
```

The <init> portion is any initializing action. A typical action is to create and assign a value to a loop counter. Here's one we'll use all the time:

```
for ( int i = 0; <condition>; <end action> )
{
    <statements>
}
```

The <condition> is a logical expression. While the condition is true, the looping continues. Here's the one we will use in our assignment of eight border characters:

```
for ( int i = 0; i < 8; <end action> )
{
    <statements>
}
```

The <end action> is anything that you want to happen at the end of each iteration of the loop. Typically, you use it to increment a counter, which is just what we'll do:

```
for ( int i = 0; i < 8; i++ )
{
    <statements>
}
```

For our simple assignment, we don't need a block statement. One assignment statement will do:

```
for ( int i = 0; i < 8; i++ )
    border[i] = brdr[i];
```

The other statements in the constructor just assign the parameters to the appropriate data members of the box object that is being created. Listing 4-8 shows the complete constructor.

Listing 4-8: TEWIN.CPP

```
// mainline for testing only
    int main()
    {
        return 0;
    }
```

```
box::box( int lf, int tp, int rt, int bt,
        char* brdr,
        int out_clr, int con_clr )
{
    lft = lf;
    top = tp;
    rgt = rt;
    btm = bt;

    for ( int i = 0; i < 8; i++ )
        border[i] = brdr[i];

    outline_clr = out_clr;
    contents_clr = con_clr;
}
```

```
// end of TEWIN.CPP
```

Again, just use Alt+F9 to check your work. The real testing will have to wait until we implement the draw() method.

The Destructor

So far, we haven't done anything that really needs a destructor. If we had allocated another object, such as a title string, we would need to delete it in the destructor. But we haven't, so for the moment, there's nothing for the destructor to do.

Regardless, I add the destructor shell that you see in Listing 4-9.

Listing 4-9: TEWIN.CPP

```
box::box( int lf, int tp, int rt, int bt,
        char* brdr,
        int out_clr, int con_clr )
{
    lft = lf;
    top = tp;
    rgt = rt;
    btm = bt;

    for ( int i = 0; i < 8; i++ )
        border[i] = brdr[i];

    outline_clr = out_clr;
    contents_clr = con_clr;
}

box::~box()
{
    // nothing to do
}
```

```
// end of TEWIN.CPP
```

The compiler takes care of freeing the space allocated to the fixed-length members of a structure or object. In our box class, that's 12 bytes for 6 integers and 8 bytes in our border[] string. (It also includes whatever overhead C++ adds for its internal bookkeeping.)

The Draw Method

We're already about 95 percent of the way to a completed draw() method, with our box_draw() procedure. To create the draw() method efficiently, you'll need to work with BOX_DRAW.CPP and TEWIN.CPP simultaneously.

For fast two-file work, open both files with F3. Press F6 to switch from one to the other. If there are any other windows open, press Alt+F3 to close the unwanted window after pressing F6 transfers you to it. Use F6 and Alt+F3 as needed to close everything but the two windows you want to work with. Then copy to the clipboard (highlight text and press Ctrl+Ins) from one window and paste from the clipboard (position the cursor and press Shift+Ins) in the second window.

The following steps are the ones that you need to take to create the draw() method.

S T E P   B Y   S T E P

1. Add the line #include <CONIO.H>, which you see at the top of Listing 4-10.

2. Copy the blanks[] array lines from BOX_DRAW.CPP into TEWIN.CPP, as shown at the top of Listing 4-10.

3. Copy the entire box_draw() procedure from BOX_DRAW.CPP into TEWIN.CPP.

4. Change the line "void box_draw(...)" to the simple line "box::draw()," as shown near the center of Listing 4-10.

Listing 4-10: TEWIN.CPP

```
// TEWIN.CPP—Tiny Editor windowing capabilities
// Copyright 1995, Martin L. Rinehart

#include <CONIO.H>


char blanks[] =  // 80 space chars
    "                                                                                "
    "                                                                                ";
```

```
class box

...
```

```
void box::draw()
{
/*
```

```
COORDINATES MUST BE WITHIN SCREEN.   MINIMUM BOX IS 4 COLS
BY 3 ROWS.   DRAWING FAILS IF YOU GO TO BOTH SCREEN RIGHT AND
SCREEN BOTTOM.
```

```
...
```

```
    // repairing blanks[]
        i = rgt-lft;
        blanks[0] = blanks[i] = blanks[i+1] = ' ';
}
```

```
// end of TEWIN.CPP
```

This code will *not* compile, yet. Our box_draw() called itself to clear its center. In this context, this step is better done using fresh code, taking advantage of the for loop.

To get a routine that compiles, stub out the center drawing code with an empty statement, like this:

```
    // repaint the center
        if ( outline_clr != contents_clr )
            ;
```

That semicolon on a line by itself (it could also come at the end of the previous line) is a null statement. The if needs to be followed by a statement, and the semicolon is a syntactically complete statement.

Now let's write some code that will complete the job of painting the box center. Listing 4-11 shows code that will do the job.

Listing 4-11: TEWIN.CPP

```
    // repaint the center
        if ( outline_clr != contents_clr )
        {
            textattr( contents_clr );
            int i, j;
            for ( i = top+1; i < btm; i++ )
            {
                gotoxy( lft+1, i );
                for ( j = lft+1; j < rgt; j++ )
                    putch( ' ' );
            }
        }


    // repairing blanks[]
```

The first item of business is to reset the text attribute to the contents color. Then we use nested for loops. An outer for loop sets the counter i from the line after the top to the line before the bottom. After i is set, the gotoxy() function positions the cursor just inside the left border at line i. Then another loop steps the counter j from the column just inside the left edge to the one just before the right edge. As j is incremented, we putch() a blank, which is written in the proper color.

You can check your work with Alt+F9. To start serious testing, you need to create a mainline that creates a box and then calls the box.draw() method.

To do this, we'll add a little to the syntax we've discussed so far. You've seen that you can create an object just as you create a variable of one of the built-in types. For examples:

```
int i;
char c;

box b;
```

This syntax is very straightforward, but it doesn't work when you need to pass arguments to a constructor function. For that purpose, you can add arguments, in parentheses, after the variable name, like this:

```
    int i;
    char c;

    box b( <constructor params> );
```

Listing 4-12 shows a mainline routine that uses this syntax to create a box.

Listing 4-12: TEWIN.CPP

```
// mainline for testing only
    int main()
    {
        textattr( 7 ); // white on black
        clrscr();

        // 62 is yellow on cyan, 23 is white on blue
        box b( 1, 5, 45, 15, "┌┐│┘─└│", 62, 23 );

        b.draw();

        return 0;
    }
```

This mainline clears the screen to black and then creates and draws a box. Figure 4-4 shows my result.

T I P

The border string is available in BOX_DRAW.CPP. You can copy it from that file using the same two-file technique you used to build the draw() method.

Press Ctrl+F9 and your program will draw the box. You'll have to press Alt+F5 to view the DOS screen.

Debugging

There shouldn't be much need for debugging this code, since we've used already debugged code. This is a good time, however, to experiment with F7 and F8.

Figure 4-4: A box object on the DOS screen.

We've used F7 already to step through our code one line at a time. After you press F7, TCLite's status line (the bottom line) switches to suggest these choices:

▶ F1—Help

▶ F7—Trace

▶ F8—Step

▶ F9—Make

▶ F10—Menu

Both F7 and F8 will step through a program, one line at a time. The difference is that F7 will trace into a subroutine if the line calls one, and F8 will step over the subroutine.

The most dramatic way to see the difference between the keys is to use F8 to step through your whole program. You'll see the highlight step through your code, one line at a time. It skips the lines that do not correspond to actual generated code, such as blanks and comments.

Complete the program using F8. Then repeat the process using F7. This time the line that creates a box (box b(1, 5, ...)) skips your cursor right into the constructor, box::box(). This is, of course, exactly the sequence your program is following.

You can trace into your constructor, still using F7. You'll need eight steps to complete the loop that assigns border characters. Go ahead and use Ctrl+F7 to set watches whenever you want.

Once your constructor has run to completion, if you continue to press F7 you'll trace into the draw() method. As you'll see, tracing into draw() is tedious, due to the loops.

The way to step through a loop when you are debugging is to look at it once or twice with F7 taking you through each step. When you are confident that it is working correctly, position your cursor at the line after the loop and press F4 to run to the cursor. This will run the loop at full speed, stopping at the line where you positioned your cursor. Then you can resume stepping with F7 or F8 to continue.

When you are confident that your box object is being created correctly, let's go on to place a handful of boxes on the screen.

USING BOX OBJECTS

Your program now creates and uses your very first object. We could leave it here and charge forward, but I don't want to. First, I think you're entitled to pat yourself on the back and have a little fun with the code you've created.

Second, this is a good point to introduce another preprocessor directive, since you'll see that it can make your programming much easier.

#define Your Colors

We saw one example of defined constants when we used textmode(), setting C80 or C4350. You can define your own constants whenever they will make your code clearer or your coding easier. A good example is in the use of colors supplied as text attributes.

So far, our code has depended on having comments accompany some fairly meaningless numbers—62 is yellow on cyan, for example. Another way to achieve the desired effect, readable code, is to use #define to create a defined, meaningful synonym for 62.

The #define preprocessor directive is similar to a text editor's search and replace command. The preprocessor will replace your defined term with its definition. The syntax is:

```
#define <term> <definition>
```

Here's an example:

```
#define YELLOW_CYAN 62
```

With this definition, you can use the defined term YELLOW_CYAN anyplace in the code. The preprocessor will substitute the value 62. (This is done by straight text substitution, just as a text editor would execute a search and replace command.)

Listing 4-13 uses #define to create some constants and then uses the defined constants in the code, in place of the numbers.

Listing 4-13: TEWIN.CPP

```
// TEWIN.CPP—Tiny Editor windowing capabilities
// Copyright 1995, Martin L. Rinehart

#include <CONIO.H>

char blanks[] =  // 80 space chars
    "                                                      "
    "                                                      ";

#define WHITE_BLACK   7
#define YELLOW_CYAN 62
#define WHITE_BLUE   23

class box

...

// mainline for testing only
    int main()
    {
        textattr( WHITE_BLACK );
        clrscr();

        box b( 1, 5, 45, 15, "┌┐┘─└│",
            YELLOW_CYAN, WHITE_BLUE );

        b.draw();

        return 0;
    }
```

As Listing 4-13 shows, not only is this code more readable, it saves you the trouble of adding a comment with every color number you use. Let's use this technique to add a bunch more boxes.

Drawing Lots of Boxes

We can create lots of boxes by taking one box and putting it in several different places. To do this, we'll need a method to move a box. Listing 4-14 shows one that moves the box but doesn't change its size.

Listing 4-14: TEWIN.CPP

```
class box
{
private:
    int lft, top, rgt, btm;

    char* border;

    int outline_clr, contents_clr;

public:
    box( int lf, int tp, int rt, int bt,
        char* brdr,
        int out_clr, int con_clr );
    ~box();

    void draw();
    void moveto( int new_lft, int new_top );
};


...


void box::moveto( int new_lft, int new_top )
{
    rgt = rgt + new_lft - lft;
    lft = new_lft;

    btm = btm + new_top - top;
    top = new_top;
```

```
}
```

```
// end of TEWIN.CPP
```

This is a very simple routine. You'll find, by the way, that many object methods are just as simple as this one.

Listing 4-15 shows how you can use this routine. Don't follow my example too faithfully—have some fun putting boxes where you like them. But don't push your box off the screen.

W A R N I N G

Most memory managers expect DOS code to respect the boundaries of the screen. Writing, for example, to line 51 will probably overwrite other code or data that your memory manager thought it could squeeze into an unused corner of memory above the first 640K. If you are going to do much box moving, you'll want to add boundary checking code.

Listing 4-15: TEWIN.CPP

```
// mainline for testing only
   int main()
   {
       textattr( WHITE_BLACK );
       clrscr();

       box b( 1, 5, 45, 15, "┌┐│┘─└│",
           YELLOW_CYAN, WHITE_BLUE );

       b.draw();

       b.moveto(  5,  8 ); b.draw();
       b.moveto( 10, 10 ); b.draw();
       b.moveto( 15, 12 ); b.draw();

       return 0;
   }
```

When you press Ctrl+F9, you should get boxes artistically placed around your screen. (You did do it artistically, didn't you?) Figure 4-5 shows my version.

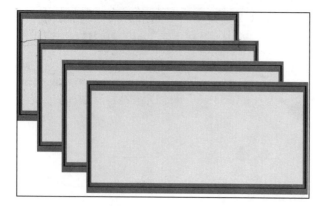

Figure 4-5: Drawing a set of boxes on the screen.

Another way to get different boxes is to create several box objects and draw them all. Listing 4-16 shows an example.

Listing 4-16: TEWIN.CPP

```cpp
// mainline for testing only
    int main()
    {
        textattr( WHITE_BLACK );
        clrscr();

        box b( 1, 5, 45, 15, " ⌐⌐|⌐—⌐|",
            YELLOW_CYAN, WHITE_BLUE );

        b.draw();

        b.moveto(  5,  8 ); b.draw();
        b.moveto( 10, 10 ); b.draw();
        b.moveto( 15, 12 ); b.draw();
```

```
box c( 10, 1, 20, 15, "□|⌐¬|",
    WHITE_BLUE, YELLOW_CYAN );
c.draw();


box d( 30, 1, 40, 15, "□|⌐¬|",
    WHITE_BLUE, YELLOW_CYAN );
d.draw();

    return 0;
}
```

Did you notice that I switched the colors on the last two boxes? Try something like that yourself.

#define Border Strings

One of the most tedious bits of work you can do in DOS programming is to look up border characters to put together your boxes. You can do this by running CHARS to find your characters, translating their coordinates to decimal, and then using the numeric keypad to enter these characters.

N O T E

Some editors have a direct way of entering characters above 128. With most of the others, holding the Alt key down while you tap three digits on the numeric pad sends a high character. For example, holding Alt down and tapping 201 generates the upper-left corner of a double-line box.

To save you all this trouble, there is a tiny file called BORDERS.CPP in your SAMPLES\ subdirectory. For the work here, get that file and copy it into TEWIN.CPP, as Listing 4-17 shows.

Listing 4-17: TEWIN.CPP

```
// TEWIN.CPP—Tiny Editor windowing capabilities
// Copyright 1995, Martin L. Rinehart
```

```
#include <CONIO.H>

char blanks[] =  // 80 space chars
    "                                                        "
    "                                                        ";

#define WHITE_BLACK  7
#define YELLOW_CYAN 62
#define WHITE_BLUE  23
```

```
#define SINGLE    "┌┐│┘─└│"
#define DOUBLE    "╔╗║╝═╚║"
#define SING_DOUB "╒╕│╛═╘│"
#define DOUB_SING "╓╖║╜─╙║"
```

```
...

// mainline for testing only
    int main()
    {
        textattr( WHITE_BLACK );
        clrscr();

        box b( 1, 5, 45, 15, SINGLE,
            YELLOW_CYAN, WHITE_BLUE );

        b.draw();

        b.moveto(  5,  8 ); b.draw();
        b.moveto( 10, 10 ); b.draw();
        b.moveto( 15, 12 ); b.draw();

        box c( 10, 1, 20, 15, DOUBLE,
            WHITE_BLUE, YELLOW_CYAN );
        c.draw();

        box d( 30, 1, 40, 15, SING_DOUB,
            WHITE_BLUE, YELLOW_CYAN );
        d.draw();
```

```
        return 0;

    }
```

Try these border strings in your own code. You'll see that they make it simple to use different border strings.

H I N T

I call the style with single-line verticals and double-line horizontals SING_DOUB. The contrary is DOUB_SING, of course. I never could remember which was which, though. If you have a better idea than mine, go right to it. Figure 4-6 shows a sampling of different box outline strings.

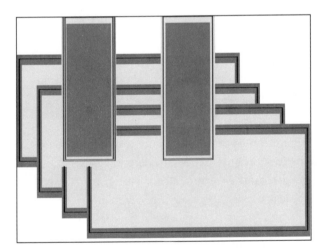

Figure 4-6: Using different outline strings.

Okay, we've had enough fun, and we've learned to #define constants that make our code more readable (and easier to type). We're ready to move on. For your reference, my version of TEWIN at this point is in your SAMPLES\ subdirectory as 06TEWIN.CPP.

04

SUMMARY

You're another big step on your way at this point. You've built a box class and can decorate your screen with it. In the next chapter we'll be putting it into use as the base for dialog boxes.

While you were here, you learned about the old-style structures that didn't have member functions. We then went on to C++-style structures and classes, which have data and code members.

While we were looking at these topics, you built structure and class definitions. You used these definitions to create structure and object variables. You declared these variables, initialized them, and used them.

We looked at the difference between object variables and pointers to objects. You saw the member access operators, dots and arrows, that are used with objects and pointers, respectively.

You used the scope resolution operator to define member functions. These included constructor and destructor functions. You used the *new* and *delete* operators, along with constructors and destructors, to create and remove objects.

You saw how the private and public member access specifications distinguished structures and classes and could be used in both to control access to members.

You saw how variables are scoped to the block in which they're declared, and how objects' destructors are called when those objects go out of scope.

You learned more about procedural programming, using the for loop and defining constants with the #define preprocessor directive.

You did your work using the built-in debugger. You used F7 to trace into routines and both F7 and F8 to step through your program. You also used Ctrl+F8 to toggle breakpoints and Ctrl+F7 to set watches.

That's certainly a lot of new material, but don't worry about remembering it. We'll be using all of it constantly throughout the rest of this book.

In the next chapter, we'll start using one of the most powerful concepts in object-oriented programming: inheritance.

All modern UIs depend on dialog boxes as one of their primary means of communicating with the user. We'll use dialog boxes to communicate with ourselves in our Tiny Editor.

In this chapter we'll build a dialog box class, using inheritance—a powerful feature of object-oriented programming. While we do this, you'll:

- Use class inheritance
- Learn about base and derived classes
- Use escape characters in strings
- Use the gettext() and puttext() functions
- Learn about base and derived constructors
- Pass parameters to base constructors
- Learn about base and derived destructors
- Use address and dereferencing operators
- Use protected access in base classes
- Use the *new* operator to create buffers
- Create your own #include header file
- Use strlen() and strcpy() functions from STRING.H
- Overload member functions
- Learn about pre- and post- increment and decrement operators

5

Dialog Boxes
Inherit from Boxes

We've built a box class. Boxes are a useful part of many things, including dialog
boxes. A dialog box will need to know how to draw a box, such as the ones we
programmed in the last chapter. C++ provides a very convenient mechanism for
one class to incorporate the capabilities of another class. It's called *inheritance*.

WHAT IS INHERITANCE?

When one class inherits from another, it incorporates all of that class's data
members and member functions. Our dialog box classes, for example, will inherit from the box class. That means that they will "know" how to draw themselves. (Of course, it really means that they will have access to the draw()
method that we've programmed, as well as access to the data members that the
draw() method depends on.)

Base and Derived Classes

We'll create a dialog class that inherits from the box class. The dialog class is said to be *derived* from the box class. Put another way, the box class is called a *base class* for the dialog class.

The base class provides all its members to the derived class. This means that all the methods of the base class will be methods of the derived class. Of course, the reason for deriving a new class from a base is to add new functionality.

For example, we'll derive message, yes/no, and other dialogs from the base dialog type. The message dialog will display a message and wait for a keypress before returning control to the program that launches this dialog.

The yes/no dialog is a little more strict. It will wait for a Y or N keypress before it returns control. Of course, it will have an appropriate usage tip requesting one of these keypresses. The message dialog will have a "press any key" usage tip.

By inheriting from a base class and then adding these specific behaviors, we'll have objects that do precisely what we want. We'll use them as if they were fundamental components of our C++ programming language, as soon as we've made them work.

Subclasses and Other Misnomers

There's nothing really complex about inheritance, but the unfortunate term "subclass" has also been applied to derived classes. In fact, a derived class inherits all the members, data and code, of its base class and then it adds some of its own. The derived class's data and methods are supersets of the base class's data and methods.

Unfortunately, standard object terminology uses the term "subclass" for a derived class. I don't use this term because it's dead wrong. A derived class is a superset, not a subset, of the base class.

W A R N I N G

A subclass is a derived class. There is nothing "sub" about a subclass. Derived classes are supersets of their base classes. When you hear the term "subclass," mentally delete it and insert the more descriptive term "derived class."

The term "subclass" will not appear again in this book. I don't recommend that you use it unless you have a good reason to want to confuse people.

PROGRAMMING POPUP BOXES

The first thing that would be nice for our boxes is the ability to pop up over other things on the screen. Actually, that popup capability isn't really what a popup does, at all.

To simulate the popup functionality, a popup box saves the screen that was behind itself. When it is time for your popup to pop back down, it restores the original screen. The effect is that the popup is popping up over whatever else is on the screen and then popping down, revealing the former screen.

What we'll want is a popup class that is derived from the box class. It will know how to draw itself, as boxes do, but it will also be smart enough to save and restore the screen.

Deriving a Class

The syntax for deriving one class from another is simple enough:

```
class <derived class name> : <base class name>
{
    // new data and methods here
};
```

Remember that the derived class inherits all the data and methods of the base class, so you don't repeat any of the base class's members. Skipping details, this is what the popup class definition could look like:

```
class popup : box
{
private:
    char* screen_save_buffer

public:
    // constructor, destructor and other methods here
};
```

The popup class with that definition has a character buffer for saving the screen that we will create in the popup's constructor and free in the popup's destructor function. It also has the members of the box class—lft, top, and all the rest.

Base and Derived Constructors

When you derive a class, its base class's constructor is called (if the base class has a constructor) before its own constructor (if any) is called. Let's create our first example and test this behavior.

To yield neater output, I'm going to use *escape characters* in the output string. Escape characters are provided primarily for characters that you can't type into a string or character constant, such as carriage returns and control characters.

You create an escape character by starting with the backslash character, which is not interpreted as a character but as a signal that an escape character definition is starting. Some common escape characters are:

▶ \n—newline

▶ \r—return

▶ \l—linefeed

▶ \b—backspace

▶ \f—formfeed

▶ \'—single quote

▶ \"—double quote

▶ \\—backslash character

▶ \t—tab

You can also use either octal or hexadecimal numbers for escape characters.

▶ \ooo—octal character

▶ \xhh—hex character

For example, an escape character (decimal 27) could be defined in either of these ways:

```
esc = '\33'  // octal 33 == decimal 27
esc = '\x1B' // hex   1B == decimal 27
```

Listing 5-1 shows a simple example of a base class and a derived class. Their constructors simply announce that they are in business. The code is all new, so it's not on disk. Enter and run it with Ctrl+F9.

Listing 5-1: T.CPP

```cpp
// t.cpp

#include <conio.h>

class base
{
public:
    base();
};

class deriv : base
{
public:
    deriv();
};

int main()
{
    clrscr();

    deriv d;
    getch();

    return 0;
}

base::base()
{
    cprintf( "in base constructor\n\r" );
}

deriv::deriv()
{
    cprintf( "in deriv constructor\n\r" );
}

// end of t.cpp
```

When you run this program, it will give the result shown in Figure 5-1. The base constructor runs first, followed by the derived class's constructor.

```
in base constructor
in deriv constructor
```

Figure 5-1: Exploring constructors and destructors.

Parameters to Constructors

Our abstract classes in Listing 5-1 had simple constructors that did not use parameters. Let's add parameters, since we'll need parameters for a popup box (to initialize coordinates, a border, and colors, as you need to do for the base box).

There is nothing new here in the syntax of the class definition, but there is one thing to watch for. Your constructor in the derived class must pass all the parameters that the base class's constructor needs, so all the parameters for both the base and derived classes must be included in the derived class's constructor.

There is a bit of syntax added to the constructor function's definition in the derived class. It is written like this example:

```
deriv::deriv( int p1, int p2, char p3, ... ) :
    base( p1, p2 )
{
    ... //deriv constructor logic here
}
```

The base class constructor's function call appears, following a colon, after the parameters to the derived class's constructor. The arguments passed to the base class's constructor must be parameters of the derived class, or constants, or expressions using only those parameters and constants.

H I N T

The rule for arguments passed to the base class constructor seems restrictive, at first, but makes sense if you think about it. Besides constants and the values passed as parameters to the derived class constructor, what data would the base class's constructor have to work with?

Let's try an example. Listing 5-2 adds parameters to the classes you built in
Listing 5-1. A good way to check your work is to set a breakpoint (Ctrl+F8) at
the getch() line in main() and run the program to that point.

Listing 5-2: T.CPP

```cpp
// t.cpp

#include <conio.h>

class base
{
private:
    int b1, b2;

public:
    base( int p1, int p2 );
};

class deriv : base
{
private:
    int d1;

public:
    deriv( int p1, int p2, int p3 );
};

int main()
{
    clrscr();

    deriv d( 1, 2, 3 );
    getch();

    return 0;
}

base::base( int p1, int p2 )
```

```
{
    b1 = p1;
    b2 = p2;

    cprintf( "in base constructor\n\r" );
}

deriv::deriv( int p1, int p2, int p3 ) :
    base( p1, p2 )
{
    d1 = p3;
    cprintf( "in deriv constructor\n\r" );
}

// end of t.cpp
```

If you stop the code in Listing 5-2 at the getch() line (with a breakpoint, or by putting the cursor there and pressing F4), you can take a look at d, the deriv class object. These are the data members that you can look at in the Watch window:

```
d.b1
d.b2
d.d1
```

The value of these three data members should be 1, 2, and 3, respectively. You can see in your Watch window that you address the data members of the base class as if they were defined in the derived class. In fact, when you told the compiler that the derived class was inheriting from the base, you *were* defining these data members in the derived class.

Base and Derived Destructors

When you delete an object, you call its destructor function, as we have already seen. When you delete a derived object, you call its destructors in the reverse order of the constructors. The derived class's destructor, if any, runs, and then the base class's destructor, if any, runs.

Listing 5-3 adds destructors that show this sequence clearly. Add the new lines to T.CPP and use Ctrl+F9 to test. (You should remove the breakpoint.)

Listing 5-3: T.CPP

```cpp
// t.cpp

#include <conio.h>

class base
{
private:
    int b1, b2;

public:
    base( int p1, int p2 );
    ~base();
};

class deriv : base
{
private:
    int d1;

public:
    deriv( int p1, int p2, int p3 );
    ~deriv();
};

int main()
{
    clrscr();

    deriv d( 1, 2, 3 );
    delete &d;

    getch();

    return 0;
}

base::base( int p1, int p2 )
```

```
    {
        b1 = p1;
        b2 = p2;

        cprintf( "in base constructor\n\r" );
    }
```

```
base::~base()
{
    cprintf( "destroying base\n\r" );
}
```

```
deriv::deriv( int p1, int p2, int p3 ) :
    base( p1, p2 )
{
    d1 = p3;
    cprintf( "in deriv constructor\n\r" );
}
```

```
deriv::~deriv()
{
    cprintf( "destroying deriv\n\r" );
}
```

```
// end of t.cpp
```

The line that deletes your deriv object uses the address operator, the ampersand. The *delete* operator works on addresses, not on objects. It is designed for use like this:

```
obj_type* foo = new obj_type

... // use pointer foo

delete foo;
```

In this case, foo is not an object; it is a pointer to the object. The *delete* operator requires a pointer to the object. The value of the pointer to an object is the address of the object. This is equivalent code:

```
obj_type foo; // foo is an obj_type variable

... // use object foo

delete &foo; // &foo is the address of foo -- a pointer
```

In many ways, the address operator and the dereferencing operator can be thought of as a pair. Consider this statement:

```
char* cptr = "ABCDE";
```

You usually think of a pointer variable like this as pointing to a string such as "ABCDE"—which is what it does. But more precisely, cptr is pointing to the first letter, "A," in the string. For example:

```
char* cptr = "ABCDE";

putch( *cptr );      // outputs an 'A'
putch( *(cptr+1) ); // outputs a 'B'
```

The dereferencing operator and the address operator invert each other's operations:

```
char* cptr = "ABCDE";

printf( &(*cptr) ); // same as printf( cptr )
```

When you have a pointer, you can use the dereferencing operator, *, (called star), to refer to the contents of the address. When you have a nonpointer variable, you can use the address operator, &, when you want the address of the variable. This is another way of stating it:

```
any_type  var;
any_type* ptr;

ptr = &var;

f1( var );  // call f1() with an any_type var
f1( *ptr ); // same

f2( &var ); // call f2() with a pointer to any_type
f2( ptr );  // same
```

Back to our example, T.CP. When your destructors are called (deleting a derived class calls both destructors) the logic in the derived class's destructor is run first. Then the logic in the base class's destructor is run.

A Popup Class

Now that you know how constructors and destructors are handled with base and derived classes and how to handle parameters for the constructors, let's go on to write a popup class and test it.

First, let's add the popup class to TEWIN.CPP. I'll give it a constructor and a destructor and ask them to tell me they're there when I hope they should be.

Listing 5-4 shows the code I've added to TEWIN.CPP. Add the new popup class definition above the mainline, below the box class definition. Then add the declaration and initialization of the popup variable to the mainline. Finally, add the constructor and the destructor just above the end of the file. Use Ctrl+F9 to test, and check your result with Alt+F5.

Listing 5-4: TEWIN.CPP

```
// TEWIN.CPP -- Tiny Editor windowing capabilities


...


class popup : box
{
public:
    popup( int lf, int tp, int rt, int bt,
        char* brdr,
        int out_clr, int con_clr );
    ~popup();
};

// mainline for testing only
    int main()
    {
        textattr( WHITE_BLACK );
        clrscr();

        box b( 1, 5, 45, 15, SINGLE,
            YELLOW_CYAN, WHITE_BLUE );
```

```
        b.draw();

        b.moveto(  5,  8 ); b.draw();
        b.moveto( 10, 10 ); b.draw();
        b.moveto( 15, 12 ); b.draw();

        box c( 10,  1, 20, 15, DOUBLE,
            WHITE_BLUE, YELLOW_CYAN );
        c.draw();

        box d( 30,  1, 40, 15, SING_DOUB,
            WHITE_BLUE, YELLOW_CYAN );
        d.draw();

        popup pu( 3, 5, 35, 10, DOUB_SING,
            WHITE_BLACK, WHITE_BLACK );

        return 0;
    }

...


popup::popup( int lf, int tp, int rt, int bt,
        char* brdr,
        int out_clr, int con_clr ) :
    box( lf, tp, rt, bt, brdr, out_clr, con_clr )
{
    cprintf( "\n\rbuilding popup" );
}

popup::~popup()
{
    cprintf( "\n\rdeleting popup" );
}

// end of TEWIN.CPP
```

When you run this code, you should get the "building popup" and "deleting popup" messages in addition to all the boxes that we've painted. With this framework, the next job is to actually make the popup appear to pop up and down.

Popping up is easy. All we have to do is draw the box. Almost all we have to do is to call the draw() method of the popup class (inherited from box), and we've popped our box up.

I did say almost. Add the two lines in Listing 5-5 to main(), press Ctrl+F9, and look at the error. What's wrong?

Listing 5-5: TEWIN.CPP

```
        popup pu( 3, 5, 35, 10, DOUB_SING,
            WHITE_BLACK, WHITE_BLACK );

    pu.draw();
    getch();


        return 0;
```

The error message tells you that box::draw() is not accessible from main(). The good news is that adding a single word to the code will fix the problem.

The problem comes in the treatment of access rights when a derived class inherits from a base class. By default, all the members of the base class (public, private, and protected) become private members of the derived class.

The error message tells you that the method exists but is private. It's just as if you had coded this:

```
class foo
{
private:
    void meth();
};

int main()
{
    foo f;
    f.meth();  // can't do this!
}
```

You can call a private method only from another method within the same class. This fact is generally useful when you have a complex method that requires its own supporting subroutines. Here is an example:

```
class foo
{
public:
    void do_it();
private:
    void do_it_subr1();
    void do_it_subr2();
};

int main()
{
    foo f;
    f.do_it(); // this is OK!
}

void foo::do_it()
{
    do_it_subr1();
    do_it_subr2();
}

void foo::do_it_subr1()
{
... // private, called from object's method
}

    ... // ditto for do_it_subr2()
```

For example, suppose we had broken box.draw() into two parts, coded in their own functions. One part could draw the outline, and the other could clear the contents. The draw() method could be public, and it could call the private methods, draw_outline() and draw_contents().

Apart from this situation, however, you generally want your methods to be public. In fact, you commonly want everything that is public in a base class to be public in a derived class as well. The way to make this work is to add the public keyword ahead of the base class name in the function definition:

```
class deriv : public base
```

This makes all the public members of base public members of deriv. The private members of base remain private. The alternative is to define the base class as private:

```
class deriv: private base // default!
```

This is the default access, with all members of base made private in deriv.

T I P

Since private is the default access, you can skip the access permission word, but don't. If you always explicitly call your derived class public or private, you'll avoid errors such as the one you just saw, calling a method that was inadvertently left private.

This long explanation points to the short fix for your program. Add the public keyword, as shown in Listing 5-6.

Listing 5-6: TEWIN.CPP

```
class popup : public box
{
public:
    popup( int lf, int tp, int rt, int bt,
        char* brdr,
        int out_clr, int con_clr );
    ~popup();
};
```

With public access, main() can call pu.draw(), and your box has popped up as you specified. Now we have to get it to pop back down. To do that, we'll need to save the screen behind the popup.

There are two places we could do this. We can save the screen when we run the constructor, or we can save it just before we draw the popup. I'll do the save in the constructor. Bear in mind that this wouldn't be satisfactory if we were going to change the box's location after running the constructor.

Let's take a look at the new constructor and destructor code we need to save and restore the screen under our popup. It takes only five lines. Enter the code in Listing 5-7 and test it with Alt+F9. It won't work, but don't worry.

Listing 5-7: TEWIN.CPP

```
popup::popup( int lf, int tp, int rt, int bt,
        char* brdr,
        int out_clr, int con_clr ) :
    box( lf, tp, rt, bt, brdr, out_clr, con_clr )
{
    int bufsize = (rgt-lft+1)*(btm-top+1)*2;

    screen_save_buf = new char[ bufsize ];

    gettext( lft, top, rgt, btm, screen_save_buf );
}

popup::~popup()
{
    puttext( lft, top, rgt, btm, screen_save_buf );

    delete screen_save_buf;
}

// end of TEWIN.CPP
```

The first thing to do is calculate the size of the buffer we need for the screen save. This is the width times the length of the rectangle, in characters, doubled.

H I N T

Each character on screen requires two bytes of video memory. One byte holds the character's own value (for instance, an 'A'), and the other byte holds the character's text attribute (foreground and background color, intensity, and blink status).

The *new* operator is used here in a way you haven't seen up to now. It allocates a buffer large enough to hold an array that you specify. The syntax is:

```
<var> = new <type>[ <size> ];
```

The <var> is a variable of the appropriate type. The <type> is any valid type, such as an int, a char, or a class you have defined. The <size> is the number of elements of the type you have specified. Asking for char[100] will get a buffer of 100 bytes (plus a few more that C++ uses internally for its own accounting). An int[100] buffer will be 200-plus bytes long, since each integer needs two bytes.

There are two new functions, both declared in CONIO.H. You've probably guessed what they do. The gettext() function gets text from video memory and places it into your buffer. Conversely, puttext() returns text from your buffer, writing it into video memory. There's no trick to using gettext() and puttext(), but if you misuse them, you can get rather spectacular and definitely unwanted results.

The efficiency of gettext() and puttext() is the key to the performance of your text-mode programs. As a consequence, they are written in assembly and tuned for speed. They assume that you call them with sensible parameters. The coordinates from which you gettext() must be on the screen. The buffer into which you gettext() must be large enough. Similarly, you must puttext() into a location that is on the screen from a buffer that is as large as necessary.

If you misuse these functions, you will be launching an assembly language program that is moving data from who knows where overwriting who knows what. Before we leave this section, we'll experiment with a very minor error in the puttext().

H I N T

Write your gettext() calls carefully. Copy the line with the gettext() call and change the "get" to "put" for a puttext() that correctly matches the gettext(). Don't retype the arguments unless you are very fast, are very accurate, and have a very reliable disk backup procedure.

Now, what about those compile errors? Each one tells you something like "box::lft is not accessible in function popup::popup(...)." The word "accessible" should give you a clue that we have another access problem.

When we first used private and public access, I told you that there was a third type, *protected*. Here we need that third type. A private member is strictly private. It is accessible only within member functions of its own class. This does *not* include member functions of a derived class, such as our popup::popup() constructor.

On the other hand, the protected access specification makes members available to all derived classes but otherwise private. A protected base member is a private member of both the base class and the derived class. Again, we need to change just one word to fix the problem. Actually, I'll change two words, since I know that the *private* specification in the popup class will also cause a problem later on.

Listing 5-8 shows the changes. Both the private: lines have been changed to protected:.

Listing 5-8: TEWIN.CPP

```
class box
{
protected:
    int lft, top, rgt, btm;

    char* border;
```

```
        int outline_clr, contents_clr;

public:
    box( int lf, int tp, int rt, int bt,
        char* brdr,
        int out_clr, int con_clr );
    ~box();

    void draw();
    void moveto( int new_lft, int new_top );
};


class popup : public box
{
protected:
    char* screen_save_buf;

public:
    popup( int lf, int tp, int rt, int bt,
        char* brdr,
        int out_clr, int con_clr );
    ~popup();
};
```

With this change, you can compile successfully. Alt+F9 will report success.

Before we leave this point, let me summarize. If a base class is not declared public, all its members will be private—not accessible in the derived class. The private access of the whole base class overrides the access declared within it for any of its members.

Similarly, if a member is declared private in the base class, it will be private—not accessible in a derived class—even if the base is declared public by the deriving class.

Protected base class members are accessible in a public base class's derived class. You should make a habit of always using protected, rather than private, access except in special situations where you need to make your base class members inaccessible.

Public base class members in a public base class are also public in a derived class. This is the access you normally want for your methods.

Now let's look at main(), making it pop our box up and down. Since we are using the constructor and destructor, we'll need to use *new* and *delete*, which means using a popup pointer, not a popup variable. Listing 5-9 shows how this can be done.

Listing 5-9: TEWIN.CPP

```
// mainline for testing only
   int main()
   {
       textattr( WHITE_BLACK );
       clrscr();

       box b( 1, 5, 45, 15, SINGLE,
           YELLOW_CYAN, WHITE_BLUE );

       b.draw();

       b.moveto(  5,  8 ); b.draw();
       b.moveto( 10, 10 ); b.draw();
       b.moveto( 15, 12 ); b.draw();

       box c( 10, 1, 20, 15, DOUBLE,
           WHITE_BLUE, YELLOW_CYAN );
       c.draw();

       box d( 30, 1, 40, 15, SING_DOUB,
           WHITE_BLUE, YELLOW_CYAN );
       d.draw();

       popup* pu = new popup( 3, 5, 35, 10, DOUB_SING,
           WHITE_BLACK, WHITE_BLACK );

       getch();

       pu->draw();
       getch();
```

```
      delete pu;
      getch();

      return 0;
  }
```

This code creates pu, a pointer to a popup, using the same parameters that we were using for the pu popup variable. It waits for a keypress before drawing the popup, then draws it (popping up), and then pauses again. At your next keypress, it deletes pu, visually appearing to pop it down.

Got this running? Your popup class is now in business! We'll apply it to create dialog boxes, starting in the next section of this chapter. Before we do, I want to show you a very small error in a puttext() argument.

In the popup destructor's puttext() call, add just 1 to the address of screen_save_buf. Make it look like this:

```
  puttext( lft, top, rgt, btm, screen_save_buf+1 );
```

With that single-byte offset, press Ctrl+F9 again. Your boxes draw properly; you press a key and your popup pops up properly; you press another key and boom! Instead of your popup popping down, your screen is redrawn with a spectacular pattern of colors you don't like and characters you've never seen before.

By getting the pointer wrong by one byte, you've tricked puttext() entirely. It thinks the characters are video attribute bytes, and it thinks the video attributes are characters. It's also going to write whatever byte happened to be just past the end of screen_save_buf into the last character on your screen.

I hope you get the idea that this sort of mistake can be dangerous to your computer's health.

Get rid of that extra +1, and let's go on to building a dialog class.

PROGRAMMING A DIALOG CLASS

The dialog class is a type of popup used in good user interfaces. There are lots of different kinds of dialog boxes. Common ones include information boxes, warning boxes, and help boxes. The interaction can be just reading a message and pressing a key to continue, it can be selecting a yes or no answer, or it can be more complex.

By this time, you should suspect that what we need is a base dialog class from which we can inherit to add any of these other capabilities. We'll start with a dialog class that inherits from the popup class.

Using Header Files

Before we go on, let's create our own header file to clean up the TEWIN.CPP file and give ourselves more flexibility. A header file is given the extension .H by tradition. Although nothing in C++ compels you to use any particular extension, I suggest that you stick to this convention. It's as good as any other convention.

H I N T

The C language and the UNIX operating system share a common heritage. C was written in part to develop UNIX. UNIX was written in C, and almost all UNIX work is done in C. C++ was created from C in the UNIX universe. Filenames in UNIX don't have DOS-style extensions—they are just names. The period is like any other character in a UNIX filename. Still, the UNIX tradition is to separate the main part of the filename from a suffix part with a period, as we do in DOS. The suffixes .C, .CPP, and .H are used in UNIX just as they are as extensions in DOS.

I'll refer to header files or include files or .H files as we go along, using these names as synonyms. Let's get it correct before we get sloppy.

An include file is any file brought in with the preprocessor #include directive. This directive tells the preprocessor to incorporate the include file as if it were typed in its entirety at the spot of the #include directive.

A header file is an include file used at or near the beginning of a source file—thus it gets its name. A #include directive, and therefore an include file, can appear anywhere in your source, although the top of the file is the common location.

The extension .H is used by convention for a header file, although any extension acceptable to the operating system is acceptable to C++. With that said, we can go on talking about .H, include, and header files as if they were all the same—which is the common habit among C++ programmers.

There is a minor difference between the standard .H files that come with TCLite and those of all other C++ programming systems, as well as the ones that you write yourself. Typically, you write your own header files in your own working directory. It is very convenient to put your .H files in the same directory as your .CPP files. TCLite lets you use the \TCLITE directory for this purpose.

The header files that are part of the system are put in the INCLUDE\ directory. The syntax for specifying the location of the header file is this:

```
#include <CONIO.H> // system INCLUDE\ directory
#include "MYHDR.H" // working directory
```

You set your working directory in TCLite by changing to whatever directory you like before you launch TCLite. (Once you are in TCLite, you can use the File|DOS Shell menu choice to shell out to DOS and change working directories.)

The location of the system header files defaults to \TCLITE\INCLUDE. You can change this using the Options|Directories... menu choice.

T I P

While you use TCLite, don't confuse your learning by creating directory problems. The default choices are good ones until your projects get complex. For complex projects, of course, you'll want to upgrade from TCLite to the latest TC++ or other professional C++ system.

Items that are commonly found in header files include:

▶ #define constants

▶ Function declarations

▶ Class and structure definitions

Let's move our defined constants and class definitions into TEWIN.H. This move will shorten our TEWIN.CPP file, making it more handy. As you'll see when we add source files to the TE system, it's almost mandatory to have these items in a header file, since multiple source files will need the class definitions.

Begin with a skeleton .H file, as you see in Listing 5-10. (It's all new, so there's no 05-10.CPP on disk.)

Listing 5-10: TEWIN.H

```
// TEWIN.H -- windowing header for Tiny Editor
// copyright 1995, Martin L. Rinehart


// end of TEWIN.H
```

With TEWIN.H prepared, I set up the files as shown in Figure 5-2.

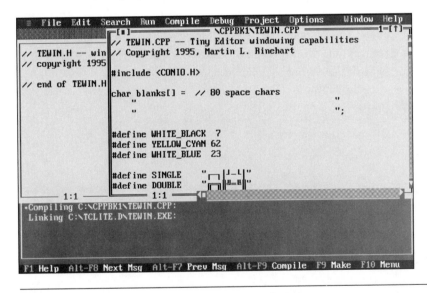

Figure 5-2: Header and source files in the IDE.

This setup lets me see the #defines and class definitions in the left-hand window while I work on the source code in the window to the right. This arrangement is often all I need, for instance, to check on how I spelled a member name or defined a method. When you need to switch windows, it's very easy to jump back and forth with a mouse click.

Once your setup is suitable, choose Options|Save so that your setup will be automatically loaded the next time you load TCLite.

To create the working header and source combination, follow these steps:

S T E P   B Y   S T E P

1. By dragging with your mouse, or by using the arrow keys while you hold down Shift, highlight the #defines and the class definitions in TEWIN.CPP. Use Shift+Del to cut these to the clipboard.

2. Switch to TEWIN.H; position the cursor between the top and bottom comments and press Shift+Ins to paste the lines from the clipboard.

3. Add a new line—#include "TEWIN.H"—to TEWIN.CPP.

4. Your results should be those shown in Listing 5-11 and Listing 5-12. In TEWIN.CPP, press Ctrl+F9 and one of two things will happen. One possibility is that the program will work just as it did before you made these changes, which is exactly what you want.

Listing 5-11: TEWIN.H

```
// TEWIN.H -- windowing header for Tiny Editor
// copyright 1995, Martin L. Rinehart


#define WHITE_BLACK   7
#define YELLOW_CYAN  62
#define WHITE_BLUE   23

#define SINGLE    "┌│┘─└│"
#define DOUBLE    "╔║╝═╚║"
#define SING_DOUB "╒│╛═╘│"
#define DOUB_SING "╓║╜─╙║"

class box
{
protected:
    int lft, top, rgt, btm;

    char* border;

    int outline_clr, contents_clr;
```

```
public:
    box( int lf, int tp, int rt, int bt,
        char brdr[8],
        int out_clr, int con_clr );
    ~box();

    void draw();
    void moveto( int new_lft, int new_top );
};

class popup : public box
{
protected:
    char* screen_save_buf;

public:
    popup( int lf, int tp, int rt, int bt,
        char* brdr,
        int out_clr, int con_clr );
    ~popup();
};
```

// end of TEWIN.H

Listing 5-12: TEWIN.CPP

```
// TEWIN.CPP -- Tiny Editor windowing capabilities
// Copyright 1995, Martin L. Rinehart

#include <CONIO.H>

#include "TEWIN.H"

char blanks[] =  // 80 space chars
    "                                                                                "
    "                                                                                ";


// mainline for testing only

...
```

The other possibility is that you got dozens of error messages. If you look closely, somewhere in the mess in the Message window may be a message that there was a problem finding the .H file. If that is your problem, click on the TEWIN.H window or use F6 to switch to it and press F2 to save it. Return to the TEWIN.CPP window and try Ctrl+F9 again. Everything should be back in business.

If you got it right the first time, try this. Add a little deliberate damage to the #include line and try Ctrl+F9 again. Putting a bogus character on the line, like this "x," will do:

```
x#include "TEWIN.H"
```

In your Message window you get a host of messages telling you that symbols are undefined and that functions should have prototypes. Remember this symptom. It looks like something went horribly wrong, but it just means that there is a problem using an include file. Something as simple as deleting the offending character from the #include line (which you should do now) will fix all these problems at once.

Adding the Dialog Class

Now that our files are structured to use both a header file and a main source file, we can go on to add the dialog class. The dialog class is a popup box with a title centered in the top of the outline. We'll use it as a base to create other classes, such as a message dialog and a yes/no dialog.

First, we need to add the dialog class definition to the header file. Listing 5-13 shows the code to add to TEWIN.H.

Be careful when you come to the constructor function's declaration in this class definition. Pay some attention to what I've left out. I've decided to adopt a common color and border scheme for my dialog boxes, so I've omitted those parameters.

Listing 5-13: TEWIN.H

```
// TEWIN.H -- windowing header for Tiny Editor
// copyright 1995, Martin L. Rinehart

#define WHITE_BLACK  7
#define YELLOW_CYAN 62
```

```
#define WHITE_BLUE   23

#define DIAG_OUT_CLR 59 // Hi cyan on cyan
#define DIAG_CON_CLR 63 // Hi white on cyan

#define SINGLE     " ⌐┐|┘—└||"
...
class dialog : public popup
{
protected:
    char* title;

public:
    dialog( char* ttl, int lf, int tp, int rt, int bt );
    ~dialog();
};
```

```
// end of TEWIN.H
```

Add the #defines for the dialog colors near the #defined colors at the top of
the file and add the class definition near the end. You can test your work with
Alt+F9 in the header file window, but Ctrl+F9 will always fail.

If you inadvertently try Ctrl+F9 in a header file, you'll get an error from the
linker. The linker will be trying to find a code module named main(), which is
the name that C++ assigns to your main() function. Of course, the header file
doesn't have a main(), so the linker won't find one. Remember that the linker
isn't called if the compilation fails.

H I N T

There is a subtle difference between Ctrl+F9's invoking the linker and your getting a "success" report from Alt+F9. The run command implied by Ctrl+F9 lets
compiler warning messages pass without telling you. (It halts on errors but pro-
ceeds on warnings.) The Alt+F9 combination lets you see any warning messages.

Now let's go on to the additions we need to make to TEWIN.CPP. We'll be using a pair of string functions, strlen() and strcpy(). As their names suggest, strlen() finds the length of a string, and strcpy() copies strings. The string functions are declared in STRING.H, logically enough. We need to #include this header file.

Of course, we'll have to change main() so that it launches a test dialog box instead of the test popup that it is launching currently. And, finally, we'll actually have to write constructor and destructor functions for the dialog class. All of this work is probably less trouble to do than to talk about.

Listing 5-14 shows the additions and changes you need to make. When you test with Ctrl+F9 you should get a popup dialog with a title.

Listing 5-14: TEWIN.CPP

```
// TEWIN.CPP -- Tiny Editor windowing capabilities
// Copyright 1995, Martin L. Rinehart

#include <CONIO.H>
#include <STRING.H>

#include "TEWIN.H"
...
        box d( 30, 1, 40, 15, SING_DOUB,
            WHITE_BLUE, YELLOW_CYAN );
        d.draw();


        getch();

        dialog* d1 = new dialog( " Testing ",
            3, 5, 35, 10 );

        getch();

        delete d1;
        getch();

        return 0;
...
```

```
popup::~popup()
{
    puttext( lft, top, rgt, btm, screen_save_buf );

    delete screen_save_buf;
}
```

```
dialog::dialog( char* ttl,
    int lf, int tp, int rt, int bt )
    : popup( lf, tp, rt, bt, SINGLE,
    DIAG_OUT_CLR, DIAG_CON_CLR )
{
    title = new char[ strlen(ttl) + 1 ];
    strcpy( title, ttl );

    draw();

    int tlen = strlen( ttl );
    int tloc = ( rt - lf + 1 - tlen ) / 2;

    textattr( DIAG_OUT_CLR );
    gotoxy( lf+tloc, tp );
    cprintf( title );
}

dialog::~dialog()
{
    delete title;
}
```

// end of TEWIN.CPP

The built-in strlen() function reports the length of a string, excluding the trailing null. For example, "abcde" is 5 long. When we ask the *new* operator for space for the title, we need to add in the extra character we'll need for the trailing null.

The strcpy() called in the constructor copies from a source (the second argument) to a destination (the first argument). Since the title string was allocated with the *new* operator in the constructor, it has to be freed with the *delete* operator in the destructor.

The other job of the constructor is to draw() the box and then add the title. The title is centered in the top line by taking the width of the box, rt − lf + 1, and subtracting the length of the string, tlen. This gives the blank space, which is divided by 2 to find the starting point for the title.

There are two points to look at here. First, division truncates any fractional part if you are doing arithmetic with integers. The result will work fine here, but in many applications you'll want a result like 1.5 rounded up to 2.0, not truncated to 1.0.

Second, I never get these calculations right the first time. (When I wrote this one, I initially forgot to add the 1.) To test a bit of arithmetic like this, go to your mainline and reduce the length of the rt argument to something that just barely fits the title on the top line. You'll quickly find if you have correctly centered it or not. Put the original form back when you are done testing.

Figure 5-3 shows my dialog box.

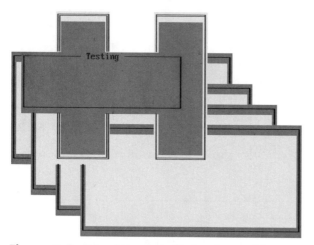

Figure 5-3: Popping up a dialog box object.

Bear in mind that this code will give an ugly result if your box isn't big enough to allow for your title. This is fine since you'll always want either to create a box that's large enough or to rewrite your title so that it's small enough to fit.

Using Optional Parameters

Before we leave this dialog box, let's assume that many of our dialogs will fit nicely in a standard size. (That's many, but not all of them.) It would be nice to be able to omit the coordinates in the common case. To allow this, we can assign default values to parameters. Here's an example:

```
type myfunc( int p1 = 1, int p2 = 2, int p3 = 3 )
{
    ... // use params here
}
```

When your calling programs use this function, arguments can be omitted. Omitted arguments will assume the default values, but included arguments will take the values explicitly provided. For example:

```
myfunc( 4, 5, 6 );  // p1=4, p2=5, p3=6
myfunc( 4, 5 );     // p1=4, p2=5, p3=3
myfunc( 4 );        // p1=4, p2=2, p3=3
myfunc();           // p1=1, p2=2, p3=3
```

As the examples show, arguments that are supplied are handed to the parameters in the order they are written. If one argument is given, the first parameter is assigned that value—the other parameters are given the default values.

This ordering means that you can omit arguments only from the right side of the argument list. You can't do this:

```
myfun( 4, ,6 ); // ERROR!
```

This is why I chose to make the first parameter the title string and provided the coordinates after the title in our dialog class. Listing 5-15 shows the dialog constructor redefined to provide default coordinates. Make this change in the class definition in TEWIN.H:

Listing 5-15: TEWIN.H

```
class dialog : public popup
{
protected:
    char* title;

public:
    dialog( char* ttl,
```

```
        int lf=15, int tp=8, int rt=65, int bt=15 );
    ~dialog();
};
```

After you make this change, return to the TEWIN.CPP file window and try Ctrl+F9 again. There should be no change from the previous time, since your mainline is still supplying all the coordinates. Now modify the mainline to supply just the title, as shown in Listing 5-16.

Listing 5-16: TEWIN.CPP

```
    d.draw();

    getch();

    dialog* d1 = new dialog( " Testing " );

    getch();

    delete d1;
```

With this change, when you press Ctrl+F9 you'll get a dialog box waiting just above the center of the screen, in a very good position for typical uses. Figure 5-4 shows my version.

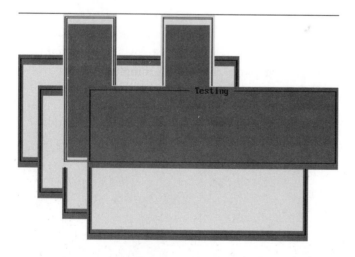

Figure 5-4: A dialog box with default coordinates.

In the next two sections, we're going to create two very useful dialog box types derived from this class.

WRITE A MESSAGE CLASS

To begin, we'll create a message-type dialog box. This will be useful whenever you want to display a message but don't need a particular confirming keystroke. (The yes/no dialog we'll get to in the next chapter stays on the screen until it gets either a yes or a no answer. The message dialog is willing to take any keystroke.)

The interesting feature of our message class is how it allows us to write a one-line message or a message of more than one line. We'll achieve this capability using a C++ feature called *overloading*.

In C++, as in many languages, the plus (+) operator is *overloaded*. That means it can operate intelligently on different types of operands. For example, plus can add two integers, or two floating-point numbers, or an integer and a float. It can also add an integer to a pointer. (You used that feature when you added 1 to the address of your screen-save buffer in the last chapter.)

The C++ compiler lets you write your own overloaded functions, too. This simply means that a function of one name can operate on different types or numbers of parameters. This is a powerful capability that gives you a lot of flexibility in the way you create functions.

Overloading Basics

Let's go back to our old friend T.CPP and try a simple example of overloading. Let's create a function that can accept either an int or a char as an argument. Listing 5-17 (all new, so it's not on disk) shows you one example:

Listing 5-17: T.CPP

```
// t.cpp

#include <conio.h>

// declare a pair of foo functions
    void foo( int i );
    void foo( char c );
```

```
int main()
{
    clrscr();

    foo( 2 );   // call the int version
    foo( 'b' ); // call the char version

    getch();

    return 0;
}

// define the foo functions
    void foo( int i )
    { cprintf( "\n\rInt function here" ); }

    void foo( char c )
    { cprintf( "\n\rChar function here" ); }

// end of t.cpp
```

When you run this function, you'll get the appropriate message displayed for each call. C++ manages this job by a process called *name mangling*, which means that C++ assigns its own names to the versions of your functions that it compiles. Logically speaking, this works as follows:

```
void foo( int i );  // compiles as vfoo_i();
void foo( char c );  // compiles as vfoo_c();
```

These aren't the real internal names, of course. They're here to give you the idea, not the details.

H I N T

When you go on with your C++ work, you'll learn enough to pick out the actual mangled names. Don't do it! There is no standard for the precise mangling mechanism, and there is no guarantee that the compiler vendor won't change mangling methods from one version of the compiler to the next.

The compiler will pick the correct function to call based on the arguments that you supply in your code. Try commenting out one of the versions of foo() in the above example and see what happens when you attempt to compile your code.

Another way to overload a function is to assign different numbers of parameters. Actually, the default parameters that we used in the previous section were a special case of this more general technique. Listing 5-18 shows T.CPP from the above example modified to show how this works.

Listing 5-18: T.CPP

```cpp
// t.cpp

#include <conio.h>

// declare a pair of foo functions
    void foo( int i );
    void foo( int i1, int i2 );

int main()
{
    clrscr();

    foo( 2 );    // call the int version
    foo( 2, 3 ); // call the 2 int version

    getch();

    return 0;
}

// define the foo functions
    void foo( int i )
    { cprintf( "\n\rInt function here" ); }

    void foo( int i1, int i2 )
    { cprintf( "\n\rTwo int function here" ); }

// end of t.cpp
```

When you run this code, you'll see that the compiler also matches the number of arguments in the function call to the number of parameters in the function definition. Let's go back to TEWIN and implement our message class using this technique.

Writing the Basic Message Class

We'll start with a simple message class that doesn't have any message lines at all. It just provides the basic functionality as if we had a message to display. First, add the new color #define and the new class definition in Listing 5-19 to TEWIN.H.

Listing 5-19: TEWIN.H

```
// TEWIN.H -- windowing header for Tiny Editor
// copyright 1995, Martin L. Rinehart

#define WHITE_BLACK   7
#define YELLOW_CYAN  62
#define WHITE_BLUE   23

#define DIAG_OUT_CLR 59 // Hi cyan on cyan
#define DIAG_CON_CLR 63 // Hi white on cyan
#define DIAG_TIP_CLR 48 // Black on cyan

#define SINGLE      "┌┐│┘─└│"
...
class message : public dialog
{
public:
    message();
};

// end of TEWIN.H
```

We'll display a "press any key to continue" message for the user in the DIAG_TIP_CLR color. By putting this into a message with no other lines of message, we can test our work before moving this functionality into a function called by all the message constructors.

Now, let's turn to TEWIN.CPP. In the mainline, modify the lines that created and used a dialog object to create and use a message object. Then add the definition of the message constructor near the bottom of the file, and you are ready to hit Ctrl+F9 again.

These changes are shown in Listing 5-20.

Listing 5-20: TEWIN.CPP

```
        d.draw();

        getch();

        message* ms = new message();

        getch();

        delete ms;
        getch();
...
dialog::~dialog()
{
    delete title;
}

message::message() :
    dialog( " Message " )
{
    textattr( DIAG_TIP_CLR );
    gotoxy( rgt-25, btm-1 );
    cprintf( "press any key to continue" );
}

// end of TEWIN.CPP
```

When you run this code, you'll get an empty dialog titled "Message" that will tell you to "press any key to continue." Figure 5-5 shows my version.

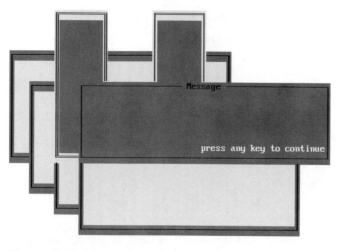

Figure 5-5: An empty message object.

One of the things that you should have noticed by now is that we are building a hierarchy of classes, and that every time we have added another class to the hierarchy, the complexity of the calling arguments has been reduced.

T I P

How did I know that rgt–25 would position the character string in just the right place? I used to count carefully and try to figure this out. Now I just toss in anything that seems more or less sensible and run the code. When the computer screen shows you your message hanging off the right, or too far to the left, it's easy to adjust a little bit and try again. This is much faster than counting.

Right now we're at zero arguments. Unfortunately, we'll have to begin adding more, since we can hardly have fewer.

Adding Messages

Let's begin with a single-line message. First, we'll need another version of the constructor, one that accepts a message string and displays it in the center of the dialog box. I'll assume that the message will fit. (If it won't fit on a single line, divide it into two lines, for example, and call the two-line message constructor.)

Start by adding the additional constructor declaration to TEWIN.H's class definition, as you see in Listing 5-21.

Listing 5-21: TEWIN.H

```
class message : public dialog
{
public:
    message();
    message( char* msg1 );
};


// end of TEWIN.H
```

Now let's add a definition of this constructor in TEWIN.CPP and call the new version from main(). Listing 5-22 shows these changes.

Listing 5-22: TEWIN.CPP

```
        getch();


        message* ms = new message(
            "This is a sample message." );


        getch();

...
message::message( char* msg1 ) :
    dialog( " Message " )
{

    gotoxy( lft+2, top+(btm-top)/2 );
    // textattr( DIAG_CON_CLR );
    cprintf( msg1 );

    textattr( DIAG_TIP_CLR );
    gotoxy( rgt-25, btm-1 );
    cprintf( "press any key to continue" );

}

// end of TEWIN.CPP
```

I've taken advantage of the fact that the last color specified by box::draw() is the contents color. When you cprintf() the message line, you don't need to set this color again. But I've put the appropriate line of code in as a comment, so that later on when something changes, we'll see what we are depending on. (You could need this code if, for instance, you change the box::draw() function.)

When you run this version, you'll get the test message neatly centered in the message dialog box. It will stay on the screen until you press a key, when it will neatly pop down. Figure 5-6 shows a single-line message object.

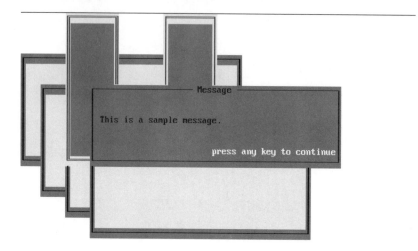

Figure 5-6: A single-line message box popped up.

This is beginning to look like exactly what we need. Perhaps the best news is that anytime we want a message dialog like this, we'll just add three lines of code to our system:

```
message* ms = new message( "This is a sample message." );
getch();
delete ms;
```

Of course, when these three lines seem like too much trouble, it will be easy enough to write a function that does all this work with only one line in the calling program, like:

```
pop_a_message_box( "This is the message I want." );
```

Right now, though, let's move that general-purpose tip line from the constructor into its own function and get rid of the no-message constructor.

First, in the message class definition in TEWIN.H, remove the no-message constructor declaration and add a private function, tip_line(). Note that you have to give tip_line() a type when you declare it. Listing 5-23 shows how this is done:

Listing 5-23: TEWIN.H

```
class message : public dialog
{
public:
    message( char* msg1 );

private:
    void tip_line();
};


// end of TEWIN.H
```

N O T E

Constructor and destructor functions cannot be given a type in their declarations or definitions. They cannot return values, either. All other functions *must* be given a type. Those that don't return values must be declared and defined as void functions.

Now delete the entire definition of the no-parameter message constructor from TEWIN.CPP. Move the three lines that actually display the tip line from the other message constructor into their own function, message::tip_line(). Call this function from the message constructor. Listing 5-24 shows these changes.

Listing 5-24: TEWIN.CPP

```
dialog::~dialog()
{
    delete title;
```

```
}


message::message( char* msg1 ) :
    dialog( " Message " )
{
    gotoxy( lft+2, top+(btm-top)/2 );
    // textattr( DIAG_CON_CLR );
    cprintf( msg1 );

    tip_line();


}


void message::tip_line()
{
    textattr( DIAG_TIP_CLR );
    gotoxy( rgt-25, btm-1 );
    cprintf( "press any key to continue" );
}
```

// end of TEWIN.CPP

With these changes, you should get exactly the same result as before when you press Ctrl+F9. However, you are now nicely set up to add provisions for additional message constructors supporting more lines of message.

Two- and Three-Line Message Objects

If you have used other languages where variable numbers of parameters are simply supported, you'll be disappointed to find that C++, like C before it, has only a primitive way of supporting this feature. There is no standard way of supporting variable parameters except through the use of predefined macros in a header file.

Even with the defined macros, certain seemingly simple processes, such as passing a variable number of parameters from one routine to another, are not possible in any straightforward manner. On the other hand, writing a handful of routines to support different numbers of parameters is a simple, straightforward task. Let's continue from one-parameter message dialogs to two- and then three-parameter versions. You should be able to take over from there.

In fact, if you're feeling confident already, go ahead and try these on your own and check your work against the examples here. If you're not feeling confident yet, or if today's a "bad code day," go right ahead and follow the examples here.

First, add declarations for two more constructors in the message class in TEWIN.H. Listing 5-25 shows these two new lines.

Listing 5-25: TEWIN.H

```
class message : public dialog
{
public:
    message( char* msg1 );
    message( char* msg1, char* msg2 );
    message( char* msg1, char* msg2, char* msg3 );

private:
    void tip_line();
};


// end of TEWIN.H
```

With the declarations in place, add definitions in TEWIN.CPP, and add calls to these functions in main().

For these definitions, we'll use the preincrement operator, ++. You've already used the postincrement operator to increment a variable, this way:

```
i++;
```

We've used this operator on a line by itself as a statement. It can also be combined with other operators and operands in expressions:

```
array[ i++ ] = ...;
```

In this case, array[i] is assigned some value, and then the variable i is incremented. This operator is called the postincrement operator because the variable is used in the expression and then incremented, after it is used.

The preincrement operator does the increment first and then uses the variable in the expression. This is a parallel example:

```
array[ ++i ] = ...;
```

In this case, i is incremented, and then the value of array[i] (the incremented i) is assigned a value.

N O T E

Using ++ before a variable (++i) increments the variable before it is used in an expression. Using ++ after a variable (i++) increments the variable after it is used in an expression. The – operator works the same way. Using –i decrements i before it is used, whereas i– decrements i after it is used.

Listing 5-26 shows the additions to TEWIN.CPP. The new constructors use the preincrement operator to adjust the row on which the message lines are displayed. (The extensive additions to main() are simpler than they look if you start by copying the one-line message lines. Similarly, the two new message constructors can be created quickly if you start by making copies of the existing one.)

Listing 5-26: TEWIN.CPP

```
message* ms = new message(
    "This is a sample message." );

getch();

delete ms;
getch();

ms = new message(
    "This is a sample",
    "two-line message." );

getch();

delete ms;
getch();

ms = new message(
    "This is a sample",
```

```
                "three-line message",
                "being tested." );

        getch();

        delete ms;
        getch();

        return 0;
...
message::message( char* msg1 ) :
    dialog( " Message " )
{
    gotoxy( lft+2, top+(btm-top)/2 );
    // textattr( DIAG_CON_CLR );
    cprintf( msg1 );

    tip_line();
}
```

```
message::message( char* msg1, char* msg2 ) :
    dialog( " Message " )
{
    int msg_row = top+(btm-top)/2 - 1;
    gotoxy( lft+2, msg_row );
    // textattr( DIAG_CON_CLR );
    cprintf( msg1 );

    gotoxy( lft+2, ++msg_row );
    cprintf( msg2 );

    tip_line();
}

message::message( char* msg1, char* msg2, char* msg3 ) :
    dialog( " Message " )
{
    int msg_row = top+(btm-top)/2 - 1;
```

```
    gotoxy( lft+2, msg_row );
    // textattr( DIAG_CON_CLR );
    cprintf( msg1 );

    gotoxy( lft+2, ++msg_row );
    cprintf( msg2 );

    gotoxy( lft+2, ++msg_row );
    cprintf( msg3 );

    tip_line();
}
```

```
void message::tip_line()
```

When you try Ctrl+F9 with these additions, you should get a program that pops up three separate message dialogs in turn. They each disappear on any keypress. Figure 5-7 shows the last of the three on screen.

You can write any expression using pre- or postincrement (or -decrement) operators with multiple statements, and sometimes nested expressions can be clearer than successive statements.

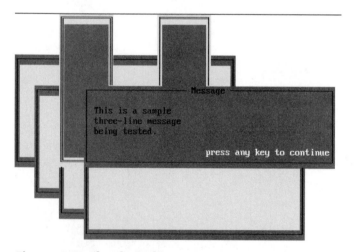

Figure 5-7: The three-line message popped up.

```
gotoxy( lft+2, ++msg_row );

    // the above is the same as:
```

```
msg_row++;   // or ++msg_row;
gotoxy( lft+2, msg_row );
```

Use two statements whenever the results appear more clear. Many times you can use either pre- or postincrement to achieve the same result. Here's one of the constructors rewritten using postincrement:

```
message::message( char* msg1, char* msg2 ) :
    dialog( " Message " )
{
    int msg_row = top+(btm-top)/2 - 1;
    gotoxy( lft+2, msg_row++ );
    // textattr( DIAG_CON_CLR );
    cprintf( msg1 );

    gotoxy( lft+2, msg_row );
    cprintf( msg2 );

    tip_line();
}
```

In this case, the postincrement form looked to me as if it was hiding the manipulation of msg_row, whereas the preincrement form seemed more explicit. There aren't any firm laws about good style, but the goal is always to write clear code.

W A R N I N G

Never write clever code! If your code is not obvious, rewrite it in an obvious way, even if that takes more lines of source or results in a slower running program. (If your clever code is too wonderful to omit, add enough comments so that we can completely understand how it works.)

At this point, you've created a class hierarchy. Your boxes are built into popups, your popups become dialogs, and your dialogs have been built into the message class.

In the next chapter, we'll branch out from a linear hierarchy, branching from dialogs into yes/no dialogs.

S U M M A R Y

You've learned a lot more about C++ in this chapter. We started with the basics of class inheritance. It may have been new to you then, but it isn't new to you any more. We've used it repeatedly, and we'll continue to do that.

Looking at the basics of inheritance, you learned that base class constructors are called before the logic of the derived constructor is run. In opposite fashion, the logic of the derived destructor runs before the base class destructor is run. While you were studying these effects, you also learned to pass parameters through the derived class to the base class's constructor.

We used escape characters in strings to add returns and linefeeds. You also saw that other special characters, including octal and hexadecimal characters, can be written this way.

You used the gettext() function, defined in CONIO.H, to get a block from the screen and save it in your own character buffer. You used the companion puttext() function to do the reverse.

We took a brief look at the address and dereferencing operators, seeing that they reverse each other's functions. You used the address operator to apply the *delete* operator to an object variable—*delete* expects a pointer, or address, variable.

We saw how the access to members of base classes works. It defaults to private, and this feature kept us from accessing base-class members we needed. We

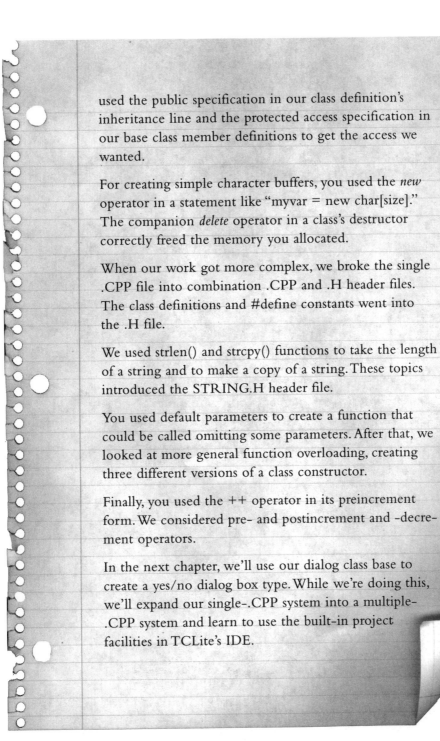

used the public specification in our class definition's inheritance line and the protected access specification in our base class member definitions to get the access we wanted.

For creating simple character buffers, you used the *new* operator in a statement like "myvar = new char[size]." The companion *delete* operator in a class's destructor correctly freed the memory you allocated.

When our work got more complex, we broke the single .CPP file into combination .CPP and .H header files. The class definitions and #define constants went into the .H file.

We used strlen() and strcpy() functions to take the length of a string and to make a copy of a string. These topics introduced the STRING.H header file.

You used default parameters to create a function that could be called omitting some parameters. After that, we looked at more general function overloading, creating three different versions of a class constructor.

Finally, you used the ++ operator in its preincrement form. We considered pre- and postincrement and -decrement operators.

In the next chapter, we'll use our dialog class base to create a yes/no dialog box type. While we're doing this, we'll expand our single-.CPP system into a multiple-.CPP system and learn to use the built-in project facilities in TCLite's IDE.

In this chapter, we're going to add more dialog boxes. While we're doing it, we'll switch from our single-file program to using multiple files, under control of the project manager built into TCLite. You'll see that the Borland IDE makes this delightfully simple.

While we're doing this, we'll:

► Create multiple .CPP files

► Create a project file to manage your .CPPs

► See that integer data are used for logical answers

► Work with relational and logical operators

► Use the else statement with if statements

► Use the break statement with an "infinite" loop

First, we'll consider the simple process of popping up a dialog box and waiting for a yes-or-no answer.

chapter

6

More Dialogs, Project Style

There's nothing particularly difficult about looking for a yes-or-no answer. The getch() function that we've been using to pause input returns the character that is pressed, although we've ignored its return values thus far. Checking for a 'y' response can be as simple as this:

```
char c = getch();
if ( c == 'y' ) ... // you got a yes response
```

Of course, you'll want to allow an uppercase or lowercase answer and otherwise add more details to this code, but this example illustrates the basics.

But let's look ahead at what a good user interface may feature.

USER COMMAND MANAGEMENT

I like to be able to respond to the user interface as my work progresses. I also like to be able to build macros that incorporate common sequences that I can trigger with a single keypress. It's nice to be able to get inputs from a file or even from a controlling program.

We won't add all these complications as we build our Tiny Editor, but I want the structure to allow me to go back and add these features when time permits, or when adding one of these features will save more time than it costs.

The Hierarchy of Commands

A sophisticated command processor might look through these command sources, in this order:

▶ A command program

▶ A file of commands

▶ A command macro

▶ Keyboard keystrokes

▶ Mouse events

If a command program is active, the command processor could go to it for commands. It would be in charge until the program terminates.

If no command program is running, commands could come from a file. Some editors, for example, echo all your keystrokes to a file. If a crash occurs in the middle of a long edit session, you can restore the original text file and play back the commands from this command file to repeat your session.

Absent a command file, a simple macro record/playback mechanism should be available. For example, I've recorded the string "C++," and as I type this text I can play it any time just by pressing Ctrl+F6. (More sophisticated macro capabilities come under the heading of command programs, discussed above.)

If none of the above are active, a request for input could look for keystrokes in the keyboard buffer. This would put the program in direct touch with your keystrokes.

When the keyboard buffer is empty, your program could also accept input from mouse events. If you have programmed your user interface flexibly, all mouse event-driven activities can also be triggered from the keyboard. This approach provides alternatives that are desirable in themselves, and it also means that all the higher-level command sources can use just the keyboard-equivalent commands to drive your program.

A Single Source for Commands

Implementing all of these command sources makes for a sophisticated command processor. We'll start with a simple command processor, such as this one:

```
int user_cmd()
{
    return getch();
}
```

This may seem like needless overhead. Your program could just call getch() directly and eliminate this layer. But there's a very important advantage to programming this way.

Our program will always call user_cmd() when it needs input. With user_cmd() defined as above, our program will initially be just getting the return from a getch(), but we can easily extend the user_cmd() function, as this pseudocode shows:

```
int user_cmd()
{
    if ( macro input is not turned on )
        return getch();

    // macro input is turned on!
    return next_macro_char();
}
```

Then we can add logic to record macros. A special keystroke (Alt+M, perhaps) can toggle macro recording. Our user_cmd() function will trap this special character, so our program won't have to worry about it. It will take care of recording macros and assigning a playback keystroke.

The user_cmd() function will also then check for the playback character and turn on macro playback when it is pressed. This work all will happen in the user_cmd() function so our Tiny Editor, or any other program, will not have to be aware of this activity.

At some later date we can enhance our user_cmd() function with the other input capabilities we've been discussing, without changing a line in the rest of the Tiny Editor program. We can build the command module for Tiny Editor and use it for every other program we write so that they all have a consistent command capability. If we add a file input feature for any one of our programs, we'll have added it for all our programs.

To get this potential advantage, we'll need to restructure our Tiny Editor source from a single .CPP file to a multifile, project-style structure.

ADDING MAINLINE AND COMMAND SOURCE FILES

First, create a mainline file, TE.CPP.

TIP

F3 is quicker than File I New, since it lets you skip the Save As... step. Just enter TE for the name. The .CPP extension is supplied by default.

As Listing 6-1 shows (all new, so it's not on disk), start with a basic file skeleton.

Listing 6-1: TE.CPP

```
// TE.CPP—Tiny Editor
// Copyright 1995, Martin L. Rinehart


// end of TE.CPP
```

To use the dialog objects you've been creating, you'll need the class definitions. To use them, just add the TEWIN.H header to your new mainline, as Listing 6-2 shows.

Listing 6-2: TE.CPP

```
// TE.CPP—Tiny Editor
// Copyright 1995, Martin L. Rinehart


#include "TEWIN.H"


// end of TE.CPP
```

Next, remove main() from TEWIN.CPP and put it in TE.CPP. Listing 6-3 shows the new TE.CPP. On your own, make sure that main() is deleted from TEWIN.CPP. I've also removed the "for testing" comment and one level of indentation from the entire function.

Listing 6-3: TE.CPP

```
// TE.CPP—Tiny Editor
// Copyright 1995, Martin L. Rinehart


#include "TEWIN.H"

int main()
{

    textattr( WHITE_BLACK );
    clrscr();

...


    delete ms;
    getch();


    return 0;
}
```

```
// end of TE.CPP
```

If you try Ctrl+F9 in the TE.CPP window at this point, you get a bunch of "should have a prototype" errors. All these come from calls to CONIO.H functions. Without a listing, add the #include <CONIO.H> line to TE.CPP and try Ctrl+F9 again.

At this point, you should have a host of linker messages, all complaining about "undefined symbol" errors. All the offending symbols are your classes' member functions. The problem is, of course, that the linker has no idea where it should look to find these symbols. (Computers have *very* short memories, don't they?)

What we need to do is create a project file. When you create a project, you need to tell TCLite about the .CPP files that are part of your project. TCLite will find the include files on its own. (Actually, the preprocessor will tell TCLite about them as it comes to #include lines.)

To build a project, follow these steps:

STEP   BY   STEP

1. Choose Project | Open project from the menus.

2. Enter TE into the Load Project File dialog box. This dialog will supply the default extension, .PRJ, for you.

3. You'll see the Project: TE window shown in Figure 6-1. The control keys, such as Ins and Del, work here just as they do in the Watch window.

4. Press Ins to launch the Add Item to Project List dialog.

5. Type TE and press Enter. This adds TE.CPP to the project list.

6. Type TEWIN and press Enter to add TEWIN.CPP to the project list.

7. Press Esc or click Cancel to exit from the Add Item to Project List window.

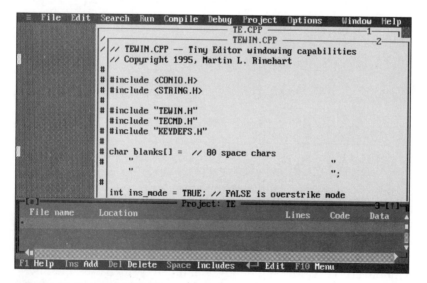

Figure 6-1: Defining the TE project.

Your project is now defined. Try Ctrl+F9 to check. Your program should run exactly as it did before. Your main() is now part of TE.CPP, calling the objects and functions you've defined in TEWIN.CPP and TEWIN.H. This change should not make any visible difference, however.

From now on, you can add .H files with an appropriate #include statement. When you add a .CPP file, however, you need to return to the Project window and use Ins to add the .CPP through the Add Item to Project dialog.

That's all you need to do to manage multiple-file projects. It's hard to see how this could be made any easier.

Now we're ready to use this new structure to get on to adding the yes/no dialog boxes we'll need later.

RETURNING YES OR NO

It's not quite enough to simply restrict the message dialog to popping down on only Y and N keypresses. We need to tell the calling program which choice the user made, of course.

One of the things that a constructor function can't have is a type, so one of the things that it can't do is return a value. This means that popping a message box up with its constructor isn't going to be all we need for a yes/no dialog.

We have choices. For one, we could create an ask_yn() method that will pop the dialog up and return an answer. An alternative is to use the constructor, as we've done with the message dialog, but add an answer data member to a yes_no class. After we create the yes_no dialog, it will take care of running itself.

Our calling program will only need to create the dialog; it can then look at the answer.

Adding a Command System

To get a keystroke, we've been calling getch() directly. As we discussed previously, a much more flexible method will be to ask a command processor to return the keystroke. This will also be what we need when it is time to get our yes-or-no answer.

Let's put our command processor in a file called TECMD.CPP. Start with a skeleton for the file, as shown in Listing 6-4 (all new, so it's not on disk).

→ add to project

Listing 6-4: TECMD.CPP

```
// TECMD.CPP—command processor for Tiny Editor
// coypright 1995, Martin L. Rinehart


// end of TECMD.CPP
```

With TECMD.CPP created, you'll also need to create a TECMD.H. For now, TECMD.CPP will be simple enough, but the .H file will be necessary for any of our other source files that need to call the user_cmd() function we'll write. TECMD.H will have that function's declaration, which our other source files will need to include.

So go ahead and create TECMD.H, as shown in Listing 6-5 (also all new, and not on disk).

Listing 6-5: TECMD.H

```
// TECMD.H—command processor header in Tiny Editor
// Copyright 1995, Martin L. Rinehart


// end of TECMD.H
```

At this point, your screen has five file windows and some number of other windows, including the Project window, the Message window, and perhaps a Watch or other window. Use Alt+F3 to close them all. You'll be given a chance to save any of the file windows that have been modified (including the ones you just created) since last saved.

You want to eliminate every window from your IDE's desktop. When you are windowless, open your code windows in this order:

▶ TE.CPP

▶ TEWIN.CPP

▶ TEWIN.H

▶ TECMD.CPP

▶ TECMD.H

The order in which you open your windows will correspond to the window numbers that TCLite will assign. You can switch to a window by pressing Alt plus its window number. With the order above, Alt+1 will switch to TE.CPP, Alt+2 will switch to TEWIN.CPP, and so on.

After opening my windows in order, I arrange them as shown in Figure 6-2.

The .H files are cascaded on the left, and the .CPP files are cascaded on the right. By cascading them you can get a setup that lets you click with the mouse

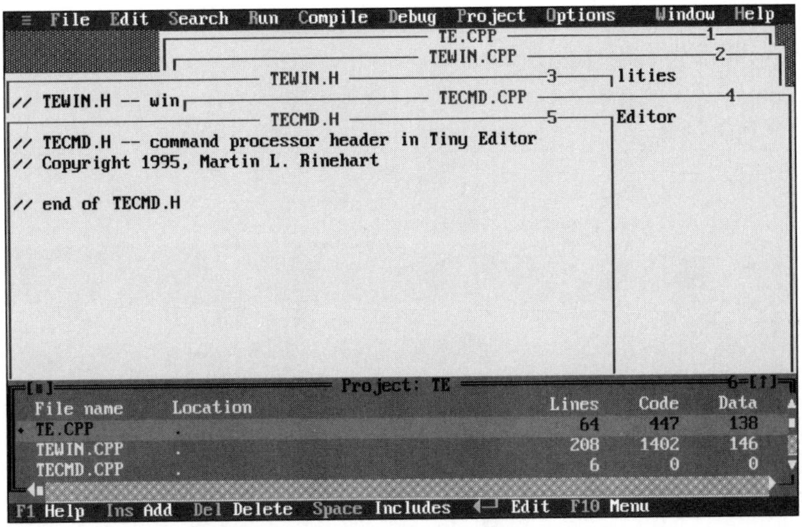

```
 ≡  File  Edit  Search  Run  Compile  Debug  Project  Options    Window  Help
┌─────────────────────────────── TE.CPP ──────────────┬─1─┐
│                              ┌─────── TEWIN.CPP ───────────┴─2─┐
│                     ┌──────── TEWIN.H ────────────┬─3──┐lities │
│ // TEWIN.H -- win┌──┴───────────── TECMD.CPP ──────────┴─4─┐    │
│                  │────── TECMD.H ──────────┬─5──┐Editor  │    │
│ // TECMD.H -- command processor header in Tiny Editor │    │    │
│ // Copyright 1995, Martin L. Rinehart            │    │    │    │
│                                                  │    │    │    │
│ // end of TECMD.H                                │    │    │    │
│                                                  │    │    │    │
│                                                  │    │    │    │
│                                                  │    │    │    │
│                                                  │    │    │    │
│                                                  │    │    │    │
│                                                  │    │    │    │
│                                                  │    │    │    │
│                                                  │    │    │    │
│                                                  │    │    │    │
│                                                  │    │    │    │
│                                                  │    │    │    │
├─[■]───────────────── Project: TE ═════════════════6═[↑]─┤
│  File name    Location                  Lines   Code   Data ▲
│ • TE.CPP        .                          64    447    138 ■
│   TEWIN.CPP     .                         208   1402    146 ▼
│   TECMD.CPP     .                           6      0      0 ▼
│◄■                                                        ►
 F1 Help  Ins Add  Del Delete  Space Includes  ◄─┘ Edit  F10 Menu
```

Figure 6-2: File windows in two cascades.

on any window on screen. (The lower-numbered windows poke out at the upper left, and the higher-numbered windows poke out at the lower right when they are not on top.)

This arrangement lets you use either the mouse or the Alt+*number* keystroke to switch quickly to the window you want. Since we'll be adding code in all these windows as we go, this will become very important.

Once you have your setup done to your liking, choose Options|Save so that TCLite will continue to arrange your desktop this way.

With this setup in place, let's use it to add the simplest possible user_cmd() function to TECMD. Start by adding a function declaration as shown in Listing 6-6.

Listing 6-6: TECMD.H

```
// TECMD.H—command processor header in Tiny Editor
// Copyright 1995, Martin L. Rinehart
```

```
int user_cmd();
```

```
// end of TECMD.H
```

After adding the declaration in the header, add the definition in TECMD.CPP, as shown in Listing 6-7.

Listing 6-7: TECMD.CPP

```
// TECMD.CPP—command processor for Tiny Editor
// coypright 1995, Martin L. Rinehart

#include <CONIO.H>

#include "TECMD.H"

int user_cmd()
{
    return getch();
}
```

```
// end of TECMD.CPP
```

Now you have the structure and your simplest possible command function. The remaining step is to put this code to work. Return to TE.CPP (Alt+1) and add the new #include as shown in Listing 6-8.

Listing 6-8: TE.CPP

```
// TE.CPP—Tiny Editor
// Copyright 1995, Martin L. Rinehart

#include <CONIO.H>

#include "TEWIN.H"
#include "TECMD.H"

int main()
```

Without a listing, also change every occurrence of getch() in TE.CPP to a call to user_cmd(). (The IDE editor's search and replace, launched with Ctrl+Q, A, will do this nicely.)

When you press Ctrl+F9, all the affected modules are automatically recompiled, and your program will run, once again, just as it did before. Of course, this version is taking its input from user_cmd(), not directly from getch().

Now our structure is in place, so we can write a function that returns a yes-or-no command.

Checking for Y or N

Your user_cmd() will be the general function that gets the next command. It goes to the keyboard now, but it could go to a macro, a mouse, or whatever when you get around to improving it. We can also add specific functions to our command processor that will return only selected commands.

The yes-or-no command is a good example of how you can do this.

To write a yes-or-no command, we'll need to look a little more closely at C++'s logical expressions. The first thing to know is that C++ does not have a logical data type.

Like C, C++ uses integer data types, such as ints, to represent logical values. A zero value is considered false, and all other values are considered true. The value that appears inside the ()s or an if or a while statement is interpreted this way.

Here are some examples:

```
if ( i < top ) ... // comparison returns 1 or 0
if ( i == top )... // true when i equals top
if ( i != top )... // != means NOT equal


if ( 0 ) ...        // never!
if ( 1 ) ...        // always!
while ( 1 ) ...     // loop forever
```

Here are some other tests you could write:

```
i = ...          // some value assigned to i

if ( i != 0 ) // same as the following:
if ( i )

if ( i == 0 ) // same as:
if ( !i )
```

The ! operator—not—represents logical negation. It reverses the logical value of its argument. Not true is false; not false is true. More precisely, in C++ (!i) returns zero if i is nonzero; (!i) returns nonzero if i is zero.

Most of the time you can think of 1 as the true value, but you can never safely depend on this. Any nonzero value is interpreted as true. The value of !0 may be 1, or it may be any other nonzero value (and −1 is a strong possibility).

These remarks also apply to the middle expression in a for loop:

```
for ( int i = 100; i > 0; i-- ) ... // same as:
for ( int i = 100; i    ; i-- ) ...
```

Among C++ programmers, testing for (i != 0) or for (i == 0) is considered amateurish. Personally, I think that it makes your code more readable, but all C and C++ programmers soon learn to read the more cryptic tests for (i) or for (!i).

Before we go on to the code, let's add the else statement to our understanding of the if statement. In full, this is the syntax:

```
if ( <condition> ) <statement>
[ else <statement> ]
```

The statement following the else can, as always, be any C++ statement, including a block statement or another if statement. Here's a typical example:

```
if ( <condition> )
{
    ...;  // stuff to do
    ...;  // when <condition> is true
}
else
{
    ...; // stuff to do
    ...; // when <condition> is false
}
```

When you have more than one if statement preceding an else, the else applies to the nearest preceding unmatched if. This is an example:

```
if ( <condition1> )
{
```

```
      if ( <condition2> )
          statement;
      else // <condition2> is false
  }
```

If you want to match an else to a particular if, other than the immediately previous one, be sure to use block statements:

```
  if ( <condition1> )
  {
      if ( <condition2> )
          statement;
  }
  else // <condition1> is false
```

We'll use if and else statements to build our test for a yes-or-no answer. Before we start, let's look at some relational and logical operators.

== equal

!= not equal

&& logical and

|| logical or

! logical not

In these examples, the relational and logical operators are mixed, and parentheses are used to make the order of evaluation explicit:

```
  (a==2) || (b==3) // true if a equals 2 or b equals 3
  (a==2) && (b==3) // true if both a==2 and b==3

l1 = ... // l1 is assigned a true or false value
l2 = ... // l2 is also true or false

l1 || l2     // true if l1 or l2 is true
!l1          // true if l1 is false, false if l1 is true

!(l1 || l2)     // true only if l1 and l2 are both false
 (!l1) && (!l2) // same
```

```
!(l1 && l2)      // false only if l1 and l2 are both true
 (!l1) || (!l2) // same
```

Let's get on to writing a function that returns true if a keystroke is a yes-or-no answer. Begin by defining logical constants and adding a function declaration in TECMD.H, as shown in Listing 6-9.

Listing 6-9: TECMD.H

```
// TECMD.H—command processor header in Tiny Editor
// Copyright 1995, Martin L. Rinehart

#define TRUE   1
#define FALSE  0

int user_cmd();
int yn_cmd();

// end of TECMD.H
```

The constants TRUE and FALSE are often defined this way. As you'll see in Listing 6-10, these definitions can make some logical functions more clear.

In the yn_cmd() function we'll use one more new statement, break. The break statement exits from a loop or a switch. To be technically correct, it exits from the most recently enclosing loop or switch. We've used while and for loops; we'll soon get to switches, where the break statement will be critical.

T I P

For the coming work, remember that Alt+1 switches to TE.CPP; Alt+4 switches to TECMD.CPP, and Alt+5 switches to TECMD.H. If you forget, Alt+0 gives you a list of all your windows.

Add the new function shown in Listing 6-10 to TECMD.CPP.

Listing 6-10: TECMD.CPP

```
// TECMD.CPP—command processor for Tiny Editor
// coypright 1995, Martin L. Rinehart

#include <CONIO.H>

#include "TECMD.H"

int user_cmd()
{
    return getch();
}

int yn_cmd()
{
    int retval;

    while ( TRUE )
    {
        char c = user_cmd();
        if ( c == 'y' || c == 'Y' )
        {
            retval = TRUE;
            break;
        }
        else if ( c == 'n' || c == 'N' )
        {
            retval = FALSE;
            break;
        }
    }
    return retval;
}

// end of TECMD.CPP
```

The loop, while(TRUE), is a deliberate infinite loop. This code is a typical example of break statements being used to end an otherwise infinite loop. The result is that this function will keep asking for another keypress (actually, a user_cmd(), which is a keypress for now) until 'y', 'Y', 'n', or 'N' is typed.

Another way to write this function is:

```
int yn_cmd()
{
    while ( TRUE )
    {
        char c = user_cmd();
        if ( c == 'y' || c == 'Y' )
            return TRUE;

        else if ( c == 'n' || c == 'N' )
            return FALSE;
    }
}
```

By using a return statement you break out of the loop when an acceptable value is available, and you save the trouble of creating an extra variable. Some theorists object to multiple returns in a single function, however. In this case, both versions look clear to me.

However you've coded it, let's go on to test it in TE.CPP. For now, let's do a trivial change just to be sure that yn_cmd() is looking for the right keypresses. Listing 6-11 shows how you can switch the first message box into a temporary yn_cmd() test.

Listing 6-11: TE.CPP

```
user_cmd();

message* ms = new message(
    "This is a yes/no message." );

yn_cmd();

delete ms;
user_cmd();
```

```
ms = new message(
    "This is a sample",
    "two-line message." );


user_cmd();
```

I've used the first, single-line, message for this test. I made a slight change to the message so that it would be appropriate and then changed the user_cmd() call to a yn_cmd() call.

When you press Ctrl+F9, your single-line message should pop up and then refuse to respond until you type 'y', 'Y', 'n', or 'N'.

If you want to be sure that your return value is correctly TRUE or FALSE (actually, 1 or 0), slip in a variable and use F4 to run to the spot of the assignment. Set a watch with Ctrl+F7 and then use F7 to step forward one line. This is the code you need:

```
int temp;
    temp = yn_cmd();
```

Use F4 to stop at the second of those lines. (Without assigning to a temporary variable, you've nothing to display in the Watch window.)

When you are satisfied that your yn_cmd() is working, go on to building the yes/no dialog box.

BUILD THE YES/NO DIALOG BOX

A convenient yes_no object would just need to be launched so that we would have the user input we want. Since we're going to be our own customers for this class, let's make it convenient.

Start with TEWIN.H. Add a class similar to the message class. Again, we can overload the constructor to support one-, two-, or three-line messages. Listing 6-12 shows my version.

Listing 6-12: TEWIN.H

```
class message : public dialog
{
public:
    message( char* msg1 );
```

```
      message( char* msg1, char* msg2 );
      message( char* msg1, char* msg2, char* msg3 );

private:
      void tip_line();
};
```

```
class yes_no : public dialog
{
public:
    int ans;

    yes_no( char* msg1 );
    yes_no( char* msg1, char* msg2 );
    yes_no( char* msg1, char* msg2, char* msg3 );

private:
    void tip_line();
};
```

```
// end of TEWIN.H
```

These classes are very similar. Aside from the name, the visible difference here is the addition to yes_no of an integer member, ans, to hold the answer (yes or no, recorded as true or false) that we get.

One difference that you might overlook is the fact that the tip_line() private function here is a totally separate function from the tip_line() in the message class. A yes_no object won't even know that there is a tip_line() method for any class except itself.

With the class defined, go on to adding the constructor functions and the new tip_line() to TEWIN.CPP, as shown in Listing 6-13.

TIP

One way to create the new code in Listing 6-13 is to do a lot of typing. Another way is to copy the message class functions and do a small amount of editing.

Listing 6-13: TEWIN.CPP

```
void message::tip_line()
{
    textattr( DIAG_TIP_CLR );
    gotoxy( rgt-25, btm-1 );
    cprintf( "press any key to continue" );
}

yes_no::yes_no( char* msg1 ) :
    dialog( " Yes or No " )
{
    gotoxy( lft+2, top+(btm-top)/2 );
    // textattr( DIAG_CON_CLR );
    cprintf( msg1 );

    tip_line();
}

yes_no::yes_no( char* msg1, char* msg2 ) :
    dialog( " Yes or No " )
{
    int msg_row = top+(btm-top)/2 - 1;
    gotoxy( lft+2, msg_row );
    // textattr( DIAG_CON_CLR );
    cprintf( msg1 );

    gotoxy( lft+2, ++msg_row );
    cprintf( msg2 );

    tip_line();
}

yes_no::yes_no( char* msg1, char* msg2, char* msg3 ) :
    dialog( " Yes or No " )
{
    int msg_row = top+(btm-top)/2 - 1;
    gotoxy( lft+2, msg_row );
    // textattr( DIAG_CON_CLR );
```

```
    cprintf( msg1 );

    gotoxy( lft+2, ++msg_row );
    cprintf( msg2 );

    gotoxy( lft+2, ++msg_row );
    cprintf( msg3 );

    tip_line();
}

void yes_no::tip_line()
{
    textattr( DIAG_TIP_CLR );
    gotoxy( rgt-14, btm-1 );
    cprintf( "answer Y or N" );
}
```

```
// end of TEWIN.CPP
```

With your class defined and the class methods defined, it's time to call these functions from main(). Listing 6-14 shows the code to change in TE.CPP. If you change the references to "message" to read "yes_no" and change the "ms" names to "yn" you'll have made most of these changes.

Listing 6-14: TE.CPP

```
user_cmd();
```

```
yes_no* yn = new yes_no(
    "This is a yes/no message." );
```

```
yn_cmd();
```

```
delete yn;
user_cmd();
```

```
yn = new yes_no(
    "This is a sample",
    "two-line yes/no." );
```

```
    user_cmd();

    delete yn;
    user_cmd();

    yn = new yes_no(
        "This is a sample",
        "three-line yes/no",
        "being tested." );

    user_cmd();

    delete yn;
    user_cmd();

    return 0;
}


// end of TE.CPP
```

When you try Ctrl+F9 you should have one-, two-, and three-line yes_no
objects pop up and wait for your response. Figure 6-3 shows the first one
popped up.

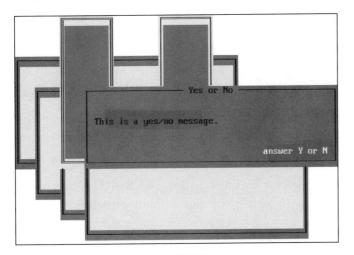

Figure 6-3: A one-line yes_no object popped up.

If you test a little, you'll see that only the first call actually insists on a yes or no answer, however.

To perfect our class, let's ask the yes or no question in the constructor and just look at the answer after we pop up this dialog box. Since all the constructors call the tip_line() private function, tip_line() is a good place to do this work.

Make the two additions shown in Listing 6-15 to TEWIN.CPP. Then delete the yn_cmd() and user_cmd() function calls that *follow* the yes_no constructor calls in TE.CPP. Your resulting TEWIN.CPP should look like the one in Listing 6-15.

Listing 6-15: TEWIN.CPP

```
// TEWIN.CPP—Tiny Editor windowing capabilities
// Copyright 1995, Martin L. Rinehart

#include <CONIO.H>
#include <STRING.H>

#include "TEWIN.H"
#include "TECMD.H"

char blanks[] =  // 80 space chars
...
void yes_no::tip_line()
{
    textattr( DIAG_TIP_CLR );
    gotoxy( rgt-14, btm-1 );
    cprintf( "answer Y or N" );

    ans = yn_cmd();
}

// end of TEWIN.CPP
```

If you don't immediately see the need for the #include "TECMD.H" directive, you should try adding the call to yn_cmd() without including the header. Press Alt+F9 and the compiler will tell you that it needs the header file.

As an aside, tip_line() is doing more than just adding the tip line, so it's not a very well-named function. Normally I would have given it a better name, but I wanted you to see that you could have separate functions with a single name in as many classes as you like.

N O T E

Your two tip_line() functions are completely separate. The name of a function in one class has nothing to do with any similar or identical names in other classes. A much fancier way to say this is that the lexical scope of method names is their class. The lexical scope of an identifier refers to the dictionaries, or name lists, that the compiler creates and uses. The compiler builds a separate dictionary for each class.

Listing 6-16 shows part of main() with more deeply shaded blank lines where the function calls get removed.

With these changes, when you run your program each yes_no dialog will stop and wait for you to type a 'Y' or 'N' answer.

To test the changes, use Ctrl+F8 to set a breakpoint on each of the "delete yn" lines and then run the program with Ctrl+F9. At the first break, use Ctrl+F7 to set a watch on yn->ans. You should see the value be 1 or 0 depending on whether you type 'Y' or 'N'.

ADD user_cmd() TO THE MESSAGE DIALOGS

On your own, add a call to user_cmd() in the message class's tip_line() function. This will simplify the calling. All you'll need to do with a message object is create it and then delete it. It will take care of interacting with the user without further instructions from your program.

Add one or two message boxes to main() in TE.CPP to test your work. Got it?

Congratulations. You're becoming a real C++ programmer. In the next chapter we'll add a dialog box that includes a text field. This will come in handy for such purposes as getting filenames from the user.

Listing 6-16: TE.CPP

```
user_cmd();

yes_no* yn = new yes_no(
    "This is a yes/no message." );
```

```
delete yn;
user_cmd();

yn = new yes_no(
    "This is a sample",
    "two-line yes/no." );
```

```
delete yn;
user_cmd();

yn = new yes_no(
    "This is a sample",
    "three-line yes/no",
    "being tested." );
```

```
delete yn;
user_cmd();

return 0;
```

SUMMARY

When you began this chapter you were working with a simple, single-.CPP structure. As you know, serious programming means working with multiple source files.

In this chapter, you switched to a serious, multifile structure. You kept your screen I/O classes in TEWIN.CPP and added TE.CPP, the mainline, and TECMD.CPP, the user input command processor.

You built a project file, using the TCLite IDE's Project window, to manage these files. One of your more pleasant discoveries was that TCLite really makes this as simple as possible.

After we went to a multifile source structure, we dove into logical data. You saw that there really isn't a logical data type, but integers with zero or nonzero values serve the purpose.

We looked at == and != operators and the way these combine with logical operations, such as !, &&, and ||.

You mixed the logical and relational operators in if and else statements to create a basic function that returns true or false in response to 'Y' or 'N' (or 'y' or 'n') values.

While you wrote this function, you used an "infinite" while loop and you used the break statement to keep it from being really infinite.

In the next chapter, we'll create a dialog box that reads in a text field. This dialog will serve nicely when we need a filename. While you build this dialog, we'll be writing our first code that will actually be doing the basics of text editing.

In this chapter we're going to add a dialog that reads in a text field. While we implement this functionality, we'll:

- ▶ Use a do while loop
- ▶ Create formatted printf() output
- ▶ Use unsigned and signed chars and ints
- ▶ Define inline functions with #define
- ▶ Use the switch statement with case and default
- ▶ Manipulate the cursor with _setcursortype()
- ▶ Run sample programs from the Help file
- ▶ Use the ternary conditional operator
- ▶ Study operator precedence and associativity

To make our editor work, we'll need to handle navigation and other commands from the keyboard, which is where we'll begin.

chapter

7

▼ ▼ ▼ ▼

A Single-Line Editor

The text field object that we'll build is actually a very small editor, used for entering and editing a single line.

Even though our new object handles just a single line, it responds appropriately to many editing commands, including:

▶ Cursor forward/backward one character.

▶ Toggle insert and overstrike modes.

▶ Insert and overstrike characters.

▶ Delete character under/behind cursor.

▶ Cursor forward/backward one word.

▶ Delete next word.

▶ Cursor to line start/end.

R E A D I N G   K E Y S T R O K E S

Up to now we've tested for printable characters, such as 'Y' and 'N'. To do any editing, however, we're going to need to look for characters that don't have typescript equivalents, such as the left-arrow key and Ctrl+F.

These keys all are reported by the getch() function, but their values are, to put it nicely, not intuitive. We'll need to begin with a little utility program that we can use to find the values for these keys. My version uses three features that we haven't used yet.

The do while Loop

The first feature is a new control structure, the do while statement. We've worked with the while statement:

```
while ( <condition> )
    <statement>
```

A similar loop, called do while, provides a similar control function:

```
do
    <statement>
while ( <condition> );
```

Here's how we'll use this loop:

```
char c;
do
    {
        c = getch();
        ... // display c's value
    }
while ( c != 27 ); // 27 == Esc
```

As with the other loops, the most common <statement> is a block statement, which this example shows. The difference between do while and while is the location of the condition.

The while statement is immediately followed by the condition. If the condition is false (zero) at the outset, the code in the loop is never executed. This kind of loop is called a *top-tested* loop.

On the other hand, do while is a *bottom-tested* loop. The code in the loop is executed before the while condition is tested. This means that the code is always executed at least once, even if the first test yields a false value.

In the example above, that's exactly what we want. If we press the Esc key, it is read and displayed before the exit test. If we used a top-tested loop, we'd never get the exit keystroke to be displayed.

Formatted Printing

The second feature is one that is key to the printf() function. The "f" stands for formatted. The printf() function will do jobs much more complex than the simple examples we've seen so far.

T I P

The cprintf() function does everything that printf() does, in almost exactly the same way, except that it uses some Borland-specific console I/O functions that we've ignored. Note that cprintf()'s declaration is in CONIO.H, whereas printf()'s declaration is in STDIO.H; you can pick one based on whatever header file is handier.

The printf() function takes a format string followed by a list of values to use to fill in the formats. The list of values should be as long as the number of format specifiers in the format string. The format specifiers start with a percent sign. Some common ones are:

▶ %d—a number

▶ %s—a string

▶ %c—a character

Here are some examples:

```
int i;
char c;
string s;

printf( "The number is: %d", i );
printf( "The character is: %c", c );
printf( "The string is: %s", s );

printf( "The employee named %s is paid %d.", s, i );
```

We'll use this feature to print the character as a number, as in:

```
c = getch();
printf( "%d", c );
```

Chars Are Numbers

In C++, as in C before it, an integer is not defined to be a particular size. The compiler implementers are free to pick a size that makes sense for the architecture of the machine their compiler will run on. The Intel CPUs, going back to the 8088 (circa 1980) work well with 16-bit integers, so PC C and C++ compilers all use 16-bit integers for the int type.

A char is an integer, too, only smaller. Our chars are 8-bit integers. You probably think of them as bytes, or as characters. To the compiler, though, they're just smaller integers.

All integers can be signed (the default) or unsigned. A signed 16-bit integer is a number from negative 32K up to positive 32K − 1. An unsigned integer ranges from 0 to 64K − 1. (These are PC values. A machine with a different integer size would, of course, have a different range of values.)

The syntax for declaring an unsigned integer is simple. You just use the "unsigned" keyword in front of the "int" keyword:

```
int i;            // -32k <= i < 32k
unsigned int j; //   0  <= j < 64k
```

For many integers, this distinction is unimportant. For char variables, however, it can be very important. Assume that you use getch() and the user enters character 128 (holds Alt down and presses 1, 2, 8 on the numeric keypad). Do you want your display routine to show that value as 128? I do.

Computers, of course, are not smart. They will dutifully transfer whatever bit pattern is in the keyboard buffer (for 128, that's a 1 and then 7 zeros) to your variable. When getch() prints it out, it will dutifully translate that pattern to its numeric value—negative 128, if your variable is an 8-bit, signed integer.

It is almost always preferable to define your chars as unsigned so that this sort of confusion is avoided. When you want to be explicit, you can use the "signed" keyword:

```
unsigned char c; //    0 <= c < 256
                 // binary 10000000 == decimal 128
```

```
signed char c;    // -128 <= c < 128
                  // binary 10000000 == decimal -128
```

Many compilers give you a switch that uses unsigned chars as a default. The contemporary default is, according to the proposed international C++ standard, signed. Older compilers often defaulted to unsigned.

In other words, you can't be sure what you'll have until you test a specific compiler, so the smart thing to do is to always be explicit.

T I P

Even after you test your compiler and *know* what it does with chars, it's smart to be explicit. If you omit the signed keyword because that's your compiler's default, your code may fail when you move it to an environment with a different compiler. This sort of trivial failure can be incredibly hard to find, too. If you explicitly label your chars, this will never be a problem.

Building a Test Program

With all that prologue, let's go on to building a simple keyboard test program. You'll need to clear out TCLite before you proceed. Begin by closing your project (choose Project|Close from the menus).

When your project is closed, you need to close all your open source files. The fast way is to simply hold Alt+F3 down until your desktop is clear. If there are any unsaved files open, you'll get an appropriate dialog. It will pop up and down and nothing bad will happen, regardless of how long you hold Alt+F3, so be fearless.

When your desktop is clear, enter the code in Listing 7-1 as KEYS.CPP. When it's in, test it with Ctrl+F9. (It's all new, so it's not on disk.)

Listing 7-1: KEYS.CPP

```
// KEYS.CPP-keystroke numeric value utility
// copyright 1995, Martin L. Rinehart

#include <CONIO.H>
```

```
int main()
{

    unsigned char c;
    cprintf ( "\n\rpress a key (ESC exits)\n\r" );

    do
    {
        c = getch();
        cprintf( "%d \n\r", c );
    }
    while ( c != 27 ); // 27 == Esc

    return 0;
}


// end of KEYS.CPP
```

When you run this program, you'll see the integer value of each key that you press. However, if you test keys such as the left-arrow key, you'll see a peculiar result. Figure 7-1 shows my trial run.

```
C:\CPPBK1>exit

press a key (ESC exits)
97
98
99
100
101
102
103
0
75
0
75
```

Figure 7-1: A run of KEYS.CPP.

When you press the left-arrow key, you get two separate values from successive calls to getch(). The first is zero, and the second is what is called the *scan code* of the key you pressed.

The scan codes were codes that IBM originally assigned to the keys on the PC keyboard in 1981. Each key was numbered, working roughly from left to right and top to bottom. The Esc key, which was in the upper-left corner, was given scan code 1, the numeral 1 coded 2, and so on. These scan codes are still used to address special keys, such as those on the numeric keypad.

The getch() function returns a zero value when you press an arrow key. If you call the getch() function a second time, it then returns the scan code for the key you pressed.

Experiment with the special function keys, Alt key combinations, shifted keys, and Ctrl key combinations. You'll see that some report a single value and others report a zero followed by a scan code. For example, the numeral 1 (keyboard top row) reports a value 49, but if you try Alt+1, it reports 0 followed by 120.

The scan code for the 1 is 2, not 120. Borland has taken some liberties to ensure that all these key combinations return unique values.

If you check the online documentation, you'll see that getch() is an integer function. Borland sees that it never returns values that exceed 255, so that you can catch its return with a char, if you like.

A more handy way to proceed is to cover getch() with a little logic that checks for the zero value return. If you get a zero value, call getch() again and add 256 to the result. This gives you an int value that you can use in your program without any problems. Listing 7-2 shows KEYS.CPP modified to always return an int result.

Listing 7-2: KEYS.CPP

```
// KEYS.CPP—keystroke numeric value utility
// copyright 1995, Martin L. Rinehart

#include <CONIO.H>

int main()
{
    unsigned int c;
    cprintf ( "\npress a key (ESC exits)\n\r" );

    do
    {
        c = getch();

        if ( !c )
            c = 256 + getch();
```

```
        cprintf( "%d \n\r", c );
    }
    while ( c != 27 ); // 27 == Esc

    return 0;
}


// end of KEYS.CPP
```

Figure 7-2 shows the updated program returning single values for the control and navigation keys.

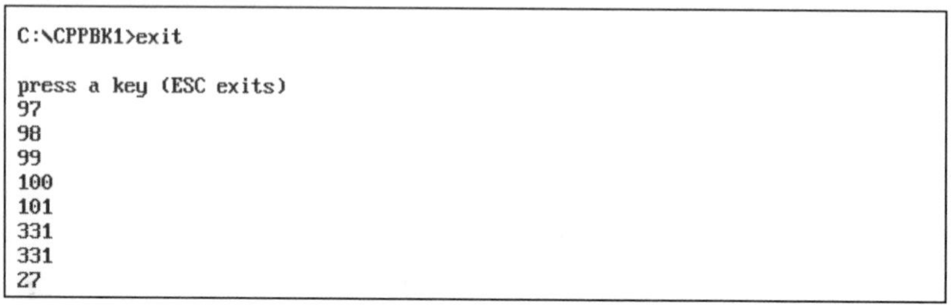

```
C:\CPPBK1>exit

press a key (ESC exits)
97
98
99
100
101
331
331
27
```

Figure 7-2: Improved results from KEYS.CPP.

With this program, we can begin to build a file of key definitions that will let us write code with defined constants, such as LF_ARROW, instead of cryptic values, such as 331.

Building KEYDEFS.H

Let's start by defining the arrow keys and some critical keyboard keys. The quickest way to build this list is to spend some time running your KEYS program and recording results with paper and pencil, then entering the results into your file.

Listing 7-3 shows a start.

Listing 7-3: KEYDEFS.H

```
// KEYDEFS.H—getch() value MACRO definitions
// Copyright 1995, Martin L. Rinehart

#define LF_ARROW        331
#define RT_ARROW        333
```

```
#define UP_ARROW        328
#define DN_ARROW        336

#define HOME            327
#define END             335

#define PGUP            329
#define PGDN            337

#define INS             338        insert  X
#define DEL             339        delete  X

#define ENTER            13
#define BKSP              8
#define ESC              27                  15 keys

#define TAB               9
#define BKTAB           271


// end of KEYDEFS.H
```

After you get those keys defined, continue with the Ctrl key combinations of the same keys. When you try these, you'll see the problem that I've hinted at in the comment near the bottom of Listing 7-4.

Listing 7-4: KEYDEFS.H

```
#define CTRL_LF_ARROW   371
#define CTRL_RT_ARROW   372
#define CTRL_UP_ARROW   397
#define CTRL_DN_ARROW   401
#define CTRL_HOME       375
#define CTRL_END        373
#define CTRL_PGUP       388           11 keys  with CNTRL
#define CTRL_PGDN       374
#define CTRL_ENTER       10
#define CTRL_BKSP       127
// #define CTRL_ESC            27
#define CTRL_TAB        404
// #define CTRL_BKTAB         404
```

As you see in the comments, I get the same value for Ctrl+Esc that I got for Esc, and the same for Ctrl+Shift+Tab that I got for Ctrl+Tab. The problem here is not Borland's getch() implementation, it's Microsoft's DOS. Some keystrokes, such as Ctrl+Esc, aren't really returned by the BIOS (Basic Input Output Service) calls that getch() depends on. This means that there are certain keystrokes that you may use in Windows, for instance, that you cannot access in a DOS program. You just have to design around that problem.

Next, let's add the special function keys. Listing 7-5 is rather long, but I'm sure that you'll see how to speed up entering this list with a little creative copying.

Listing 7-5: KEYDEFS.H

```
#define F1          315
#define F2          316
#define F3          317
#define F4          318
#define F5          319
#define F6          320
#define F7          321
#define F8          322
#define F9          323
#define F10         324

#define SHIFT_F1    340
#define SHIFT_F2    341
#define SHIFT_F3    342
#define SHIFT_F4    343
#define SHIFT_F5    344
#define SHIFT_F6    345
#define SHIFT_F7    346
#define SHIFT_F8    347
#define SHIFT_F9    348
#define SHIFT_F10   349

#define CTRL_F1     350
#define CTRL_F2     351
#define CTRL_F3     352
#define CTRL_F4     353
#define CTRL_F5     354
```

```
#define CTRL_F6    355
#define CTRL_F7    356
#define CTRL_F8    357
#define CTRL_F9    358
#define CTRL_F10   359

#define ALT_F1     360
#define ALT_F2     361
#define ALT_F3     362
#define ALT_F4     363
#define ALT_F5     364
#define ALT_F6     365
#define ALT_F7     366
#define ALT_F8     367
#define ALT_F9     368
#define ALT_F10    369
```

The final list adds the Alt key numbers that Borland's IDE uses to switch windows. Listing 7-6 shows the Alt+*digit* combinations.

Listing 7-6: KEYDEFS.H

```
#define ALT_0      385
#define ALT_1      376
#define ALT_2      377
#define ALT_3      378
#define ALT_4      379
#define ALT_5      380
#define ALT_6      381
#define ALT_7      382
#define ALT_8      383
#define ALT_9      384
```

With these values added, your list should meet most of your needs for DOS text-mode programming. Before we leave it, let's add one more feature of well-written programs to this header file.

You've already seen that we're using #include to use the same .H files in several .CPP source files. As our headers get longer, this can become a problem. One header file may #include another header. If several headers #include KEYDEFS.H, for example, the compiler may start spending a large part of its time reading and rereading this one file.

For this reason, and others, a good feature of a header file is to check to see that it has not already been included and to only include itself once.

This task is done by defining a keyword and then using conditional preprocessor directives. Here's what conditional preprocessor directives can look like:

```
#IFNDEF have_read_keydefs
    #define have_read_keydefs

    #define LF_ARROW        331
    #define RT_ARROW        333
    . . .
#ENDIF
```

The first directive, #IFNDEF, can be read, "IF Not DEFined." It checks to see if the following word has a definition. As you might guess, the code between #IFNDEF and #ENDIF is executed only if the answer is "Yes, the word is not defined."

The second line of that example uses #define to define a word. Unlike the use we've made of #define so far, it doesn't bother assigning a value. It's content just to define the word. The effect of this definition is to have #IFNDEF evaluate to false the next time it looks at this word.

These directives form a very common combination in header files. Unlike the sample here, the included header file code and preprocessor directives are not commonly indented within the surrounding #IFNDEF/#ENDIF block, since this block typically surrounds the entire header file. Listing 7-7 shows the top and bottom of the completed file, with this feature added:

Listing 7-7: KEYDEFS.H

```
// KEYDEFS.H—getch() value MACRO definitions
// Copyright 1995, Martin L. Rinehart


#ifndef KEYDEFS


#define KEYDEFS
```

```
#define LF_ARROW       331
#define RT_ARROW       333

...

#define ALT_8       383
#define ALT_9       384
```

```
#endif
```

```
// end of KEYDEFS.H
```

You'll find KEYDEFS.H to be indispensable in most of the programs that you write, beginning with the work we're about to start in the next section.

PREPARING THE CLASS

Our first step will be to build the structure we want so that we can implement a string field and, as always, test as we build. But the work we have just done shows how your testing can miss things when your knowledge is incomplete.

To get started, clear your desktop and then reopen the TE project (Project | Open). That should return the five open file windows that we carefully organized in the last chapter. Now let's go find and fix the bug.

Fixing a Bug

Before we begin work on our string field dialog, let's use what we've learned to eliminate a bug in our existing user_cmd(). It doesn't know that a single key-press can fill in two answers from getch(). To see this version fail, switch the first popup dialog in main() (in TE.CPP) from a yes_no object to a message object.

Listing 7-8 shows the changes you need to make in TE.CPP to do this conversion.

Listing 7-8: TE.CPP

```
    d.draw();

    user_cmd();

    message* ms = new message(
```

```
        "This is a message." );

    delete ms;
    user_cmd();


    yes_no* yn = new yes_no(
        "This is a sample",
        "two-line yes/no." );

    delete yn;
```

With these changes entered, use Ctrl+F9 to run your program. At the first pause, press a Ctrl combination. What happens? Your message dialog is launched and erased in a flash. If you get unlucky in your timing this could happen between screen refresh cycles so you don't even see a blink.

What's happening, of course, is that the first getch() returns a zero. Then your message is launched, and it calls another getch() in user_cmd(). This call is answered by the second part of the Ctrl combination, not by your pressing another key.

What you want, of course, is for user_cmd() to return an integer that shows the Ctrl and other nonprintable characters as numbers above 255, just as we were doing in the section above. This requires a simple modification to TECMD.CPP, as shown in Listing 7-9.

Listing 7-9: TECMD.CPP

```
// TECMD.CPP—command processor for Tiny Editor
// coypright 1995, Martin L. Rinehart


#include <CONIO.H>

#include "TECMD.H"


int user_cmd()
{
    int c = getch();
    if ( !c )
        return 256 + getch();
```

```
    else
        return c;
}
...
```

With that addition, when you run your program it will pause in the appropriate places, whatever keystrokes you use. Now let's go on to setting up a string_field class for entering strings.

Building a string_field Class

Let's move on to string_fields, another useful class for our window source file. We won't be using TECMD.CPP, so you can close its window and that of TECMD.H. (Remember to choose Options|Save if you want this change to last to your next session.)

Enter the class definition in Listing 7-10 into TEWIN.H. Most of the members of this class have obvious uses.

Listing 7-10: TEWIN.H

```
private:
    void tip_line();
};


class string_field
{
protected:
    int row, col;
    int width;    ——————  // length of str

    char* str;

    int cloc;   —> // cursor location

public:
    string_field(int c, int r, char* s);
    ~string_field();

    void show();
```

```
        void edit();
};
```

```
// end of TEWIN.H
```

We'll want to know how wide the field is, as well as where it should be placed (width, starting row and col). We'll want a character string member, too. The cloc variable will keep track of the location of the cursor in the field.

The constructor and destructor functions are standard. We'll also have a function that displays the field, and another that handles the actual editing (press the right-arrow key, and the cursor moves to the right, and so on).

With the class defined, let's write a constructor, a destructor, and the show() method. Then we can use our main() to put a string_field object on the screen and watch it as we implement the edit() method.

Listing 7-11 shows the basic string_field methods to add to TEWIN.CPP.

Listing 7-11: TEWIN.CPP

```
void yes_no::tip_line()
{
    textattr( DIAG_TIP_CLR );
    gotoxy( rgt-14, btm-1 );
    cprintf( "answer Y or N" );

    ans = yn_cmd();
}


string_field::string_field(int c, int r, char* s)
{
    col   = c;
    row   = r;
    width = strlen(s);
    str   = s;

    cloc  = col;
}
```

```
string_field::~string_field()
{
}

void string_field::show()
{
    GOHOME;
    textattr( STR_CLR );

    for ( int i = 0; i < width; i++ )
        putch(' ');

    GOHOME;
    cprintf( str );
}
```

// end of TEWIN.CPP

In the constructor, I haven't made a copy of the string. If we were doing our editing on a copy of the string, we could add a keystroke that said, "Oops! Forget these changes and go back to the way it was." On the other hand, if we were working on a copy, we'd have to make sure that we copied the changed version over the original when editing terminated normally. It's another one of those situations where you can't have your cake and eat it, too.

The destructor is empty at the moment. The show() method has a pair of newly defined macros, as the capital letters show. The GOHOME macro sends the cursor to the start of the field. Unlike the macros that we have used before now, this one expands to code, not to a data constant. (Look ahead to Listing 7-13 to see how this is done.)

There are tighter and faster ways to clear the field to blanks than the for loop written here. Use Shift+F1 and type "CONIO.H" to look at some of the available functions. (The CONIO library routines are almost all written in well-optimized assembler.)

With the routines available, let's call them from main(). The main() function has gone long enough without some spring cleaning. The version in Listing 7-12 is reduced to the essentials we need for working on our string_field class.

Listing 7-12: TE.CPP

```
// TE.CPP—Tiny Editor
// Copyright 1995, Martin L. Rinehart

#include <CONIO.H>

#include "TEWIN.H"
#include "TECMD.H"

int main()
{
    textattr( WHITE_BLUE );
    clrscr();
                          col  row
    string_field sf( 10, 5,
        "Hello, world!         " );

    sf.show();
    user_cmd();

    return 0;
}

// end of TE.CPP
```

Be careful to add a good batch of trailing blanks to the string constant in the call to the constructor. It doesn't matter how many, as long as you've got a bunch of them. I took the string's length for the width of the field (another choice that could have been done otherwise with good results in some cases), so these blanks are part of the field on the screen.

Finally, you have to add the new macros. I put mine in TEWIN.H, as you see in Listing 7-13.

Listing 7-13: TEWIN.H

```
// TEWIN.H—windowing header for Tiny Editor
// copyright 1995, Martin L. Rinehart

#define WHITE_BLACK  7
```

```
#define YELLOW_CYAN 62
#define WHITE_BLUE   23

#define DIAG_OUT_CLR 59 // Hi cyan on cyan
#define DIAG_CON_CLR 63 // Hi white on cyan
#define DIAG_TIP_CLR 48 // Black on cyan

#define SINGLE      "┌│┘─└│"
#define DOUBLE      "╔║╝═╚║"
#define SING_DOUB   "╒│╛═╘│"
#define DOUB_SING   "╓║╜─╙║"

#define STR_CLR 0x7F // hi-white on white
#define GOHOME   gotoxy( col, row );


class box
```

As you see, the GOHOME macro expands to a function call.

When you press Ctrl+F9, you should get your string_field object in the upper-left part of a blue field. Figure 7-3 shows what this should look like.

Figure 7-3: The prototype string_field object.

The string field itself is high-intensity white on a white background. (A white background is actually a shade of gray in text mode, but it's often called white, regardless.)

CONTROLLING THE CURSOR

The text-mode cursor is controlled by the video hardware. When you write to a location on the screen, you are actually updating a character in video RAM. Whenever you update a video RAM character via putch() or cprintf() the hardware cursor is positioned at the next character.

The basic input/output system (BIOS) calls that DOS supports let you control the cursor. The video BIOS calls, also known as interrupts, perform functions such as positioning the cursor and setting its size. We can call these functions directly or use the ones covered in CONIO.H.

Moving the Cursor

Let's start by moving the cursor. When we finished our show() function we left the cursor out at the right border of our string_field object. This is not really where we want it. The easiest way of moving the cursor is by calling the gotoxy() function.

Take a good look at the condition you left your cursor in (Alt+F5 to view the user screen) and then add the simple change shown in Listing 7-14 to the show() method.

Listing 7-14: TEWIN.CPP

```
void string_field::show()
{
    GOHOME;
    textattr( STR_CLR );

    for ( int i = 0; i < width; i++ )
        putch(' ');

    GOHOME;
    cprintf( str );

    GOHOME;
}

// end of TEWIN.CPP
```

This added line leaves the cursor under the first character in your string_field object, which is where you want it to start. If you check the constructor, you'll see that cloc, the variable that holds the cursor location, is initialized to col. This change has the added benefit of making cloc correct.

Now we're ready to make the cursor go left and right, in response to arrow key-strokes. These are the first two edit commands we'll implement.

Well, almost the first two! We'd better begin by implementing an edit() method. For testing, we'd better have a way of exiting from the edit method, so an escape command may be the very first one to implement.

The structure we'll need is a public method, edit(), which calls a protected method, edit_do(). As you'll see as we go along, the edit_do() routine gets all the real work, whereas the functions that use string_field objects merely call the edit() method.

Listing 7-15 shows the addition of these two routines to TEWIN.CPP.

Listing 7-15: TEWIN.CPP

```
void string_field::show()
{
    GOHOME;
    textattr( STR_CLR );

    for ( int i = 0; i < width; i++ )
        putch(' ');

    GOHOME;
    cprintf( str );

    GOHOME;
}

void string_field::edit()
{
    int done = FALSE;

    while ( !done )
    {
        done = edit_do( user_cmd() );
    }
}
```

```
int string_field::edit_do( int cmd )
{
    if ( cmd == 27 )
        return TRUE;
    else
        return FALSE;
}
```

// end of TEWIN.CPP

For the moment, our edit_do() is a trivial fellow who just decides that an escape keystroke means that it's time to quit. This method will get a lot larger as we add functionality.

Listing 7-16 shows the small addition you need to make to TEWIN.H to declare the edit_do() method.

Listing 7-16: TEWIN.H

```
class string_field
{
protected:
    int row, col;
    int width;

    char* str;

    int cloc;

    int edit_do( int cmd );

public:
```

The final change you need to make is to replace the user_cmd() call in main() with a call to the new edit() method. That's shown in Listing 7-17.

Listing 7-17: TE.CPP

```cpp
// TE.CPP—Tiny Editor
// Copyright 1995, Martin L. Rinehart

#include <CONIO.H>

#include "TEWIN.H"
#include "TECMD.H"

int main()
{
    textattr( WHITE_BLUE );
    clrscr();

    string_field sf( 10, 5,
        "Hello, world!            " );

    sf.show();
    sf.edit();

    return 0;
}

// end of TE.CPP
```

When you run this version, your string_field will stay on the screen until you press the Esc key. Now let's take a look at the control structure, the switch, that we'll actually want in our edit_do() method.

You use a switch when you want to write code that works like this:

```
get a keystroke
    if it's an escape, do ...
    if it's a right arrow, do ...
    if it's a left arrow, do ...

    ...
```

The actual syntax of the switch statement goes like this:

```
switch ( <variable> )
{
    case <value1>:
        <statement>
    case <value2>:
        <statement>
    ...
    default:
        <statement>
}
```

If we have a routine, such as edit_do(), that takes an integer parameter called cmd, this is what our switch could look like:

```
switch ( cmd )
{
    case 4: // 4 is Ctrl+D
    {
        // code to move cursor right one space
    }
    case 19: // 19 is Ctrl+S
    {
        // code to move cursor left one space
    }
    ...
    default:
        // whatever you want if none of above apply
}
```

If you're familiar with similar constructs in other languages, there's a peculiar feature you'll have to adjust to. Like C, C++ doesn't just execute the <statement> for the first case that applies; it begins executing <statement>s when a case applies and doesn't automatically stop until the end of the switch.

On the other hand, the break statement breaks out of a switch, just as it breaks out of a loop. Here's some typical code:

```
switch ( cmd )
{
    case 4: // 4 is Ctrl+D
    {
```

```
            // code to move cursor right one space
            break;
    }
    case 19: // 19 is Ctrl+S
    {
            // code to move cursor left one space
            break;
    }
    ...
    default:
            // whatever you want if none of above apply
}
```

There's a break after the code in each case. Of course, this behavior may seem strange at first, but it can be made to work for you sometimes. Supposing you've defined some common navigation keys and want to support both the navigation keys and the Wordstar-style control keys. Here's a switch that does both:

```
switch ( cmd )
{
    case 4: // 4 is Ctrl+D
    case RT_ARROW:
    {
            // code to move cursor right one space
            break;
    }

    case 19: // 19 is Ctrl+S
    case LF_ARROW:
    {
            // code to move cursor left one space
            break;
    }
    ...
    default:
            // whatever you want if none of above apply
}
```

In the early days of microcomputers we used typewriter-style keyboards, which didn't have arrow keys or a numeric keypad. Most programmers used the Wordstar word processor as their text editor. Wordstar used E, S, D, and X, in combination with the Ctrl key, as a navigation diamond. (They form a diamond shape, sort of, on the keyboard.) Through products like Borland's text editors, these keys are still with us today.

When the value following a case matches the value of the control variable, the switch stops evaluating cases and begins to execute <statement>s. Execution continues until a break statement or the end of the switch is reached. This means that if our cmd variable is either a 4 (Ctrl+D) or a RT_ARROW (defined elsewhere), the code to move the cursor one space to the right will be executed. This also shows the <statement> following each case is optional.

The code in <statement>s is not executed until one of the case values matches the control variable. If no case is matched, the default <statement> is executed.

W A R N I N G

The default <statement> in a switch does what you expect—it is executed if none of the case values match the control variable. But the <statement> following the default keyword is like any other <statement> in a switch. If you don't put a break at the end of the preceding case, the <statement> following default will be executed, too. Be sure you put the break at the end of each case.

Strictly speaking, the control variable can really be an expression. Switching on a variable, as shown here, is the most common way to work.

Any experienced C or C++ programmer can tell you stories about monumental bugs that were the result of forgetting a break statement in a switch. When you type in a switch, make a habit (or write a macro!) of typing "case : break;" for each case you anticipate. Then go back and fill in the case and the logic.

Now let's add a switch to edit_do(). To begin, without consulting a listing, #include "KEYDEFS.H" after the other #includes at the top of TEWIN.CPP. Then replace your edit_do() code with the code shown in Listing 7-18.

Listing 7-18: TEWIN.CPP

```
int string_field::edit_do( int cmd )
{
    int is_done = FALSE;
```

```
    switch ( cmd )
    {
        case ESC:
        {
            is_done = TRUE;
            break;
        }

        default:
        {
        }
    }

    return is_done;
}
```

```
// end of TEWIN.CPP
```

Again, when you run this revised code (Ctrl+F9) your string_field object *Run !*
should stay on the screen until you press the Esc key. Now we're ready to begin
adding to this switch, and we can get to moving the cursor. (Remember moving
the cursor? That's how we started this section.)

The code in Listing 7-19 shows just how simple this code would be if we didn't
have to worry about end conditions. Enter it and test, but be sure not to press
the left-arrow key if you are already at the left side of the field nor to press the
right arrow at the right side.

Listing 7-19: TEWIN.CPP

```
    int string_field::edit_do( int cmd )
{
    int is_done = FALSE;

    switch ( cmd )
    {
        case ESC:
        {
```

```
                is_done = TRUE;
                break;
        }

        case LF_ARROW:
        {
            gotoxy( --cloc, row );
            break;
        }

        case RT_ARROW:
        {
            gotoxy( ++cloc, row );
            break;
        }

        default:
        {
        }
    }

    return is_done;
}


// end of TEWIN.CPP
```

As you see, all we really have to do is preincrement or predecrement cloc and then use gotoxy(). This moves our cursor and records its new location in one simple step. Of course, it will barge right past the left or right edge, too.

Listing 7-20 shows a more robust implementation.

Listing 7-20: TEWIN.CPP

```
        case LF_ARROW:
        {
            if ( cloc > col )
                gotoxy( --cloc, row );

            break;
```

```
        }

    case RT_ARROW:
        {
            if ( cloc < (col + width - 1) )
                gotoxy( ++cloc, row );

            break;
        }

    default:
```

With that code, when you press Ctrl+F9 you can stand on your left- and right-arrow keys as long and hard as you like, and no harm will come of it. Your field editor is beginning to come to life.

Now let's treat that cursor a little more formally.

Turning the Cursor Off

One of the hallmarks of a good user interface is that the cursor (or in graphics, the insertion point) seems to be there when you want it and to be invisible the rest of the time. One of the things that may have been annoying you (it was annoying me) about the dialog boxes we've put up so far was that the cursor never left us alone.

Up to now, though, hiding the cursor has been more of a nicety than a necessity. However, we're going to want the cursor to change size when we switch our editor from insert to overstrike mode, so we'll definitely want control of it. Let's begin by learning how to turn it off.

Our main() function in TE.CPP doesn't have much company, at the moment. It's typical of object-oriented programs that the job of main() is to launch an object or two and then wait patiently until the objects and the user are done with their work. So the main file is a good place to put startup and shutdown routines.

Let's add a startup routine that sets the screen background color and turns the cursor off. Before I show you, suppose that you have just reached the end of this book. The rest of the book is gone and you are on your own. How do you get control of the cursor yourself?

To begin, where might you look? For help, Help is a good place to start. Press Shift+F1 for the help index and type "cur" to get to "cursor." (Try this out as you're reading.)

What happens? You find that there is no entry in the index for "cursor." In general, the index has all the topics as they appear in the system, but not much in the way of generic entries. If the function that sets the cursor is setcursor(), for example, you'll find it by looking for "set" but not under "cur." (Try looking for "set," and you'll find that the right function isn't called "setcursor()," either!)

What you need to do is to look for something you know you'll find that will lead you further. Since the cursor is a console-related item, CONIO.H is a promising place to start. Again try Shift+F1 and look up "conio."

TIP

Help windows are windows, just like all the rest. F6 circles among the open windows. F5 toggles between normal and full-screen views. Alt+0 lists all windows.

When you get "CONIO.H" in the index, press Enter (or double-click) and you will see the screen shown in Figure 7-4.

```
≡ File  Edit  Search  Run  Compile  Debug  Project  Options     Window  Help
┌[■]══════════════════════════════ Help ══════════════════════════3═[↕]═┐
│ CONIO.H                                                               ▲│
│ ▬▬▬▬▬▬▬                                                               │
│                                                                       │
│ Functions                                                             │
│                                                                       │
│ cgets          clreol          clrscr          cprintf               │
│ cputs          cscanf          delline         getch                 │
│ getche         getpass         gettext         gettextinfo           │
│ gotoxy         highvideo       insline         kbhit                 │
│ lowvideo       movetext        normvideo       putch                 │
│ puttext        _setcursortype  textattr        textbackground        │
│ textcolor      textmode        ungetch         wherex                │
│ wherey         window                                                 │
│                                                                       │
│                                                                       │
│ Constants, data types, and global variables                          │
│                                                                       │
│ BLINK          COLORS          directvideo    text_info   text_modes │
│                                                                       │
│ See also                                                              ▼│
│[◄]□                                                                  [►]│
└ F1 Help on help  Alt-F1 Previous topic  Shift-F1 Help index  Esc Close help
```

Figure 7-4: Help for CONIO.H.

The functions are listed in alphabetical order, which is less than ideal if you don't know the name of a function, but there are few enough that you can scan the list to pick out a promising one.

In this list, one entry that looks good (in fact, the only one that looks remotely plausible, too) is "_setcursortype()." Since it's highlighted in the help screen, you can jump right to the reference by double-clicking with the mouse. (You can get to _setcursortype() from the keyboard by using Tab and/or the arrow keys and then pressing Enter.)

When you get to help on "_setcursortype()," you see that it gives you three interesting choices, covered by macros in the CONIO.H header file:

▶ _NOCURSOR—just what it says

▶ _NORMALCURSOR—the standard underscore cursor

▶ _SOLIDCURSOR—a large rectangle or a solid block

You also get a sample program. The help windows are read-only edit windows. You can position the cursor with the mouse or arrow keys, and you can highlight text by dragging with the mouse or by using Shift plus arrow keys. Let's test the sample program with the following steps:

S T E P   B Y   S T E P

1. Highlight the entire sample program.

2. Copy the highlighted text to the clipboard with Ctrl+Ins (Shift+Del doesn't work in a read-only edit window).

3. Close your project (Project|Close).

4. Close all your other windows (hold Alt+F3 until your desktop is clean).

5. Use F3 to open a new window for TT.CPP.

6. Use Shift+Ins to copy the sample program into TT.CPP.

7. Run the sample with Ctrl+F9.

All this should take about 30 seconds, once you get used to it. After you're done, use File|DOS Shell to go out and delete TT.*. (On my machine, TT.* eats 20K of disk space. These losses can mount up if you don't clean house.)

If you've read the sample program you just ran, you see how to use
_setcursortype() to choose one of the three available cursor styles. Listing 7-21
shows how I've created a startup() function and used it to clear the screen and
turn the cursor off.

Clear your desktop again and reopen your TE project. Then make the changes
in TE.CPP. Choose your own background color, but be sure to make it something distinctive while we're working on TE.

Listing 7-21: TE.CPP

```
// TE.CPP—Tiny Editor
// Copyright 1995, Martin L. Rinehart

#include <CONIO.H>

#include "TEWIN.H"
#include "TECMD.H"

void startup();

int main()
{
    startup();
    string_field sf( 10, 5,
        "Hello, world!          " );

    sf.show();
    sf.edit();

    return 0;
}

void startup()
{
    textattr( WHITE_BLUE );
    clrscr();

    _setcursortype(NOCURSOR );
```

—NOCURSOR

```
}
```

```
// end of TE.CPP
```

To maintain a consistent style, you could put the function declaration into a header file, TE.H. I don't generally create a header file until I'm convinced that the scope of the source code makes this extra trouble worthwhile.

When you run your program, it will not have a cursor. Of course, that's not what you want when you edit a string_field object. As it stands, you can press the left and right arrows, but the cursor you're moving is completely invisible. We'll fix this effect next.

[handwritten: Run ! No Cursor !]

Selecting Cursor Size

In DOS, the standard became an underscore cursor for overstrike mode and a larger cursor for insert mode. In TCLite, the standard is not observed. TCLite uses the underscore cursor for insert mode and a larger cursor for overstrike mode.

I try to observe standards whenever possible. In this case, I'm going to set my principles aside and go with the TCLite version. There's a simple reason for this choice.

We're going to work with the underscore cursor and a large block cursor to show overstrike and insert modes. I spend almost all my time in insert mode. The large block cursor gets very annoying, very quickly. So I'll opt for the underscore cursor as the one I see most often. You'll have no trouble doing the opposite, if you prefer.

N O T E

Through the video interrupt, interrupt 0x10, you can set the cursor to any size your hardware accepts. The set cursor size service is function 1. Registers CH and CL get the start and end scan lines. You can find the support functions to do this (no assembly language required) in DOS.H. You might want to come back to this after you've got the rest of TE working.

Before we add this capability, think about where you want to attach it. You could make insert/overstrike mode a function of the edit object, or you could make it an editor-wide setting. If it's a function of the edit object, you could have one editor window in insert mode and another editor window in overstrike mode.

You could toggle overstrike mode in one string_field object but revert to insert mode when you switch to the next string_field or editor window. This may be exactly the sort of sophisticated control you want. On the other hand, this may be a source of continuing frustration.

I'm going to implement the mode choice with a system-wide variable. When I toggle between modes, I'll have the choice maintained until I toggle back. If you want to allow different modes in different windows, make the variable a data member in each class, so that each object will know what mode it is in, and don't forget to reset the cursor type when you switch among your objects.

To implement the cursor choice, I'll use the most complex of the C++ operators, the conditional operator. The conditional operator returns one of two values, based on a condition.

N O T E

Unary operators take one operand. The logical not (!) is a common unary operator. *Binary* operators, such as logical or (||) and plus (+), take two operands. The conditional operator (?:) is the sole *ternary*, or three-operand, operator.

Here are some ternary operators at work:

```
sales_tax = is_taxable ? (rate*amt) : 0;

shirt = (Fahrenheit>72) ? "tee shirt" : "sweatshirt";

printf( end_page ? NEW_PAGE : NEW_LINE );

alices_tea_party = today ? "never jam today" : "jam!";
```

In each case, the conditional operator evaluates two of three expressions. It starts with the condition, the expression preceding the question mark. If the condition is true, the expression preceding the colon is evaluated and its result is returned. If the condition is false, the expression following the colon is evaluated and its result is returned.

When you use the conditional operator, pay attention to your spacing. As the examples show, extra blanks around the **?** and **:** can make conditional operators much more readable. Eliminating blanks in the component expressions also helps.

Now let me take a moment to introduce the notion of operator precedence. In C++, as in most programming languages, multiplication takes precedence over addition.

```
a = b*c + d;   // takes the product of b and c, then adds d
a = b * c+d;   // ditto!  spacing is for humans only

a = b * (c+d); // parentheses force addition first
```

As in most computer languages, you can use parentheses to specify the exact order of operations. Unlike many languages, C++ has inherited a rich set of operators from C, and along with them, it has inherited a detailed operator precedence table. For example, these two statements are equivalent:

```
sales_tax = is_taxable ? (rate*amt) : 0;

sales_tax = is_taxable ? rate * amt : 0;
```

They are equivalent because multiplication has a higher precedence than the conditional operator. However, although the two statements are identical to the compiler, the first form is completely unambiguous to the human reader.

In any expression, you can use parentheses to specify the order of operations explicitly. The parse phase of compilation is responsible for, among other things, eliminating the parentheses and leaving the operations in their specified order. Surplus parentheses have no cost in the compiled code, so use them.

If you ever take a C++ test where you are questioned about your knowledge of the precedence of C++ operators, give a failing grade to the author of the test.

Find employment somewhere else—somewhere that code readability is thought more valuable than trivial programmer cleverness.

There is only one precedence rule that you should know and use. Parentheses tell both the compiler and human readers exactly how you want your expression evaluated. Always use parentheses, and you will never have a problem with precedence.

Associativity specifies the order of evaluation. In this example, associativity of the plus operator is irrelevant:

```
a = b + c;
```

This statement does the expected work. It adds b and c and assigns the result to a. Since the equal sign is an operator, it does depend on precedence, too. (This is one bit of precedence where I break my own rule about parentheses. This statement works the same way in almost every computer language.)

Now let's look at an example where associativity may be relevant:

```
a = foo() + bar();
```

Since we don't have the definitions of foo() and bar() to inspect, we can't be sure that the order of their evaluation won't make a difference in the result. (Suppose, for example, that foo() increments a global variable and bar() doubles the same variable.)

What is certain is that if the associativity is important, the code should be much more explicit. Here's an example written decently:

```
tmp1 = bar(); // doubles glob_var
tmp2 = foo(); // increments glob_var

a = tmp1 + tmp2;
```

With all that in the background, let's go on to use the conditional operator to implement cursor control. Listing 7-22 shows the addition of the global variable and the addition to the edit() method, both in TEWIN.CPP, that turn on the appropriate cursor.

Listing 7-22: TEWIN.CPP

```
...
char blanks[] =  // 80 space chars
```

```
                 "                                            "
                 "                                          ";

int ins_mode = TRUE; // FALSE is overstrike mode

box::box( int lf, int tp, int rt, int bt,
...
void string_field::edit()                    ins_mode
{
    _setcursortype(
        insmode ?   _NORMALCURSOR : _SOLIDCURSOR );

    int done = FALSE;

    while ( !done )
    {
        done = edit_do( user_cmd() );
    }
    _setcursortype(_NOCURSOR );
}
```

This code implies a rule that we'll enforce on all our objects. Any object that wants a cursor has to turn it on and position it. The object also has to turn the cursor off when it is done using the cursor.

By the way, if you aren't quite sure that this all works as it should, add a getch() after sf.show() and another after sf.edit() in main(). For a little less work you could just press Alt+F5 after your program is completed. Either way, you'll see that your code is turning the cursor on and off correctly. You can't see that it is properly reflecting insert or overstrike mode, but this is the next item on our agenda.

Selecting Insert/Overstrike Mode

Our final task before we leave the cursor is to toggle insert and overstrike modes. I want to do this with either Ctrl+V or the Ins key. The toggle will have to change the global variable and change the cursor to reflect this status. Listing 7-23 shows the code to add to the string_field::edit_do() method in TEWIN.CPP.

Listing 7-23: TEWIN.CPP

```
case RT_ARROW:
{
    if ( cloc < (col + width - 1) )
        gotoxy( ++cloc, row );

    break;
}

case INS:
case 22:  // Ctrl+V
{
    ins_mode = !ins_mode;
    _setcursortype( insmode ?
        _NORMALCURSOR : _SOLIDCURSOR );
}

default:
{
}
```

Isn't it delightfully easy to add something like this, when you don't have to stop and learn a new handful of features? You're well on your way to becoming a real C++ programmer at this point.

ENTERING CHARACTERS

Now that we can toggle insert and overstrike modes, it's time to actually do some inserting and overstriking. As we work on these features you'll get some solid experience with using pointers. Let's make a quick review.

These two statements are identical in effect:

```
char a[] = "vwxyz"; // a is an array of characters

char* a = "vwxyz";  // a is a pointer to a string
```

The only difference between those two lines is the way we choose to think about them. In both cases the value of a is the address of the string. In both cases, the array of characters (or string, if you prefer) is six characters long. The compiler adds a trailing null character to the five characters enclosed in quotes.

These two statements are also the same in effect:

```
char c = a[0]; // c is 'v', the first element in the array
char c = *a;   // c is 'v', the item a points to
```

We can address the other elements of the array with a pointer or with a subscript, too:

```
c = a[1];   // c is 'w'
c = *(a+1); // also 'w'


c = a[2];   // c is 'x'
c = *(a+2); // also 'x'


// etc.
```

In some cases, working with subscripts is more clear. In other cases, pointers make more sense. Old-time C programmers use pointers almost exclusively, because old compilers generated poor code for subscripts. Contemporary C++ programmers write their code as clearly as possible and let the compiler look after itself.

Let's begin by programming an overstrike capability, since it is simpler than insert mode. Overstrikes seem to program very simply using subscript notation. We need to tend to three things when the user presses a key.

Overstriking Characters

First, we need to place the new character into the string in memory. Second, we need to put the character into the string on the screen. Finally, we need to update the cursor.

Updating the cursor includes two distinct possibilities. When we putch() the character onto the screen, the hardware cursor is advanced to the next location on screen, where we often want it. We just have to increment our cloc variable. On the other hand, if we were at the last character in the field, the cursor would be pushed out past the end of the field. We'll leave cloc alone, but we need to bring the hardware cursor back into bounds.

Listing 7-24 shows the basic code, although it has a pair of bugs. Add this code into the switch logic in the string_field's edit_do() method in TEWIN.CPP.

Listing 7-24: TEWIN.CPP

```
        default:
        {
            if ( ins_mode )
            {
                ; // code tk
            }
            else // overstrike
            {
                str[ cloc-col ] = cmd;
                putch( cmd );

                if ( cloc < col + width - 1 )
                    cloc++;
                else
                    gotoxy( cloc, row );
            }
        }
    }


    return is_done;
}


// end of TEWIN.CPP
```

Run

One bug is that this default code is executed not just for characters typed in but for unrecognized control codes, function keys, and whatever else you might press. Don't even test this. Stick to left- and right-arrows, Ins (or Ctrl+V), and regular keyboard keys.

Another bug is more interesting. Run this program and strum some keys with the underscore cursor visible at the left. Nothing happens, which is what we want. We haven't supplied code for insert mode yet.

Now tap the Ins key and watch. Did you get a capital R, followed by a cursor advance? I did. Take a minute to find that error, before you read on.

see pg 250 bots

Where did k come from ?

Run

Got it? The problem is above the default keyword. There's no break statement at the end of the insert code. I told you that this was a classic bug. This is a typical example, except that it is harmless and easy to fix.

Listing 7-25 shows fixes for both bugs. As you see, we've now got just a little code for the main process and quite a lot of code worrying about end conditions and special cases. User interface work is like that.

Listing 7-25: TEWIN.CPP

```
case INS:
case 22:  // Ctrl+V
{
    ins_mode = !ins_mode;
    _setcursortype( insmode ?
        NORMALCURSOR : SOLIDCURSOR );
    break;
}


default:
{
    if ( (cmd < 256) && (cmd>=32) )
    {
        if ( ins_mode )
        {
            ; // code tk
        }
        else // overstrike
        {
            str[ cloc-col ] = cmd;
            putch( cmd );

            if ( cloc < col + width - 1 )
                cloc++;
            else
                gotoxy( cloc, row );
        }
    }
}
```

```
        }

    return is_done;
}


// end of TEWIN.CPP
```

In the above listing, I moved all the interior logic to the right by one tab stop to accommodate the added if statement. The shifted lines are not shown as new, since the only thing added is a leading tab character.

T I P

This code is becoming a good example of the necessity for maintaining consistent standards for indenting and formatting. If you don't take the trouble to make everything line up neatly, your code will quickly become unusable.

With these corrections, you should get a line editor with a correct and robust implementation of overstrike mode. Now it's time to get on to insert mode.

Inserting Characters

Inserting a character is a bit more complicated than just overstriking. First, if we are not at the end of the field, we have to slide characters in the string starting at the cursor to the right by one, except the trailing null. The old last character (the last non-null, that is) gets dropped.

Then the new character can be written into the memory string, and the right side of that string, starting with the new character, can be printed.

Last of all we have to adjust cloc and the hardware cursor as we did in the overstrike case. This process is nontrivial. We can simplify the code by treating the insertion of spaces into a string as a routine that we'll want for our library. Then the insert characters case can call that routine to do the hardest part.

To create this routine, first declare it in TEWIN.H, as shown in Listing 7-26.

Listing 7-26: TEWIN.H

```
#define STR_CLR 0x7F // hi-white on white
#define GOHOME  gotoxy( col, row );

void ins_chars( char* s, int nchars=1 );

class box
```

Note that I've used a default value of 1 for the number of chars to insert. This means that we can call the routine with one or two parameters. In our first use, we'll be inserting a single space, so one calling parameter will work.

You should test your library routines thoroughly before you put them into service. In lieu of asking you to test this one, I'll explain it thoroughly after the next listing.

Listing 7-27 shows the new code in TEWIN.CPP. The necessary logic has been added to the insert case, and the new ins_chars() library routine has been added after the last of the object methods.

Listing 7-27: TEWIN.CPP

```
        default:
        {
            if ( (cmd < 256) && (cmd>=32) )
            {
                if ( ins_mode )
                {
                    char* ip = str+cloc-col; // insert ptr
                    ins_chars( ip ); // insert one space
                    *ip = cmd;        // replace the space

                    gotoxy( cloc, row );

                    cprintf( ip );
                    if ( cloc < col+width-1 )
                        cloc++;
```

```
                              gotoxy( cloc, row );
                }
                else // overstrike
                {
                    str[ cloc-col ] = cmd;
                    putch( cmd );

                    if ( cloc < col + width - 1 )
                        cloc++;
                    else
                        gotoxy( cloc, row );
                }
            }
        }
    }

    return is_done;
}
```

```
void ins_chars( char* s, int nchars )
{
// insert nchars of spaces on left
// drop nchars from right

// nchars must be <= strlen(s)
// nchars defaults to 1

    char* p2 = s  + strlen(s) - 1; // point to last char
    char* p1 = p2 - nchars;

    while ( p1 >= s )
        *p2-- = *p1--; // copy existing chars to the right

    while ( p2 > p1 )
        *p2-- = ' ';    // fill hole with spaces
}
```

```
// end of TEWIN.CPP
```

The new insert logic starts by creating a pointer, ip, to the position in str where the insertion will take place. It then calls ins_chars() to do the work.

The ins_chars() routine has four working statements. The first sets a pointer, p2, which points to the last character in the string. The second sets another pointer, p1, which points to the character that will replace the one pointed to by p2.

The next two statements are while loops. The first replaces the character at p2 with the one at p1 and then decrements both pointers. It continues doing this until it reaches the beginning of the string. This approach depends on a little trick:

```
char* all = "abcde"; // strlen( all ) == 5

char* mid = all+2;    // mid points to 'c'
                      // printf( mid ) prints "cde"
                      // strlen( mid ) = 3
```

In the edit_do() code, ip is set to point somewhere into the middle (or maybe an end—it doesn't matter) of our string. But we call ins_chars() with ip, so ins_chars() always works at the start of its string.

The final loop in ins_chars() backs p2 up toward p1, replacing every character in between with spaces. Here's an example:

```
char* all = "abcde";

char* ip = all+1;  // points to "bcde"

ins_chars( ip, 2 ); // changes ip to "  bc"
                    // so all is    "a  bc"
```

The rest of the logic in the insert case is the same type. Set a breakpoint (Ctrl+F8) at the char* ip line and step through these statements with F7. Use Ctrl+F7 to set watches on all the variables.

Got it running? Congratulations. You're getting your single-line editor past its most difficult functions. In the next chapter we're going to go on to add more functions, such as moving the cursor by words and deleting text.

SUMMARY

In this chapter we started to build a string_field entry object, which is an editor for single-line text fields.

When we started, we used the do while loop to read in and report on the keystrokes we'll need. You saw that the do while loop is appropriate when you want to run the loop code once before you first test your loop's condition.

To look at our keys, we used the printf() function's formatting capability. Actually, we used cprintf(), one of printf()'s siblings with the same formatting capabilities.

We saw that chars and ints are both integer data, but of different lengths. You used unsigned chars to avoid having char values over 127 misinterpreted as negative numbers.

When we got back to our Tiny Editor code, we used #define to create the GOHOME macro. GOHOME inserts a function call when we use it, unlike our earlier macros, which inserted data values.

The key to responding to user input is acting on one of a variety of commands. The switch statement, with its components case and default, is ideally suited to this situation. You started with just an if/else test but replaced this with the switch so we could move forward.

We set the cursor to reflect insert or overstrike status (although in a nonstandard way). You used the _setcursortype() function to actually address the hardware through the BIOS.

While we were learning about _setcursortype(), you copied a sample program out of a help screen and then compiled and ran it. You saw that the help screens were read-only edit windows that respond to the standard editing commands, excluding those that change things.

You used the ternary (three-operand) conditional operator to choose between two possible values within an expression. While we were coding with the conditional operator, we took a look at operator precedence and associativity. You decided (I hope!) to use parentheses to keep the order of execution completely explicit.

You've mastered a lot of the C++ language at this point. You'll see in the next chapter that you'll be spending your time using what you know to add the functionality you want to your string_field objects.

At the end of the last chapter, our string_field object let us move the cursor and enter text in either insert or overstrike mode. Now that we've got a very simple edit capability, you'll see that we are most of the way to having a robust set of edit capabilities.

In this chapter we're going to add these functions:

- ▶ Del delete (under cursor)
- ▶ Backspace delete (behind cursor)
- ▶ Cursor forward/backward a word at a time
- ▶ Delete word
- ▶ Jump to field start/end
- ▶ Exit on exit commands

While we're adding these functions we'll be building on the knowledge of C++ you've accumulated so far. We won't be learning more of the language—we'll be using what we've learned. While we do this, we'll consider the difference between exhaustive and exhausting testing, and you'll get a lot more experience with pointers as we manipulate strings.

8

More Single-Line Edit Functions

DEL DELETES UNDER THE CURSOR

There are lots of ways to implement commands in a text editor, but the most standard is the Del keypress. It deletes the character under the cursor in almost every product that has any text-editing capability.

To implement Del, we'll need a support function like ins_chars(), but it will have the opposite effect. We want to delete characters, of course. (The Del key will delete just one character, but it's very little extra trouble to write a more general routine that deletes multiple characters.)

Actually, del_chars() is just the opposite of ins_chars(). The latter function removed characters from the right end of the string and added blanks at the left end. The del_chars() process is to remove characters from the left and add blanks on the right.

In the preceding chapter, I gave you a completed version of ins_chars(). That was a bit of a cheat, which we're not going to repeat here. Let's build this one from scratch.

The key to building library or support routines is to build them and test them exhaustively before you use them. As you'll see, exhaustive testing is often a very simple matter—it takes thought but not a lot of hard work.

Begin by closing your TE project and closing all your open windows. Then open a T.CPP window and enter the test code in Listing 8-1. (It's all new, so there's no listing on disk.)

Listing 8-1: T.CPP

```
#include <stdio.h>

void del_chars( char* s, int nchars=1 );

int main()
{
    char* test;

    test = "abcdefg";
    printf( "\n'%s'", test );

    test = "abcdefg";
    del_chars(test);
    printf( "\n'%s'", test );

    test = "abcdefg";
    del_chars(test, 2);
    printf( "\n'%s'", test );

    test = "abcdefg";
    del_chars( test+5, 2 );
    printf( "\n'%s'", test );
```

```
        return 0;
}


void del_chars( char* s, int nchars )
{
        // code tk
}
```

Enter and run this code, and you'll have tested your test routine. All the tests, of course, simply repeat the input at this point. Now let's see what you've learned this far. Before you go on to the next listing, change that *tk* comment to code that actually does the job. Remember, we don't really want to delete characters; we want to make the field look like we've deleted characters.

T I P

The *tk* comment is an old author's code for "to come." It means you haven't written something. It's very handy in code since *tk* isn't a string you're likely to find used anywhere else. You can search for it and almost always find exactly the right spot.

Making characters appear deleted means that the job is to slide characters from the right toward the left and then add blanks at the right end to preserve the original length. Go ahead now and try your hand at this before you go on.

There are a lot of ways to write any function. I've written mine as you see in Listing 8-2.

Listing 8-2: T.CPP

```
void del_chars( char* s, int nchars )
{
// delete chars on left end of s, adding equal
// number of spaces on right end

// nchars must be <= strlen(s)
// nchars defaults to 1
```

```
    char* p1 = s;
    char* p2 = s + nchars;

    while ( *p2 )
        *p1++ = *p2++;

    while ( p1 < p2 )
        *p1++ = ' ';
}
```

Does your code handle all three tests correctly? If it does, and if your comments are reasonable, you've completed an exhaustive test.

Testing exhaustively doesn't mean that you run lots and lots of tests. It means that you think about the possible cases that your routine will handle, and test each case.

For instance, deleting one character on the left is certainly one case for del_chars(). Your first test checks that case. You could pass del_chars() a hundred more strings as arguments for that case and check the results, but that would simply check the same functionality over and over again.

By examining your code, you can list the possible cases. For my code, they are:

► Deleting one character (pass one argument)

► Deleting multiple characters (two arguments)

► Deleting to the end of the string

Our tests check all these possibilities. They do not check behavior for invalid inputs, but that doesn't need to be done. I've included the comment that says nchars can't be greater than the length of the string.

Some people would also code for the condition where nchars exceeded the length of the string. This would, it's claimed, make the function more *robust*. That may be true, but it would let calling routines off the hook in the matter of providing valid inputs. That would let the robust support function hide bugs in the calling functions, a situation that will not contribute to a robust system.

With that routine thoroughly tested, you can add it to the TEWIN.CPP code, along with a Del case that uses it. Begin by adding a prototype for del_chars() in TEWIN.H, as shown in Listing 8-3.

Listing 8-3: TEWIN.H

```
#define STR_CLR 0x7F // hi-white on white
#define GOHOME gotoxy( col, row );

void ins_chars( char* s, int nchars=1 );
void del_chars( char* s, int nchars=1 );


class box
```

With the function declaration in place, add a new case and the function's definition in TEWIN.CPP, as shown in Listing 8-4.

Listing 8-4: TEWIN.CPP

```
        case INS:
        case 22:  // Ctrl+V
        {
            ins_mode = !ins_mode;
            setcursortype( insmode ?
                NORMALCURSOR : SOLIDCURSOR );
            break;
        }


        case DEL:
        case 7:    // Ctrl+G
        {
        //shift rest of string one space left
            del_chars( str+cloc-col );

        // redisplay and reposition cursor
            gotoxy( col, row );
            cprintf( str );
            gotoxy( cloc, row );

            break;
        }

        default:
...
```

```
void del_chars( char* s, int nchars )
{
// delete chars on left end of s, adding equal
// number of spaces on right end

// nchars must be <= strlen(s)
// nchars defaults to 1

    char* p1 = s;
    char* p2 = s + nchars;

    while ( *p2 )
        *p1++ = *p2++;

    while ( p1 < p2 )
        *p1++ = ' ';
}
```

// end of TEWIN.CPP

When you run TE with these additions, your single-line editor should respond appropriately when you tap the Del key. Be sure to test it with a Del keypress on the first character in the field, on any middle character, and on the end character. (Those three tests check all the possibilities.)

BACKSPACE DELETES TO THE LEFT

If you're like me, having the Del key functioning makes you want to have a standard backspace delete functionality, too. The Backspace key almost always deletes the character to the left of the cursor, since this behavior provides a simple way of correcting typing mistakes.

Since we have the Del key and the supporting del_chars() function hooked up, the Backspace key is simple. You might want to try it yourself before you look at my code.

Listing 8-5 shows the addition of a new case in edit_do(), TEWIN.CPP, that gives you backspace delete capability.

Listing 8-5: TEWIN.CPP

```
case DEL:
case 7:    // Ctrl+G
{
//shift rest of string one space left
    del_chars( str+cloc-col );

// redisplay and reposition cursor
    gotoxy( col, row );
    cprintf( str );
    gotoxy( cloc, row );


    break;
}


case BKSP:
{
    if ( cloc > col )
    {
        cloc-;

    // shift rest of string one space left
        del_chars( str+cloc-col );

    // redisplay and reposition cursor
        gotoxy( col, row );
        cprintf( str );
        gotoxy( cloc, row );
    }
    break;
}

default:
```

Again, be sure to test this on the first character, the last character, and a middle character. Unlike with Del, nothing should happen if you press the Backspace key at the left end of the string.

That was almost trivial, wasn't it? Our next job won't be quite as simple.

MOVING BY WHOLE WORDS

I've been a long-time fan of Sammy Mitchell's commercial and shareware editor, Qedit. Its footprint is only about 50K, and it provides a good set of text-editing capabilities. Other text editors tilt the scale at 10 or even 100 times the weight of Q, but they don't provide anything like 10 times more power.

But there's one feature of Q that I don't like: its definition of a word. It's not that Sammy's definition of a word is wrong or unintelligent; it just doesn't match my idea. The nice thing about having your own editor is that you'll never have to say that it doesn't match your idea.

I'm going to write this editor my way. I hope that you'll look at it very critically as we go along. I've structured it so that you can implement your own definition of a word just by changing the left_word() and right_word() functions. Do it your way.

The Next Word on the Right

When you command the cursor to hop to the next word on the right, what do you really mean? If your cursor is in the middle of whitespace and there's a word on the right, the answer is simple: You want the cursor to hop to the start of that word.

But what do you want to happen if your cursor is not in the middle of whitespace? Suppose it's in the middle of a word? What about punctuation characters? Do you want to treat them like alphanumeric characters, or like whitespace?

I prefer an almost trivially simple definition of a word: Any string (one or more) of nonwhitespace characters is a word. A word ends with the first whitespace character or at the end of the field, if there isn't a whitespace character following the word.

I use the same definition for either end of the word, so I don't care if the direction is to the left or to the right. On the other hand, I want my word-left and word-right commands both to find the beginning character in a word. My word-left command will find the first letter in the current word, if the cursor is in the middle of a word. If the cursor is at the first letter (on the left) of a word, or in whitespace between words, the cursor will move left until a word starts and then continue to the first letter of that word.

Going to the right, I want the cursor to get out of a word if it's in one (move right looking for a whitespace character). Then I want it to pass over all white-space until it finds a nonwhitespace character.

Of course, going either left or right, the cursor should stop at the end of the field, if it gets there before it would stop otherwise. If it starts at the end of the field, it should stay put, of course. Now let's look at the code that I use to find the start of the next word on the right. It looks like this:

```
while ( *here > 32 )                    space
    here++;                // Point 1

while ( *here < 33 )       // 2
{
    if ( ! *here )
        return --here;     // 3    at the end (null), return previous to null
    here++;                // 4
}

return here;
```

The first while loop (point 1) moves the here pointer to the right (increments it) as long as *here (the character here points to) is greater than 32. (32 is the ASCII space character; this is an ASCII-specific algorithm.)

The next loop (2) continues while the character, *here, is white. (Characters less than 33 include space, tab, enter, and linefeed, in addition to a lot of others that shouldn't be part of a text file.)

If the character is zero (! *here is true) we're at the end of the string, so --here (the last address before the terminating null) is returned (3).

Finally the loop (2) continues after incrementing the here pointer (4). The pointer will keep marching to the right until it finds the next nonwhitespace character or the end of the string.

In Listing 8-6, I've added declarations for both word_right() and word_left() to TEWIN.H. Listing 8-7 shows the word_right() code and the appropriate case added to TEWIN.CPP's edit_do() method.

Listing 8-6: TEWIN.H

```
void ins_chars( char* s, int nchars=1 );
void del_chars( char* s, int nchars=1 );

char* left_word( char* left, char* here );
char* right_word( char* here );

class box
```

Listing 8-7: TEWIN.CPP

```
        case BKSP:
        {
            if ( cloc > col )
            {
                cloc--;

                // shift rest of string one space left
                del_chars( str+cloc-col );

                // redisplay and reposition cursor
                gotoxy( col, row );
                cprintf( str );
                gotoxy( cloc, row );
            }
            break;
        }

        case 6:              // ^F
        case CTRL_RT_ARROW:
        {
            char* cp = right_word( str+cloc-col );
            cloc = col + cp - str;
            gotoxy( cloc, row );
            break;
        }

        default:
...
```

```
char* right_word( char* here )
{
/* find left end of word on the right
   Finds left end of next word to the right.

   If in white space, finds next nonwhite.

   If in nonwhite, finds first nonwhite following
   first white.

   Returns pointer to last char (preceding null) in
   string if there is no word to the right.

   Assumes ASCII (space == 32, 33 is first nonwhite)
*/

// exit current word, if any
   while ( *here > 32 )
       here++;

// pass over current white space
   while ( *here < 33 )
   {
       if ( ! *here )
           return --here;
       here++;
   }

   return here;
}
```

```
// end of TEWIN.CPP
```

Once you enter these lines, you'll have to add some text to your test field. You can do this in main(), or you can do it by typing directly into the field itself.

Be sure you test finding the next word from the start of a word, from the middle, from the last character, and from within whitespace. Repeat these tests when there is no next word, and you'll have exhaustively tested your new functionality.

The Next Word on the Left

Working to the left is similar to working to the other direction, of course. I'll let you examine the word_left() function on your own. Don't enter any of it until you are confident that you understand how it works.

Don't be afraid to pull either of these functions into a separate T.CPP and to test them on their own. Use the debugger to step through them with F7 and F8 to watch if you want to check any details.

Listing 8-8 shows the additional code to add to the edit_do() method in TEWIN.CPP. This case and the word_left() function are the ones to add.

Listing 8-8: TEWIN.CPP

```
case 6:                  // ^F
case CTRL_RT_ARROW:
{
    char* cp = right_word( str+cloc-col );
    cloc = col + cp - str;
    gotoxy( cloc, row );
    break;
}


case 1:                  // ^A
case CTRL_LF_ARROW:
{
    char* cp = left_word( str, str+cloc-col );
    cloc = cp - str + col;
    gotoxy( cloc, row );
    break;
}


default:
...
```

```
char* left_word( char* left, char* here )
{
/* find left end of word on the left
   Finds left end of current word, if in word but not
   at left end.

   Finds left end of previous word if at left char in
   word or in space(s) between words.

   A "word" is a set of consecutive nonwhite chars.

   Warning: string in which this works must be two or
   more characters long!

   Assumes ASCII (space == 32, 33 is first nonwhite)
*/

// exit if at left end
    if ( left == here )
        return left;

// move one char left
    here--;

// if at space, find non-space
    while ( *here < 33 )
    {
        if ( left == here )
            return left;
        here--;
    }

// find next space
    while ( *here > 32 )
    {
        if ( left == here )
            return left;
        here--;
```

```
    }

// return preceding non-space
    return ++here;
}
```

// end of TEWIN.CPP

With this code in place, you should be hopping happily to the left and to the right. Make sure you test both the letter combinations (Ctrl+A and Ctrl+F) and the arrow-key combinations.

DELETING WHOLE WORDS

You've implemented the key support routines that you'll need to delete whole words. I think.

Before we can really talk about implementation, as always, we have to decide exactly what we are going to implement. If your cursor is at the start of a word and you press the delete-word command, the word to the right of the cursor should disappear, of course.

But what about the whitespace trailing that word? What should happen if your cursor is in the middle of a word? Suppose the cursor is in whitespace between words?

Again, these questions don't have right answers; they have personal opinions. One opinion that I don't hold, but that is completely reasonable, is that if your cursor is in a word, the delete-word command should delete that word. I don't do this because I like to position my cursor in a word and delete the right-hand portion, not the whole word.

I also like to see the whitespace on the right of a word deleted along with the word. This works very well if you want to delete two or three words in the middle of a line. You'll be left with the remaining words neatly separated by a single whitespace character.

Of course, if you delete the trailing whitespace and you use my behavior when you're in the middle of a word (delete the right side of the word), you pack the next word into the remaining part of the word with the cursor. You can make it a rule to delete the trailing whitespace only if there is a whitespace character to the left of the cursor, but then what about the case where your cursor is at the left edge?

You decide how you want your own editor to behave. One thing I'll recommend is that you follow my example in going for a single, consistent rule. Your editor may not always do precisely what you want, but if it always does precisely what you expect, you'll be well ahead of someone trying to remember all the exceptions. Your code will be a lot simpler, too.

With all that said, take a look at Listing 8-9. It's my delete-word command case in the edit_do() method in TEWIN.CPP.

Listing 8-9: TEWIN.CPP

```
case 1:                 // ^A
case CTRL_LF_ARROW:
{
    char* cp = left_word( str, str+cloc-col );
    cloc = cp - str + col;
    gotoxy( cloc, row );
    break;
}


case 20:                // ^T -- delete word
{
    char* cp1 = str + cloc - col;
    char* cp2 = right_word( cp1 );
    del_chars( cp1, cp2-cp1 );
    cprintf( cp1 );
    gotoxy( col + cp1 - str, row );
    break;
}


default:
```

I begin by setting a pointer, cp1, to the character at the location of the cursor. A call to right_word() sets a second pointer to the start of the next word on the right. Then del_chars() gets rid of the intervening characters. The next two lines print the string from the point of the deletion and reposition the cursor.

This process gets easier as you master C++, and as you build the support routines that do the hard work.

JUMPING TO HOME AND END

Among the easiest of all the keystroke commands are the ones that move the cursor to the left or right end of the field. Home and End are commonly used for these, although you may prefer some other commands.

NOTE

Do you want two-key commands, such as Ctrl+Q followed by another letter? Trap the prefix key (Ctrl+Q, for instance) in your user_cmd() routine in TECMD.CPP. When you get the prefix key, call getch() again for the following letter. Combine the result into an integer (you can assign freely from about 1,000 up to 32,000!) and return the integer. In KEYDEFS.H, #define your two-key commands just as you've #defined other commands.

Before you look at my code, try Home and End (or whatever keys you've picked) on your own.

Listing 8-10 shows the two cases I added to the edit_do() method in TEWIN.CPP for Home and End.

Listing 8-10: TEWIN.CPP

```
case 20:                 // ^T -- delete word
{
    char* cp1 = str + cloc - col;
    char* cp2 = right_word( cp1 );
    del_chars( cp1, cp2-cp1 );
    cprintf( cp1 );
    gotoxy( col + cp1 - str, row );
    break;
}

case HOME:
{
```

```
        cloc = col;
        gotoxy( col, row );
        break;
    }

case END:
{
        cloc = col + strlen(str) - 1;
        gotoxy( cloc, row );
        break;
    }

default:
```

I hope your version worked out as neatly as this. Before we call this object complete, I'll tidy up with some keystrokes that I'm used to. You'll want to add some or all of these to your own version.

RECOGNIZING EXIT COMMANDS

The Esc exit was handy when we started with a test program. Now we ought to think about it. It often means, "Ignore what I just did." Frequently, Enter or Tab is used to signify that you have finished with the field and want to exit, leaving changes intact.

If you'll want your mainline code to check the manner of exit (for example, to restore an edited field that was exited via an Esc keypress), add a data member called exit_key or something similar to the string_field object. Before you actually exit, store the current keystroke (cmd value) in this data member.

I'll skip this detail, since it's no trouble to go back and add it later if I really want it. For now, I just want to be able to leave my field with a wider set of choices. I certainly want to exit with Esc, Enter, and Tab. Of course, if Tab works, so should Shift+Tab.

I also want to exit with an up- or down-arrow keypress. With just a single field, these keys don't have any natural meaning. If there were two or three fields, though, the up-and down-arrow keys might reasonably be expected to navigate from one field to the next. For now, I'll be content with just leaving the current field.

The same argument also applies, for me, to the Ctrl+E and Ctrl+X keystrokes, which are synonyms for the up- and down-arrow keys in the old Wordstar command set.

The same logic also tells me to exit on a PgUp or PgDn keypress. That applies, too, to the Ctrl+R and Ctrl+C Wordstar equivalents of these navigation keys.

The good news about implementing leaving the line is that actually adding these keystrokes is easier than thinking through which ones you like. Listing 8-11 shows the new lines you need to add to edit_do() in TEWIN.CPP.

Listing 8-11: TEWIN.CPP

```
switch ( cmd )
{
    case ESC:
    case ENTER:

    case PGUP:
    case PGDN:

    case UP_ARROW:
    case DN_ARROW:

    case 5:  // Ctrl+E
    case 24: // Ctrl+X

    case 18: // Ctrl+R
    case 3:  // Ctrl+C

    case TAB:
    case BKTAB:

    {
        is_done = TRUE;
        break;
    }
```

All you have to do, as Listing 8-11 shows, is add lines that list each exit key as a new case, where the ESC case was doing the job. The bad news is that you should test every one of these additions individually.

For me, it's very tempting just to put these in as a group and check a couple. After all, what could go wrong?

Speaking from sad experience, I'll report that it is far easier to test these, one at a time, than to discover the answer to that rhetorical question, "What could go wrong?" The answer to the question is that neither you nor I know what could go wrong, but Mr. Murphy (the guy with the famous Law) knows what can go wrong, and he's just waiting for a chance to prove it.

One final bit and we'll call this object a finished product. That's the Ctrl+D and Ctrl+S keystrokes. Do these suggest Done or Save to you? If so, add them into this list. To me they suggest Wordstar diamond commands. (The TCLite editor interprets them this way, too.)

I've added cases for them to the left- and right-arrow cases, as Listing 8-12 shows.

Listing 8-12: TEWIN.CPP

```
    case 19:            // Ctrl+S
    case LF_ARROW:
    {
        if ( cloc > col )
            gotoxy( --cloc, row );

        break;
    }


    case 4:             // Ctrl+D
    case RT_ARROW:
    {
        if ( cloc < (col + width - 1) )
            gotoxy( ++cloc, row );

        break;
    }
```

With those additions, our single-line editor now responds to a reasonable selection of both Wordstar-compatible commands and navigation key commands. I'm ready to put it into service.

SUMMARY

When we started this chapter, we had a primitive string_field object. It let us move the cursor and insert or overstrike characters. In this chapter, you built a professional string_field object, starting from that base.

We made a separate test routine and considered what constituted an exhaustive test as we added delete capabilities. We added a delete function that could handle any number of characters and tested it this way.

You used the delete function to implement the expected actions for the Del and Backspace keys.

After deletions, we went on to write routines that found the next word to the left or right of the cursor. I showed you how I did mine and discussed some of the ways that you may prefer to implement yours.

We used the word-oriented routines to move the cursor left and right by whole words. We also used them in combination with the delete routine to implement a delete-word capability.

The simplest addition was hooking the Home and End keys up to hop to the beginning or end of the field.

Finally, we took advantage of the flexibility of the switch statement to add a selection of exit commands and to add Wordstar-diamond control-key commands as synonyms for arrow-key cursor-movement commands.

We've done all this work on the methods that are part of our string_field object. It's been a typical example of how classic, C-style procedural code is still alive and well as the implementation layer for C++ objects' methods.

In this chapter we're going to:

- ▶ Build a string_dialog class
- ▶ Get a filename with our string_dialog
- ▶ Use a public method to access protected data
- ▶ Access protected members with a *friend* class
- ▶ Experiment with iostreams
- ▶ Learn about typedefs, including the FILE stream typedef
- ▶ Check short and long integer types with the sizeof() operator
- ▶ Open a file with fopen() and read it with fgets()
- ▶ Terminate our program with exit()
- ▶ Learn about singly and doubly linked lists
- ▶ Use file utility functions rewind(), feof(), and fclose()
- ▶ Use Alt+F4 to access the Inspect feature of the debugger

▼ ▼ ▼ ▼

Reading Text Files

Now that we have a string_field class, we can create a dialog box that asks for a filename. Then, of course, the next step is to open and read in the file, and this step is our current project.

Before we're done here, your mainline will pop up a dialog requesting a filename, wait while you enter a name, open the named file, and read its contents from disk into a linked-list structure in memory.

While we're working on all this, we'll be building support functions and objects. As we go along, pay attention to the size (or rather, the lack of size!) of the main() routine that directs all this work.

Let's get started.

LAUNCHING A FILENAME DIALOG BOX

The very first thing our Tiny Editor will need is the name of a file. I really like the modern Common User Access (CUA) filename dialogs that let you find just

about any file on your disk with only mouse clicks. (The dialog box you get
when you press F3 in TCLite is a good example.)

On the other hand, I really like short, to-the-point programs. I'll let Borland
and the other software vendors write the all-encompassing programs, while I
write simple, "do it my way" programs that don't need a whole hard disk just to
install. For our Tiny Editor, let's just use a string_field where you can type in
your filename, not a fancy dialog box.

With our string_field object, we can also cheat while we are debugging our
Tiny Editor. We'll have the string_field initialized with the name of a standard
test file, so we don't have to type it in all the time. Let's begin with another dialog box class, the string_dialog.

My string_dialog is a dialog box with a string_field object. It's very handy for
things like filenames. Listing 9-1 shows the class definition to add to TEWIN.H.

Listing 9-1: TEWIN.H

```
class string_dialog : public dialog
{
private:
    int sf_col, sf_row;

    string_field* sf;

public:
    string_dialog( char* fld, char* ttl );
    ~string_dialog();

};
```

```
// end of TEWIN.H
```

The variables sf_col and sf_row hold the position of the string_field object.
We'll use these to position the string_field, based on the position of the dialog
box. The other data member is the string_field object.

I should warn you that there are going to be some problems doing precisely
what we want, here. I'm going to let them appear before I explain how to solve
them.

With this class definition, let's add a constructor and destructor to TEWIN.CPP.
Listing 9-2 shows a first try.

Listing 9-2: TEWIN.CPP

```
}

string_dialog::string_dialog( char* fld, char* ttl )
    : dialog( ttl )
{
    sf_col = 2 + lft;
    sf_row = 3 + top;
    sf = new string_field( sf_col, sf_row, fld );

    sf->show();
    sf->edit();
}

string_dialog::~string_dialog()
{
    delete sf;
}
```

```
void ins_chars( char* s, int nchars )
```

You see that the constructor for the string_dialog positions the string_field two columns from the left and three rows down from the top of the dialog box. It then creates the string_field, displays it, and gives the user control to interact with it.

When this works, all the mainline will need to do is create a string_dialog box and then read the value of the string. Everything else will happen automatically. Let's try it. You need to change TE.CPP so that it creates a string_dialog. Listing 9-3 shows the necessary changes.

Listing 9-3: TE.CPP

```
// TE.CPP -- Tiny Editor
// Copyright 1995, Martin L. Rinehart

#include <CONIO.H>

#include "TEWIN.H"
```

```
#include "TECMD.H"

void startup();

int main()
{
    startup();

    string_dialog* sd = new string_dialog(
        "test.fil                              ",
        " Open File " );

    delete sd;

    return 0;
}

void startup()
{
    textattr( WHITE_BLUE );
    clrscr();

    setcursortype(NOCURSOR );
}

// end of TE.CPP
```

When you run this code, your string dialog should pop up just as you've asked it to and let you manipulate your filename until you choose to press one of the exit keys (such as Enter) that terminates a string read. This is precisely what we want. There's only one more small detail.

Our main() function doesn't know what the result of our string editing is. It needs to ask the string_dialog object for the final status of the str member of sf (the string_field object member) in the string_dialog. Let's have the mainline report that value to us.

Listing 9-4 has some code that looks like it will tell us, but it won't work. Add it to TE.CPP and see what problems come up.

Listing 9-4: TE.CPP

```
int main()
{
    startup();

    string_dialog* sd = new string_dialog(
        "test.fil                          ",
        " Open File " );

    // test: report file name
        gotoxy( 1, 1 );
        cprintf( sd->sf->str );
        getch();

    delete sd;

    return 0;
}
```

Figure 9-1 shows the error I get when I try to compile this code.

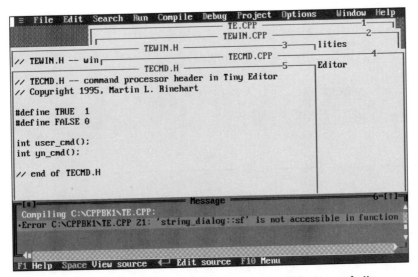

Figure 9-1: An object member is not accessible in main().

The problem is that your main() function does not have access to the private members (you had declared sf as a private data member of string dialog class) of the string_dialog object. A simple way to fix the problem is to make sf public, but that's generally not a good practice.

Making a data member public gives the whole world read and write access to that member, which is seldom what you want. (Even if you are the only member of "the whole world," it still makes it too easy for you to do something wrong.) What you want is a function that returns the value of the string. Try adding a function, sval(), that returns this value.

Listing 9-5 shows sval() added to the string_dialog class definition in TEWIN.H. Listing 9-6 shows the definition of sval() in TEWIN.CPP. Listing 9-7 shows TE.CPP making use of this value. This all uncovers the next problem—it still doesn't work.

Listing 9-5: TEWIN.H

```
class string_dialog : public dialog
{
private:
    int sf_col, sf_row;

    string_field* sf;

public:
    string_dialog( char* fld, char* ttl );
    ~string_dialog();

    char* sval();

};
```

Listing 9-6: TEWIN.CPP

```
string_dialog::~string_dialog()
{
    delete sf;
}
```

```
char* string_dialog::sval()
{

    return sf->str;

}
```

```
void ins_chars( char* s, int nchars )
```

Listing 9-7: TE.CPP

```
// test: report file name
    gotoxy( 1, 1 );
    cprintf( sd->sval() );
    getch();
```

This is the sort of access that is always recommended in any discussion of object design. Or at least it would be if it worked. The problem is the same one as before, except that we've moved it—this time it's the string_dialog object that doesn't have access to the protected members of the string_field class.

Remind yourself of just how dumb computers really are. Our string_dialog and string_field objects sound, to us, as if they should be working together. To the C++ compiler, there is no such relationship, of course. We could use the same solution, creating a function to access the data member of the string_field class, but there is a way to tell the C++ compiler directly that our classes should work together.

We can declare a class to be a *friend* of another class. Classes that are friends are permitted access to data members that would otherwise be inaccessible. The class that grants *friend* status is granting access to its members, but only on a very selective basis.

For us, we'd like our string_field class to allow the string_dialog class to access string_field's members. More exactly, we'd like the string_field class to allow members of the string_dialog class to access the members of string_field objects. It's very simple to do. Add the one line shown in Listing 9-8 to the definition of the string_field class in TEWIN.H.

Listing 9-8: TEWIN.H

```
class string_field
{
```

```
friend class string_dialog;

protected:
    int row, col;
    int width;

    char* str;

    int cloc;

    int edit_do( int cmd );
public:
    string_field(int c, int r, char* s);
    ~string_field();

    void show();
    void edit();
};
```

That one line does the trick:

```
    friend class string_dialog
```

This tells the compiler that string_dialog objects can access the members of string_field objects, just as if they were member functions of the string_field class. This is precisely what we want in this situation.

Now when you press Ctrl+F9, you can run your string_dialog, and your main() can report the result of your work. Figure 9-2 shows my user screen after playing with the filename.

Now we have a tool to get a filename, so let's move on to using it.

O P E N I N G   A   F I L E

Let's begin with a small text file, TEST.FIL. Here's mine:

```
    partridge in pear tree

    turtle doves
```

French hens

calling birds

diamond rings

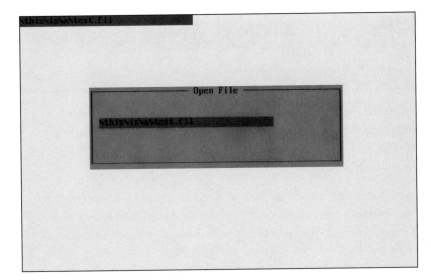

Figure 9-2: Reporting the results of editing the filename.

Any text will do, but be sure that it has some natural order, so you'll know when it's getting scrambled and when it's coming out right.

Create your file in the same directory as your C++ projects. Before we can open it, let's take a look at files and data streams.

Files and Streams

In C++, the printf() family has been substantially replaced by the object-oriented iostreams family. Using iostreams, you can write programs like the one in Listing 9-9 (all new, so it's not on disk). Call this one T1.CPP.

Listing 9-9: T1.CPP

```
#include <iostreams.h>


int main()
```

```
{
    char name[] = "Martin Rinehart";

    cout << '\n' << name;

    char temp;
    cin >> temp;

    return 0;
}
```

This program outputs (via cout and the << operator) the name, preceded by a
newline. Then it reads (via cin and the >> operator) a single character into
temp. The character you enter must be a nonblank, printable one, so this isn't
quite the same as using getch().

I won't teach you iostreams input and output because almost no professional
C++ systems actually use streams this way. For a clue to the reason, enter the
nearly equivalent program shown in Listing 9-10 (also all new, so not on disk).
Call this one T2.CPP.

Listing 9-10: T2.CPP

```
#include <conio.h>

int main()
{
    char name[] = "Martin Rinehart";

    cprintf( "\n%s", name );

    getch();

    return 0;
}
```

After you run this, use the File|DOS Shell menu choice and run a directory of
your .EXE files. On my machine, T1.EXE, the iostreams version, takes 35,542
bytes, whereas T2.EXE, the conio version, takes 11,290 bytes.

Another reason to use the classic printf() instead of the object-oriented iostreams is that the former is still useful as you move into Windows and other GUI environments. The sprintf() function works like printf(), but it sends its output to a string in RAM and so provides a very common way of formatting strings of mixed text and numeric data. These formatted results can then be displayed by a GUI using whatever fancy fonts or other techniques the GUI supports.

However, streams have taken the place of straight DOS file accesses for most disk I/O, and here we will take advantage of them.

The FILE Typedef

When you work with DOS file streams, you work with FILEs. The FILE typedef is defined in STDIO.H. It is:

```
typedef struct {
    short           level;
    unsigned        flags;
    char            fd;
    unsigned char   hold;
    short           bsize;
    unsigned char   *buffer, *curp;
    unsigned        istemp;
    short           token;
} FILE;
```

This introduces a number of topics, such as typedefs, that we need to discuss before we go on to open our file. Let's start with the simplest, first.

Short and Other Integers

There is another type of integer that we haven't discussed, the *short*. C and C++ are the languages of UNIX, as well as of DOS-based computers. In the UNIX world, there are lots of different computer architectures.

Most modern architectures are settling around word lengths that are powers of two. Intel CPUs support 8-, 16-, and 32-bit words directly. DEC's Alpha and others go up to 64- and even 128-bit words. But ten years ago, this was not the case.

Computer words used to come in all sizes. You still see an echo of this in C's and C++'s support for octal (three-bit) constants. C was originally defined to support four vague integer sizes. In order, they are: char, short, int, and long. The only thing that was guaranteed about these integers was that the size order was as specified. (A long was as big as or bigger than an int. An int was not longer than a long, nor shorter than a short, and so on.)

The original DOS-based C compilers were built when Intel CPUs primarily supported 16-bit words and 8-bit bytes, along with providing some support for operations on 32-bit double words. The meaningful sizes were then 8, 16, and 32 bits, so a char has 8 bits, shorts and ints have 16 bits, and longs have 32 bits.

If you get to writing code that is intended for porting to different machine architectures, you should remember that these are DOS-based sizes as currently implemented, not C++-defined sizes. For portable code, C++ supports the sizeof() operator. It looks like a function, but it doesn't require a declaration.

Listing 9-11, also all new and so not on disk, uses the sizeof() operator to report the lengths of various integer types.

Listing 9-11: T.CPP

```
#include <conio.h>

int main()
{

    char      c;
    short     s;
    int       i;
    signed    g;
    unsigned  u;
    long      l;

    clrscr();

    cprintf( "\n\rsize of char     is %d", sizeof(c) );
    cprintf( "\n\rsize of short    is %d", sizeof(s) );
    cprintf( "\n\rsize of int      is %d", sizeof(i) );
    cprintf( "\n\rsize of signed   is %d", sizeof(g) );
    cprintf( "\n\rsize of unsigned is %d", sizeof(u) );
    cprintf( "\n\rsize of long     is %d", sizeof(l) );

    getch();
```

```
    return 0;
}
```

When you run this program, you'll see that the sizeof() operator reports a size in bytes. A char is 1 byte, an int is 2, and a long is 4. Short, signed, and unsigned ints are all 2 bytes long. Figure 9-3 shows the results this program gives in TCLite.

```
size of char     is 1
size of short    is 2
size of int      is 2
size of signed   is 2
size of unsigned is 2
size of long     is 4
```

Figure 9-3: Sizes of integral types in TCLite.

T I P

Remember that sizeof(int) or sizeof() any of the other integer types is not defined in CH. The reason sizeof() is included in the language is so that you can use it to write portable code covering multiple hardware platforms.

We've looked at the signed and unsigned keywords as modifiers to types such as int and char. They can also be used, as they are here, as synonyms for unsigned int and signed int.

To be complete, the keywords long and short can also be used as modifiers to the basic type int, as in:

```
    short s;         // a short int
    short int si;    // another short int

    long l;          // a long int
    long int li;     // another long int
```

As we have noted, the default for an int is signed. The signed keyword can be used along with int, short, or long if you like. In practice, most C++ programmers just use char, int, and long for PC work.

Defining Pointers

Another topic illustrated in the FILE definition is the declaration of multiple pointers on a single line. Let's begin with the basics. The asterisk can be positioned adjacent to the data type, as we have been doing, or adjacent to the variable name, which was the common style for C programmers, as this shows:

```
char* cpp_style; // pointer declared, C++ style

char *c_style;   // same meaning, but C style
```

In this case, both positions for the asterisk are correct in both C and C++. The style has changed, but both forms have always worked.

You can also declare multiple variables of a single type on one line:

```
char c1, c2, c3; // three char variables

int  i1, i2, i3; // three int variables
```

But what do you do when you want two pointers? This should clarify your choices:

```
char* cp1, * cp2; // two pointers to chars

char *cp1, *cp2;  // same, in the older style
```

You must include the asterisk if you want a pointer. If you omit it, you have a char (or other) variable:

```
char* cp1, c2;   // c2 is a char, not a pointer to char

char c1, *cp1;   // c1 is a char, cp1 is a pointer to char
```

☢

───

W A R N I N G

───

Remember to include the asterisk when you want a pointer. It's easy to mistake *char* cp1, cp2 for a declaration of two pointers to char. Without the asterisk, the second variable is a char, not a pointer to char, even though its name suggests otherwise.

───

Typedefs

A typedef is a way of defining a new word for an old type. Suppose you are writing a program for piloting boats and you are dealing with distances in miles. You can define a Distance type, as:

```
typedef unsigned char Distance;
```

This could make some of your code more readable. For example:

```
Distance miles_traveled = ... ;
Distance miles_remaining = ... ;
```

When you head away from shore, you may need to allow for greater distances. All you need to do to adapt your piloting program for offshore navigation is change the typedef:

```
typedef unsigned int Distance;
```

The typedef is one example where the C++-style of writing the asterisk with the type makes your meaning clearer:

```
typedef char* String; // String means char*
typedef char *String; // String still means char*!

String last_name; // last_name is a pointer to char

    // same as: char* last_name, or char *last_name
```

Many authorities suggest that you use an initial capital letter, as these examples do, when you create a typedef. The FILE typedef does not conform, unfortunately. In the following example, a typedef defines a struct:

```
typedef struct
{
    int x_coord;
    int y_coord;
} Point;
```

This is the way FILE is defined. This usage predates C++ and is not generally considered good C++ style. It still works, of course, and we'll make use of it with all our file I/O. You use this sort of typedef just as you use any other:

```
Point p;
```

Opening the File

With all that background, you can now read the FILE definition. It defines a new word, FILE, which tells the compiler that the following variable is a structure of the defined type. You can manipulate the member variables (default access to a struct is public), but you don't have to. In fact, it would probably be better if FILE's members were private or protected. You really don't want to manipulate them directly.

If you let TCLite's runtime functions take care of the FILE stream, you'll have a very easy time with text files. We can start with opening the file. Before we leave this part of the project, we'll encapsulate this functionality in an appropriate object. For now, though, let's just open the file in the mainline.

The fopen() built-in function takes a filename and mode as arguments and returns a FILE pointer or null value. The mode values include "r" for read, "w" for write, and "a" for append. They also combine with "b" for binary files or "t" for text files. (See the online help for a full list.)

We'll open a text file for reading with a call like this:

```
char* fname = "test.fil";
FILE* infile = fopen( fname, "rt" ); // Read, Text mode
```

When it's time to write the file, we'll use a call like this:

```
FILE* outfile = fopen( fname, "wt" ); // Write, Text mode
```

Opening a disk file for reading fails (returns null) if the file does not exist. Opening for writing creates a new file or overwrites an existing file. The fclose() built-in function closes files.

TIP

When you write an fopen(), make a habit of immediately writing the corresponding fclose(), too. Leaving files open does *not* cause an error until you have run out of DOS file handles. You can forget to close a file and not find out about it until you really need to open another one. (We'll need another handle, for example, when it's time to save our edited file back to disk.)

Listing 9-12 shows the file opening code in TE.CPP. Don't overlook the extra #include directive or the fact that the debugging code is extended to report the pointer value.

Listing 9-12: TE.CPP

```
// TE.CPP -- Tiny Editor
// Copyright 1995, Martin L. Rinehart

#include <CONIO.H>
#include <STDIO.H>

#include "TEWIN.H"
#include "TECMD.H"

void startup();

int main()
{
    startup();

    string_dialog* sd = new string_dialog(
        "test.fil                      ",
        " Open File " );

    FILE* infile = fopen( sd->sval(), "rt" );
```

```
// test: report FILE pointer
    gotoxy( 1, 1 );
    cprintf( "Pointer to %s is %d.",
        sd->sval(), infile );
    getch();


if ( infile )
    fclose( infile );
```

```
    delete sd;


    return 0;
}
```

When you run this program, you should get a positive integer value for your FILE* variable. Run the program a second time and specify a file that doesn't exist: "\no\such.fil" should do the trick. With a nonexistent file, your pointer will be zero.

DISPLAYING THE FILE

Now that we have an open file, let's list our file in a box on the screen. In the next section, we'll build a linked-list class to hold the contents of the file in RAM, and all our permanent display code will work with the linked-list structure. This is just a quick test to see how the record=reading routines work.

To display the file, we'll need a character buffer big enough to fit the largest line in our file, and we'll need a routine to read a record at a time from a text file. The buffer is simple enough to create, and the text file read routine is built in, so this step won't be much trouble.

The fgets() Function

The text read routine is fgets(). It is called like this:

```
#define MAX_CHARS 1024

char inbuf[ MAX_CHARS ];
...
fgets( inbuf, MAX_CHARS, infile );
```

The first argument (inbuf, above) is the buffer that will be filled from the file. The second argument is an integer specifying the maximum number of characters to read. The last argument is the FILE* variable that points to the open file stream.

The fgets() call reads in text one line at a time. It reads from the current position up through the first newline character in the file.

N O T E

In DOS, text records are separated by carriage return–linefeed pairs ("\r\n"). In UNIX, the mother system for C and C++, a single linefeed character separates lines. On the Macintosh, a single return character does the job. The fgets() function is portable across all these platforms if you program for the newline ("\n") and let the library code handle the system-specific translation.

Your buffer is filled by fgets() with the text line plus a newline character and a trailing null. There are two exceptions, however. For one thing, if the maximum number of characters are written into your buffer, reading and writing stop. If either the newline or the null or both don't fit, they are discarded.

The other exception has to do with the end of the file. If your file has been read through the end, subsequent calls to fgets() do nothing. (You can rewind your file or otherwise reposition the file pointer if you want to reread data, of course.)

Creating a Box for Our Display

All of this is more trouble to explain than it is to use. Listing 9-13 shows the start of some sample read and display code in TE.CPP.

Listing 9-13: TE.CPP

```
// TE.CPP -- Tiny Editor
// Copyright 1995, Martin L. Rinehart

#include <CONIO.H>
#include <STDIO.H>
#include <STDLIB.H>
```

```cpp
#include "TEWIN.H"
#include "TECMD.H"

void startup();

int main()
{
    startup();

    string_dialog* sd = new string_dialog(
        "test.fil                              ",
        " Open File " );

    FILE* infile = fopen( sd->sval(), "rt" );

    if ( !infile )
    {
        printf( "\nCouldn't open file" );
        getch();
        exit( 1 );
    }

    // display file
        dialog* show_fil = new dialog(
            sd->sval(), 15, 3, 75, 23 );

        getch();
        delete show_fil;

    fclose( infile );

    delete sd;

    return 0;
}
```

In this code, I've used the exit() built-in function, defined in STDLIB.H. As its name suggests, exit() terminates the program, returning to the operating system.

The argument is the code to return to the operating system. In DOS, that's the value of the errorlevel variable that you can use in batch files.

The exit() routine actually calls the C++ exit code. Among other jobs, the exit code is responsible for closing all open files and returning all allocated memory back to DOS. This fact lets you use exit() anywhere in a program, without worrying about these clean-up details.

H I N T

You may want to call your own cover function for exit(), such as my_exit(). While exit() takes care of low-level clean-up, you may want to tidy up the screen or handle error messages with more grace. The error message "Couldn't open file" in the listing is a good example of one that has no grace.

After checking that a file was opened, this code continues, using the dialog object as a handy way of popping up a box to display the file. If you recall, we programmed the dialog with optional position parameters, which we are taking advantage of now.

Displaying the Text

With a popup box on the screen, now we just need to call fgets() and position the results. Since this is temporary code, we'll ignore such difficulties as lines that are too long and more lines than will fit.

Listing 9-14 shows the extra code to add to TE.CPP that displays your text file in the box. This code uses the feof() function, which works just as you would expect.

Listing 9-14: TE.CPP

```
void startup();

#define MAX_CHARS 1024

char inbuf[ MAX_CHARS ];

int main()
```

```
{
    startup();

    string_dialog* sd = new string_dialog(
        "test.fil                        ",
        " Open File " );

    FILE* infile = fopen( sd->sval(), "rt" );

    if ( !infile )
    {
        printf( "\nCouldn't open file" );
        getch();
        exit( 1 );
    }

    // display file
        dialog* show_fil = new dialog(
            sd->sval(), 15, 3, 75, 23 );

        int row = 4;
        while ( !feof(infile) )
        {
            fgets( inbuf, MAX_CHARS, infile );
            gotoxy( 17, row );
            cprintf( inbuf );
            row++;
        }

        getch();
        delete show_fil;

    fclose( infile );

    delete sd;

    return 0;
}
```

Enter and run this code. It may work beautifully. On the other hand, it may show the bug that you see in Figure 9-4.

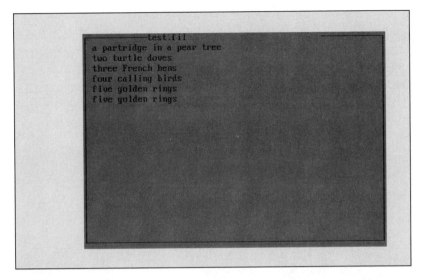

Figure 9-4: File display, with double reporting of last line.

If your version doesn't double up the final line, edit your TEST.FIL. Make sure there is a return at the end of the last line. Run again and you'll see the bug. Delete the return so that eof() comes at the end of the last line and your code works correctly.

T I P

You can use F3 to open and edit your TEST.FIL. This is very convenient, but it reveals a minor bug in TCLite. If you change nothing but TEST.FIL and use Ctrl+F9 to run again, you get a "Source modified?" dialog question. Just choose the No answer and continue.

To guard against this mistake, we'll have to manipulate our input buffer. We want to be able to check that fgets() actually wrote into the buffer. (The doubled last line appears because nothing was written into the buffer, so our code is just rewriting the previous buffer values.)

We can make this check by putting a zero in the first character of the buffer and testing to see if it has been overwritten. Listing 9-15 shows how this can be done.

Listing 9-15: TE.CPP

```
// display file
    dialog* show_fil = new dialog(
        sd->sval(), 15, 3, 75, 23 );

    int row = 4;
    *inbuf = 0;

    while ( !feof(infile) )
    {
        fgets( inbuf, MAX_CHARS, infile );
        if ( *inbuf )
        {
            gotoxy( 17, row );
            cprintf( inbuf );
            row++;

            *inbuf = 0;
        }
    }

    getch();
```

With this change, your display should be correct, with or without a return character following the last line of text.

May I return to the subject of programming practice for just a minute? This is an excellent example of how going very slowly gets your work done quickly. By taking the time to do a sample file read, we uncovered the rather tricky problem of fgets() behavior when a newline ends the file. If we had charged straight ahead into our linked-list class, we could have spent hours trying to find the nonexistent bug in our linked-list code, before we discovered that we were looking at a peculiarity in the fgets() routine.

With that said, let's get on to building a linked list from our text file and developing the classes we need for our editor.

USING A LINKED-LIST CLASS

To begin with, if you haven't used a linked-list structure, you're probably wondering what it is and why we are interested in using it for an editor application.

Linked Lists Explained

There are several types of linked lists. They all permit a lot of flexibility in keeping a lot of data in RAM. For many applications, they are a better structure than the arrays you might first think of using.

Singly Linked Lists

At its simplest, a linked list is a list of things where each thing contains a link to the next thing in the list. Here's a structure that holds one book record in a linked list of book records:

```
struct book
{
    book* next_book;

    char* title;
    char* author;
    ...
};
```

Here's an example of a routine that could print the titles of all the books in a list, given a pointer to the first book in the list:

```
void titles( book* first_book )
{
    book* this_book = first_book;
    do
    {
        printf( this_book->title );
        this_book = this_book->next_book;
    }
    while ( this_book );
}
```

The line that assigns this_book->next_book to this_book is typical of code that works with linked lists. That assignment lets you march down the list.

Doubly Linked Lists

Singly linked lists are almost never found in practice. When we say "linked list," we almost always are referring to a doubly linked list. A doubly linked list (which I'll just call a linked list from now on) has pointers to the next and previous elements of the list.

Let's build a linked list of zoo animals:

```
struct animal
{
    animal* next_animal;
    animal* prev_animal;

    char* name;
    . . .
};


. . .


animal* first_animal = new animal();
first_animal->name = "aardvark";
. . .
```

The advantage of a doubly linked list is, of course, that you can navigate forward or backward through the list. This makes operations like insertions and deletions relatively simple. Here's the relevant part of a routine that inserts animals in our zoo software:

```
void insert_animal( animal* existing, animal* added)
{
    added->prev_animal = existing;
    added->next_animal = existing->next_animal;

    existing->next_animal = added;
    added->next_animal->prev_animal = added;

    . . . // add added->name, etc.
}
```

As you see, the added animal is linked into the list by assigning pointers. The added animal points to the existing animal (prev) and the existing animal's original forward link (next). Then the forward link of the existing animal and the backward link of the original next animal are pointed to the added animal.

These four assignments insert a new element into a linked list. This sequence can be orders of magnitude faster than using an array. Supposing our zoo software used an array structure. Here's equivalent code to insert a new animal:

```
animal animals[MAX_ANIMALS];
int last_animal;

...

void insert_animal( int existing, animal* added )
{
    if ( last_animal < MAX_ANIMALS )
    {
        for ( int i = last_animal; i > existing; i- )
            animals[i+1] = animals[i];
    }
    else ... // error: no more animals!

    ... copy data from new to animals[existing]
}
```

As you see, inserting an animal involves moving all the following animals in the array. As the array grows, this can be a time-consuming operation. It gets slower as you add animals, and (if you keep your animals in alphabetical order) it can be much slower to add an aardvark than it is to add a zebra.

By contrast, the linked-list operation is virtually instantaneous, and it doesn't depend on a predetermined limit like MAX_ANIMALS. (It depends on having enough RAM, but both methods have that requirement.)

Other Linked Lists

For one operation, an array is a much better structure: finding the *n*th element. With the array of animals, finding animal 500 is as simple as:

```
animals[500]
```

With a linked list, finding the 500th animal requires that we start at the first animal and then skip forward 499 times. Other forms of linked lists have been implemented that speed up this operation.

For example, you could add *skip links* to your linked list. A skip link, as its name implies, points to a list member some distance away, skipping intervening list members. (Skip links are used in addition to, not in lieu of, next and previous links.) Using skip links that point 25 elements ahead or backward can make finding the *n*th element much faster.

On the other hand, the more complexities, such as skip links, that you add to the linked-list structure, the more the whole process is slowed as you maintain these links.

Linked Lists and Text Editors

The linked-list structure is one of the most common ones to use for implementing a text editor. Let's consider one operation: moving a group of lines. With a linked-list structure, you can view this process in steps. First, we'll delete the lines from their current location. Second, we'll insert these lines into their new location.

Deleting a Group of Lines

To remove a group of lines, you simply link the line that precedes the deletion to the line that follows the deletion. If you are deleting lines 6 through 9, you link line 5 to what was line 10, and your deletion is complete.

Of course, you'll want to take some clean-up action with respect to the deleted lines. You can free their memory, or you could save them for use in an undo operation. If you are moving them, you'll save a pointer to the first line in the deleted group.

H I N T

There is seldom any reason to move lines in memory if you use a linked-list structure. When you *delete* lines, you just unlink them from the text file and relink them to the clipboard or some other location.

Inserting a Group of Lines

Let's insert a group of lines between the current lines 2 and 3. To do this, all we have to do is link line 2 to the first line in the insertion group and link the former line 3 to the last line in the insertion group. If the lines we are inserting are the ones we just deleted, these steps will complete a move operation.

We will have adjusted three or four pointers when we *delete* the lines from one location, and we will have updated four pointers when we *insert* the lines into their new location. All told that's seven or eight pointers. The whole operation is virtually instantaneous. The only process that requires measurable computer time is updating the screen.

Other Operations

Many of the operations that occur constantly during editing are ideally suited to a linked-list structure. Inserting and deleting individual lines are typical examples.

About the only operation that is not well-suited to a linked list is the command to jump to a particular line number. However, you'll find that on a modern computer, even this command executes quickly enough that this is not a practical problem.

Reading Text into a Linked List

Are you ready to build a linked-list class? Let's start with two classes, memfile and memline. The memfile object will keep track of the start and end of a linked list of memline objects. It will also remember what file the text was read from.

Defining the Objects

The memline objects each contain one line of text from the file, in addition to backward and forward list pointers. Listing 9-16 shows definitions for these two classes. I'm putting these definitions into a new file, TEFIL.H. We'll add the associated code to TEFIL.CPP, of course. TEFIL.H is all new, so it's not on disk.

Listing 9-16: TEFIL.H

```
// TEFIL.H -- file-related classes, Tiny Editor
// Copyright 1995, Martin L. Rinehart

struct memline // all public members!
{
    memline* prev, * next;
    char* text;

    memline( memline* after_line, char* txt );
    ~memline();
```

```
};

class memfile
{
protected:
    FILE* text_file;
    memline* head_line, * tail_line;

public:
    memfile( FILE* tf );
    ~memfile();

    memline* hline() { return head_line; };
};

// end of TEFIL.H
```

There's nothing really new here except that we haven't discussed the role of a wrapper class for our linked lists, such as the memfile class. This class's job, as you'll see, is to read the text from its FILE* member into RAM in a linked list of memline objects. It also keeps track of the head and tail of the list. Of course, later on we'll also ask it to take care of storing the modified text back to disk, but that part can wait a while.

The Memline Constructor

Listing 9-17 shows the new TEFIL.CPP and its first function, the memline constructor. It's all new, so it's not on disk.

Listing 9-17: TEFIL.CPP

```
// TEFIL.CPP -- file-related classes, Tiny Editor
// copyright 1995, Martin L. Rinehart

#include <STDIO.H>
#include <STRING.H>

#include "TEFIL.H"

memline::memline( memline* after_line, char* txt )
{
```

```
    if( after_line )
    {
        prev = after_line;
        next = after_line->next;

        prev->next = this;
        next->prev = this;

        int len = strlen( txt );

        text = new char[len+1];
        strcpy( text, txt );

        char* endp = text+len-1;
        if ( *endp == '\n' )
            *endp = 0;
    }
    else // this is the 1st line
    {
    }
}

// end of TEFIL.CPP
```

The memline() constructor has two parts, chosen by the if test. The else part is chosen when you call the function with a null for the after_line, the line the new one is inserted after. Although that is the second part of the code, let's consider it first.

As you see, the code simply assigns nulls to the pointers to the previous and next lines in the linked list, as well as to the line's text. This action just creates an empty line that can be used as the start of the list.

Here's a quick quiz to test yourself.

```
// the constructor says:
    prev = next = NULL;
    text = NULL;

// why not just:
    prev = next = text = NULL;
```

Can you figure out what the compiler will say about the second form? Try it to find out (or to confirm your answer, if you saw the answer).

If you noticed that text is a pointer to char whereas the other two variables are pointers to memlines, you got the right answer. You can assign NULL (zero) to any pointer, but you can't assign a pointer of one type to any other type.

The error message refers to char near* and memline near*. Pointers can be near or far, depending on the *memory model* you use. (TCLite supports only the *small* model, where all pointers are automatically near pointers.) In TCLite, you can't use far pointers, so you don't need to worry about this fact. When you move on to other C++ systems, you'll be able to use more memory, but you'll have to choose your pointer types more carefully.

The other part of the memline constructor inserts a new line after an existing one. It first assigns its own object's prev and next pointers, and then it reassigns the pointers of the memlines it falls between.

After assigning the pointers, it copies the string into a new string object. You can't just copy the pointer, because that will always be to a single location: inbuf. You have to move the data from inbuf into individual character arrays.

The last operation is replacing the terminal newline character with a null.

H I N T

The strlen() function returns 5 for the string "abcde"—it does not count the terminating null. On the other hand, "abcde"[5] is the terminating null character, since "abcde"[0] is the letter 'a'.

The if test is needed only for the last line in the file. All lines except the last in a text file are terminated with a newline character. More precisely, a newline character separates each text line in a file, and the fgets() function returns the newline separator following each line it reads.

The Memline Destructor
Unfortunately, we can't really test this constructor until we've added more code. Let's continue with the memline destructor, also in TEFIL.CPP. We won't use this function for a while, but it is a good example of working linked-list code. Listing 9-18 shows this code.

Listing 9-18: TEFIL.CPP

```
}

memline::~memline()
{
    delete text;

    if ( prev )
        prev->next = next;

    if ( next )
        next->prev = prev;
}
```

```
// end of TEFIL.CPP
```

This destructor deletes text (the character array) and then resets the pointers of the surrounding memline objects.

The Memfile Constructor and Destructor

Now we're ready to build a memfile object, beginning with writing a constructor function. Listing 9-19 shows the constructor, also in TEFIL.CPP.

Listing 9-19: TEFIL.CPP

```
}

memfile::memfile( FILE* tf )
{
    text_file = tf;
    head_line = new memline( NULL, "" );

    memline* curline = head_line;
    char inbuf[1024];
    *inbuf = 0;

    rewind( tf );

    do
```

```
    {
        fgets( inbuf, 1024, text_file );
        if ( !*inbuf )
            break;

        curline = new memline( curline, inbuf );
        *inbuf = 0;
    }
    while ( !feof(text_file) );
}


memfile::~memfile()
{
}
```

// end of TEFIL.CPP

The memfile constructor copies the FILE stream pointer into text_file (tf) and then builds a null memline for the head_line member. It also creates a pointer to the current line, initially the head_line, which we'll use when we read the file.

I've also included an input line buffer in the memfile object. If you are writing reentrant code, you cannot put buffers like this into global variables. In fact, you shouldn't use any global variables at all. This example shows how you can avoid them without imposing too much overhead on your small programs.

N O T E

Reentrant code is code that can be run in multiple, independent copies. For example, a multithreaded operating system might have interrupted the reading of text from disk into the memfile/memlines construct we're using here. The operation that interrupted this one might just have been another read from disk into a memfile/memlines construct. A single, global input buffer would probably have gotten our files' contents mixed. (The interrupting program would work, but the interrupted one would find data from the wrong file in inbuf when it resumed operation.) Using a separate input buffer for each memfile will eliminate this source of bugs.

The rewind() operation is another function defined in STDIO.H. While the name suggests a tape operation, in fact the function performs an instantaneous resetting of the file pointer to the beginning of the file. This is probably not needed here, but it could solve a problem later on if we allow editing or viewing a single file in two or more windows at once.

The actual read operation shows just how clean code using a linked list can be. The key line is:

```
curline = new memline( curline, inbuf );
```

This line creates a new memline object, linked into the list after the current memline object. The new memline becomes the current memline right after it is created (to be used in the next pass through the loop).

This simple line shows how effectively object-oriented design and code can push the gritty details of an operation out of sight of the code that uses the object.

A null destructor function serves to remind us that there is no code written for this function, as yet. We'll come back to this problem when it's time to close a file.

Reading the Data

Now we have the code we need to read a text file into a linked list in memory. The remaining job is to call the code and then to test it thoroughly. Listing 9-20 shows the changes needed in TE.CPP's main() to actually read your test data into memory.

Listing 9-20: TE.CPP

```
// TE.CPP -- Tiny Editor
// Copyright 1995, Martin L. Rinehart

#include <CONIO.H>
#include <STDIO.H>
#include <STDLIB.H>

#include "TEWIN.H"
#include "TECMD.H"
#include "TEFIL.H"
```

```
void startup();

#define MAX_CHARS 1024

char inbuf[ MAX_CHARS ];

int main()
{
    startup();

    string_dialog* sd = new string_dialog(
        "test.fil                          ",
        " Open File " );

    FILE* infile = fopen( sd->sval(), "rt" );

    if ( !infile )
    {
        printf( "\nCouldn't open file" );
        getch();
        exit( 1 );
    }

    memfile* mf = new memfile( infile );

    fclose( infile );

    delete mf;

    return 0;
}
```

Add the new #include directive and then replace all the old test code with the line that calls the memfile constructor. Finally, replace the delete call with the one shown here. If you test this code with Ctrl+F9, you'll be asked for a filename, as before. After you provide the filename, the program will finish so fast you may think that it hasn't done anything at all.

What you need to do is to run this under the debugger, this time using the Inspect capability. Follow these steps:

STEP BY STEP

1. Position your cursor on the "new memfile" line and press F4 to run to that line. (Press Enter to accept your default TEST.FIL name.)

2. Press F7 to step into the memfile constructor.

3. Press F8 until you arrive at the line that assigns zero to *inbuf. (We really want to look at the results of the assignment to curline, just above this line. If we stop at the "curline = ..." line, the assignment won't have been made.)

4. Press Alt+F4 and type the name "curline" into the Data Inspect box. A box labeled "Inspecting curline" will pop up.

You are now looking at the object pointed to by curline. You can see the actual value of the prev and next pointers. This is shown in Figure 9-5. Your pointers will probably be different from mine, except for the next pointer, which should be pointing to NULL. The first line of your TEST.FIL should be reported where mine says "partridge in pear ...".

```
 =  File  Edit  Search  Run  Compile  Debug  Project  Options     Window  Help
                                      TE.CPP                  1
                       rewind( tf );     ┌─[■]─── Inspecting curline ─┐─[↑]─┐
                                         │Register (DI) » ds:1010           ▲│
// TEWIN.H -- w        do                │prev                      ds:1006 ■│
                       {                 │next                         NULL ▓│
// TECMD.H -- c            fgets( inbuf, 1│text ds:101A "a partridge in a pear▼│
// Copyright 19           if ( !*inbuf ) │◀█                               ▶ │
                            break;        │memline(memline near*,char near*) 8│
#define TRUE  1                           │~memline()                8BFC:1149│
#define FALSE 0          curline = new m │struct memline *                  ▼│
                          *inbuf = 0;    └──────────────────────────────────┘
int user_cmd();        }
int yn_cmd();           while ( !feof(text_file) );
                     }
// end of TECMD

                     memfile::~memfile()
                     {
                   ── 64:1 ────
 ── 1:1 ──
 F1 Help  Alt-I Set index range  F10 Menu
```

Figure 9-5: Inspecting curline during a test run.

To test this code more completely, continue this way:

1. Press Ctrl+F8 to set a hard breakpoint at the "*inbuf = 0" line.

2. Press Ctrl+F9 to run to this breakpoint. You'll see the Inspecting... box change as you read in the next record.

3. Press Ctrl+F9 two or three more times to read in more of your file.

Your screen should still look similar to the one shown in Figure 9-5, but you will be several lines farther into the file. Now let's use the Inspect capability to look at our linked list.

With your mouse, position the cursor over the line that says "prev" in the Inspecting... box. Double-click with the left mouse button. You'll get another Inspecting... box to pop up, only this one will be inspecting the object pointed to by prev.

Grab the title bar of this new Inspecting... box and position it below the first one. Then double-click on prev in the second Inspecting... box. This will pop up a third Inspecting... box, showing the object pointed to by prev in the second Inspecting... box.

Again, position the third box so you can read all three. What you are doing is following the prev pointers backward through the linked list. Continue this until you come to head_line. (You'll know you're at head_line when the text pointer points to NULL, not a text string.)

I've done this, and my result is shown in Figure 9-6.

Repeat this whole process, following the list forward by clicking on the next pointers, starting in the head_line box. You should reverse the steps. If you go forward and backward correctly, your list is correctly linked. (If not, use F7 to step into the memline constructor and see what you did wrong.)

Carefully check each pointer. Each memline's next pointer should lead to the next line of your file. Each prev pointer should lead to the prior line.

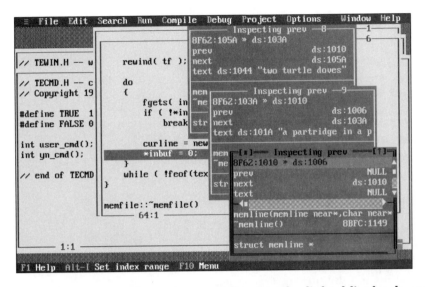

Figure 9-6: Inspecting... boxes following the linked list backward.

When the code works correctly, congratulate yourself. In the next chapter, we'll combine our memfile with a window so we can view all this on the screen, and you'll begin to see our Tiny Editor take shape.

SUMMARY

We started by adding the string_field class we created in the last chapter to the dialog box class we built earlier to produce a string_dialog class. This dialog box makes it easy to pop up a box that accepts a text field, such as a filename.

We used this dialog box class to get a filename in our main() front end to our future editor. You saw that once the class worked, it took almost no work in main() to pop up and use one of these dialogs.

When it came time to use the filename, we found out that there were problems associated with limiting access to the data members of an object. We overcame these problems by using a data access function and by making one class a friend of another.

We experimented briefly with the iostreams facilities of C++. We decided to use streams to access our disk files, but to continue with the older, C-based methods for console input and output, since they require a lot less space in the .EXE file.

The streams concept for disk input/output led us into the FILE typedef. We learned about typedefs and about short and long integers, signed and unsigned. We used the sizeof() operator in an experimental program, looking at the size of the various types of integers.

Then we went on to use the FILE stream pointer when we opened our file on disk. After we opened the file with fopen(), we read text lines with fgets(). Through an experimental front-end program, we discovered that there are some significant quirks in fgets() that impact the reading of the final line. These quirks were simple to work around, once we understood them.

We dipped into STDLIB.H for the exit() function. We used exit() to prematurely terminate our program when we couldn't find the specified file for opening.

Then we looked at singly and doubly linked lists. Doubly linked lists, the type normally meant when you say *linked list*, are ideally suited to the type of operations typical of a text editor.

We implemented a memline class and a memfile class to read our text lines from disk into a linked-list structure in memory. Along the way, we used file functions defined in STDIO.H, including rewind(), feof(), and fclose().

Finally, we tested our linked-list class by running our code in the TCLite debugger. We made heavy use of the Inspect feature (Alt+F4) to check the objects that we were creating.

Now that we can get our text files into memory, the next step is to get them onto the screen where we can see them. Once we can see a file, of course, we'll be on our way to editing it.

In the last chapter we opened a text file and read it into a linked list in memory. In this chapter, we're going to use that linked list, along with a dialog box, as the base for the critical display code that is fundamental to our Tiny Editor.

Beginning in this chapter, you'll be spending more time coding and less time learning, since you've already been exposed to a great deal of the C++ language. Still, we'll meet our share of new topics, including:

► Declaring, but not defining, class names

► Using and adding to the list of C++ keywords

► Using complex constructors with default base class parameters

► Using functions, like toupper(), from CTYPE.H

► Adding to an existing class without breaking existing code

► Building a simple message-passing executive

► Using the compound assignment operators in C++

► Recognizing lvalues

Let's dive right into development.

chapter 10

Displaying Text Files

I call the file window class object a file_win. Actually this isn't correct. What we're building is a window to display a portion of the linked list we built in memory from the text file on disk. But if we're going to talk about this class we'll want to call it something short, which is where file_win comes in.

A file_win has two basic components: a dialog object and a memfile object. The windows surrounding text files have been with us since long before the term *dialog box* became common, so we're not used to thinking of file windows as a type of dialog box. But they are.

If you think about it, you'll see that a text file is just another type of content for a dialog box, not really fundamentally different from a display showing a message, or asking yes or no, or getting a filename in a string_field object. And if you consider our dialog box's basic capabilities, such as popping up and back down, you'll see that the dialog box is exactly the right object to contain the display of our file (the display of our memory-based, linked-list copy of our file, to be technical).

Defining the File Window Class

Let's begin, as we always do, in our header file with a definition for the class. Add the definition in Listing 10-1 to TEFIL.H. (If you try Alt+F9, you'll see that this won't compile.)

Listing 10-1: TEFIL.H

```
// TEFIL.H -- file-related classes, Tiny Editor
// Copyright 1995, Martin L. Rinehart

class file_win : public dialog
{
protected:
    memfile* mem_file;

    memline* top_line;
    memline* cur_line;

    int curx, cury; // window-relative cursor location

    int ins_mode;

public:
    file_win( char* file_name, FILE* tf );
    ~file_win();

    void show_all( memline* startline );
    void show_line( int row, char* str );
};

struct memline // all public members!
```

In general, you can't use Alt+F9 on a header file if you're using the structure we're using here. None of the needed include files are available in the .H unless you use it as part of the .CPP. The first error you get when you try to compile this file is the "type name expected" mistake in the definition line of the file_win class. The problem is that the compiler has no idea what that word "dialog" is supposed to mean. (If you preceded this code with a definition of a dialog class, this problem would be solved. To #include TEWIN.H does the trick, but we do this in our .CPP file.)

The second error is more interesting, however. The same problem shows up with the "memline* memfile;" line. The compiler has no idea what a memline is. (The fact that it would find out if it read a little more of this file doesn't enter our compiler's thoughts.) What do you do when you want to refer to a class or structure that hasn't been defined?

One way to solve the problem is to rearrange your definitions to keep your compiler happy. I don't like to do this, and it won't always work, either. I prefer to put my class and structure definitions into my files in the way that I find most sensible. Right now I know I'll be working on the file_win class, so having it right at the top of the .H makes sense.

Sometimes, too, class A will have a member of class B, and class B will have a member of class A. In that case (or in more involved cases where the definitions are circular, via membership or inheritance) there is simply no way to order the definitions to keep the compiler happy. For both these reasons, C++ supports a stub class definition:

```
class <classname>;
```

If you want to tell your compiler that memfile and memline are classes (and tell it to take that on faith—you'll get around to the actual definitions when it suits you!) do it like this:

```
class memfile;
class memline;


... // now you can do these:
    // memfile* ...
    // memline ml = ...
```

This explains the addition to TEFIL.H shown in Listing 10-2. Make the addition and try Alt+F9 again. It eliminates a dozen of the 16 errors you get without it.

Listing 10-2: TEFIL.H

```
// TEFIL.H -- file-related classes, Tiny Editor
// Copyright 1995, Martin L. Rinehart
```

```
class memfile;
class memline;
```

```
class file_win : public dialog
```

This use of the "class" keyword is analogous to a function declaration. Like a function declaration, it tells the compiler what to expect but leaves the actual definition for later.

C++ reserves *keywords* for itself. You cannot name a variable "int," for instance—"int" can be used only as a type specifier; "while" can be used only in looping statements; and so on. When you declare or define a class name, that name becomes another keyword.

T I P

Don't try to memorize the current list of C++ keywords. It changes over time. If you inadvertently use a keyword as a variable or other name, you'll get inexplicable compiler messages. If you suddenly leave the rational world, try changing your names. For a definitive check, use Shift+F1 to look up "if," for example, in TCLite's index. TCLite tells you that it is a keyword.

With our file_win object defined, let's go on to writing the constructor function.

Constructing a File Window Object

The constructor for our file_win class will have an exceptionally long top line. Before we get to the code, let's think about how we have been defining our constructors with optional arguments. We've been using a technique like this:

```
base::base( specify this, specify that,
    optional thing1=1, optional thing2=2, ... )
```

This means that our working calls to build a *base* are mostly done this way:

```
base b = new base( this, that );
```

All the other parameters take their default values. Now we're going to build a new class, inheriting from base, that doesn't use the defaults. It has a new set of defaults. We'll do it this way:

```
deriv::deriv( specify this, specify that ) :
    base( this, that, 101, 102, ... )
```

In the first line of the deriv constructor, you specify the call to the base class's constructor. We'll be putting in all the values here.

Listing 10-3 shows the constructor added to TEFIL.CPP. It derives the file_win object from the dialog object, but it doesn't accept any of the old defaults that we've been using to make dialog objects easy to use.

Listing 10-3: TEFIL.CPP

```
// TEFIL.CPP -- file-related classes, Tiny Editor
// copyright 1995, Martin L. Rinehart


#include <STDIO.H>
#include <STRING.H>


#include "TEWIN.H"
#include "TEFIL.H"


file_win::file_win( char* file_name, FILE* tf ) :
    dialog( file_name, 5, 2, 75, 20 )
{
    mem_file = new memfile( tf );
}

file_win::~file_win()
{
    ; // tk
}


memline::memline( memline* after_line, char* txt )
```

The header line specifies creating a file_win object with a filename and a text file stream. In turn, it inherits from the base dialog class, passing the filename on as a title for the dialog window and then specifying a much larger box than our default dialog.

After creating the underlying box (a dialog object is a popup object, which is, in turn, a box object) we proceed to build the file_win by creating a memfile from the text file stream. Remember that this will actually read the disk file into the linked list.

We'll fill in the destructor when it comes time to implement commands like exit and quit. For now, let's create a file_win in the mainline and see what we've got.

Trying the File Window Object

Listing 10-4 shows the new TE.CPP, building a file_win object (and pausing after the build). Try Alt+F9 on this and see if you can fix the bug on your own.

Listing 10-4: TE.CPP

```
if ( !infile )
{
    printf( "\nCouldn't open file" );
    getch();
    exit( 1 );
}


file_win* fw = new file_win( sd->sval(), infile );
getch();


fclose( infile );


delete fw;


return 0;
```

I get a whole bunch of errors, beginning with an *undefined symbol* error. The root cause of each error is the same: We didn't include the TEFIL.H header file in TE.CPP. Without my troubling you with a listing, just go ahead and add this file and see what happens.

T I P

An *undefined symbol* sometimes means a simple typo, but more often than not it means you forgot to include a header file. Don't waste time on the other errors until you've included all the header files. Leaving just one header out typically causes a cascade of errors.

With TEFIL.H included, your program should run and pop up a large window, similar to the one shown in Figure 10-1.

CNTL+F9

OK.

Figure 10-1: The first file_win pops up.

We're certainly heading in the right direction, but I'm not really pleased with the result. It wants some improvement.

Making It Look Professional

To begin our improvements, the filename is, to be polite, not a very attractive window title. Let's start by doing a nice job on this title.

Improving the Title

If you look at the TCLite file windows, you'll see that they use the title, neatly centered. There is a single space on either side of the title, and it's written in all caps. Let's do our own title this way.

I've created a routine called new_titleize(). Its job is to take a string and make it suitable for use as a window title. That means having one blank on either end and capitalizing all the letters. The prefix "new" reminds me that it uses the *new* operator to create a character array, so I should use the *delete* operator as soon as I'm done with it.

If our supply of routines like this one were larger, we'd create a library file and add to it. For now, however, it's enough just to add this routine to TE.CPP. Listing 10-5 shows the function to add.

Listing 10-5: TE.CPP

```
void startup()
{
    textattr( WHITE_BLUE );
    clrscr();


    setcursortype( _NOCURSOR );
}


char* new_titleize( char* text )
{
/* returns pointer to copy of text changed as follows:

One leading blank precedes 1st non-blank.
One trailing blank follows last non-blank.
All letters are capitalized.

*/

    char* nb1, * nb2;   // pointers to non-blanks

    nb1 = text;         // start at beginning

    while ( *nb1 )      // find first non-blank
    {
        if( (*nb1) > 32 )
```

```
            break;

        nb1++;
    }

    nb2 = nb1 + strlen(nb1); // start at end

    while ( nb2 >= nb1 )         // back up to last non-blank
    {
        nb2--;
        if ( (*nb2) > 32 )
            break;
    }

// copy trimmed string into new char array
        char save = *(++nb2);
        *nb2 = 0;               // damages source

        int len = nb2 - nb1 + ③; string, blank, NULL

        char* ret = new char[ len ];

        *ret = ' ';
        strcpy( ret+1, nb1 );

        *nb2 = save;         // repairs damage

    // end new char array correctly
        *(ret+len-2) = ' ';
        *(ret+len-1) = 0;

    // capitalize string
        char* cp;
        for ( cp = ret+1; *cp; cp++ )
            *cp = toupper( *cp );

    return ret;
}
```

// end of TE.CPP

I didn't build the original in one big chunk, as you probably know by now. But I'll let you put it in all at once so we can move on with our work. The to-upper() function is a built-in, defined in CTYPE.H.

Listing 10-6 shows the changes you need to make to main(), in TE.CPP, to use this function.

Listing 10-6: TE.CPP

```
// TE.CPP -- Tiny Editor
// Copyright 1995, Martin L. Rinehart

#include <CONIO.H>
#include <STDIO.H>
#include <STDLIB.H>
#include <STRING.H>
#include <CTYPE.H>

#include "TEWIN.H"
#include "TECMD.H"
#include "TEFIL.H"

void startup();
char* new_titleize( char* );

#define MAX_CHARS 1024

char inbuf[ MAX_CHARS ];

int main()
{
    startup();

    string_dialog* sd = new string_dialog(
        "test.fil                              ",
        " Open File " );

    FILE* infile = fopen( sd->sval(), "rt" );

    if ( !infile )
```

```
    {
        printf( "\nCouldn't open file" );
        getch();
        exit( 1 );
    }

    char* title = new_titleize( sd->sval() );
    file_win* fw = new file_win( title, infile );
    delete title;

    getch();

    fclose( infile );
```

Once you have entered this code, run it again and see what you think of the result. I think it's looking a lot more professional.

Text Files Need Their Own Colors and Border

Before we leave the display code, I'd like to change the colors of this box to ones more conducive to text editing. While we're at it, I'd also like to choose a distinctive border style to distinguish our file windows from other dialog boxes.

The problem that we face is one of planning. More exactly, the problem is lack of planning. We didn't build the dialog box so that you could modify the underlying box colors or border string. We need to retrofit this capability.

We're not really in the sort of trouble that you'll meet later on, but let's attack the problem as if we were. Assume that your dialog box class is in use in lots of places—enough places so that it will be a real problem to find them all, never mind changing them. You want to make any changes in such a way that existing uses of the dialog class are not affected.

Here's one example of a change that will add a capability but won't impact existing code:

```
// existing code:
    void foo()
    {
        int i1 = 1;
        int i2 = 2;
        ...
```

```
// more flexible code:
    void foo( int i1=1, int i2=2 )
    {
        . . .
```

In the existing code, in the example, the two integer variables are always initialized to 1 and 2. In the more flexible version, the two optional parameters default to the same values when you call the function without arguments. But they also let you provide these values as arguments, if you want to change them.

In general, adding optional parameters (they must come after any existing parameters) lets you enhance your code without impacting the routines that use the existing version.

First, let's just assume that we've enhanced our dialog box with additional optional parameters. Listing 10-7 adds the border style and colors we'll need in the file_win constructor in TEFIL.CPP.

Listing 10-7: TEFIL.CPP

```
file_win::file_win( char* file_name, FILE* tf ) :
    dialog( file_name, 5, 2, 75, 20,
    SING_DOUB, FILE_WIN_OUT_CLR, FILE_WIN_CON_CLR )
{
    mem_file = new memfile( tf );
}
```

We haven't defined these color constants yet, but we'll get to that when we improve the dialog constructor. This is our next job. Begin by adding the two #defines shown in Listing 10-8 to TEWIN.H.

Listing 10-8: TEWIN.H

```
#define DIAG_CON_CLR 63 // Hi white on cyan
#define DIAG_TIP_CLR 48 // Black on cyan

#define FILE_WIN_OUT_CLR 126 // Hi yellow on white
#define FILE_WIN_CON_CLR   7 //    white   on black

#define SINGLE    " ┌─┐│─└┘│ "
#define DOUBLE    " ╔═╗║═╚╝║ "
```

Then, also in TEWIN.H, change the declaration of the dialog constructor to include the extra optional parameters, as shown in Listing 10-9.

Listing 10-9: TEWIN.H

```
class dialog : public popup
{
protected:
    char* title;

public:
    dialog( char* ttl,
        int lf=15, int tp=8, int rt=65, int bt=15,
        char* brdr=SINGLE,
        int oc=DIAG_OUT_CLR, int cc=DIAG_CON_CLR );
    ~dialog();
};
```

Last, add the new parameters to the dialog constructor in TEWIN.CPP. Listing 10-10 shows this change.

Listing 10-10: TEWIN.CPP

```
dialog::dialog( char* ttl,
    int lf, int tp, int rt, int bt,
    char* brdr, int oc, int cc )
    : popup( lf, tp, rt, bt, brdr, oc, cc )
{
```

Now run this code, and you should get the good-looking box shown in Figure 10-2. Of course, this run also uncovers a small bug—the title is not written in the correct color.

That last bug is simple enough. Can you find it?

In the dialog constructor in TEWIN.CPP, the dialog box color was hard-coded. Replace the textattr() line with the one shown in Listing 10-11, and you'll be set.

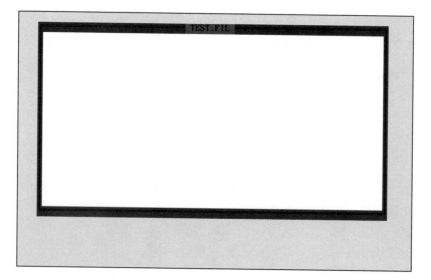

Figure 10-2: An attractive title and border for the file_win box.

Listing 10-11: TEWIN.CPP

```
int tloc = ( rt - lf + 1 - tlen ) / 2;

textattr( oc );
gotoxy( lf+tloc, tp );
cprintf( title );
```

With this last change, our file_win dialog box is just right. We've fixed this up without any impact on the other routines that use the dialog class, too. (You've been testing that as you go, of course. Every time you run the code, the file-name dialog box double-checks a previous dialog object.)

It's time to get on to displaying the text file in this box.

DISPLAYING THE FILE

If our text file would appear in the box, I'm sure you'd start thinking that we were really going to create an editor. We'll handle that in this section.

We've written a complete intra-line editor for our string_field object, but we're not going to use that code here. To keep focused on the task at hand, I ignored the complication of scrolling when we wrote that code. For a text editor, we can't ignore that. So we're going back to square one. The good news is that we can use some of those support routines, like left_word() and right_word(), to help us along.

T I P

Make a mental note to replace the string_field code with a special case of the code we're working on now, when you go on to improve this editor after you finish this book. It will save some space. More important, having less code simplifies maintenance.

Our first routine, one that we'll use constantly, displays the text inside the box. We'll want it to start by clearing the box. Then we'll start writing from a line passed as a parameter, and we'll quit writing lines when we come to the end of the text or to the end of the box.

Displaying All Lines

Before we look at the top-level routine, let's take a look at its main part. It's very simple. A show_line() routine is responsible for displaying each line. This function takes care of details like starting at the correct character (the screen can scroll left and right) and stopping just before the right border, if the whole line doesn't fit.

A variable, cl, points to the current line. It is initialized with a pointer to whatever line is passed into the starting line parameter. Skipping from line to line in the text is as simple as this:

```
cl = cl->next;
```

As usual, doing the typical work is only a small part of the code. We can skip from one line to the next this way, but we have to be sure we don't skip right on past the end of the file. The whole skip code looks like this:

```
if ( cl->next )
    cl = cl->next;
else
    break;
```

The break statement breaks out of a loop that passes over all the rows in the window. By now you should be recognizing that condition as C-programmer shorthand, as these statements illustrate:

```
if ( cl->next ) ...

// same as:

if ( cl->next != NULL ) ...
```

The whole working part of the show_all() function is this:

```
for ( int row = top+1; row < btm; row++ )
{
    show_line( row, cl->text );

    if ( cl->next )
        cl = cl->next;
    else
        break;
}
```

This is all it takes to march down the window, writing line after line of text, stopping when we run out of text or out of window. Of course, we have other work to do, to clean up all the exceptions.

First, we initialize our linked-list structure with a starting line. This isn't actually text, so we can't write it out. We have to skip over this memline if it is the line passed as an argument. (Without this line, you'll have trouble when you delete all the lines in your file. You need one extra or your whole linked list will be lost.) This code skips past that line if it can, but it doesn't skip if there are no lines of text following:

```
memline* cl = startline;

if ( !cl->prev )          // at start of memfile
{
    if ( cl->next )       // has 1 or more lines
        cl = cl->next;
}
```

Second, and a related problem, show_all() could be called to display an empty list. That contingency is handled this way:

```
if ( (!cl->text) && (!cl->next) ) // at end
    return;
```

Again, you should be recognizing this C idiom:

```
if ( !cl->text ) ...


// same as:


if ( cl->text == NULL ) ...
```

Third, there's bookkeeping and housecleaning to be done. You have to keep track of which line is at the top of the display, you have to clear the display, and so on. Again, the working part of the code is not the largest part.

Listing 10-12 shows the routine, added to TEFIL.CPP. (We'll add to TEFIL.H in just a bit—you can't compile or run this yet.)

Listing 10-12: TEFIL.CPP

```
file_win::~file_win()
{
    ; // tk
}

void file_win::show_all( memline* startline )
{
    memline* cl = startline;

    if ( !cl->prev )        // at start of memfile
    {
        if ( cl->next )      // has 1 or more lines
            cl = cl->next;
    }

    top_line = cl;

    textattr( FILE_WIN_CON_CLR );
```

```
    clear();

    if ( (!cl->text) && (!cl->next) )  // at end
        return;

    for ( int row = top+1; row < btm; row++ )
    {
        show_line( row, cl->text );

        if ( cl->next )
            cl = cl->next;
        else
            break;
    }
}
```

```
memline::memline( memline* after_line, char* txt )
```

This code depends on the show_line() routine to do its actual display. This is our next concern.

Displaying a Single Line

As was the case with show_all(), the working part of the show_line() function is simple:

```
gotoxy( lft+1, row );
    cprintf( str );
```

Here, the row and str variables are parameters passed into show_line(). The lft variable is a data member of the file_win object. (Actually, lft comes from the box object, inherited by the popup, in turn inherited by the dialog, and finally inherited by file_win.)

Unfortunately, real-life code is never as simple as the working part, and this is no exception. First, we check to see if the string is empty (a blank line). If it is, we're done before we start:

```
if ( !*str )
    return;
```

Software engineering purists object to having more than one return in a function. I often use a return at the top of a function after a "do we need to do this work?" check. Try rewriting the show_line() function (Listing 10-13) with a single return at the bottom and see which form you prefer. Both ways will work, and both can be clean, maintainable code. But you should pick just one style and stick to it.

N O T E

C++ functions return from the closing brace at the very end of the function, even if there is an explicit return statement in the code. You can see this clearly by using F7 to step through a function in the debugger. The closing brace is where local variables are released. If the local variables are structures or objects, their destructors are called here.

If we don't beat a hasty retreat for having no text, we need to check the length of the string and declare it to a new data member of file_win, lchar. The lchar (left character) variable holds the column number (counting from the right) of the leftmost displayed character of the string. (If lchar equals zero, the window is scrolled all the way to the left. Higher values are the number of characters scrolled to the right.)

If the starting display character is past the end of the string, again there's nothing to display, so we exit. On the other hand, if the starting character is in the text, we move the pointer up to this character and adjust the remaining string length:

```
int len = strlen( str );

if( len <= lchar )
    return;

str = str + lchar;
len = len - lchar;
```

The str variable is a parameter. This means it is local to this function. When you pass variables to a C++ function, they are passed by value, so str is a copy of the address of a string. (It's actually the address of a data member of memline, a linked-list object, but your local copy doesn't know anything about that.) When you fiddle with str (say, by adding lchar as we do here) you don't change the calling value.

N O T E

C++ provides another way of using arguments to call by reference, not value. A call by reference lets the called routine manipulate the actual values in the calling routine. This may be precisely what you want to do, or it may be an invitation to write truly horrible, unmaintainable software.

At this point we've skipped over any null text or text that has been scrolled off to the left. Now we can worry about text that is too wide to fit. If the text is too wide, we'll drop a temporary null into the character that would have fallen on the right border of the box. Then we can write the string. If we drop this temporary null in, we have to save the character we overwrote and replace it after we do the string write.

Listing 10-13 shows the full code, also in TEFIL.CPP.

Listing 10-13: TEFIL.CPP

```
}

void file_win::show_line( int row, char* str )
{
    if ( !*str )
        return;

    int len = strlen( str );

    if( len <= lchar )
        return;

    str = str + lchar;
    len = len - lchar;
```

```
    int toobig = len > lwid;
    char save;

    if ( toobig )
    {
        save = *(str+lwid);
        *(str+lwid) = 0;
    }

    gotoxy( lft+1, row );
    cprintf( str );

    if ( toobig )
        *(str+lwid) = save;
}
```

memline::memline(memline* after_line, char* txt)

Clearing the Display

The final support routine is the one that clears the display. (In our first use of
show_all(), we'll be writing the text into an empty box, so clearing isn't necessary. But we'll also use show_all() when we scroll up and down, when clearing
will be very necessary.)

This one isn't really interesting except for one problem: how do you test a
clear() routine when it's working on a box that is already clear?

My solution was to write the clear() code to clear exactly one character more
than was necessary. This extra character will overwrite the right border of the
box. When you run this in the debugger, you can see the right border disappear,
one character at a time, as you step through the display loop. If that works, you
can then change clear() to start one character too far to the left. That will wipe
out the left border as you step through the loop. Then you can put the original
value back and be confident that your routine works.

Listing 10-14 shows the clear() routine, which you should add to TEFIL.CPP.

Listing 10-14: TEFIL.CPP

```
}

void file_win::clear()
{
    blanks[lwid] = 0;

    for ( int row=top+1; row < btm; row++ )
    {
        gotoxy( lft+1, row );
        cprintf( blanks );
    }

    blanks[lwid+1] = ' ';
}
```

```
memline::memline( memline* after_line, char* txt )
```

Remember to set a breakpoint at the for loop in clear() when you first start to test. You should completely test this routine before you go on to write the actual text. (Alternatively, you can comment out the call to clear() and write the text first. Then go back and test clear() thoroughly.)

Putting the Display Together

Now that all our code is in place, we've got to add our new features to the class definition and then watch the code run. You have the big advantage here of using routines that I've already debugged, but it's still a good idea to step through them in the debugger. We're both human, after all.

First, let's add what we need to TEFIL.H. Listing 10-15 shows the additions you need to make.

Listing 10-15: TEFIL.H

```
// TEFIL.H -- file-related classes, Tiny Editor
// Copyright 1995, Martin L. Rinehart


#define TRUE  1
#define FALSE 0
```

```
class memfile;
class memline;

class file_win : public dialog
{
protected:
    memfile* mem_file;

    memline* top_line;
    memline* cur_line;

    int lchar, lwid;
    char* blanks;

    int curx, cury; // window relative cursor location

    int ins_mode;

public:
    file_win( char* file_name, FILE* tf );
    ~file_win();

    void show_all( memline* startline );
    void show_line( int row, char* str );
    void clear();
};

struct memline // all public members!
{
    memline* prev, * next;
    char* text;

    memline( memline* after_line, char* txt );
    ~memline();
};

class memfile
```

```
{
```

```
friend class file_win;
```

```
protected:
```

With these changes in the header, you can go on to the constructor in
TEFIL.CPP. Listing 10-16 shows those additions.

Listing 10-16: TEFIL.CPP

```
file_win::file_win( char* file_name, FILE* tf ) :
    dialog( file_name, 5, 2, 75, 20,
    SING_DOUB, FILE_WIN_OUT_CLR, FILE_WIN_CON_CLR )
{
    mem_file = new memfile( tf );

    lchar = 0;
    lwid = rgt - lft - 1;

    blanks = new char[81];
    for ( char* cp=blanks; cp < blanks+80; cp++ )
        *cp = ' ';
    blanks[81] = 0;

    curx = cury = 0;
    ins_mode = TRUE;

    show_all( mem_file->head_line );
}

file_win::~file_win()
{
    delete blanks;
}

void file_win::show_all( memline* startline )
```

Run this code in the debugger, beginning by setting your cursor at the call to *Run!* show_all() and pressing F4. Continue with F7 to step into show_all() and step on through it. Don't forget to run the tests on clear() that I suggested. You want to be sure that this routine is perfect, since it will be a real workhorse in all the code that follows.

Got it all? I tested mine by fiddling with some of the constants. In the file_win constructor, you can try shrinking the default window to one that won't fit all the lines in your test file. That tests another case.

Combine that test with shrinking the width until it fits some, but not all, of your text lines. Test a width that just fits all of at least one line, to be sure you handle the right edge correctly.

We can't scroll the window yet, but you can simulate scrolling by assigning an initial lchar value that's greater than zero. Again, test several values, to see what happens as you scroll the screen to the left.

Don't forget to test an empty input file. When you are done, and you are confident your display code is really solid, we can go on to turning on the cursor and moving it around the window.

MOVING THE CURSOR

Now you've had your first taste of the Tiny Editor that we're building. It's time to actually implement the editing structure. The cursor movement routines are simple to code, so they're a good place to get started.

Turning the Cursor On and Off

Before you can move the cursor, you have to turn it on, of course. When we turn it on, we'll want to be complete and turn it back off again. Let's start with a simple routine that sets the cursor to the same block or underscore that we've used before.

Again, we're defying the normal DOS convention and using the block cursor for overstrike mode and the small cursor for insert mode, which is consistent with the behavior of TCLite's built-in editor. We'll do this work from an empty edit() method, to get a head start on the structure that we'll need for editing.

Listing 10-17 shows the additions to the class definition in TEFIL.H, and Listing 10-18 shows the code you need to add to TEFIL.CPP to get this working.

Listing 10-17: TEFIL.H

```
class file_win : public dialog
{
protected:
    memfile* mem_file;

    memline* top_line;
    memline* cur_line;

    int lchar, lwid;
    char* blanks;

    int curx, cury; // window relative cursor location

    int ins_mode;

public:
    file_win( char* file_name, FILE* tf );
    ~file_win();

    void show_all( memline* startline );
    void show_line( int row, char* str );
    void clear();
    void edit();
    void show_cursor();
};
```

Listing 10-18: TEFIL.CPP

```
}

void file_win::edit()
{
    show_cursor();

    getch(); // editing goes here!

    setcursortype( _NOCURSOR );
```

```
}

void file_win::show_cursor( )
{
    setcursortype(
        insmode ?   _NORMALCURSOR : _SOLIDCURSOR );
}
```

```
memline::memline( memline* after_line, char* txt )
```

With these additions, you'll have everything ready. Finally, (you don't need a listing, do you?) add a call to edit(), just after the show_all() call in the file_win constructor. That will display your cursor, set for the normal insert mode.

You can change the default ins_mode assignment in the constructor from TRUE to FALSE, to test the other possible call to show_cursor(). The only problem that remains is that the cursor is displayed exactly where we left the hardware cursor after the last write—at the end of the last line of text.

It would be nice to have the cursor start at the upper-left corner of the text file, wouldn't it? For that, let's implement a go() method that positions the cursor. Since many of our operations will depend on knowing the location of the cursor, we'll ask go() to keep track of where it sets things. Also, we'll call go() with window-relative coordinates (1, 1 is the top-left writable position), so go() will have to convert these to screen-based coordinates. Listing 10-19 shows the code to add to TEFIL.CPP.

Listing 10-19: TEFIL.CPP

```
void file_win::show_cursor( )
{
    setcursortype(
        insmode ?   NORMALCURSOR : SOLIDCURSOR );
}

void file_win::go( int x, int y )
{
    curx = x;
    cury = y;
```

```
    gotoxy( 1ft+x, top+y );
}
```

```
memline::memline( memline* after_line, char* txt )
```

That's simple enough, isn't it? Now add a declaration of go() in the header file, TEFIL.H. Add the following two lines between the show_all() and the edit() calls in the constructor, and you'll be in business:

```
go( 1, 1 );
cur_line = top_line;
```

Got it? Good. I'm going to be asking you to do more and more work on your own, since by now you are becoming a C++ programmer and don't need a listing for every minor operation.

T I P

Did you get stuck on something you thought you knew but couldn't make work on your own? Look through the later disk listings to find out exactly how I've done something. This isn't really very convenient, but it isn't supposed to be, either. Trying on your own will quickly show you what you know and what you only thought you knew.

If you're like me, that cursor blinking happily in the corner makes you really want to press a key and have something happen. We'll start by getting our structure set up.

Building the Editing Structure

Actually, we've just about built the edit structure. The way we built our string_field is the way we'll build editing here. Again, you'll have the edit() routine call an edit_do() routine that will actually do all the hard work.

The one new wrinkle is that we'll have the TECMD code pass edit commands, rather than keystrokes. This will simplify our code in edit_do(). More important, it will give us considerable flexibility in implementing the commands.

For example, you may want a one-key command for something that I prefer to do with a two-key sequence. That just means that you'll have slightly different code in your TECMD than I do. This means that you'll do it your way, I'll do it my way, and we'll both be happy. In the long run, it also means that you can add a keyboard customization feature or a mouse without needing to rebuild the editor itself.

Let's begin by creating a header file of edit commands that we can include in both TECMD.CPP and TEFIL.CPP. My starting file is shown in Listing 10-20. I've named it EDITCMDS.H. It's all new, so it's not on disk.

Listing 10-20: EDITCMDS.H

```
// EDITCMDS.H -- edit command defs in Tiny Editor
// Copyright 1995, Martin L. Rinehart

#define EXIT           1000
#define NOP            1999


#define CURSOR_UP      1001
#define CURSOR_DN      1002
#define CURSOR_LF      1003
#define CURSOR_RT      1004


// end of EDITCMDS.H
```

You can see that I've adopted the integers from 1000 to 1999 for edit command identifiers, beginning with EXIT and ending with NOP. In between these values we can just assign numbers as we add commands.

N O T E

Assembly language programmers sometimes need to pad a program. For example, some instructions must start on a full word boundary, which may require an extra byte if the last instruction ends in the middle of a word. The instruction NOP (pronounced "no op" since it means *no operation*) is provided for this purpose. Even when you don't need padding, a NOP command can be handy as you construct a program.

Next, we'll want to improve the TECMD.CPP code so that it has a specific function to return edit commands. This will include another switch, but it will use the #defined names in KEYDEFS.H as input and the #defined names in EDITCMDS.H as outputs. Listing 10-21 shows the additions, including the new edit_cmd() function.

Listing 10-21: TECMD.CPP

```cpp
// TECMD.CPP -- command processor for Tiny Editor
// copyright 1995, Martin L. Rinehart

#include <CONIO.H>

#include "TECMD.H"
#include "KEYDEFS.H"
#include "EDITCMDS.H"

int user_cmd()
{
    int c = getch();
    if ( !c )
        return 256 + getch();
    else
        return c;
}

int edit_cmd()
{
    int c = user_cmd();

    switch ( c )
    {
        case ESC:
            return EXIT;

        case UP_ARROW:
        case CTRL_E:
            return CURSOR_UP;
```

```
        case DN_ARROW:
        case CTRL_X:
            return CURSOR_DN;


        case LF_ARROW:
        case CTRL_S:
            return CURSOR_LF;


        case RT_ARROW:
        case CTRL_D:
            return CURSOR_RT;


        default:
            return NOP;

    }
}
```

```
int yn_cmd()
```

After you add the new #includes and edit_cmd() to TECMD.CPP, go ahead and add a declaration for edit_cmd() to TECMD.H. Next, we'll add the edit_do() function to TEFIL.CPP.

Listing 10-22 shows the new edit_do(). It should remind you of the edit_do() method we built into the string_field object. Also, the revised edit() method is also shown in this listing.

Listing 10-22: TEFIL.CPP

```
void file_win::edit()
{
    show_cursor();


    int done = FALSE;


    while( !done )
    {
        done = edit_do( edit_cmd() );

    }
```

```
        setcursortype(_NOCURSOR );
}
```

```
int file_win::edit_do( int cmd )
{
    int done = FALSE;

    switch ( cmd )
    {
        case EXIT:
        {
            done = TRUE;
            break;
        }


    }


    return done;
}
```

```
void file_win::show_cursor( )
```

Before you can run this code, you'll need to #include both TECMD.H and
EDITCMDS.H in TEFIL.CPP. You'll also need to add the declaration for
edit_do() in TEFIL.H. I've added the edit_do() declaration as a private method,
under the other methods.

H I N T

You can mix methods and data members together in a class definition, but this
arrangement doesn't lead to easily readable code. If you keep them separate,
your maintenance will be easier.

We added the declaration of edit_do() in the string_field class in a separate private section, which is just what I've done again with this edit_do(). I use this technique:

```
class whatever
{
protected:
     data member 1;
     data member 2;
     etc.;

public:
     whatever();
     ~whatever();
     more public methods( go, here );

private:
     private method1();
     etc.;
};
```

This arrangement makes the private methods stand out when you look at the class definition. As in so many cases, you can do it this way or you can do it some other way that suits you, but you should always do it the same way.

When you run this code, you'll get an editor that can respond appropriately to the Esc key. It will wait patiently while you press every other key on your keyboard. It returns a NOP or one of the cursor movement commands for any other keystroke. Your edit_do() routine, of course, ignores everything except EXIT, which is only sent in response to the Esc key.

Next, except for one little detail, we'll teach the edit_do() routine to actually move the cursor around. First, though, there is an extra pause that happens after you press Esc. You can see that the Esc leaves edit(), since it turns your cursor off. This is fine. But the extra wait is a nuisance. It comes from a getch() in TE.CPP. Get rid of this one before you go on. (Don't get rid of the getch() after the error message—it's the one that precedes fclose() that you want to remove.)

Moving the Cursor

With all that setup work behind us, we can bring the cursor to life easily. Let's start by teaching it to go down. The edit_cmd() function already sends a CUR-SOR_DN message if you press the down-arrow key or Ctrl+X. The only job left is to teach edit_do() to respond appropriately.

Before you do that, add the debugging msg() routine to your TEFIL.CPP, as shown in Listing 10-23.

Listing 10-23: TEFIL.CPP

```cpp
// TEFIL.CPP -- file-related classes, Tiny Editor
// copyright 1995, Martin L. Rinehart

#include <STDIO.H>
#include <CONIO.H>
#include <STRING.H>

#include "TECMD.H"
#include "TEWIN.H"
#include "TEFIL.H"
#include "EDITCMDS.H"

void msg( char* debug )
{
    // debugging message
    int x, y;
    x = wherex(); y = wherey();

    gotoxy( 1, 1 );
    cprintf( "                                      " );
    gotoxy( 1, 1 );
    cprintf( debug );

    gotoxy( x, y );
}

file_win::file_win( char* file_name, FILE* tf ) :
```

By adding this function at the top of the file, you don't even need a function declaration. We'll get rid of msg() when we are done debugging. It uses the top line to write whatever message we want. This will come in very handy as we build functionality into edit_do().

We'll start with CURSOR_DN. The first thing we want to know is that our system is all working together, passing messages correctly. (It's passing messages, like CURSOR_DN, internally. Our msg() function lets us take a look at what it's doing, externally.)

Start by adding the two cases shown in Listing 10-24 to edit_do().

Listing 10-24: TEFIL.CPP

```
int file_win::edit_do( int cmd )
{
    int done = FALSE;

    switch ( cmd )
    {
        case EXIT:
        {
            done = TRUE;
            break;
        }

        case CURSOR_DN:
        {
            msg( "cursor down" );
            break;
        }

        case NOP:
        {
            msg( " " );
            break;
        }

    }
```

```
    return done;
}
```

The CURSOR_DN case will just tell you what it is supposed to do. The NOP case will clear the message area. This lets you conveniently test both the down-arrow key and Ctrl+X, without needing to run the program twice. When you run this code, it should respond to either of these keypresses by showing the "cursor down" message on the top line, as shown in Figure 10-3.

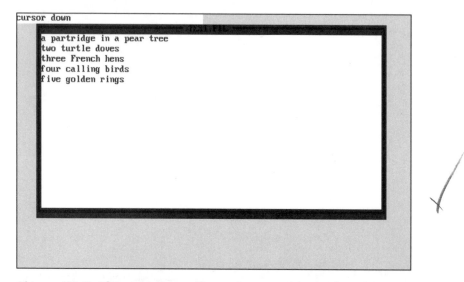

Figure 10-3: The message tells us that our internal messages are working.

Now we can actually get to work on moving the cursor down. As usual, this is quite simple, but we'll have more code for the exceptions than for the operation itself. To go down, we'll need to move the cursor down one line and record the new location in the data members we've created to keep track of the cursor. We also need to note the new current line in the linked-list memfile.

The exceptions are that we can't move down if we're at the last text line or if we're already on the bottom line of the window. If we're on the bottom line of the window, but not at the last line of text, we'll want to scroll the screen, but this can wait for later. For now, we'll need some support code.

Let's start with a move() routine. We can write one that looks like our go() routine but takes an incremental approach. This is how it will work:

```
move(  1,  0 ); // move right one column
move(  0,  1 ); // move down  one row

move( -1,  0 ); // move left  one column
move(  0, -1 ); // move up    one row
```

Like go(), move() will update the curx and cury variables, in addition to actually moving the cursor. Also like go(), it will just do as it's told, presuming that the operation makes sense. (If you tell it to move past the edge of the window, it will go right ahead and do so.) Listing 10-25 shows the move() routine in TEFIL.CPP.

Listing 10-25: TEFIL.CPP

```
void file_win::go( int x, int y )
{
    curx = x;
    cury = y;

    gotoxy( lft+x, top+y );
}

void file_win::move( int dx, int dy )
{
/* Calling routine MUST ensure that result of move
   is within the window!
*/
    curx += dx;
    cury += dy;

    gotoxy( lft+curx, top+cury );
}

memline::memline( memline* after_line, char* txt )
```

The move() routine makes use of the += assignment operator. It is defined this way:

```
x += add_this;

// same as:

x = x + add_this;
```

You can also do assignments that subtract, multiply, divide, shift, and so on. For a complete list of these assignment operators, press Shift+F1 and press first the = sign and then Enter.

N O T E

The assignment operator is defined in the documentation using the term *lvalue*. The definition avoids circularity but is quite obscure. Speaking circularly, an lvalue is a value that you can put on the left side of an assignment operator. A simple variable is an lvalue. A pointer is an lvalue. An arithmetic expression is *not* an lvalue. The thing pointed to by a pointer (*ptr) is an lvalue if it is something like a char or an int. It is not an lvalue if it is something like a string_dialog object.

When you add move(), also add a declaration for it in TEFIL.H.

Now let's add is_*xxx*_line() routines, where the *xxx* is either "top" or "bot." These will let us test before performing an up or down command. Listing 10-26 shows these two functions in TEFIL.CPP.

Listing 10-26: TEFIL.CPP

```
void file_win::move( int dx, int dy )
{
/* Calling routine MUST ensure that result of move
   is within the window!
*/
    curx += dx;
    cury += dy;
```

```
    gotoxy( lft+curx, top+cury );
}
```

```
int file_win::is_top_line()
{
    if ( !cur_line->prev )
        return TRUE;
    else
        return ( !cur_line->prev->prev );
}

int file_win::is_bot_line()
{
    if ( !cur_line )
        return TRUE;
    else
        return ( !cur_line->next );
}
```

```
memline::memline( memline* after_line, char* txt )
```

Don't forget to add declarations for these functions in TEFIL.H. They can be declared as private methods.

As our last piece of preparation, let's add some #defines that will make it easy to write code to check on our window edges. Add these to TEFIL.H, as shown in Listing 10-27.

Listing 10-27: TEFIL.H

```
// TEFIL.H -- file-related classes, Tiny Editor
// Copyright 1995, Martin L. Rinehart

#define TRUE  1
#define FALSE 0

#define AT_TOP_WIND  ( cury == 1 )
#define AT_BTM_WIND  ( (top+cury) == (btm-1) )
```

```
#define AT_LFT_WIND   ( curx == 1 )
#define AT_RGT_WIND   ( (lft+curx) == (rgt-1) )


class memfile;
class memline;
```

Now let's go ahead and move the cursor down! Revise the CURSOR_DN case in edit_do(), TEFIL.CPP, as shown in Listing 10-28.

Listing 10-28: TEFIL.CPP

```
        case CURSOR_DN:
        {
            if( !is_bot_line() )
            {
                if ( !AT_BTM_WIND )
                {
                    cur_line = cur_line->next;
                    move( 0, 1 );
                }
                else
                {
                    msg( "at window bottom" );
                }
            }
            else
            {
                msg( "at EOF line" );
            }
            break;
        }

        case NOP:
```

With this code added, you can actually press the down-arrow key (or Ctrl+X) and watch the cursor go down! I'll bet that really makes you want to press the up-arrow key and watch it go back up, doesn't it? Finally, we've got all our infrastructure in place, so that is dead simple. Add the new edit_do() case shown in Listing 10-29 to TEFIL.CPP, and your cursor will be bidirectional.

Listing 10-29: TEFIL.CPP

```
case EXIT:
{
    done = TRUE;
    break;
}


case CURSOR_UP:
{
    if ( !AT_TOP_WIND )
    {
        cur_line = cur_line->prev;
        move( 0, -1 );
    }
    else
    {
        if ( is_top_line() )
            msg( "at BOF" );
        else
            msg( "scroll up" );
    }
    break;
}


case CURSOR_DN:
```

Doesn't that feel good? While we're on a roll, let's see if that infrastructure won't take us right and left, too. Add the two new cases in Listing 10-30 to edit_do() in TEFIL.CPP and try those directions, too.

Listing 10-30: TEFIL.CPP

```
case CURSOR_DN:
{
    if( !is_bot_line() )
    {
        if ( !AT_BTM_WIND )
        {
```

```
                    cur_line = cur_line->next;
                    move( 0, 1 );
                }
                else
                {
                    msg( "at window bottom" );
                }
            }
            else
            {
                msg( "at EOF line" );
            }
            break;
        }

        case CURSOR_RT:
        {
            if ( !AT_RGT_WIND )
                move( 1, 0 );
            else
                msg( "scroll right" );


            break;
        }

        case CURSOR_LF:
        {
            if ( !AT_LFT_WIND )
                move( -1, 0 );
            else
            {
                if ( lchar == 0 )
                    msg( "at left" );
                else
                    msg( "scroll left" );
            }
            break;
        }
```

```
case NOP:
{
    msg( "  " );
    break;
}
```

With these cases in place, you can move in all four directions. Of course, testing some more exception conditions would be nice, but I'm not going to worry about that just yet.

If you could resize the screen, you could test all the exception conditions, just by choosing an appropriate screen size and then moving the cursor. So instead of doing some more tests now, I'm going to go right ahead and implement screen resizing first. Then we can do exhaustive testing on our cursor movement code.

For now, our editor is finally under way. You're really becoming a C++ programmer.

SUMMARY

In this chapter, we focused on writing C++, not learning about C++. From here on we'll be spending a lot more of our time doing it than we'll spend learning new features.

Our task was to build a file window. We used our dialog box for the window and added a memfile object member, to get the file. (Of course, that's really the in-memory, linked-list copy of the file.)

We declared class name variables in advance of defining our classes, so that the compiler could handle memfile and memline references in the file_win class definition. We saw that these names, once we define or declare them, become additional C++ keywords, just like "while" or "int."

We used a complex constructor for our file_win class. The inherited dialog base class constructor was called with a full list of parameters, instead of the optional parameters assuming their default values.

We used the CTYPE.H header file for the first time. We wanted to improve the appearance of our file_win titles by putting the filename in all uppercase letters. The toupper() function defined in CTYPE.H was the right one for this job.

We had to modify the constructor of a base class to pass additional arguments through to a deeper base. We did this by adding optional parameters. This is one way that we can improve an existing class without affecting the existing uses of the class.

We added a layer to our TECMD input processor. Instead of passing keystrokes to our file_win's edit() method, it passes integer messages for each of the available edit commands. This message-passing structure is more flexible and maintainable than a keystroke-based structure.

We used the += operator and briefly considered the other compound assignment operators. We also discussed the term *lvalue,* defining it circularly as anything acceptable on the left side of an assignment operator. (The online documentation has a noncircular, but quite complex, definition.)

While we were doing this, we built the workhorse display routine, show_all(), that our Tiny Editor will depend on. We finished up by getting the cursor to move around the screen in response to messages from TECMD.

In the next chapter, we'll continue developing the Tiny Editor, beginning with commands to adjust the size of the screen.

We've built our Tiny Editor up to the point where we can read in a file, keep track of the text in a linked list in memory, and display the linked list in a dialog box. Within the dialog box, we can move the cursor.

Our next job is to make the window resizable. When you can adjust the window's size, you'll be able to see, without much trouble, if the display functions are completely debugged. We'll also be able to add the window scrolling and movement features that are currently stubbed out with debugging messages.

While we do this, we'll:

▶ Use enum to create an enumeration data type
▶ Use sprintf() to format results into a string
▶ Use the *else if* idiom as if it were a C++ statement
▶ Use the textmode() function to enter 50-line mode
▶ Distinguish multiple functions with the scope resolution operator
▶ Use polymorphic functions
▶ Let short-circuit expression analysis help our code
▶ Use multiple inline assignments

Even more than before, however, we'll be using what we know to write more code. Let's get started.

Resizing, Moving, and Scrolling

In TCLite, you've probably been using the mouse to grab the lower-right corners of the edit windows (or other windows, too) and drag them to size your windows. Did you know that you can also size your windows from the keyboard?

RESIZING THE WINDOW

If you haven't done this yet, select any file window and press Ctrl+F5 (or, from the menus, choose Window | Size). Your bottom-line status message changes to give you your options. You can move the window with any arrow key. You can size the window with Shift plus any arrow key. Enter (or Esc) signals completion. The rest of the keyboard sends NOPs.

F5 is, more or less, TCLite's window manipulation key. F5 alone toggles the current window between part- and full-screen display. Alt+F5 switches from TCLite to the DOS program screen. Ctrl+F5 enters move/resize mode. Shift+F5 is a NOP.

Since Ctrl+F5 is TCLite's choice, let's use it for our Tiny Editor, too. (If you have a preference for another favorite keystroke, by all means do it your way. One of the main reasons for having your own editor is so that it works exactly the way you want it to.)

Unfortunately, if you really want to respond to the Shift+arrow key combinations you're going to have to do some fancy programming. The getch() routine doesn't return unique values for the Shift+arrow keys. It does, however, return unique values for the Alt+arrow key combinations. Use these to add #defines for ALT_LF_ARROW and the other three to KEYDEFS.H:

```
ALT_LF_ARROW    411
ALT_RT_ARROW    413
ALT_UP_ARROW    408
ALT_DN_ARROW    416
```

H I N T

The BIOS interrupt 16h is for the keyboard. Function 0 tells you what key was pressed, and function 2 tells you the status of each of the shift-type keys (Left and Right Shift, Ctrl, Alt, and so on). At any rate, they're supposed to. DOS's proprietor has reserved many keystrokes for its own use (such as Alt+Tab for switching programs) and doesn't pass these keystrokes on to our programs. The problems with getch() aren't Borland's fault.

By the way, I got these keystroke values by running our KEYS utility. Let's continue by adding message definitions for the window commands.

Programming the Messages

Listing 11-1 shows the additions I made to EDITCMDS.H to support the window size and move commands. Go ahead and add them to your version.

Listing 11-1: EDITCMDS.H

```
// EDITCMDS.H -- edit command defs in Tiny Editor
// Copyright 1995, Martin L. Rinehart

#define EXIT            1000
#define NOP             1999

#define CURSOR_UP       1001
#define CURSOR_DN       1002
#define CURSOR_LF       1003
#define CURSOR_RT       1004

#define WIN_MOVE_UP     1901
#define WIN_MOVE_DN     1902
#define WIN_MOVE_LF     1903
#define WIN_MOVE_RT     1904

#define WIN_SIZE_UP     1911
#define WIN_SIZE_DN     1912
#define WIN_SIZE_LF     1913
#define WIN_SIZE_RT     1914

// end of EDITCMDS.H
```

With the messages available, we need to add to TECMD.CPP. The CTRL_F5 keystroke triggers a new keystroke loop. Inside this loop, we'll send WIN_MOVE or WIN_SIZE messages until the moving and sizing is finished (by an Enter or Esc keypress).

This means we'll need one switch for plain edit commands and another switch for window move/size commands. The edit_cmd() routine can become a top-level function that picks the right switch routine based on the current mode. The mode is ideally suited for implementation via an *enum* construct.

Here's one way to do modes:

```
#define NORMAL    0
#define WIN_MODE 1

int in_mode = ... // NORMAL or WIN_MODE
```

This is the way we've done our keystrokes and messages. But there's another way:

```
enum mode { normal, winmode };

mode in_mode = ... // normal or winmode
```

The enum construct creates a new data type (I've called the sample "mode") and it creates, within the braces, variables of that type. The compiler will assign each item within the enum a unique integer value, beginning with zero. You can initialize the enum values yourself, if you want:

```
enum days { sat=6, sun, mon=1, tues, wed, thur, fri };
```

The compiler increments the value for each entry in an enum list, so in this example sat==6, sun==7, mon==1, tues==2, and so on. There are two advantages to using an enum as opposed to #defining your own constants.

First, you don't have to worry about the integers. The compiler assigns them and they are all different. You can think exclusively in terms of "normal" versus "winmode" or whatever names are appropriate for the problem you're working on.

Second, the enum creates a new data type. This is a limited integer type, which should be assigned values of its own type only. Here's a sample:

```
enum mode { normal, winmode };

mode in_mode = normal;   // OK
mode in_mode = winmode;  // OK

mode in_mode = 4;        // don't do this!
mode in_mode = i-1;      // don't do this, either!
```

One of the nicest things about an enum is that you can add to it at any time. Here's a sample:

```
enum mode { normal, winmode, othermode }; // addition!

mode in_mode = normal;   // OK
mode in_mode = winmode; // OK

mode in_mode = othermode; // now this is OK, too
```

With that said, let's put an enum to work for us in TECMD.CPP. Start by renaming edit_cmd() to be plain_cmd() and then add the new edit_cmd(). Listing 11-2 shows all the additions.

Listing 11-2: TECMD.CPP

```
// TECMD.CPP — command processor for Tiny Editor
// copyright 1995, Martin L. Rinehart

#include <CONIO.H>

#include "TECMD.H"
#include "KEYDEFS.H"
#include "EDITCMDS.H"

enum mode{ normal, win_mode };

mode in_mode = normal;

int user_cmd()
{
    int c = getch();
    if ( !c )
        return 256 + getch();
    else
        return c;
}

int edit_cmd()
{
    switch ( in_mode )
    {
        case normal:
```

```
                    return plain_cmd();

        case win_mode:
            return win_cmd();
    }
}

int plain_cmd()
{
    int c = user_cmd();

    switch ( c )
    {
        case ESC:
            return EXIT;

        case UP_ARROW:
        case CTRL_E:
            return CURSOR_UP;

        case DN_ARROW:
        case CTRL_X:
            return CURSOR_DN;

        case LF_ARROW:
        case CTRL_S:
            return CURSOR_LF;

        case RT_ARROW:
        case CTRL_D:
            return CURSOR_RT;

        case CTRL_F5:
        {
            in_mode = win_mode;
            return win_cmd();
        }
```

```
        default:
            return NOP;
    }
}

int win_cmd()
{
    int cmd = user_cmd();

    switch ( cmd )
    {
        case LF_ARROW:
            return WIN_MOVE_LF;

        case RT_ARROW:
            return WIN_MOVE_RT;

        case UP_ARROW:
            return WIN_MOVE_UP;

        case DN_ARROW:
            return WIN_MOVE_DN;

        case ALT_LF_ARROW:
            return WIN_SIZE_LF;

        case ALT_RT_ARROW:
            return WIN_SIZE_RT;

        case ALT_UP_ARROW:
            return WIN_SIZE_UP;

        case ALT_DN_ARROW:
            return WIN_SIZE_DN;

        case ENTER:
        case ESC:
        {
```

```
            in_mode = normal;
            return plain_cmd();
        }


    default:
        return NOP;
    }
}
```

```
int yn_cmd()
```

Add a declaration for the new functions to TECMD.H, too.

With that done, we can test the whole thing with an addition to our edit_do() in TEFIL.CPP. Listing 11-3 shows all the new cases, stubbed out with msg() calls.

Listing 11-3: TEFIL.CPP

```
case NOP:
{
    msg( " " );
    break;
}

case WIN_MOVE_LF:
{
    msg( " win move left " );
    break;
}

case WIN_MOVE_RT:
{
    msg( " win move right " );
    break;
}

case WIN_MOVE_UP:
```

```
    {
        msg( " win move up " );
        break;
    }

    case WIN_MOVE_DN:
    {
        msg( " win move down " );
        break;
    }

    case WIN_SIZE_LF:
    {
        msg( " win size left " );
        break;
    }

    case WIN_SIZE_RT:
    {
        msg( " win size right " );
        break;
    }

    case WIN_SIZE_UP:
    {
        msg( " win size up " );
        break;
    }

    case WIN_SIZE_DN:
    {
        msg( " win size down " );
        break;
    }
}

return done;
```

When you've entered these lines, run the program again. Pressing Ctrl+F5 will drop you into win_mode. In win_mode you'll get messages when you press an arrow key or an Alt+arrow key combination. Esc or Enter will drop you back into normal mode.

TCLite is nice about changing the border of the window you're working on when you go into its equivalent of our win_mode. I'll leave it up to you to add that feature if you want it. I like it, but we've got more work to do.

Now that we've got our messages coming through correctly, we can get on to the work of actually implementing the commands.

Resizing the Window

To resize our window, we'll first need to pop it down (restoring the screen behind it). Next, we'll change its size as per the message we've received. Last, we'll redraw the window in its new size. This actually sounds like more work than it will turn out to be.

We can write one routine that does the work and then just call the routine with appropriate arguments in edit_do(). Let's start by checking on this structure, making sure our new routine is called correctly. The sprintf() function (STDIO.H) is useful for this job. The sprintf() function writes formatted output to a string buffer in memory, like this:

```
void foo( int n )
{
    char* outbuf = "                        ";
    sprintf( outbuf, "the answer is: %d", n );
    ...
}
```

Like printf(), sprintf() inserts values of zero or more arguments into the same number of %-based specifiers in the template. It starts with an extra first argument, the string into which the output is placed. Listing 11-4 shows how sprintf() can be used with a function like msg() that needs a single string argument.

Listing 11-4: TEFIL.CPP

```
    case WIN_SIZE_LF:
    {
        win_size( -1, 0 );
```

```
            break;
        }

    case WIN_SIZE_RT:
        {
            win_size( 1, 0 );
            break;
        }

    case WIN_SIZE_UP:
        {
            win_size( 0, -1 );
            break;
        }

    case WIN_SIZE_DN:
        {
            win_size( 0, 1 );
            break;
        }

    }

    return done;
}

void file_win::win_size( int dx, int dy )
{
    char* m = "                                    ";
    sprintf( m, "sizing %d, %d", dx, dy );
    msg( m );
}

void file_win::show_cursor( )
```

Don't forget to add the declaration of win_size() in TEFIL.H before you run this code. Although win_size() could be made private right now, I made mine public since I think we'll have other uses for it later on.

In this starting version of win_size(), I use a simple character string, m, as an output buffer for the sprintf() function. The sprintf() call writes a formatted string into this buffer, which you can then show on the screen with the msg() function.

When you have this code running, let's move on to the implementation of win_size(). Our first job is to check to see if the new size is acceptable. There are actually four separate checks, only one of which is applicable in any one instance. We'll be either shrinking or growing in the x or y dimension. To pick one of the four checks, we can use an idiom from C that looks like a new statement but isn't.

The *else if* idiom is an if statement, following an else. Here's how it works:

```
// standard if/else:
    if ( whatever )
        do_this();
    else
        do_that();


// else followed by if/else:
    if (whatever )
        do_this();
    else
        if ( another_choice )
            do_another_this();
        else
            do_another_that();


// another way to write the above example:
    if (whatever )
        do_this();
    else if ( another_choice )
        do_another_this();
    else
        do_another_that();
```

The general case can be written this way:

```
if <cond1>
    <code for cond1>
```

```
else if <cond2>
    <code for cond2>
...
else if <condn>
    <code for condn>
else
    <code if none of above are true>
```

To avoid ambiguity, the C rule, carried through to C++, is that the else keyword is matched to the nearest preceding open if. Try writing a complex set of nested if statements this way:

```
if <cond1>
    <code for cond1>
else
{
    if <cond2>
        <code for cond2>
    else
    {
        <cond3>
            ...
    }
}
```

Then carefully eliminate redundant braces, using the rule that the else is matched to the nearest preceding open if. You'll see that you can reduce the complex set of nested ifs to a set of *else if* constructs.

Using the *else if* idiom, here's what our sizing test will look like:

```
if ( dx > 0 )
    // check for expanding, right
else if ( dx < 0 )
    // check for shrinking, left
else if ( dy > 0 )
    // check for expanding, down
else
    // check for shrinking, up
```

Remember that this construct works for mutually exclusive cases. It wouldn't work if, for instance, we called our win_size() routine with nonzero values for both dx and dy. But since each WIN_SIZE_*xxx* message is for only one direction, we only call win_size() for one direction at a time.

Let's put this approach into practice. First, though, we're going to need to know how big our screen is. We can record the screen size in global variables.

N O T E

Object-oriented software engineering frowns on global variables. Don't let this fact talk you out of using them for items, such as the screen width, that are truly global. Since your code runs on a single screen, it would be a design mistake *not* to use a global variable for the screen width.

I'm going to assume that our startup() routine sets a 50-line screen (more on this in a minute). Let's reserve the bottom line for future use as a status line, giving our editor 49 lines to work with. I'm also assuming that our screen width is 80 characters. To avoid a bug in the Borland screen-output code, I'm not going to write to the last column, so we'll only use 79 characters width. Add these two lines as global variables, outside of all the functions in TEFIL.CPP, as shown in Listing 11-5.

Listing 11-5: TEFIL.CPP

```
// TEFIL.CPP-file-related classes, Tiny Editor
// copyright 1995, Martin L. Rinehart

#include <STDIO.H>
#include <CONIO.H>
#include <STRING.H>

#include "TECMD.H"
#include "TEWIN.H"
#include "TEFIL.H"
#include "EDITCMDS.H"

int screen_width  = 79;
int screen_height = 49;

void msg( char* debug )
```

Now we can write our size test code. I start by writing my function with comments:

```
void file_win::win_size( int dx, int dy )
{
// check the size, exit if not ok


// restore the screen


// resize and repaint the box
}
```

And then I continue by expanding a comment. This is where I put that if/else idiom into practice:

```
void file_win::win_size( int dx, int dy )
{
// check the size, exit if not ok
    if ( dx > 0 )        // grow right
    else if ( dx < 0 ) // shrink left
    else if ( dy > 0 ) // grow down
    else // ( dy < 0 ) // shrink up
// restore the screen
```

And finally I add the details:

```
void file_win::win_size( int dx, int dy )
{
// check the size, exit if not ok
    if ( dx > 0 )        // grow right
    {
        if ( rgt == screen_width )
            return;
    }
    else if ( dx < 0 ) // shrink left
    {
        if ( rgt - lft == 2 )
            return;
    }
    else if ( dy > 0 ) // grow down
    {
```

```
            if ( btm == screen_height )
                return;
        }
        else // ( dy < 0 ) // shrink up
        {
            if ( btm - top == 2 )
                return;
        }


    // restore the screen

    // resize and repaint the box
    }
```

It's in the nature of this code that it will be easy to check after the rest of the function is working. We can just shrink or expand until we hit these limits. Since there's nothing subtle here, I'll go right ahead and leave the testing for later.

Repainting the screen will take some work, so I'll stick that step into its own method. To test this much code, I'll stub the repaint() with a line that redraws the underlying box. This will lead to interesting bugs, but at least it will let us test the code.

Listing 11-6 shows the new code in win_size() and the stub repaint() method, both in TEFIL.CPP.

Listing 11-6: TEFIL.CPP

```
void file_win::win_size( int dx, int dy )
{
// check the size, exit if not ok
    if ( dx > 0 )        // grow right
    {
        if ( rgt == screen_width )
            return;
    }
    else if ( dx < 0 ) // shrink left
    {
        if ( rgt - lft == 2 )
            return;
```

```
        }
        else if ( dy > 0 ) // grow down
        {
            if ( btm == screen_height )
                return;
        }
        else // ( dy < 0 ) // shrink up
        {
            if ( btm - top == 2 )
                return;
        }

// restore the screen
    puttext( lft, top, rgt, btm, screen_save_buf );

// resize and repaint the box
    rgt += dx;
    btm += dy;
    repaint();
}

void file_win::repaint()
{
    draw(); // box only, rest tk
}
```

void file_win::show_cursor( )

When you run this code, you should see the general idea working. Ctrl+F5 enters window size/move mode. Alt+arrow keys change the window's size. In addition to the fact that our redraw routine only draws the box, our screen restore code behaves peculiarly. Your size routine should correctly respect three of the four boundary conditions, but the screen isn't in 50-line mode, so boxes that are over 24 lines cause problems, too.

Let's fix the last problem first. I do all my text editing in 50-line mode. Actually, there isn't a 50-line mode on the PC. It does 43 lines in EGA video and 50 lines in VGA (or better) video. Determining which you're in is a problem, but it is a problem disappearing as the last of the old EGA video devices are going to the computer graveyards.

If you need to support EGA devices, the simple way is just to use a 42-line screen_height. If you run on an old-fashioned laptop with very low resolution, you may even prefer 24 lines. Your Tiny Editor will be more portable if you don't go beyond the 49 lines suggested here, even if your main computer can support more.

The screen mode can be selected at startup time by adding the code in Listing 11-7 to TE.CPP's startup() routine.

Listing 11-7: TE.CPP

```
void startup()
{
    textmode( C4350 );

    textattr( WHITE_BLUE );
    clrscr();

    setcursortype(NOCURSOR );
}
```

If you want to know more about the text modes you can select, press Shift+F1 to bring up the help index and then choose "conio" and press Enter to get to the right topic. In the CONIO.H help screen, you can double-click on "textmodes" to see the complete selection.

With the screen in 50-line mode, use Ctrl+F5 followed by enough Alt+down arrows to test your bottom-of-screen limit. While you're doing this test, your screen restores will produce spectacular results in the lower part of your screen.

The bottom limit should be correct, even though the screen restores are non-sensical.

The problem with the screen restores is simple. We're not resaving the screen after we change window sizes. This means that we're writing whatever's in RAM to the video display—bytes out past the ones that our screen save recorded. What we need to do is to save the correct size screen area after we restore the screen but before we draw the box.

We can put the resave into the repaint() method, since this will be necessary with the screen moves, too. For sizing, though, we also need to throw out the old screen_save_buf and get a new one, since the size of this buffer will be shrinking or expanding.

Listing 11-8 shows the changes to TEFIL.CPP that will make the screen saves/restores behave sensibly.

Listing 11-8: TEFIL.CPP

```
// restore the screen
    puttext( lft, top, rgt, btm, screen_save_buf );

// resize and repaint the box
    rgt += dx;
    btm += dy;

    delete screen_save_buf;
    screen_save_buf = new char[
        (rgt-lft+1) * (btm-top+1) * 2 ];

    repaint();
}

void file_win::repaint()
{
    gettext( lft, top, rgt, btm, screen_save_buf );
    draw(); // box only, rest tk
}
```

When you compile and run with this code in place, everything should work except our incomplete repaint() routine. That's our last step, and the window size commands will be complete.

Let's get right to it. Go back to TEWIN.CPP and look at the constructor for the dialog class. You see that we centered and displayed the title in the constructor. If we had done that in a separate routine, we could reuse that code now. This would be even more interesting if we had named that routine draw(). Let me explain.

More than one class in a hierarchy can have a routine named, for example, draw(). You can use the scope resolution operator, ::, to explicitly select one of the draw routines, this way:

```
dialog::draw(); // draw() in the dialog class
box::draw();    // draw() in the box class

draw();         // ambiguous?
```

Actually, the compiler will have no problem with a draw() that is not qualified with the scope resolution operator. If you are in a dialog method, then it will choose draw() from the dialog class. If you are in a popup or box method, then it will choose draw() from the box class.

In general, the compiler looks to the current class first. If it can't find a method, it looks in the current class's base class. If it still can't find a method, it searches the base class's base class, and so on.

Of course, if you use the scope resolution operator to explicitly name the class, then the compiler just does what you've told it. Listing 11-9 moves the draw-type code out of the dialog class constructor into a separate draw() method for the dialog class. If you copy the code from the constructor to the new routine, be sure you change the names of the parameters to the names of the data members. For example, the parameter ttl becomes the data member title, lf becomes lft, and so on. (The shaded line in the constructor marks the old location of the drawing code.)

Listing 11-9: TEWIN.CPP

```
dialog::dialog( char* ttl,
    int lf, int tp, int rt, int bt,
    char* brdr, int oc, int cc )
```

```
    : popup( lf, tp, rt, bt, brdr, oc, cc )
{
    title = new char[ strlen(ttl) + 1 ];
    strcpy( title, ttl );

    draw();
```

```
}

dialog::~dialog()
{
    delete title;
}
```

```
void dialog::draw()
{
    box::draw();

    int tlen = strlen( title );
    int tloc = ( rgt - lft + 1 - tlen ) / 2;

    textattr( outline_clr );
    gotoxy( lft+tloc, top );
    cprintf( title );
}
```

```
message::message( char* msg1 ) :
```

Add a declaration for dialog::draw() in TEWIN.H, too. In the constructor, the
line, draw(), used to call box::draw() because there was no other draw() in the
hierarchy. Adding a dialog::draw() changes the meaning of this line. Now it will
call dialog::draw().

In the dialog::draw() function, if we had just said draw(), our function would
have called itself. Sometimes a function can call itself (recursion) and this will
do precisely what you want. In this case, however, this would be an infinite
loop. You need to specify box::draw(), telling the compiler exactly which draw()
you mean.

F5 ?

When you press Ctrl+F9 and go into window-sizing mode, you'll see an interesting result. As you resize your window, the title is correctly redisplayed, too. That's because the file_win's repaint() calls draw(). Again, the meaning of that draw() has been changed. It too finds dialog::draw(), since the dialog class is the immediate base of the file_win class.

So we have done exactly what we meant to do, with very little trouble. Isn't object-oriented code wonderful? In this case, it helps us find the next bug much faster than we could have, otherwise.

Have you tested very small file_win sizes? If you do, you'll see that our dialog::draw() makes the implicit assumption that its title will fit. Of course, this is no longer a valid assumption, so we have to do something about it.

You could do something much nicer than my fix, but why don't you make a mental note and continue right on? For now, the fix shown in Listing 11-10 just suppresses the title altogether if it doesn't fit.

Listing 11-10: TEWIN.CPP

```
void dialog::draw()
{
    box::draw();

    int tlen = strlen( title );
    int tloc = ( rgt - lft + 1 - tlen ) / 2;

    if ( tloc > 0 )
    {
        textattr( outline_clr );
        gotoxy( lft+tloc, top );
        cprintf( title );
    }
}
```

Now that our title is fixed up, courtesy of a dialog::draw() routine, we need only redisplay the text and we are back in business. Fortunately, we wrote a display routine in our file_win class that is there for the calling.

Listing 11-11 shows the simple addition to file_win::repaint() in TEFIL.CPP that redisplays the text file inside our dialog box. Unfortunately, the job isn't quite that simple.

Listing 11-11: TEFIL.CPP

```
void file_win::repaint()
{
    gettext( lft, top, rgt, btm, screen_save_buf );
    draw(); // dialog box

    lwid = rgt - lft - 1;
    show_all( top_line );
}
```

Try this change and see what works, and what is left to be done. Got it? (You may also want to change the comment after the draw() call, as long as you're here. I have, although it's not flagged.)

This change correctly redisplays the window, including properly revealing the screen behind the window. But it doesn't correctly reposition the cursor. It should put the cursor back where it was in the simple case. If the window shrinks past the cursor's position, it should reposition the cursor. Let's add that logic to complete this step.

Listing 11-12 shows the addition to file_win::repaint() in TEFIL.CPP that correctly keeps track of the cursor and, when needed, the cur_line (pointer to the current memline).

Listing 11-12: TEFIL.CPP

```
void file_win::repaint()
{
    gettext( lft, top, rgt, btm, screen_save_buf );
    draw(); // dialog box

    lwid = rgt - lft - 1;
    show_all( top_line );

    if ( curx > lwid )
        curx = lwid;
```

```
    if ( cury > btm-top-1 )
    {
        cury-;
        cur_line = cur_line->prev;
    }
    gotoxy( lft+curx, top+cury );
}
```

With that final change, our window sizing commands all work correctly. Now that we can size the window, let's go on to moving the window.

Moving the Window

As we did with the window sizing commands, we can create a new file_win method, win_move(), that does the work in moving the window. Unlike the sizing, however, moving the window will be dead simple because we have already met and conquered all the difficulties that came up along the way.

Moving is just like sizing, except that you don't ever have to discard the old win_save_buf. (Since you aren't changing the window's size, the old buffer is always just the right size for the new screen save.) The repaint() method that handles sizing will also handle moving.

As before, let's begin by creating a stub win_move() and calling it in response to the appropriate commands. Listing 11-13 shows the changes to file_win::edit_do() in TEFIL.CPP that call the new method.

Listing 11-13: TEFIL.CPP

```
    case WIN_MOVE_LF:
    {
        win_move( -1, 0 );
        break;
    }

    case WIN_MOVE_RT:
    {
        win_move( 1, 0 );
        break;
```

```
        }

    case WIN_MOVE_UP:
    {
        win_move( 0, -1 );
        break;
    }

    case WIN_MOVE_DN:
    {
        win_move( 0, 1 );
        break;
    }
```

Listing 11-14 (from disk, use 11-13.CPP) shows the new win_move() method to add to TEFIL.CPP.

Listing 11-14: TEFIL.CPP

```
    return done;
}

void file_win::win_move( int dx, int dy )
{
    char* m = "                        ";

    sprintf( m, "move: %d %d", dx, dy );
    msg( m );
}

void file_win::win_size( int dx, int dy )
```

After you enter and run the code with this addition, your move commands (plain arrow keys) in the Ctrl+F5 mode will report that they want to move the window. We're ready to implement the win_move() method.

Again, start with checking that the requested move fits within the borders of the screen. Then go on to add the rest of the logic. Since it's so similar to the win_size() code, I'll just show the whole method at once.

Listing 11-15 shows the full win_move() function in TEFIL.CPP.

Listing 11-15: TEFIL.CPP

```
void file_win::win_move( int dx, int dy )
{
// exit if the move is not in the screen
    if ( dx < 0 ) // move left
    {
        if ( lft == 1 )
            return;
    }
    else if ( dx > 0 ) // move right
    {
        if ( rgt == screen_width )
            return;
    }
    else if ( dy < 0 ) // move up
    {
        if ( top == 1 )
            return;
    }
    else                    // move down
    {
        if ( btm == screen_height )
            return;
    }

// restore the screen
    puttext( lft, top, rgt, btm, screen_save_buf );

// move and repaint the dialog box
    lft += dx;
    rgt += dx;

    top += dy;
    btm += dy;

    repaint();
```

```
}

void file_win::win_size( int dx, int dy )
```

With this code added to the file_win class's capabilities, you can both move and size your file_win dialog boxes. Go ahead and test it thoroughly, before we move on.

Remember that we didn't check our display routine for all the possible overflows? Testing these routines thoroughly tests the display routine, too.

SCROLLING

Next on our list of jobs to complete is scrolling the display. When we scroll, the secret to avoiding bugs is simple. You have to pay close attention to the file_win data members that track your current position. When you scroll, you must correctly update these variables:

▶ top_line—the top line on the screen

▶ cur_line—the current (cursor location) line

▶ curx and cury—the location of the cursor

▶ lchar—the leftmost character position

This job is simplified by the fact that in most scrolling, curx and cury are not changed. (Picture your cursor at one edge or the other of the screen when you press the arrow key that would move it into the edge. The cursor stays put while the display moves underneath it.)

Similarly, there are two very different scrolls: horizontal and vertical. In a horizontal scroll, lchar changes, but top_line and cur_line are unchanged. In the vertical scroll, top_line and cur_line change, but lchar remains the same.

With that said, let's do the scrolling. There are two jobs to handle here. First, we'll scroll in response to bumping the cursor into an edge of the screen. Then we'll scroll in response to explicit cursor commands (such as PgUp).

Bumping into the Edges

To handle the single row/column cursor movements, start with a stub win_scroll() that will report its planned activity. Listing 11-16 shows my version of the related changes in edit_do() in TEFIL.CPP. Listing 11-17 (from disk, use 11-16.CPP) shows the win_scroll() method added to TEFIL.CPP.

Listing 11-16: TEFIL.CPP

```
case CURSOR_UP:
{
    if ( !AT_TOP_WIND )
    {
        cur_line = cur_line->prev;
        move( 0, -1 );
    }
    else
    {
        if ( is_top_line() )
            msg( "at BOF" );
        else
            win_scroll( 0, -1 );
    }
    break;
}

case CURSOR_DN:
{
    if( !is_bot_line() )
    {
        if ( !AT_BTM_WIND )
        {
            cur_line = cur_line->next;
            move( 0, 1 );
        }
        else
        {
            win_scroll( 0, 1 );
        }
    }
    else
    {
        msg( "at EOF line" );
```

```
            }
        break;
    }

    case CURSOR_RT:
    {
        if ( !AT_RGT_WIND )
            move( 1, 0 );
        else
            win_scroll( 1, 0 );

        break;
    }

    case CURSOR_LF:
    {
        if ( !AT_LFT_WIND )
            move( -1, 0 );
        else
        {
            if ( lchar == 0 )
                msg( "at left" );
            else
                win_scroll( -1, 0 );
        }
        break;
    }
```

Listing 11-17: TEFIL.CPP

```
    gotoxy( lft+curx, top+cury );
}

void file_win::win_scroll( int dx, int dy )
{
    if ( dx > 0 )
        msg( "scrolling right" );
    else if ( dx < 0 )
        msg( "scrolling left" );
```

```
    else if ( dy > 0 )
        msg( "scrolling down" );
    else // dy < 0
        msg( "scrolling up" );
}
```

```
void file_win::show_cursor()
```

When you test this code, you'll find the ability to shrink the window down to a small size is invaluable in generating the scroll messages. Until we can actually scroll down, however, there's no way to generate a scroll up message. That will come soon.

Let's start with the horizontal scroll. This just requires changing lchar and then redisplaying the whole screen. None of the other four key data members (curx, cury, top_line, and cur_line) are affected. Listing 11-18 shows the improvements needed in win_scroll() in TEFIL.CPP.

Listing 11-18: TEFIL.CPP

```
void file_win::win_scroll( int dx, int dy )
{
    if ( dx > 0 )
    {
        lchar++;
        show_all( top_line );
        gotoxy( lft+curx, top+cury );
    }
    else if ( dx < 0 )
    {
        lchar--;
        show_all( top_line );
        gotoxy( lft+curx, top+cury );
    }
    else if ( dy > 0 )
        msg( "scrolling down" );
    else // dy < 0
        msg( "scrolling up" );
}
```

With these lines in place, you should scroll left and right. Now let's try up and down. The trick here is to adjust top_line and cur_line. If you remember show_all(), you know that it sets top_line, so all we really need to handle is cur_line. This is made considerably simpler by the fact that our cursor movement code in edit_do() doesn't call the scroll routine if we are at the eof or bof lines.

Listing 11-19 shows this addition to win_scroll() in TEFIL.CPP.

Listing 11-19: TEFIL.CPP

```cpp
void file_win::win_scroll( int dx, int dy )
{
    if ( dx > 0 )
    {
        lchar++;
        show_all( top_line );
        gotoxy( lft+curx, top+cury );
    }
    else if ( dx < 0 )
    {
        lchar--;
        show_all( top_line );
        gotoxy( lft+curx, top+cury );
    }
    else if ( dy > 0 )
    {
        show_all( top_line->next );
        cur_line = cur_line->next;
        gotoxy( lft+curx, top+cury );
    }
    else // dy < 0
    {
        show_all( top_line->prev );
        cur_line = cur_line->prev;
        gotoxy( lft+curx, top+cury );
    }
}
```

You should now be scrolling successfully in all four directions. Once again, the window resize commands make testing this code possible. Our last scrolling project is to take care of the explicit scrolling commands.

Explicit Scrolling Commands

While the meanings of PgUp and PgDn are almost universally accepted, there is no such agreement on the right way to get to the top or bottom of a file. TCLite uses Ctrl+Home to go to the top of the screen and Ctrl+PgUp to go to the top of the file. I'll do it the same way, but if you have a different preference, go right ahead and do it your way.

PgUp and PgDn

Let's start with PgUp and PgDn. Before we can go down a page, we'll need to know if the last line of the file (the in-memory, linked-list copy of the file, of course) is already on the screen. This will be simple if we have the show_all() routine keep track of the last line it has written.

Start by adding a pointer to a memline, called bot_line, to the file_win class definition in TEFIL.H. I added mine to the line that defines top_line. Next, you want to record bot_line when show_all() finishes writing lines. (It already has the logic to check on how far it can go without going past the end of the linked list.)

Before you can do that, though, you have to eliminate the midfunction return statement. The relevant part now reads, in pseudocode:

```
show_all

... preliminaries

if ( at end of linked list )
    return;

show the lines
```

We need to change this to the following form:

```
show_all

... preliminaries
```

```
if ( NOT at end of linked list )
{
    show the lines
}
assign bot_line
```

First, note that the form of the if test is now:

```
if ( (!cond1) && (!cond2) ) ...
```

That can also be written this way:

```
if ( !(cond1 || cond2) ) ...
```

N O T E

Be careful when you apply mathematical laws to C++ logical expressions. C++ uses *short circuit* evaluation for logical expressions. If the first operand of an and expression (&&) is false, the second operand is ignored—the expression is false. Similarly, if the first operand of an or (||) expression is true, the whole expression is true and the second operand is not evaluated. In either case, if the second operand calls a function or includes an increment (++) or decrement (–) operator, the chance of bugs is substantial.

This means that this is true:

```
if ( (!cond1) && (!cond2) ) ... // test for end of file

    // if the above is true, then:

if ( cond1 || cond1 ) ...    // tests for NOT end of file
```

With that in mind, Listing 11-20 shows the show_all() routine modified to assign bot_line the correct value.

Listing 11-20: TEFIL.CPP

```
void file_win::show_all( memline* startline )
{
    memline* cl = startline;
```

```
    if ( !cl->prev )            // at start of memfile
    {
        if ( cl->next )         // has 1 or more lines
            cl = cl->next;
    }

    top_line = cl;

    textattr( FILE_WIN_CON_CLR );
    clear();

    if ( (cl->text) || (cl->next) ) // not at end
    {
        for ( int row = top+1; row < btm; row++ )
        {
            show_line( row, cl->text );

            if ( cl->next )
            {
                if ( (row+1) < btm )
                    cl = cl->next;
            }
            else
                break;
        }
    }
    bot_line = cl;
}
```

Don't forget to change the comment at the end of the if statement. Make this change and then retest, before you proceed.

How are you doing? Getting this? Here's a pop quiz. What's the difference between these two blocks of code:

```
// this works:
        if ( cl->next )
        {
```

```
        if ( (row+1) < btm )
            cl = cl->next;
    }
    else
        break;

// this doesn't:
        if ( cl->next )
            if ( (row+1) < btm )
                cl = cl->next;
        else
            break;
```

In both examples, I want to check to be sure that there is another item in the linked list (cl->next is nonzero). If there is another item (line of text) I want cl to move to it, except when we are at the very last line in the window.

T I P

Did you get the answer to the quiz? Don't worry if you didn't. Your author wasted a good thirty minutes staring at the wrong version before he figured out how he tricked himself!

The second version looks like it should work because the indentation suggests the correct operation. But the C++ compiler doesn't read indentation, of course. The C++ compiler matches the else with the nearest preceding if. Here's what the second version really says:

```
// this doesn't work:
        if ( cl->next )
            if ( (row+1) < btm )
                cl = cl->next;
        else
            break;

// because the compiler reads it as this:
        if ( cl->next )
```

```
            {
                if ( (row+1) < btm )
                    cl = cl->next;
                else
                    break;
            }
```

The braces in the correct example (around the embedded if) are needed to get the else matched to the first if, which is what our logic demands. This sort of little bug yields to patient use of the debugger, including use of Alt+F4 to inspect and Ctrl+F7 to set watches.

Let's go on. With bot_line recorded, PgDn is much simpler and is parallel to PgUp. Begin by adding appropriate message definitions to EDITCMDS.H, as shown in Listing 11-21.

Listing 11-21: EDITCMDS.H

```
#define CURSOR_RT          1004

#define GO_PGUP            1011
#define GO_PGDN            1012
#define GO_BOF             1013
#define GO_EOF             1014

#define WIN_MOVE_UP        1901
```

Then we need to report these messages in response to their keystroke equivalents. Listing 11-22 shows the new cases to add to plain_cmd() in TECMD.CPP.

Listing 11-22: TECMD.CPP

```
        case RT_ARROW:
        case CTRL_D:
            return CURSOR_RT;


        case PGUP:
            return GO_PGUP;


        case PGDN:
            return GO_PGDN;
```

```
        case CTRL_PGUP:
            return GO_BOF;


        case CTRL_PGDN:
            return GO_EOF;
```

```
        case CTRL_F5:
```

Next, I want to improve the is_*xxx*_line() functions. Our existing version reports on the cur_line. We'll need to be able to ask if the bot_line or top_line is the bottom or top of the file, too. To do that, let's try overloading the function. This is the general case, similar to using optional arguments. We'll define the functions twice, with and without a parameter.

Listing 11-23 shows the private member functions of the file_win class, defined in TEFIL.H.

Listing 11-23: TEFIL.H

```
private:
    int edit_do( int cmd );
    int is_top_line();
    int is_top_line( memline* ml );
    int is_bot_line();
    int is_bot_line( memline* ml );
};
```

Add these two new function declarations to the class definition. Remember, these are new functions. They share the name of an existing function, but they have different parameters, so they are different functions.

Listing 11-24 shows the definition of the new functions in TEFIL.CPP.

Listing 11-24: TEFIL.CPP

```
void file_win::move( int dx, int dy )
{
/* Calling routine MUST ensure that result of move
   is within the window!
*/
```

```
        curx += dx;
        cury += dy;

        gotoxy( lft+curx, top+cury );
}
```

```
int file_win::is_top_line()
{
    return is_top_line( cur_line );
}

int file_win::is_top_line( memline* ml )
{
    return ( !ml->prev ) || ( !ml->prev->prev );
}

int file_win::is_bot_line()
{
    return is_bot_line( cur_line );
}

int file_win::is_bot_line( memline* ml )
{
    return ( !ml ) || ( !ml->next );
}
```

```
memline::memline( memline* after_line, char* txt )
```

I've defined the no-parameter version in terms of the one-parameter version of both functions. It's important that the actual top/bottom tests are programmed only once. If you have two different checks, they might not always give the same answer for any one line, and this discrepancy is a certain source of bugs.

I mentioned *short circuit* analysis earlier. In an or (||) test, such as you see here in is_top_line() and is_bot_line(), the left operand is evaluated. If it is true, the or condition is true and so the right operand is ignored. That can be a source of bugs. On the other hand, as this example shows, you can take advantage of this behavior to get precisely the result you want.

Consider these:

```
// assume that ml is null (empty file)
   return ( !ml ) || ... ;

   // ml is false, so !ml is true
   // evaluation stops because the || is true

// assume that ml is non-null (a text line)
   return ( !ml ) || ( !ml->next );

   // ml is true, so !ml is false
   // ml->next is evaluated
```

Now we're ready to add new cases to the file_win::edit_do() routine in TEFIL.CPP. Listing 11-25 shows these.

Listing 11-25: TEFIL.CPP

```
        case CURSOR_LF:
        {
            if ( !AT_LFT_WIND )
                move( -1, 0 );
            else
            {
                if ( lchar == 0 )
                    msg( "at left" );
                else
                    win_scroll( -1, 0 );
            }
            break;
        }

        case GO_PGUP:
        {
            if ( !is_top_line(top_line) )
                win_scroll( -1 );
            else
                msg( "top showing" );
            break;
```

```
        }

    case GO_PGDN:
    {
        if ( !is_bot_line(bot_line) )
            win_scroll( 1 );
        else
            msg( "bottom showing" );
        break;
    }

    case GO_BOF:
    {
        msg( "going bof" );
        break;
    }

    case GO_EOF:
    {
        msg( "going eof" );
        break;
    }

    case NOP:
    {
        msg( " " );
        break;
    }
}
```

I've stubbed out the GO_EOF and GO_BOF cases with msg() calls. The
GO_PGUP and GO_PGDN cases call a new win_scroll() routine. Again, I've
overloaded a name. This time, the page up and down functionality is in a version
of win_scroll() called with a single parameter. Add the function's declaration to
the class definition in TEFIL.H. (It's a void function called with a single integer
parameter. I've named my parameter "direction" to reflect its purpose.)

Now we can add a stub version of the new win_scroll(), to check our work this
far. Listing 11-26 shows this function added to TEFIL.CPP.

Listing 11-26: TEFIL.CPP

```
    gotoxy( lft+curx, top+cury );
}

void file_win::win_scroll( int direction )
{
    if ( direction == 1 ) // going down
        msg( "page down" );
    else if ( direction == -1 ) // going up
        msg( "page up" );
}

void file_win::win_scroll( int dx, int dy )
```

When you run this code, you should get reliable reports on the message line about what the code intends to do. Now let's make the new version of win_scroll() smart enough to actually do its work.

We've got two distinct cases to handle, going up and going down. In both cases, we have to adjust the top_line up or down by a full page. At least we try to adjust it by a full page. The file may be too near the appropriate end for a full page movement, so we have to keep track of how far we've really moved.

Then we adjust the cur_line by the amount we really moved the top_line. In the page up case, we can always adjust the cur_line as far as we moved the top_line. When we're going down, however, there may not be enough page showing.

Consider the case where the top five lines of a six-line file are showing in a five-line window. Assume the cursor is in the third line. You can move the top_line down a full page, repositioning the file with just the sixth line showing. But you can't move the cur_line down a full five lines—you can only move it down three lines.

When you start programming these sorts of things on your own, you can do one of two things. Either think all the combinations through slowly and carefully and then start to program, or just program the simplest case and then test to see what goes wrong. Either way you'll not get it right the first time. I tend to do a little bit of thinking and then get confused. Then I program the simplest case and see what happens. The only way to do it wrong is to ignore a bug. Even a small, infrequent bug can come back to haunt you in a disastrous way if you don't chase it down.

With all that said, Listing 11-27 is a debugged (I hope!) version of the new win_scroll() in TEFIL.CPP.

Listing 11-27: TEFIL.CPP

```
void file_win::win_scroll( int direction )
{
/* direction -1 == page up,
            1 == page down
*/

    int pgsize = btm-top-1;
    int dist;

    if ( direction == -1 )
    {
    // back top_line up one page (if possible)
        for ( dist = 0; dist < pgsize; dist++ )
        {
            if ( top_line->prev )
                top_line = top_line->prev;
            else
                break;
        }

    // back cur_line up as much as top_line
        for ( int i=0; i < dist; i++ )
            cur_line = cur_line->prev;
    }

    if ( direction == 1 )
    {
    // move top_line down one page (if possible)
        for ( dist = 0; dist < pgsize; dist++ )
        {
```

```
            if ( top_line->next )
                top_line = top_line->next;
            else
                break;
        }


    // move cur_line down as far as top_line (if possible)
        for ( int i = 0; i < dist; i++ )
        {
            if ( cur_line->next )
                cur_line = cur_line->next;
            else
            {
                cury -= dist-i;
                break;
            }
        }
    }
    show_all( top_line );
    gotoxy( lft+curx, top+cury );
}
```

```
void file_win::win_scroll( int dx, int dy )
```

With this code in place, your PgUp and PgDn keys should function correctly. Now we can go on to Ctrl+PgUp/PgDn (or whatever keystrokes you chose to generate the GO_EOF/BOF messages). Before we do that, however, let's try a little cleanup.

Have you noticed that every call to show_all() is followed by a gotoxy()? Let's put that gotoxy() into the show_all() routine. Follow these steps:

STEP BY STEP

1. Copy the gotoxy() line at the end of the insert in Listing 11-27 to the end of show_all(). Retest all your keystrokes. Nothing should change.

2. Delete the gotoxy() call from repaint(). Then move the show_all() call in repaint() to the end of the function, so curx and cury are set before you call show_all(). Retest. ✓

3. Delete the gotoxy() call from the single-parameter version of win_scroll(). Retest. ✓

4. Delete the four calls to gotoxy() from the two-parameter version of win_scroll(). Do a final, thorough, test. ✓

That job shrank my .EXE file by just over 100 bytes. More important, it simplified the code, which will pay off in reducing the work we're doing, and in reducing maintenance.

H I N T

Do you sometimes get mysterious border characters for one or the other of your dialog boxes? That can happen due to a TCLite bug. To eliminate the problem, compile your modules separately with Alt+F9 and then build the executable with Ctrl+F9. If this doesn't eliminate the damage, you've got a bug in your code.

Top and Bottom of File

After the hard work you've done getting PgUp and PgDn to function, you'll be pleased to know that Ctrl+PgUp and Ctrl+PgDn (or whatever keystrokes you chose) are not a problem.

The simpler of the two commands to implement is GO_BOF. We just have to position the cur_line pointer to the top line in the linked list. If the file is empty, the null memline at the top of the list is the one we want (the mem_file->head_line). If there is text in the file, the top line is the next one in the linked list.

Listing 11-28 shows the replacement code for the GO_BOF case in edit_do(), TEFIL.CPP.

Listing 11-28: TEFIL.CPP

```
case GO_BOF:
    {
```

```
        cur_line = mem_file->head_line;
        if ( cur_line->next )
            cur_line = cur_line->next;


        curx = cury = 1;


        show_all( cur_line );

        break;

    }
```

I seldom use multiple = signs in a single statement, but this is one exception. The = operator assigns the value on the right to the <u>lvalue</u> on the left. The result assigned to the lvalue is also the result of the expression. Multiple assignments are evaluated from right to left, so these are equivalent:

```
// one way:
    curx = 1;
    cury = 1;

// the same result:
    curx = cury = 1;
```

Don't use this effect to write more complex assignments. Here's a bad way to assign 2 and 4 as dimensions of a rectangle:

```
len = 2 * wid = 2; // a bad way to write code!
```

T I P

C++, like C, makes tricky, obscure code quite easy to write. Clever code is impossible to unravel. Smart programmers have no use for clever code. Good C++ programming, like good programming in every other language, is obvious, straightforward programming.

Let's get on to GO_EOF. We could start at the top of the file and look down the linked list until we come to the end (the next pointer will be null), but there's a quicker way. When we defined the memfile class, we included a tail_line pointer, but we didn't implement it. If we implement it now, we'll be able to go directly to the end of the list. Listing 11-29 shows the line you need to add to the end of the memfile constructor in TEFIL.CPP.

Listing 11-29: TEFIL.CPP

```cpp
memfile::memfile( FILE* tf )
{
    text_file = tf;
    head_line = new memline( NULL, "" );

    memline* curline = head_line;
    char inbuf[1024];
    *inbuf = 0;

    rewind( tf );

    do
    {
        fgets( inbuf, 1024, text_file );
        if ( !*inbuf )
            break;

        curline = new memline( curline, inbuf );
        *inbuf = 0;
    }
    while ( !feof(text_file) );

    tail_line = curline;

}
```

To test that line, set a breakpoint at the closing brace, just following the assignment to tail_line. When your program reaches that point (immediately after pressing Enter in the filename dialog) use Alt+F4 to inspect tail_line. Can you describe a minimal exhaustive test? Figure 11-1 shows my screen while I'm busy testing this code.

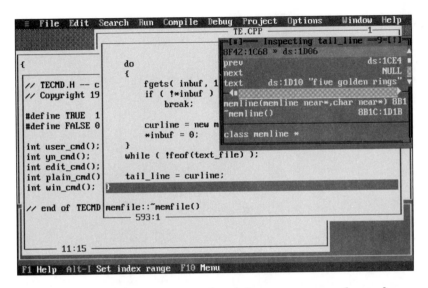

Figure 11-1: Using inspect in the debugger to test the code.

I tested an empty file, a one-line file, and a two-line file. Looking at the algorithm, that seems to test everything. (Actually, it doesn't test an out-of-memory condition, but we'll discuss that later.)

GO_EOF takes more code than GO_BOF because you have to go to the end of the file and then back up to the top of the page that contains the end of the file. Of course, you can't be sure that the file takes up a full page, so your backward trip has to watch out for the beginning of the file, too.

Still, the essence of the routine would be the same, except for the problem of positioning the cursor at the end of the final line. Going to the beginning, you can set curx to 1. At the end, you have to set curx to 1 more than the length of the last line. And just in case, you have to check to be sure that finding the end of the line doesn't require scrolling to the right.

Listing 11-30 shows the code that does all this, replacing the stub case in edit_do() in TEFIL.CPP

Listing 11-30: TEFIL.CPP

```
case GO_EOF:
    {
```

```
            if ( !cur_line->next ) // at bottom? done!
                break;


            top_line = cur_line = mem_file->tail_line;
            int pgsize = btm - top - 1;


            int backup = 1; // start at last line


            // find the top of the page
                while ( (backup < pgsize ) &&
                        (top_line->prev) )
                {
                        top_line = top_line->prev;
                        backup++;
                }


            // position to the end of the last line
                curx = strlen( cur_line->text ) + 1;


            // scroll right, if need be
                int toofar = curx - (rgt-lft-1);
                if (toofar > 0 )
                {
                        lchar = toofar;
                        curx = rgt-lft-1;
                }


            cury = backup < pgsize ? backup-1: pgsize;
            show_all( top_line );
    }
```

Enter and test this routine, completely. Again, use the ability to resize your window to test going to the bottom when the bottom is on screen and when it is not, and going to the bottom when the end of the last line fits and when it does not. As I was testing mine, I found a bug in the GO_BOF routine. Have you noticed it, yet?

If you use GO_BOF when the screen is scrolled to the right, it does not go back to the left. All that is required is a simple adjustment to lchar. Listing 11-31 shows the fix I've added to the GO_BOF case in edit_do() in TEFIL.CPP.

Listing 11-31: TEFIL.CPP

```
    case GO_BOF:
    {
        cur_line = mem_file->head_line;
        if ( cur_line->next )
            cur_line = cur_line->next;

        curx = cury = 1;
        lchar = 0;

        show_all( cur_line );

        break;
    }
```

With these commands working, there's only one more feature to add to our screen-manipulation capabilities—toggling full-screen display mode.

TOGGLING FULL-SCREEN DISPLAYS

Try running your Tiny Editor again, only don't accept the default TEST.FIL. Try it on a longer program file. TEWIN.CPP is a good candidate. If you're like me, you'll want to tap F5 to switch to full-screen view before you've tried too many commands.

That's our next and last job in this chapter. To do this, we'll start by adding a logical flag and a spare set of screen coordinates to our file_win object. As long as we're there, we may as well throw in a toggle function, too.

Listing 11-32 shows the new members to add to the file_win class definition in TEFIL.H. It also shows four new #defines that choose the size of a screen when we toggle to full-screen display. (You may later want the full-screen top to be at line 2, for example, to allow for a top-line menu bar.)

Listing 11-32: TEFIL.H

```
// TEFIL.H--file-related classes, Tiny Editor
// Copyright 1995, Martin L. Rinehart


#define TRUE  1
#define FALSE 0
```

```
#define AT_TOP_WIND  ( cury == 1 )
#define AT_BTM_WIND  ( (top+cury) == (btm-1) )
#define AT_LFT_WIND  ( curx == 1 )
#define AT_RGT_WIND  ( (lft+curx) == (rgt-1) )

#define FULL_LFT     1
#define FULL_TOP     1
#define FULL_RGT     screen_width        ✓
#define FULL_BTM     screen_height

class memfile;
class memline;

class file_win : public dialog
{
protected:
    memfile* mem_file;

    memline* top_line, * bot_line;
    memline* cur_line;

    int lchar, lwid;
    char* blanks;

    int curx, cury; // window relative cursor location

    int ins_mode;

    int full_screen_mode;              ✓
    int save_lft, save_top, save_rgt, save_btm;

public:
    file_win( char* file_name, FILE* tf );
    ~file_win();

    void show_all( memline* startline );
    void show_line( int row, char* str );
    void clear();
```

```
    void edit();
    void show_cursor();
    void go( int x, int y );
    void move( int x, int y );
    void win_move( int dx, int dy );
    void win_size( int dx, int dy );
    void win_scroll( int direction );
    void win_scroll( int dx, int dy );
    void repaint();
    void toggle_full_screen();

private:
    int edit_do( int cmd );
    int is_top_line();
    int is_top_line( memline* ml );
    int is_bot_line();
    int is_bot_line( memline* ml );
};
```

When we press F5 (again, F5 is TCLite's keystroke, but by all means suit your-self, not me or Borland) we'll check the full_screen_mode flag to see what mode we're in. If we're not in full-screen mode, we'll save the current coordinates to the save_*xxx* data members and reset the coordinates from the FULL_*xxx* values we've #defined.

We'll reverse this process when we toggle from full-screen back to normal mode. This reversal will be a little more trouble, since we need to adjust the x and y coordinates if they are outside the reduced window.

Again, we'll start by adding a new message to EDITCMDS.H. Listing 11-33 shows the new message.

Listing 11-33: EDITCMDS.H

```
#define GO_EOF          1014

#define TOGGLE_SCREEN   1801

#define WIN_MOVE_UP     1901
```

Then we move on to the plain_cmd() routine in TECMD.CPP, to add the new case, as shown in Listing 11–34.

Listing 11-34: TECMD.CPP

```
case CTRL_PGDN:
    return GO_EOF;

case F5:
    return TOGGLE_SCREEN;

case CTRL_F5:
{
    in_mode = win_mode;
    return win_cmd();
}
```

With the message added to the plain_cmd() switch, we can add a corresponding case to TEFIL.CPP as in Listing 11–35.

Listing 11-35: TEFIL.CPP

```
case NOP:
{
    msg( "  " );
    break;
}

case TOGGLE_SCREEN:
{
    msg( "toggling screen" );
    break;
}

case WIN_MOVE_LF:
{
    win_move( -1, 0 );
    break;
}
```

With this much done, you can test your work. The message line should report that it intends to toggle the screen when you press F5 or whatever key you chose.

Now we can go on to implement the toggle. We'll need to start with an addition to the file_win constructor. We need to initialize the full_screen_mode flag to false. Listing 11-36 shows this addition to file_win::file_win() in TEFIL.CPP.

Listing 11-36: TEFIL.CPP

```
file_win::file_win( char* file_name, FILE* tf ) :
    dialog( file_name, 5, 2, 75, 20,
    SING_DOUB, FILE_WIN_OUT_CLR, FILE_WIN_CON_CLR )
{

    mem_file = new memfile( tf );

    lchar = 0;
    lwid = rgt - lft - 1;

    blanks = new char[81];
    for ( char* cp=blanks; cp < blanks+80; cp++ )
        *cp = ' ';
    blanks[81] = 0;

    curx = cury = 0;
    ins_mode = TRUE;


    full_screen_mode = FALSE;


    show_all( mem_file->head_line );

    go( 1, 1 );
    cur_line = top_line;
    edit();
}
```

Next, add the new file_win method, toggle_screen(). Listing 11-37 shows this method added to TEFIL.CPP. After you add this method, change the msg() call in edit_do() to call this function (this change is not shown in the listing).

Listing 11-37: TEFIL.CPP

```
    gotoxy( lft+curx, top+cury );
}

void file_win::toggle_full_screen()
{
    // restore the screen
        puttext( lft, top, rgt, btm, screen_save_buf );

    if ( full_screen_mode ) // switch to part screen
    {
        lft = save_lft;
        top = save_top;
        rgt = save_rgt;
        btm = save_btm;

        if ( curx > (rgt-lft-1) )
            curx = rgt-lft-1;

        if ( cury > (btm-top-1) )
            cury = btm-top-1;
    }
    else // switch to full screen
    {
        save_lft = lft;
        save_top = top;
        save_rgt = rgt;
        save_btm = btm;

        lft = FULL_LFT;
        top = FULL_TOP;
        rgt = FULL_RGT;
        btm = FULL_BTM;
    }


    // resize the screen buffer
        delete screen_save_buf;
        screen_save_buf = new char[
```

```
        (rgt-lft+1) * (btm-top+1) * 2 ];

    repaint();

    full_screen_mode = !full_screen_mode;
}
```

```
int file_win::is_top_line()
```

With this code in place, you will be able to press F5 (or your key) and toggle between normal and full-screen views of your file. Our Tiny Editor is coming along nicely. In the next chapter we'll add actual editing to the features we handle.

Congratulations on getting all this done. Your skill as a C++ programmer is rapidly improving. If you want to see how well we've managed to encapsulate all this editor behavior in an editor object, go back to TE.CPP and look at your mainline again. It really doesn't take much to launch an editor, does it?

SUMMARY

When we started this chapter, our nascent editor read in a text file and let us move the cursor around. Our first job was to write a window resizing routine. We didn't add this feature merely because it was essential for a small text editor. We did it because it lets us conveniently test all sorts of boundary conditions as we add all the other features.

With resizing written, we added window moving and then went on to scrolling the display. This let our display move one column or line at a time as we moved the cursor into the borders of the display window.

With that working, we added the explicit display movement commands. We started with page up and page down, and then we added jumps to the beginning and end of the file.

Finally, we added a toggle to switch our window from normal to full-screen mode, and to switch back.

As we did this work, we added to our C++ vocabulary. We used an enum in TECMD.CPP to help us select command modes. (We'll be adding more modes to this enum as we go along.)

We used the sprintf() function defined in STDIO.H to write formatted output into a RAM-based character string buffer. This let us use our msg() debugging output to show combined text and numbers.

We took a good look at the *else if* idiom. We used it in our scroll_win() method to distinguish between a list of mutually exclusive choices.

To get 50-line mode, we used the built-in textmode() function, defined in CONIO.H. This let us switch VGA and better screens into 50-line mode.

We used polymorphism in different ways. We used draw() functions in the dialog and box classes. The scope resolution operator let us select the one we wanted. We also used multiple win_scroll() and is_*xxx*_line() functions, differing in their calling parameters—another way to take advantage of polymorphism.

The evaluation of or (||) and and (&&) logical expressions takes advantage of short-circuit analysis (not analyzing the second part of an expression if the final value can be determined from just the first part). We used this behavior to our advantage in the is_*xxx*_line() functions first to check for an empty file and then, if the file was not empty, to check a pointer.

Finally, we made judicious use of the fact that the = operator returns a value, so we can use it in multiple assignment expressions. But we avoided abusing this privilege.

In the next chapter, we're going to learn more about C++'s finer points, and we're going to teach our Tiny Editor how to insert and delete text. Before we're done, you'll really be able to able to claim that you've written a text editor in C++.

In the last chapter we started with a simple file_win class that let us move the cursor around in text. We read the text from a file into a linked list in memory. Before we were done, we had added the ability to move and resize the window, and we had text that would scroll in response to commands like PgUp and PgDn and to the cursor's moving past the edge of the visible window. The Tiny Editor project is starting to come alive.

We've created a file_win class that is beginning to look like a text editor. One of the key things that it doesn't handle yet is text editing. In this chapter we'll add the ability to insert, delete, and overwrite text. By the time we get to the end of the chapter, you'll actually have a text editor.

While we build these capabilities, we'll build within the structure we've got and almost entirely within your current knowledge of the C++ language. We'll take a quick look at unions and some of the bit-level operators, and we'll consider a subtlety of the for loop, but we'll spend almost all our time writing code.

Unlike the earlier chapters, before we're done I'll be asking you to work on your own and check your work against mine after you finish it—not just copy my work. It's getting to be time to prove how good you are, isn't it?

12

Editing with Our Editor

At the end of this chapter we won't be quite ready to replace our existing editors with the Tiny Editor, but we'll be getting closer. (The ability to save the edited text back to disk is one critical item that we'll still be missing.)

When we built the string_field class, we handled the basics of overstriking, deleting, and inserting characters within a line. It's tempting to try to use that code to handle the intra-line editing in our Tiny Editor. Unfortunately, the string_field just won't do.

In an editor, we have to be able to scroll within a limited visual window into a nearly unlimited text line. Additionally, we have special problems, such as handling characters typed when the cursor is out past the end of the text line.

Since our command of C++ was still shaky when we wrote the string_field class, I decided to avoid the extra problems that go with generalizing code. That helped us make steady progress, but now we've got some extra work to do. Still, you've seen how the insides of our text editing commands work, and you've built key library routines that we can reuse. This time around, our job will be simpler.

INSERT/OVERSTRIKE MODE

I want to code the overstrike capability first, since it's simpler than the insert capability. This requires being in overstrike mode, of course. Since we'll normally be in insert mode, this means that the first thing to code is a way to switch back and forth. While we're at it, let's pass the characters coming in either mode.

Sending a Message

First, we'll need a message that toggles insert mode. Listing 12-1 shows the new message added to EDITCMDS.H.

Listing 12-1: EDITCMDS.H

```
#define GO_EOF          1014

#define TOGGLE_SCREEN   1801
#define TOGGLE_INSERT   1802

#define WIN_MOVE_UP     1901
```

Next we need to send the TOGGLE_INSERT message to the file_win object. Listing 12-2 shows the addition to TECMD.CPP's plain_cmd() switch that will do this in response to an Ins keypress or a Ctrl+V keypress.

Listing 12-2: TECMD.CPP

```
        case CTRL_PGDN:
            return GO_EOF;

        case CTRL_V:
        case INS:
            return TOGGLE_INSERT;

        case F5:
            return TOGGLE_SCREEN;
```

To test our work, we can stub out a case in TEFIL.CPP's edit_do() switch. Listing 12-3 shows the stub code that shows us that our messages are coming through.

Listing 12-3: TEFIL.CPP

```
case NOP:
{
    msg( "  " );
    break;
}

case TOGGLE_INSERT:
{
    msg( "Toggling insert" );
    break;
}

case TOGGLE_SCREEN:
```

With this code in place, you can run the program and then press Ctrl+V or Ins. The appropriate message will pop up on our message line. To test both keystrokes, you have to clear the message line, which means forcing up another message.

Improving the Message Function

Wouldn't it be nice if the message cleared itself? Let's use the ungetch() function, defined in CONIO.H, to help us out. We'll have the msg() function display its message and then wait for a keypress. When it gets a keypress, it can blank out the message and then use ungetch() to stuff the keypress right back into the keyboard buffer. This means that the next keypress will both clear the message line and perform the next editing function.

Listing 12-4 shows an improved version of msg() at the top of TEFIL.CPP.

Listing 12-4: TEFIL.CPP

```
void msg( char* debug )
{
    // debugging message
```

```
    int x, y;
    x = wherex(); y = wherey();

    gotoxy( 1, 1 );

    char* blank = "                                        ";
    cprintf( blank );
    gotoxy( 1, 1 );
    cprintf( debug );

    gotoxy( x, y );
    int ch = getch();

    gotoxy( 1, 1 );
    cprintf( blank );
    ungetch( ch );

    gotoxy( x, y );
}
```

This version of msg() will make your remaining testing a bit easier. Now let's go on to actually toggling insert mode and, of course, changing the cursor accordingly. (Again, we're still using the unconventional block cursor to indicate overstrike and the underscore cursor for insert mode.)

Listing 12-5 shows the revised case in edit_do() in TEFIL.CPP that does all our work. This could hardly be simpler, could it?

Listing 12-5: TEFIL.CPP

```
    case TOGGLE_INSERT:
        {
            ins_mode = !ins_mode;
            show_cursor();
        break;
        }
```

With that code in place, test again and you'll see the cursor happily change, announcing the new status of the insert flag, in response to either Ctrl+V or

Ins. Now we're ready to actually use overstrike mode to do our first text editing.

OVERSTRIKING CHARACTERS

The first problem we face in overstriking (or, for that matter, inserting) characters is that the commands returned have to expand to contain two parts:

▶ A command that says "character typed"

▶ The character itself

One way to effect this expansion would be to send a message, such as CHAR-ACTER_FOLLOWS, and then return the character on the next call to edit_cmd(). A simpler, and faster, solution is to combine the command with the character. We have an integer, with 64K possible values, for the command message. Since we're working on a Tiny Editor, we can assume that we'll never come close to 64K different commands.

Experimenting with Unions

A union is a misnamed C-based construct, but it is a good possibility for this situation. With a union, you can define one place in memory in two or more ways. For example, let's define a structure of two characters:

```
struct two_chars
{
    char c1;
    char c2;
}
```

This defines a struct that contains two bytes. Of course, an int on a PC is also two bytes long. A union can define two bytes of memory that we can address as either an int or a two_chars struct:

```
union chars_int
{
    two_chars tc;
    int i;
}
```

In a class or structure, every defined item starts at the next location in memory. In our two_chars struct, for example, one byte in memory holds char c1, and the next byte holds char c2.

In contrast, every defined item in a union starts in exactly the same location in memory. In the example above, the union puts a two_chars struct and an int at a single memory location. This can be very handy when sometimes you want to pass, for example, an integer command but at other times you want to examine just one byte or the other of that command.

Let's try a union in a T.CPP. Listing 12-6 (all new, so it's not on disk) shows how a union works.

Listing 12-6: T.CPP

```
#include <CONIO.H>

struct two_chars
{
    char c1;
    char c2;
};

union chars_int
{
    two_chars tc;
    int i;
};

int main()
{
    chars_int ci;

    ci.tc.c1 = 2;
    ci.tc.c2 = 1;

    clrscr();
    cprintf( "\n\r the word's value is %d", ci.i );
    getch();

}
```

This program creates a structure that is two chars long and then defines a union that equates this structure with an integer. The union lets you address one word in memory either as a single integer or as individual bytes. For example:

```
ci.i = 1; // assignment to the whole word

ci.tc.c1 = 1; // assignment to just the first byte
ci.tc.c2 = 1; // assignment to just the second byte
```

When you run the example in Listing 12-6, you may be surprised to see that the result is 258. This is because the Intel architecture treats the first byte of an integer in RAM as the low-order byte. If we number our bytes starting with the lower number on the left, this is what that means:

Bytes in RAM	Interpretation
01 00	The integer 1
00 01	The integer 256

In our sample program:

02 01	The integer 258

Of course, writing the lower-numbered byte on the left is a human-oriented convention. It's the way most debuggers display bytes when they show them to us, for example. But it has no meaning as far as the computer is concerned. Intel's engineers chose the other order for the internals of the $80x86$ chip series.

N O T E

Some modern CPUs put the low-order byte of an integer first in RAM (assume *first* means at the location with the lower-numbered address), and some CPUs use the opposite convention. In CPU design, the debate between the methods is called the Endian controversy. The name comes from Swift's *Gulliver's Travels* in which the Lilliputians are at war: One Lilliputian state eats their boiled eggs starting from the little end, and the neighboring state starts with the big end. For us, the Endian controversy means that our code is processor-specific when we work with unions.

Our sample program assigned the two bytes and then reported the value of the resulting integer. The opposite approach works just as well. Experiment with the T.CPP example in Listing 12-7.

Listing 12-7: T.CPP

```
int main()
{
    chars_int ci;

    ci.i = 258;

    clrscr();
    cprintf( "\n\r i is %d: c1 is %d and c2 is %d", ci.i,
        ci.tc.c1,
        ci.tc.c2 );
    getch();


}
```

The distinctive feature of the union is that you can work with parts of a word (or larger piece of memory) without needing to actually work with the low-level operators C++ inherited from C. On the other hand, sometimes these low-level operators that actually fiddle with bits achieve the same result. You can shift bits, for example:

```
i = 1<<8 ; // shift 1 8 bits left (result: 256)
```

You can use the left shift operator to slide a byte into the high-order byte of an integer. You can retrieve the high-order byte of an integer by shifting to the right:

```
c = i>>8; // c == high-order byte of i
```

You can use the bitwise-and operation to mask off bits in an integer, too:

```
c = i & 0x00FF; // mask off the high-order 8 bits
```

You can also use bitwise or, not, and xor operators if you want to fiddle with bits. Try any of these that you like in a program like T.CPP. The presence of these operators in C made it the language of choice for all systems-level work that otherwise would be done in assembler.

We don't want to shift bits if our goal is simply to assign to or examine byte-sized pieces of a word. Try this assignment in your T.CPP:

```
ci.tc.c1 = 0;
ci.tc.c2 = 127;
```

You should get the value 32512 for your integer. If you raise c2 to 128, you'll get −32768, since 128 has the high bit set. You can also write 127 this way, if it seems more clear:

```
ci.tc.c1 = 0;
ci.tc.c2 = 0x7F; // same as 127
```

Either way, you're turning on all the bits in the high-order byte excepting the first one, which is the sign bit. This gives us an effective technique for sending a command in the high byte and lets us return the char value in the low byte, without needing a second call or other extra cycle expenditure.

Now try this single assignment:

```
ci.i = 0x7F00 + 12;
```

As your program shows, that puts the 0x7F in the high-order byte and the number 12 in the low-order byte. The addition operator is a straightforward way of assigning a byte when you know that the byte's value is zero before the addition. One way to pick the low-order byte from an integer is to simply assign the int to a char:

```
int i = 0x7F00 + 12;
char c = i;          // c is just 12
```

The high-order byte is simply ignored when you assign a shorter integer (such as a char) from a longer integer. These techniques are not as general as using a union, but when they suffice, they avoid machine dependencies such as the Endian controversy.

Manipulating Bytes in Code

Now let's put this idea into practice. First, let's modify TECMD.CPP so that plain_cmd() will return a compound message, including the value of the char when a character is typed.

Listing 12-8: TECMD.CPP

```
int plain_cmd()
{
    int c = user_cmd();

    if ( (c >= ' ') && (c < 256) )
        return c + 0x7F00;

    switch ( c )
    {
        case ESC:
            return EXIT;
```

Here I've combined the char in the low-order byte of the return integer and put 0x7F into the high-order byte. Doing this with addition works regardless of the way the particular CPU stores bytes. Note that I've not put this code outside the switch to avoid the need for a separate case for every possible character that might be typed.

H I N T

Switches are ideal when you have individual values, such as command keypresses. You should use *if* and *else if* constructs when you want to test for value ranges, such as typed characters.

With this new return value from TECMD, you can add a similar construct to edit_do() in TEFIL.CPP to respond to these keypresses. Listing 12-9 shows a modification that will call a new method, use_char(), when a char is received from edit_cmd().

Listing 12-9: TEFIL.CPP

```
int file_win::edit_do( int cmd )
{
    if ( cmd > 0x7F00 )
    {
```

```
        use_char( cmd );
        return FALSE;      // not done
    }
```

```
    int done = FALSE;

    switch ( cmd )
    {
        case EXIT:
```

Listing 12-10 shows a stub use_char() method that will report, if your work has been correct so far, its intention to insert or overstrike with an appropriate character.

Listing 12-10: TEFIL.CPP

```
}
```

```
void file_win::use_char( int cmd )
{
    char c = cmd; // drops high bits of cmd

    char* m = "                              ";
    if ( ins_mode )
    {
        sprintf( m, "Insert '%c'", c );
        msg( m );
    }
    else
    {
        sprintf( m, "Overstrike '%c'", c );
        msg( m );
    }
}
```

```
void file_win::win_move( int dx, int dy )
```

Add a declaration for use_char() in the file_win definition in TEFIL.H and then test this new routine. You should see a report on the intended use of each key in your message area. Now let's get on to actually overstriking some of the text in our memline objects. ✓

Padding Strings

Overstriking would be completely simple if it weren't for the fact that we have to allow for typing past the existing end of the line. When we read the text file, we created a char array long enough to hold the string. We want our editor, however, to behave as if there are an unlimited number of blanks at the end of the string that we can just type over.

What we'll need is a function that pads strings. Since we've already got library routines for strings at the end of TEWIN.CPP, I've put this new one there, too. The pad_str() function assumes that you'll call it this way:

```
char* some_string;

    ... // use some_string

some_string = pad_str( some_string ); // this is how!

    ... //it's now a completely new string
```

It's important that you call pad_str() with a call like this:

```
x = pad_str(x);
```

The old version of the string is deleted inside pad_str(), so trying to use the old version after you've run pad_str() will certainly generate peculiar, if not disastrous, results!

Listing 12-11 shows the new routine to add to TEWIN.CPP.

Listing 12-11: TEWIN.CPP

```
    return ++here;
}


char* pad_str( char* str )
{
    int len = strlen( str );

    // create a new, longer string
```

```
    char* new_str = new char[ len + PAD_STR_SIZE + 1 ];

    // copy in the old string
    strcpy( new_str, str );

    // blank fill the end of the new string
    char* cp = new_str + len;
    for ( int i=0; i < PAD_STR_SIZE; i++ )
        *cp++ = ' ';
    *cp = 0;

    // get rid of the old one
    delete str;

    return new_str;
}
```

```
// end of TEWIN.CPP
```

Overstriking Characters

With this function available, we can start to overstrike characters. Our first bit of logic checks the length of the line of text and compares it to the current cursor position. If the cursor is past the right edge of the text, it pads the line. Since you can move the cursor as far as you like to the right, it calls pad_str() in a loop, as often as needed to create enough room.

There's space in this function to scroll right when we're at the right edge, but it's not implemented yet. The last job is to putch() the character to the screen and record it in the current line's text. Since putch() moves the cursor, we also increment the curx variable.

Listing 12-12 shows this code in the file_win::use_char() method, in TEFIL.CPP.

Listing 12-12: TEFIL.CPP

```
void file_win::use_char( int cmd )
{
    char c = cmd; // drops high bits of cmd
```

```
char* m = "                        ";
if ( ins_mode )
{
    sprintf( m, "Insert '%c'", c );
    msg( m );
}
else
{
    int len = strlen( cur_line->text );

    while ( (curx + lchar) > len )
    {
        cur_line->text = pad_str( cur_line->text );
        len = strlen( cur_line->text );
    }

    if ( curx == rgt-lft-1 )
    {
    // scroll one right
    }

    putch( c );
    *(cur_line->text + lchar + curx - 1) = c;

    curx++;
}
}
```

When you test this code, don't overstrike when your cursor is at the far right column in the window. That part hasn't been implemented yet. Otherwise, you should be overstriking properly.

When this much works, try to implement the scroll on your own. Here's a hint: It's very, very simple.

Listing 12-13 shows my implementation of the scroll at the right edge. It's added to use_char() in TEFIL.CPP.

Listing 12-13: TEFIL.CPP

```
if ( curx == rgt-lft-1 )
{
// scroll one right
    lchar++;
    curx--;
    show_all( top_line );
}
```

This approach to scrolling pushes the window one character to the right, so the overstrike that follows is actually done one character before the right edge. That means that no other special code is needed.

Going Home and End

As I tested my code, I wanted to press Home and End to hop to the respective ends of the text line. As we go along we'll find other commands that are missing that we would like to have. You'll find some of your favorites that I haven't noticed, too.

Rather than wait patiently, we'll interrupt our work to add the missing commands. At this point, adding commands should be starting to get fairly routine. Follow these steps:

S T E P   B Y   S T E P

1. Add a new message to EDITCMDS.H.

2. Return the message from plain_cmd() (or whatever function is appropriate) in TECMD.CPP by adding a case for the appropriate keystroke(s).

3. Catch the message with a new case in file_win::edit_do(), in TEFIL.CPP. Use msg() to check your work this far.

4. Implement the command in edit_do() if it's very simple, or in a separate file_win method if it's more than a few lines of code.

I'll let you do most of the work without listings. Start by adding GO_HOME and GO_END messages to EDITCMDS.H. (I used numbers 1021 and 1022.) Then add a case for each of these messages to plain_cmd() in TECMD.CPP.

For a test, add stub cases in edit_do(), TEFIL.CPP, that use msg() to report the intent. Mine says "going home" and "going end." If you never make mistakes, you can skip this step. I'll bet that the people who don't skip this step get their commands implemented more quickly, though.

When the messages show appropriately in response to tapping the Home and End keys, go on to implement the commands. Home is simpler since you don't have to worry about going past the right edge of the window. Try it on your own before you look at my implementation. (The best implementation won't use show_all() unless it's needed.)

End is a bit more complicated. You have to find out where you want to put the cursor and then check to see if that is in the window. If you're outside, scrolling is needed. Again, the best implementation won't use show_all() if scrolling isn't required.

Listing 12-14 shows my implementation. I put the code right in the cases in file_win::edit_do(). If your implementation is different from mine, decide whose is better before you make changes. Yours may be better than mine, of course.

Listing 12-14: TEFIL.CPP

```
case GO_HOME:
    {
        curx = 1;

        if ( lchar == 0 )
            gotoxy( lft+1, top+cury );
        else
        {
            lchar = 0;
            show_all( top_line );
        }

        break;
    }
```

```
    case GO_END:
    {
            int slen = strlen( cur_line->text );

            curx = slen - lchar + 1;

            if ( curx < lwid )
                gotoxy( lft+curx, top+cury );
            else
            {
                curx = lwid ;
                lchar = slen - curx + 1;
                show_all( top_line );
            }
    }

        break;
    }
```

With those two commands available, you can test your overstrike capability again, just to be sure. One of the things you'll find is that the End keystroke gets you out past the last character, to the actual end of the text data member. The pad_str() function adds blanks to the end, and the strlen() function finds the location of the null, past the last blank. If you don't like this approach, write a special version of strlen() that finds the last nonblank. Alternatively, let it be.

Now that we can overstrike, let's go on to deletions.

DELETING CHARACTERS

There are four types of deletions that I want to implement immediately.

▶ Del—the character under the cursor

▶ Backspace—the character to the left of the cursor

▶ Ctrl+T—the word to the right of cursor

▶ Ctrl+Y—the current line

We can save some time by adding these in a batch, up to the point where we code the individual actions in TEFIL. Listing 12-15 shows the addition of suitable messages in EDITCMDS.H.

Listing 12-15: EDITCMDS.H

```
#define GO_HOME            1021
#define GO_END         1022


#define DEL_CHAR           1031
#define DEL_PREV_CHAR      1032
#define DEL_WORD           1033
#define DEL_LINE           1034


#define TOGGLE_SCREEN      1801
```

These are all messages that are sent from plain_cmd() in TECMD.CPP. Listing 12-16 shows these new cases.

Listing 12-16: TECMD.CPP

```
        case RT_ARROW:
        case CTRL_D:
            return CURSOR_RT;


        case DEL:
        case CTRL_G:
            return DEL_CHAR;

        case BKSP: // also CTRL_H
            return DEL_PREV_CHAR;

        case CTRL_T:
            return DEL_WORD;

        case CTRL_Y:
            return DEL_LINE;

        case PGUP:
            return GO_PGUP;
```

With TECMD sending appropriate messages, it's up to TEFIL to handle them. Again, begin by stubbing them out with msg() responses. Listing 12-17 shows the new cases in file_win::edit_do().

Listing 12-17: TEFIL.CPP

```
case GO_PGDN:
{
    if ( !is_bot_line(bot_line) )
        win_scroll( 1 );
    else
        msg( "bottom showing" );
    break;
}

    case DEL_CHAR:
    {
        msg( "del char" );
        break;
    }

    case DEL_PREV_CHAR:
    {
        msg( "del prev char" );
        break;
    }

    case DEL_WORD:
    {
        msg( "del word" );
        break;
    }

    case DEL_LINE:
    {
        msg( "del line" );
        break;
    }

case GO_HOME:
```

When you've tested this much and it works, you're ready to go on to implementing the deletions. We'll start with the character under the cursor.

Deleting under the Cursor

Deleting the character under the cursor appears to be very simple. Delete one character from the text string (just copy the right side of the string left one character) and then add a blank on the end. Redisplay this string and you're done.

Of course, that process doesn't apply if your cursor is past the end of the text string. Beyond the end, you want the delete to get rid of the invisible return character that separates lines. This means concatenating the text of the next line to the text of the current line and then redisplaying from the current line on down.

We can simplify the code a little by just calling show_all() after we concatenate the next line to the current one. But then we should really also allow the cursor to be out past the end of the current line and make it behave as if there were blanks between the cursor and the end of the current text line. Let's start, however, with just the current line of text.

You'll find that our del_chars() code, in TEWIN.CPP, serves us well. Listing 12-18 shows the simple case of deletion under the cursor, in file_win::edit_do() in TEFIL.CPP.

Listing 12-18: TEFIL.CPP

```
case DEL_CHAR:
    {
        int slen = strlen( cur_line->text );
        if ( (lchar + curx) <= slen )
        {
            char* cp = cur_line->text
                + lchar + curx - 1;
            del_chars( cp ); // deletes one char
            cprintf( cp );
            gotoxy( lft+curx, top+cury );
        }
        else
        {
            msg( "more tk" );
        }
    break;
    }
```

With this routine, you should be able to delete characters within the existing text. Let's go on to delete after the end of the text.

Although it's not true in fact, we want it to appear as if the cursor is over a '\n' character, which the Del (or Ctrl+G) keystroke deletes. A support routine, cat_next_text(), can do all the hard work, making the actual code in the DEL_CHAR case very simple. Listing 12-19 shows the added logic in the DEL_CHAR case in file_win::edit_do(), and Listing 12-20 (on disk, use 12-19.CPP) shows the new file_win method, cat_next_text(). Don't forget to add the declaration of cat_next_text() to the class definition in TEFIL.H.

Listing 12-19: TEFIL.CPP

```
case DEL_CHAR:
{
    int slen = strlen( cur_line->text );
    if ( (lchar + curx) <= slen )
    {
        char* cp = cur_line->text
            + lchar + curx - 1;
        del_chars( cp ); // deletes one char
        cprintf( cp );
        gotoxy( lft+curx, top+cury );
    }
    else
    {
        cat_next_text();
        delete cur_line->next;
        show_all( top_line );
    }
    break;
}
```

Listing 12-20: TEFIL.CPP

```
}

void file_win::cat_next_text()
{
/*
```

```
            Concatenates text from next line to text of current
            line. If cursor is beyond end of current line, blank
            pads current line out to cursor.
*/

// exit if called at eof
    if ( !cur_line->next )
        return;

// get new string buffer
    int nxt_slen = strlen( cur_line->next->text );
    char* new_str = new char[ lchar+curx+nxt_slen+1 ];

// copy in current text
    strcpy( new_str, cur_line->text );

// blank fill at end, if needed
    int slen = strlen( cur_line->text );
    char* cp = new_str+slen;

    int i = lchar + curx;
    while ( --i > slen )
        *cp++ = ' ';

// copy in next line's text
    strcpy( cp, cur_line->next->text );

// replace cur_line's text
    delete cur_line->text;
    cur_line->text = new_str;
}
```

memline::memline(memline* after_line, char* txt)

When you add this code, you should be able to go past the end of the first line (End, then right arrow) and delete to bring the second line up to form an additional part of the first line. In fact, you should be able to repeat this action until you have nothing but one long top line. Your Home and End keys will be handy in checking this one.

Now let's go on to the next delete, using the Backspace key.

Deleting behind the Cursor

Some people have the Backspace key delete left of the cursor in insert mode but just move the cursor left in overstrike mode. I'm not one of those people, but if you are, this action will be simple to implement. You've already got all the functions coded.

And for those who, like me, want the Backspace key to just delete, no matter where we are, we've also got the functions we need already coded, although not quite in the form we want.

Start by moving the logic out of the DEL_CHAR case in file_win::edit_do() and putting it into a file_win::del_char() method. Then call this method from the DEL_CHAR case. Listings 12-21 and 12-22 show these changes. (For both, use 12-21.CPP if you need a disk listing.)

Listing 12-21: TEFIL.CPP

```
case DEL_CHAR:
    {
        del_char();
        break;
    }
```

Listing 12-22: TEFIL.CPP

```
    return done;
}


void file_win::del_char()
{
    int slen = strlen( cur_line->text );
    if ( (lchar + curx) <= slen )
    {
        char* cp = cur_line->text
            + lchar + curx - 1;
        del_chars( cp ); // deletes one char
        cprintf( cp );
```

```
        gotoxy( lft+curx, top+cury );
    }
    else
    {
        cat_next_text();
        delete cur_line->next;
        show_all( top_line );
    }
}
```

```
void file_win::use_char( int cmd )
```

Of course, the code shown as new in the del_char() routine is really logic that
was cut out of the DEL_CHAR case. When you test this change, it should run
just as it did before you made the change.

However, now we can do an incredibly simple job of most of the backspace
delete logic. We just back the cursor up one space and call del_char(). Listing
12-23 shows the start of the DEL_PREV_CHAR case in file_win::edit_do() in
TEFIL.CPP.

Listing 12-23: TEFIL.CPP

```
    case DEL_PREV_CHAR:
    {
        if ( curx > 1 )
        {
            curx--;
            gotoxy( lft+curx, top+cury );

            del_char();
        }
        else
        {
            msg( "more tk" );
        }
        break;
    }
```

Run that, and you'll be delighted to see that it really works. Now we only need to handle the case where we start at the left edge of the window.

The good news is that there's a way to handle the left edge very nicely. The bad news is that things can get very complicated, very fast.

If you're at the left edge but lchar is greater than zero (your window is scrolled right), you scroll the window back one to the left, move one column left, and do a del_char(). But if you're at the left edge, you have to back up to the end of the previous line, unless you're already at the top line. Backing up to the end of the previous line may be simple, but it may require scrolling the screen to the right. The operation looks something like this:

```
if not at left edge
    back up
    delete
else if scrolled right
    scroll one left
    backup
    delete
else if not at top line
    go up one line
    go to the end of the line (scrolling if needed)
    delete
else do nothing
```

Let's work on simplifying this. First, I actually want all these actions, except the deletion, to be part of a generalized backup logic. If you'll check TCLite, for one example, you'll see that the word-left command (Ctrl+A or Ctrl+left arrow) backs up to the end of the previous line if it's given at the start of a line. Second, we've already written the logic to position the cursor at the end of a line when we programmed the GO_END case.

So we can simplify our problem by taking the logic from GO_END and putting that, too, in a separate function. While we're at it, we may as well do the same for the GO_HOME logic. As we do this, you'll see that we're actually going to be programming more and more of our logic by calling the methods that we've already written.

Add declarations for functions file_win::go_home() and file_win::go_end() in the class definition in TEFIL.H. Then move the code from the case in file_win::edit_do() in TEFIL.CPP into these new functions, as you see in Listings 12-24 and 12-25. (If you need as disk version, use 12-24.CPP for both.)

Listing 12-24: TEFIL.CPP

```
        case GO_HOME:
        {
            go_home();
            break;
        }


        case GO_END:
        {
            go_end();
            break;
        }
```

Listing 12-25: TEFIL.CPP

```
    return done;
}


void file_win::go_home()
{
    curx = 1;

    if ( lchar == 0 )
        gotoxy( lft+1, top+cury );
    else
    {
        lchar = 0;
        show_all( top_line );
    }

}


void file_win::go_end()
{
```

```
    int slen = strlen( cur_line->text );

curx = slen - lchar + 1;

if ( curx < lwid )
    gotoxy( lft+curx, top+cury );
else
{
    curx = lwid ;
    lchar = slen - curx + 1;
    show_all( top_line );
}

}
```

```
void file_win::del_char()
```

When you test this much, your Home and End keys should function correctly, just as they did before the change. Now we're ready to write a back_up() function.

To begin, I replaced my entire CURSOR_LF logic with a simple call to the back_up() method. Listing 12-26 shows my new CURSOR_LF logic in file_win::edit_do() in TEFIL.CPP, and Listing 12-27 shows the file_win::back_up() function I've added. (Use 12-26.CPP for both, if you need to work from a disk listing. Don't forget to add the declaration of back_up() in the class definition in TEFIL.H.)

Listing 12-26: TEFIL.CPP

```
        case CURSOR_LF:
        {
            back_up();
            break;
        }
```

Listing 12-27: TEFIL.CPP

```
    return done;

}
```

```
void file_win::back_up()
{

// shift one left, if not at left
    if ( curx > 1 )
    {
        curx--;
        gotoxy( lft+curx, top+cury );
        return;
    }

// scroll left, if at screen left
    if ( lchar > 0 )
    {
        lchar--;
        show_all( top_line );
        return;
    }

// go to end of previous line, if showing
    if ( cury > 1 )
    {
        cury--;
        cur_line = cur_line->prev;
        go_end();
        return;
    }

// go to end of previous line, if there is one
    if ( !is_top_line() )
    {
        cur_line = top_line = top_line->prev;
        go_end();
        return;
    }
}
```

```
void file_win::go_home()
```

The back_up() function is long, but it's not complicated. You just take one situation at a time, adding an if statement and two or three lines of working code that apply when the condition is true.

T I P

Methods like back_up() are simple to build if you only write one if test at a time. Stub out the rest of the function with a msg(), until you have handled every possibility.

When you can back_up() reliably, give a little thought to when you want to back_up(). I like to back up in response to the left arrow or Ctrl+S keypress. Many text editors, including TCLite's built-in editor, don't back up from the left end of a line. (Try it in TCLite—the cursor stops moving once it hits the left side of the line.)

If you want to turn off the back_up() functionality at the left edge, add an if statement that decides when to call back_up(). It would look something like this:

```
if ( (curx>1) || (lchar>0) )
    back_up();
```

The important point is that you decide for yourself when this function should, and should not, happen.

Now that we can back up, programming a backspace delete is not a problem. Again, you have to decide what you want the Backspace key to mean. Once you've decided, the implementation is simple.

My implementation is the soul of simplicity. You may like it this way, or you may find its behavior at the left end of a line to be disagreeable. Again, your goal isn't to write an editor my way, it's to write the editor that works your way.

Listing 12-28: TEFIL.CPP

```
case DEL_PREV_CHAR:
```

```
    {
        back_up();
        del_char();
        break;
    }
```

Add whatever extra logic you like, to make it come out your way. Be sure to think about what you want to happen if the cursor is already at the beginning of the file when the Backspace key is pressed. When you've got it where you like it, let's go on to deleting a whole word at a time.

Deleting the Current Word

When we programmed our string_field logic, we thought about deleting the next word, which entailed deciding what to do when the cursor was in the middle of a word, in whitespace between words, and so on. We can reuse that logic here. In fact, deleting a word would be very simple if it weren't for the fact that we could be responding to that command when the cursor is at, or past, the end of the line.

To do this right, we're going to need to know if the cursor is in the text line or at the end. (In the line means anyplace up to and including the last nonblank character.) I added two private member functions to file_win, in TEFIL.CPP. As Listing 12-29 shows, these are vstrlen() and is_eol().

The vstrlen() function reports strlen() for the visual portion of the line—it doesn't count trailing whitespace. The is_eol() method uses vstrlen() to see if the cursor is past the visual end of the line. (Remember, those trailing blanks are a convenience for the sake of efficiency. I don't want to be bothered thinking about them when I use the editor.)

Listing 12-29: TEFIL.CPP

```
int file_win::is_bot_line( memline* ml )
{
    return ( !ml ) || ( !ml->next );
}


int file_win::is_eol()
{
    return (lchar + curx) > vstrlen( cur_line->text );
```

```
}

int file_win::vstrlen( char* s )
{
// Visual (excluding trailing whitespace) strlen()

    int n = strlen( s );

    char* cp = s + n - 1;                    / blank

    while ( (n > 0) && (*cp <= 32) )
    {
        n--;
        cp--;

    }

    return n;
}
```

void file_win::cat_next_text()

The is_eol() function, by using vstrlen() correctly, reports TRUE when your cursor is in the trailing blanks at the end of a line, is over the underlying null character, or is off in the no-man's land to the right of the terminating null. The vstrlen() function uses the built-in strlen() and then backs up, looking for a character greater than a blank (32).

With these supporting methods, we're ready to delete a word. There are two separate problems. Our cursor may or may not be at the end of the line (more exactly, past the visible end of the line). The first part of the DEL_WORD case in file_win::edit_do(), TEFIL.CPP, handles the is_eol() situation.

If you're on the last line in the file, nothing happens. Otherwise, the appearance is that the newline character between lines is deleted, concatenating the next line to the current line. The del_char() routine has the necessary logic, so it is used. By stuffing a terminating null into the text string, the problem of trailing blanks is eliminated.

The second case is that you are in the text, so a simple word delete is called for. We handle this just as we did the string_field object. We set a pointer to the current position in the text and then use right_word() to find the start of the next word. Then we use del_chars() to get rid of the space between the current location and the start of the next word. Listing 12-30 shows the added logic. (If you need a disk listing, start with 12-29.CPP.)

Listing 12-30: TEFIL.CPP

```
case DEL_WORD:
{

    if ( is_eol() )
    {
        if ( is_bot_line() )
            break;
        else
        {
        // note: may be at a trailing blank
            *( cur_line->text +
                lchar + curx - 1 ) = 0;

            del_char();
            break;
        }
    }


    char* s1 = cur_line->text + lchar + curx - 1;
    char* s2 = right_word( s1 );

    del_chars( s1, s2-s1 );

    show_line( top+cury, cur_line->text );
    gotoxy( lft+curx, top+cury );

    break;
}
```

When you enter and run this code, don't forget to test for conditions that include shrinking the window. You want to correctly display your result when, for instance, you delete at the end of a line, connecting the next one when it doesn't fit inside the window.

Deleting the Whole Line

When you have the word deletions running, it's time to go on to deleting the whole line. I want to discuss debugging this code, but first let's start with the new logic you need to delete a line. In general, you just switch the cur_line to the former cur_line->next and then delete the old cur_line (which has become the new cur_line->prev). Redisplay and you're done.

As usual, the most common case occupies only a small part of the code. You can't switch to cur_line->next if you're at the bottom of the file already. When you delete the last line, you have to switch to cur_line->prev, instead. Of course, you can't do that, either, if you have an empty file. If you do switch to cur_line->prev, you've got to remember to decrement cury, since you've got to move the cursor up a line. And then, suppose you're deleting the last line of the file and it happens to be the only line displayed in the window and. . . .

Let's get right on to solving the problem, and then let's talk about the problem. Listing 12-31 shows the new logic to add to the DEL_LINE case in file_win::edit_do(), in TEFIL.CPP.

Listing 12-31: TEFIL.CPP

```
case DEL_LINE:
{
    if ( !is_bot_line() ) // bottom of file?
    {
        if ( cur_line == top_line )
            top_line = cur_line->next;

        cur_line = cur_line->next;
        delete cur_line->prev;
    }
    else if ( cur_line != top_line )
    {
        mem_file->tail_line = cur_line =
            cur_line->prev;
        delete cur_line->next;
```

cury--;

```
        }

        else if ( cur_line->prev )
        {
            mem_file->tail_line = cur_line =
                cur_line->prev;
            delete cur_line->next;

            top_line = cur_line;
        }


        show_all( top_line );
        break;

}
```

By the way, are you the sort who likes puzzles? If you are, take a good look at Listing 12-31. See how the work is almost the same in the second and third cases? Can you figure out a way to take advantage of that fact and write a simpler version of this logic? (I couldn't. At least not in any reasonable amount of time. I'm sure a better way will come to me just as this book goes to press.)

Bugs and Debugging

Let's think about the debugging process. I try to test everything I can think of. (Actually, you start to write the function by making a mental list of all the conditions you can think of.) Then when things don't work, I wonder why. Sometimes using a Watch or Inspect window helps. Often, all you need to do is look at the code after you see what fails. Sometimes, there's a lot of tedious work involved in tracking down the bug.

For example, I completely forgot about the mem_file->tail_line data member when I wrote the original version of this logic. I saw lots of problems crop up when I pressed Ctrl+PgDn to go to the end of the file. Of course, I had spent considerable time working on the problem before I pinned it down to the Ctrl+PgDn keystroke. When I decided that the problem might be related to the GO_EOF message, I looked at that code and saw, right away, what the problem was.

I'd deleted the last line of text, which meant that mem_file->tail_line was a tion is useful until that particular bit of memory gets reallocated for another use. Then you're in trouble.

The problem is that the cause of the trouble (in this case, not resetting the pointer to the end of the linked list) precedes the appearance of the trouble. All you can be sure of when you see trouble—in this case, random bits of memory appearing in the text file window—is that something went wrong, earlier.

One solution is to write, as we've been doing all along, a little bit of code at a time. Test as you go, and you'll have a pretty good idea of where your trouble happens. You won't have, however, 100 percent certainty.

Before I wrote this book, I wrote the code for Tiny Editor version 1.0. As I'm writing this manuscript, I'm rewriting the code, using what I learned from writing 1.0 (leaving out some of the dumber things I did). The code's still not perfect, but it's a pretty good compromise between the best possible programming and code that illustrates the parts of C++ that we're learning.

Still, I make mistakes. The big advantage I have in this medium is that I can just back up and fix them, and they disappear. We go right ahead with whatever phase of the project we're in and, hopefully, you concentrate on getting your version working while you master C++. This may make it seem like I'm so smart that I never make mistakes (which is totally false!) or that coding gets dead simple if only you learn the language thoroughly (which is partly true, and partly false).

Let's look at a couple of examples of genuine (happened while I wrote this code) bugs that are still sitting in our Tiny Editor project because I put them there. (Maybe you saw them and fixed them along the way. If you did, skim right on ahead to the next section, and accept my congratulations.)

Want to see a bug? Try this. Run your program. Use Ctrl+F5 to shrink your window horizontally to the point where a long line doesn't fit. Scroll to the left so that the right end of the line is out past the right edge of the window. Now delete a character in that line. See what happens?

You write right on past the edge of the window. If you look at the code, the offending line is easy to find. I did this:

```
cprintf( cp ); // rewrites the line from the
               // spot of the deletion
```

That, of course, is not the way to do it. It was a long time ago that we wrote the show_line() function that worries about whether the line is visible (based on the scrolling position) and whether the relevant part of the line fits. We should never write text to the screen without using the show_line() function. The best case is that if we use show_line() consistently, we won't have any bugs. The worst case is that we'll have just one function to debug, which isn't so bad.

Listing 12-32 shows the del_char() function in TEFIL.CPP with the offending cprintf() replaced by a well-mannered show_line().

Listing 12-32: TEFIL.CPP

```
void file_win::del_char()
{
    int slen = strlen( cur_line->text );
    if ( (lchar + curx) <= slen )
    {
        char* cp = cur_line->text
            + lchar + curx - 1;
        del_chars( cp ); // deletes one char

        show_line( top+cury, cur_line->text );
        gotoxy( lft+curx, top+cury );
    }
    else
    {
        cat_next_text();
        delete cur_line->next;
        show_all( top_line );
    }
}
```

After you make this change and test it, what do you think of immediately? If you don't like bugs in your programs, immediately ask yourself where else you did something just like this.

I went through TEFIL.CPP looking for instances of the string "cprintf." I found some in msg(), but they don't matter since we'll throw that one away when we're done. Otherwise, there are just two left. One is in show_line(), and the other, in clear(). Both these cprintf() calls are ones we can keep. Since there are no others, we've fixed the only bug of its kind.

While I was testing the DEL_LINE code, I also found a bug in the PgUp/PgDn logic. Sometimes it leaves the cursor one line below where it belongs. The specific symptom I saw was that the cursor was a line below the end of the file. Pressing Ctrl+Y deleted the line above the cursor. The cursor then moved up one line, but, of course, it was still one line below where it should have been.

I double-checked my DEL_LINE logic, but its treatment of cury was pretty simple. Unless you delete the last line in the file and that line is below the top line in the window, you don't change your row location. The cury member was decremented properly for the one case where it needed to be adjusted. Again, that finding led me to look elsewhere for the problem.

After a lot of experimenting, I found that the PgUp code was letting something get out of synch. Try this sequence to see for yourself:

Launch your edit window. Then use Ctrl+F5 and Alt+up arrow (or down arrow) to adjust your window so that it is one line less tall than is needed to fit your whole file. Use Enter to end the window mode and then use enough down arrows to just make your file's last line visible. Then press PgUp. You are now out of synch by one. If you press End you'll see that your cursor is checking for the end of the line of text above the one it's really on. If you press down arrow repeatedly, you'll stop one row below the last line of text.

The editor we're working on has to have everything kept synchronized, or it will fall apart quite badly. You can't leave problems like this in the code. You've got to chase them down. Begin by looking for the GO_EOF message. You'll see that it calls win_scroll(-1). This is the relevant portion of the applicable file_win::win_scroll() method:

```
// back top_line up one page (if possible)
    for ( dist = 0; dist < pgsize; dist++ )
    {
        if ( top_line->prev )
            top_line = top_line->prev;
        else
            break;
    }
```

```
// back cur_line up as much as top_line
   for ( int i=0; i < dist; i++ )
       cur_line = cur_line->prev;
```

There are two problems here. One is subtle and one is obvious. Unfortunately, the subtle one hid the obvious one when I was testing. First, the test for top_line->prev isn't the right test. We have a null memline at the head of the linked list (above the top of the file), so the following statement will back the top_line up to this null line. We want to test top_line->prev->prev, instead. That will be null when we are at the last visible top line.

The subtle problem is this:

```
int i;
for ( i = 1; i < 5; i++ ) // loop 1 thru 4
{
    if ( whatever )
        do_something;
    else
        break;
}
```

The loop counter, i, will count from 1 thru 5. When it hits 5, the loop stops. It is incremented after each iteration of the loop. This behavior can be inconsistent with the break statement in the loop.

The block above is equivalent to this one:

```
int i;
for ( i = 1; i < 5; ) // loop 1 thru 4
{
    if ( whatever )
        do_something;
    else
        break;

    i++; // END INCREMENTED
}
```

If you exit the loop via the break, your loop counter has not been incremented. If you exit via the test in the loop, your counter has been incremented. If you need to use the last value of your loop counter, you can get a different result when you make this simple change:

```
int i;
for ( i = 1; i < 5; ) // loop 1 thru 4
{
    i++; // START INCREMENTED

    if ( whatever )
        do_something;
    else
        break;
}
```

In this example, the counter is incremented before the loop tests the condition that might trigger the break. In our code, this was the test we wanted to make. Writing the loop this way allows us to decrement our counter, dist, no matter how we exit the loop. Note this small difference:

```
for ( i = 1; i < 5; i++ ) // END INCREMENTED

for ( i = 1; i++ < 5; )    // START INCREMENTED
```

In the case of the end increment, the value of i will be 1 the first time through the loop, 2 the next, then 3, and then 4. In the case of the start increment, i will be 2 the first time through the loop, then 3, 4, and 5. In both cases, the value will be 5 when the loop terminates.

That will, of course, make a difference of 1 in the value of the counter if you break out of the loop. With that fact in mind, note that Listing 12-33 has a corrected version of the win_scroll(-1) logic, which goes in TEFIL.CPP.

Listing 12-33: TEFIL.CPP

```
if ( direction == -1 )
{
// back top_line up one page (if possible)
    if ( !top_line->prev )
        return;

    for ( dist = 0; dist++ < pgsize; )
```

```
        {
            if ( top_line->prev->prev )
                top_line = top_line->prev;
            else
                break;
        }
        dist--;

    // back cur_line up as much as top_line
        for ( int i=0; i < dist; i++ )
            cur_line = cur_line->prev;
    }
```

The test has been changed to top_line->prev->prev. I added an extra check at the top to be sure that we weren't in an empty file. (If x->prev is null, x->prev->prev is a more or less random pointer—big trouble!) Finally, I changed the loop to increment dist at the start. That way, decrementing dist after the loop is complete works correctly whether we exit via the loop or from the break inside the loop.

I always try to write simple, straightforward code, not getting involved in subtleties like this. Sometimes, however, the problem just decides for itself that it will get involved in these issues. Be very careful when you check the value of a loop counter after the loop has terminated.

INSERTING CHARACTERS

Are you ready to implement insert mode? I am. If we skip the special case, the Enter (or Return) character, inserting characters is just overstriking with a little advance preparation. You slide the existing text one character to the right, from the point of the insertion to the end, and then you overstrike.

Implementing Character Insertion

Since most of the logic is common, we'll not use the structure for the use_char() function that we originally built. It's now something like this:

```
void use_char()
{
    if ( insert_mode )
```

```
        // msg() stub lives here
    else
        // overstrike logic lives here

}
```

The overstrike logic is like this:

```
// extend string if out past end

// scroll right, if at window edge

// do the overstrike
```

Here's what we need to handle insertions, as well as overstrikes:

```
void use_char()
{
// extend string if out past end

    if ( insert_mode)
    // slide text over one, to allow for insertion

// scroll right, if at window edge

// do the overstrike
```

This means we can get rid of the enclosing if and start with the overstrike logic. The extra insert logic gets added inside the existing overstrike logic.

To handle sliding the text, you need to start by deciding if there is available space already. We can just see if the last character is a blank. If it is, we don't need a longer string. If not, we need to extend the string (using our pad_str() function).

Once we've got space, we shift characters starting from the right end and stepping back to the point of the insertion. Finally, we use show_line() to display the shifted characters. Then we're ready to overstrike. Listing 12-34 has the new file_win::use_char() method in TEFIL.CPP. It's marked as all new logic, but you can see that a lot of it is carried over from the existing function.

Listing 12-34: TEFIL.CPP

```cpp
void file_win::use_char( int cmd )
{
    char c = cmd; // drops high bits of cmd

    int len = strlen( cur_line->text );

    while ( (curx + lchar) > len )
    {
        cur_line->text = pad_str( cur_line->text );
        len = strlen( cur_line->text );
    }

    if ( ins_mode )
    {
        if ( cur_line->text[len-1] != ' ' )
        {
            cur_line->text = pad_str( cur_line->text );
            len = strlen( cur_line->text );
        }

        for ( char* cp2 = cur_line->text + len - 1;
            cp2 > cur_line->text + lchar + curx - 1;
            cp2-- )
            *cp2 = *(cp2-1);

        show_line( top+cury, cur_line->text );
        gotoxy( lft+curx, top+cury );
    }

    if ( curx == rgt-lft-1 )
    {
    // scroll one right
        lchar++;
        curx--;
        show_all( top_line );
    }

    putch( c );
```

```
*(cur_line->text + lchar + curx - 1) = c;
curx++;
}
```

When you test this code, you'll be able to insert everything except newline characters.

Inserting Newline Characters

There are at least two ways to treat the newline (Enter or Return keypress). We can send it as a key and let use_char() handle it, or we can send it as a command of its own. I'm going to choose the latter course.

Some people like a distinction between pressing the Enter key in insert and in overstrike mode. I treat both cases the same. For those of you who don't agree, putting the newline character in as a separate message makes it easy to add whatever treatment(s) you like.

To get ready to program the Enter logic, follow these steps:

S T E P   B Y   S T E P

1. Add a DO_ENTER message to EDITCMDS.H. I've added mine as 1041.

2. Add an ENTER case to the plain_cmd() switch in TECMD.CPP. I've added mine right after the ESC case.

3. Add a DO_ENTER case to the switch in file_win::edit_do() in TEFIL.CPP. I've added mine right after the EXIT case. Use a msg() to announce your intention.

4. Test your work to this point.

5. Add a do_enter() method declaration to the file_win class definition in TEFIL.H. A public, void function without parameters will work nicely.

6. Add a file_win::do_enter() method definition in TEFIL.CPP. For starters, just copy the msg() from the edit_do() switch that announces your intention.

7. Change the DO_ENTER logic in edit_do() to call the new method.

8. Test your work to this point.

At this point, your function should look like this one:

```
void file_win::do_enter()
{
    msg( "Handle Enter" );
}
```

When you press the Enter key, your message announces what you want to do, if you're ready to proceed. (Don't go forward until this happens.)

Now you want to see that these things happen:

▶ A new memline is added after the existing memline.

▶ The text from the point of the Enter forward is copied to the new memline's text.

▶ The existing memline's text is truncated at the point of the insertion.

▶ The screen is redisplayed with the cursor at the left of the new line (scrolling if needed).

The question you should be asking now is this: How do we implement these objectives, one step at a time? Start by shrinking your test file so that it fits inside your default window with room to spare, if it doesn't already. That way, you can ignore details like window scrolling while you get the other logic worked out.

Then, without looking ahead to the next listing, follow these steps (all the logic is added in file_win::do_enter() in TEFIL.CPP):

S T E P   B Y   S T E P

1. Add a new memline ("new line" is adequate text for now) following the current line.

2. Add a show_all() and test. You should have a "new line" line following the current one.

3. Before the show_all(), make the new line the current line. (Adjust cur_line, curx, cury, and lchar.) You want the cursor to be displayed at the start of the line.

4. To enable adding a new bottom line, check is_bot_line(); adjust mem_file->tail_line appropriately when you're at the bottom. Test by going to

the bottom and pressing Enter. Then test with a Ctrl+PgDn (or your other GO_EOF keypress).

5. Replace "new line" with a pointer to the correct spot in the original cur_line->text. Your new line should now have the correct text.

6. Overwrite the original cur_line's text, starting at the point of the insertion, with blanks. Your insertion should now look just right, excepting screen scrolling problems.

7. Adjust for correct vertical scrolling. This is needed when your cursor is in the bottom screen line before you press Enter.

8. Test thoroughly.

Got that? Good! Now I'll show you my version, and I want you to give yourself a score. If your code is just as good as mine, give yourself an 8. If your code is more clear than mine, add a point. (Subtract a point if yours is less clear.) If your code is shorter than mine (not counting comments and blanks) add a point. If it's longer, subtract a point only if there isn't some good reason—such as increased clarity—for its being longer.

For every bug in your code that's not in mine, subtract a point. For every bug that's in my code but not in yours, subtract a point from *my* score. Okay?

Listing 12-35 shows my version of file_win::use_char() in TEFIL.CPP.

Listing 12-35: TEFIL.CPP

```
    return done;

}


void file_win::do_enter()
{
// spot of Enter keypress in text:
    char* cp = cur_line->text + lchar + curx - 1;

// create new next line
    memline* ml = new memline( cur_line, cp );

// blank out trailing part of current line
    for ( ; *cp; cp++ )
```

```
        *cp = ' ';

// make new line current
    if ( top+cury != (btm-1) )
        cury++;
    else
        top_line = top_line->next;


    curx = 1;
    lchar = 0;
    cur_line = cur_line->next;

// adjust tail_line, if necessary
    if ( is_bot_line() )
        mem_file->tail_line = cur_line;

// display
    show_all( top_line );
}


void file_win::go_word_lf()
```

Before we wrap this chapter up, let me bring up another point: I noticed two features of my go_word_rt() method that I didn't particularly like. Both happen when you're on the last word in a line. First, if the line ends at the end of the word, the cursor stops on the last character in the word. I'd prefer it to stop just past the end of the word. Second, if there are trailing blanks, it stops at the last blank. Again, I'd prefer it to stop just past the last nonblank.

To fix the first problem, you can check to see if you have gone past the visual end (last non blank) with our vstrlen() function. To fix the second problem, you can check to see if the character preceding the right-word pointer is nonblank.

You can handle these problems on your own, can't you?

SUMMARY

We began this chapter with an editor that couldn't really edit text. We ended with an editor that can really edit and can really call itself an editor! Along the way, you did more and more of the work on your own until, at the end, you were working without me.

While we were going along, we took a look at the C++ union, a structure-like thing that lets you address a single spot in memory as different data types. We also considered some of the bit-level C++ operators for achieving the same results as a union.

We also took a another good look at the for loop, seeing how you could use an increment operator at either the start or the end of each loop iteration. We didn't do this so that we could write subtle code—we did it because this subtlety was causing a subtle bug.

Mostly, we concentrated on building our editor's methods. We began with overstriking characters. Then we continued with deletions, including ones that get rid of a whole line. We concluded with insertions, including inserting lines.

If we could just save our work, we'd be able to put this editor into service. In the next chapter, we'll *not* solve this problem, though. Instead, we'll work on line groups—marking them, moving them, copying them, and deleting them.

We'll save file operations for the following chapter, since the file operations can make good use of the line group operations. You'll see how powerful and handy the linked-list structure can be.

In the last chapter we turned our file_win object into a genuine text editor, adding the ability to insert and over-strike text. We're just about to hang out the "Open for Business" sign on our Tiny Editor. What we really need now is the ability to save our work.

Before we start on the file commands, though, I want to do some serious work on the structure. We'll need to do this work to add the line group commands (mark, move, copy, and delete groups of lines).

If you can't wait to put your Tiny Editor into service, pick a keystroke—TCLite uses F2—and write a save command. It's not hard at all. Need a hint? Look up fputs() in the online help.

If you have the patience, we'll get to saving (and opening and closing multiple files, too) in the next chapter. In this one, we'll add the ability to shuffle groups of lines around, which is one of the most common text manipulation activi-ties in programming.

We'll be very busy implementing features in our Tiny Editor, so you'll be glad to know that we won't need to stop too often to consider new topics in C++. We'll pause to consider one new feature and one additional small point:

▶ Using static variables

▶ Using variable names in function declarations

Aside from these, we'll be coding. If you remember what I said in Chapter 2, you'll see how far you've come. There we were spending almost all our time worrying about C++ and just a little time coding. We've reversed that now. You know enough C++ to spend most of your time coding.

We'll begin preparing for line groups by adding new data members to our file_win class.

Manipulating Line Groups

Line groups are either very simple or very complex, depending on how you want to look at them. Let's start by considering the simple part.

When we display lines, we'll need a highlight color to show the marked group, and we'll need a logical flag set to TRUE for each line that is in the marked group. That's simple enough.

Marking is a simple matter of recording the start and end lines and setting the highlight flag in all the intervening lines. Again, that won't be a problem.

Now let's consider deleting a line group. Starting with the first line in the group, we can use our memline destructor to delete one line at a time until we've done the last line in the group. Our destructor already takes care of fixing the links between the remaining lines after a deletion, so we've already done the hard part.

But, as always, there seems to be a little detail to handle. We'll have to update the screen, of course. Here's where it starts to get complicated. Actually, it's not really complicated, but there is an almost endless list of cases to handle.

For example, the marked line group may be wholly on the current screen. If it is, the cursor may be above the group (don't move it), in the group (move it to the line before the group), or below the group (move it up, but keep it in the same line of text).

Then again, the marked line group may start above the current screen and end in the screen. Again, the cursor may be in the marked group, or it may not. Of course, the marked group may start in the current screen but end somewhere below the screen, and the cursor. . . . Well, you get the idea. And you can't forget extreme cases, such as when the marked group takes all of the current screen and more.

You'll see when we get there that the routines that move, copy, and delete line groups are as long as any we've written. Our linked-list structure lets us do the actual work quickly and easily, but the number of different situations you face for updating the screen adds lots of code.

Adding New Data Members

To handle all the different screen cases, we'll want to know where the marked group is relative to the current screen. To track that, it will help a lot if we record line numbers as we update the screen and mark the line group. Then we can write simple tests like this one:

```
// does line group start above screen?
    if ( group_start_line_no < top_line_no ) ...
```

Of course, we'll need to record the top and bottom lines (pointers to our mem-line objects) of the marked group, too. Start by adding the four new lines shown in Listing 13-1 to the file_win class definition in TEFIL.H.

Listing 13-1: TEFIL.H

```
    int full_screen_mode;
    int save_lft, save_top, save_rgt, save_btm;

    int top_line_no, bot_line_no; // screen lines
    int cur_col, cur_row;         // 1,1 is BOF
```

```
memline* group_start_line, * group_end_line;
int group_start_line_no, group_end_line_no;
```

```
public:
```

While you're adding to TEFIL.H, without a listing add a new int data member, tail_line_no, to the memfile class. We'll call head_line (the null line above the first text line) line 0, and the first line of text will be line 1. We'll initialize tail_line_no when we read in the file and update it as we add and delete lines of text.

Finally, again without a listing, add an int data member, marked, to flag the memline objects that are marked (highlighted as part of a marked line group) in the memline struct definition.

H I N T

Our memfile class definition has become crowded with data members, but our memline struct is still very simple. This is the right way to design your classes. Our Tiny Editor will typically have one or two memfile objects (a dozen would be a lot), so a crowded memfile class won't hurt. Each memfile may have thousands of memlines, however, so adding clutter to memline objects would quickly eat up available memory.

Now that you've got your data members, it's time to initialize them. Equally important, it's time to think about how you will keep track of these numbers as you work. These are the four key data points we've been working with:

▶ lchar—the leftmost visible character

▶ curx—the cursor's horizontal location

▶ top_line—the topmost visible line

▶ cury—the cursor's vertical location

You need to set these four values before doing any display updating. In addition to these four, we've depended on the cur_line pointer being set to the line that the cursor is in (so that when we type or delete a character, for example, the work is done in the right place.

Now we're going to add four data members that point out our marked line group, if any:

► group_start_line—the first memline in a group

► group_start_line_no—the start line's number

► group_end_line—the last memline in a group

► group_end_line_no—the end line's number

We can initialize the starting line number to zero and use this as a check, to see if there is any marked group. The code will look like this:

```
if ( group_start_line_no )
{
    // handle line group here
}
else
{
    // there is no line group
}
```

The commands to mark the beginning and end of a line group will be the ones that set the line group values. Additionally, whenever we add or delete lines of text we'll need to update the line numbers. (More precisely, we'll need to update those line numbers that come after the addition or deletion.) We'll also need to maintain the memfile's eof line number the same way.

Finally, let's consider these four values:

► top_line—the top line on the screen

► top_line_no—the top line's number

► bot_line—the last line on the screen

► bot_line_no—the last line's number

We call show_all() with a memline argument, which sets top_line. The show_all() function uses its parameter to set top_line, and then it sets bot_line. We can also ask it to set bot_line_no if we take care always to set top_line_no before we call show_all(). Of course, our line numbers will also need to be updated when lines are added or deleted.

T I P

The vast majority of all bugs in code such as this come from forgetting to update one of these values. Write a list or stick notes on your monitor or do whatever it takes to be sure that you always check all these values.

Going to X, Y

Let's begin by adding a display to the lower-left corner of our dialog box that tells us what column and row the cursor is in. Right now, we're constantly doing this:

```
gotoxy( lft+curx, top+cury );
```

That should suggest that a cover function would simplify our work. Let's call it goto_xy() to suggest that it is a near-relative of the built-in function. Start by adding a declaration of goto_xy() in the file_win class definition in TEFIL.H and then add a definition in TEFIL.CPP. For starters, just include that one call to the built-in gotoxy() in the definition, so that everything runs as it always has.

Continue by searching for every call to gotoxy() and replacing most of them with calls to goto_xy(). Don't adjust the calls in our temporary msg() function, and don't change the call in goto_xy() (or it will call itself, infinitely). Also, leave the calls in show_all() and show_line() alone for now.

Test all your commands to see that you've made no mistakes, and double-check that the only remaining calls to gotoxy() are in msg(), show_all(), show_line(), and goto_xy(). When you're ready, let's have goto_xy() report the cursor coordinates in the lower-left corner of the file_win window.

One complication is the case when the window is too skinny to fit the full report. The simple way around this problem is to set a limit on how skinny the window can be. (Check TCLite and you'll see that this is Borland's solution, too.) TEWIN.H is the logical place to define the minimum file_win width. While you're there, define a minimum height and add a color for the highlighted line groups, as shown in Listing 13-2.

Listing 13-2: TEWIN.H

```
#define FILE_WIN_OUT_CLR   126 // Hi yellow on white
#define FILE_WIN_CON_CLR     7 //     white  on black
#define FILE_WIN_LINE_CLR  112 //     black on white

#define FILE_WIN_MIN_HEIGHT  2  //
#define FILE_WIN_MIN_WIDTH  24

#define SINGLE      " ┌|┘─└|"
```

Go back to TEFIL.CPP and look in file_win::win_size(). You'll see that the minimums for shrinking left and up are set to numeric constants (never a good practice). Replace these constants with the new #defined constants and rerun the program, checking that your limits are being enforced.

H I N T

Being able to implement a change by modifying the code in just one place, such as by inserting the new minimum width, is a sign of good code. Having to hunt all over a source file for gotoxy() calls was a sign of bad code. Learn to enjoy the former situation and fix the latter.

Now we're ready to add a message line showing the cursor location. We can update and report the cursor location, based on the top_line_no value. (Adjust down from the top line to the current cursor location in the window, to find the current row in the file.) Of course, we haven't assigned a top_line_no value yet, so this won't work. But it's easier to put in the report first, since having that report will help us check when we go back to add the top line number.

Listing 13-3 shows a more sophisticated version of goto_xy() in TEFIL.CPP. It uses a static character buffer, which I'll explain in a minute. Get it running first.

Listing 13-3: TEFIL.CPP

```
void file_win::goto_xy()
{
```

```
    static char* loc_buf    = " 12345:1234 "; // row:col

// compute current location
    cur_row = top_line_no + cury - 1;
    cur_col = lchar + curx;

// clear bottom line
    textattr( FILE_WIN_OUT_CLR );
    gotoxy( lft+7, btm );
    for ( int i = 4; i < 12; i++ )
        putch( border[5] );

// write new value
    gotoxy( lft+3, btm );
    sprintf( loc_buf, " %d:%d \0",
        cur_row, cur_col );
    cprintf( loc_buf );

// goto x, y
    gotoxy( lft+curx, top+cury );
}
```

When you run this new version, you'll have a report of your row and column
position in the lower-left part of your box outline. At the moment, the row
number is nonsense, but we'll straighten that out soon enough. Your column
number should be accurate already.

What's a static variable? Variables declared outside your functions are file-wide
static variables. Variables declared inside your functions are local by default. A
local variable is created when your function starts running and deleted when
your function ends. A static variable is created by the compiler. The DOS loader
finds space for static variables, and DOS frees this space when your program
ends.

One use for a static variable is to create a value, such as a counter, that will not
be reinitialized every time the function is entered. Consider these:

```
void my_func()
{
    int l_counter = 0;
        // set to 0 every time encountered
```

```
    static int s_counter = 0;
        // set to 0 only when program loaded
}
```

The l_counter (dynamic) variable is set to zero every time my_func() is called. The s_counter (static) variable is initialized to zero when the program is loaded. If the value of both counters is 3 when my_func() terminates, the value of l_counter will start over at zero the next time you call my_func(). The value of s_counter will remain at 3 until you change it.

Another use for static variables is to make sure space is allocated for larger buffers at load time, so you don't have to depend on finding the space when the function is called. This is the reason for a static buffer in goto_xy(). (Actually, this buffer is so small it's hardly worth the extra bit of typing to declare it static. But you'll want to use static variables in your later work, so I'm introducing this one here.)

Now let's set the top_line_no variable, so your display isn't so foolish. Begin by setting the memfile's tail_line_no correctly in the memfile constructor. I set it to zero immediately after the rewind() and then increment it after every new memline is created. Having this value makes it simple to test for an empty file— if the tail_line's number is greater than zero, the file isn't empty.

Then I add the line shown in Listing 13-4 to the file_win constructor in TEFIL.CPP.

Listing 13-4: TEFIL.CPP

```
    full_screen_mode = FALSE;


    top_line_no = mem_file->tail_line_no > 0 ? 1 : 0;


    show_all( mem_file->head_line );
```

When you run with these changes, you'll see the top line number is correctly set to 1 when your cursor is at the top of your window. (At least it's correct until you page down. It stays at 1 as long as it's in the window's top line.)

Our last job to get this all right is to update top_line_no whenever we change the screen's top display row. Try this work on your own.

Start with PgUp and PgDn. They call the win_scroll() that has only one parameter. The simple way to modify this one is to look for these assignments:

```
top_line = top_line->prev;
```

```
top_line = top_line->next;
```

After each step backward (assigning prev) decrement the top_line_no value. Similarly, increment top_line_no after each step down to the next line (assigning next). This change should get the page movements correct.

The win_scroll() with two parameters handles single-line movements. The dy parameter specifies vertical movements. After the else statements that specify vertical movement, move the assignments to cur_line above the calls to show_all() and then slide in an appropriate increment and decrement to top_line_no.

The other two movement commands we need to handle are GO_BOF and GO_EOF. For GO_BOF, you can just assign 1 to top_line_no, right before the call to show_all(). For GO_EOF, assign mem_file_tail_line_no to top_line_no right after you assign mem_file_tail_line to top_line. Then decrement top_line_no each time you back top_line up to its prev value.

There are two more situations that could change line numbers: deleting lines and adding lines. The del_line() function almost never changes the top line's number, but there is one exception. Normally, if you delete a line on the screen, the top line number remains the same. Even if you delete the top line, a new line slides up to take its place, but the number won't change.

The exception is deleting the top line on the screen when it is the only line on the screen. Insert a statement decrementing top_line_no when this happens. (In edit_do(), the command is DEL_LINE. It's the third situation the routine handles.)

The last item to consider is adding lines. Do you want to try this without my advice?

Rewriting the Display Code

By the way, if you want my advice on adding lines, here it is: Don't do anything. You can't possibly add a line above the top line on the screen, can you? So adding lines can't change the top line's number.

On the other hand, if you tested thoroughly you saw that we were definitely doing some interesting things to the color. Sometimes we would write lines using the border color instead of the contents color. I ignored that behavior because we have to modify the display code to handle two colors in the text: the normal color and the marked line group color.

This means that we'll have to modify the show_line() code to set an appropriate color. Additionally, the places where we cheated and updated the screen directly should be changed to call show_line(), or our code will get hopelessly complicated. Let's start with the show_all() routine.

Updating show_all()

We wrote a simple show_all() that started by entirely clearing the window to the box's contents color. With marked line groups, this won't work. I want my line groups to show their lines, from the left to the right edges of the window, in the highlight color. I don't want to write just the characters in a highlight color, since I want to show that the whole area, including new text you add, is selected as part of the line group.

This requirement means that the show_line() routine will have to decide, one line at a time, what the right color is and to clear to that color before it writes text. While we're at it, we may as well teach the show_line() routine how to clear an empty line (any of the lines past the end of the file), too. That way we can dispense with the clear() routine altogether and speed up show_all() a bit.

Listing 13-5 shows the new show_all() routine in TEFIL.CPP. You can't use it yet, though. Wait until you add the matching show_line() code in the next section.

Listing 13-5: TEFIL.CPP

```
file_win::~file_win()
{
    delete blanks;
}


void file_win::show_all()
{
    memline* cl = top_line;

    if ( !cl->prev )        // at start of memfile
    {
        if ( cl->next )     // has 1 or more lines
            cl = cl->next;
```

```
        }

    top_line = cl;
    bot_line_no = top_line_no;

    for ( int row = top+1; row < btm; row++ )
    {
        show_line( row, cl );
        if ( cl->next )
        {
            if ( (row+1) < btm )
            {
                cl = cl->next;
                bot_line_no++;
            }
        }
        else
        {
            row++;

            while ( row < btm )
            {
                show_line( row, NULL );
                row++;
            }
        }
    }
    bot_line = cl;
    goto_xy();
}
```

Did you see that I dropped the parameter? This means that you'll have to
change the declaration in the class definition in TEFIL.H, too. We were almost
always calling show_all() with top_line as the argument. If the argument never
changes, we can dispense with it altogether.

When you change the argument in TEFIL.H, delete the declaration of clear().
We don't need it anymore. You should delete clear()'s definition in TEFIL.CPP,
too.

The code now does its work in a single loop, going from top to bottom. When it runs out of text (the bottom of the file comes before the bottom of the window), a little loop finishes up with calls to show_line() using a NULL memline argument. Of course, this means that the real work is now buried in the show_line() routine, which is next on our agenda.

Before you go on to show_line(), it's time to change every call to show_all(). If top_line was the argument, just delete it (as in the first example that follows). In the handful of cases where top_line was not the argument, assign the former argument to top_line before you call show_all() (as in the second and third examples).

```
    // 1st example
  show_all( top_line );     // old version

  show_all();               // new version

    // 2nd example

  show_all( cur_line );     // old version

  top_line = cur_line;      // new version
  show_all();

    // 3rd example

  show_all( top_line->prev ); // old version

  top_line = top_line->prev;  // new version
  show_all();
```

A Better show_line()

Among other changes, show_line() is going to need to choose the correct display color, so we'll have to pass it a pointer to the memline so it can check the marked flag. It will have to take care of clearing the full line, since there's no clear() to do that for it. We'll also need to teach it to handle a NULL memline so that it can clear any lines below the bottom of the text file.

All things considered, I found that rewriting from scratch was the easy way. Listing 13-6 shows my new show_line() in TEFIL.CPP. Again, since I've changed the parameters, you'll need to make an equivalent change in the declaration in TEFIL.H.

Listing 13-6: TEFIL.CPP

```cpp
        bot_line = cl;

        goto_xy();

}

void file_win::show_line( int row, memline* ml )
{
    static char* blanks =     // 80 blanks
        "                                                           "
        "                                                           ";

    char work[80];

    strncpy( work, blanks, lwid );
    work[lwid] = 0;

    char* s;

    if ( ml ) // ml is null if past end of file
    {
        s = ml->text;

        int len = strlen( s );

        if( len > lchar )
        {
            s += lchar;
            len = len - lchar;

            len = len > lwid ? lwid : len;

            strncpy( work, s, len );
        }
        textattr( ml->marked ?
            FILE_WIN_LINE_CLR : FILE_WIN_CON_CLR );
    }
    else
        textattr( FILE_WIN_CON_CLR );
```

```
    gotoxy( lft+1, row );
    cprintf( work );


}
```

```
void file_win::edit()    //
```

When you try to run this, your compiler will object that the other calls (there are three of them) to show_line() don't work. Change them this way:

```
show_line( row, some_line->text );   // old


show_line( row, some_line );             // new
```

With that done, your display should work just as it used to, except that your lines will be marked randomly. Chances are pretty good that they'll all be marked, since any nonzero bit in the marked int will effectively mark the line. In TEFIL.CPP, go back to the memline constructor and have it set marked to FALSE. Try again, and your lines should all be in the old window contents color.

Now we've got a better show_all() and show_line() team working together. For show_all() always to use the correct color, you need always to use show_line(), of course. The use_char() routine wrote single characters when it could by using putch(). This has to be changed.

In use_char(), begin by deleting the line (near the bottom) that calls putch(). Then move these two lines:

```
    show_line( top + cury, cur_line );
    goto_xy();
```

Take them from their current location, just past the for loop, to the end of the function. They should be the last two lines in the function, and you'll be in business.

Before we can move on to the line group commands, let's drop in a pair of new commands and make some detailed improvements.

A D D I N G   N E W   F E A T U R E S

When I implemented line groups for the first time, I was constantly wishing for a top/end-of-screen command pair. This time I'll be a bit smarter and start right out by adding these commands. They're almost no trouble at all.

The Top and the End of the Screen

First, let me note that I don't use the letter "B" for either end of the screen. Beginning of screen and Bottom of screen can get very confusing, so I use top and end. Follow these steps:

S T E P   B Y   S T E P

1. Add GO_TOS and GO_EOS command messages to EDITCMDS.H. I've added mine as 1023 and 1024, just after GO_HOME and GO_END.

2. Send these messages from plain_cmd(), in TECMD.CPP, in response to some appropriate keystrokes. I've copied TCLite and used CTRL_HOME for GO_TOS and CTRL_END for GO_EOS.

3. Add GO_TOS: and GO_EOS: cases in file_win::edit_do(). Use msg() to report your intention and test, before you try to implement them.

4. Implement the GO_TOS: case. Assign to cur_line and use file_win::go() to get the job done in two statements.

5. Repeat step 4 for GO_EOS. It's almost as easy.

Did you get those steps done quickly enough? I took entirely too long. I skipped the msg() step, intending to save time. Murphy's Law has *not* been repealed. In TECMD I typed GO_END when I meant to say GO_EOS. If I'd put in the msg() step, that mistake would have been obvious. As it was I couldn't figure out why my logic didn't work.

When you program slowly, you get done quickly. When you program quickly, you get done slowly.

My logic for the two new cases is shown in Listing 13-7. Yours should be similar.

Listing 13-7: TEFIL.CPP

```
case GO_END:
{
    go_end();
    break;
}

case GO_TOS:
{
    cur_line = top_line;
    go( curx, 1 );
    break;
}

case GO_EOS:
{
    cur_line = bot_line;
    go( curx, bot_line_no - top_line_no + 1 );
    break;
}

case GO_BOF:
```

With those two commands added, let's make one more fix and then get on to marking line groups.

Respecting the Visual End of a String

When you press End (or whatever key you chose to go to the end of a line), your cursor moves to the end of the line. That may be out at the end of a long string of blanks, past the visible end of the line. I'd rather have those blanks be completely invisible.

Begin with a very simple solution. In the go_end() subroutine in TEFIL.CPP, change the call to strlen() to our own vstrlen(). Then the end command will go to the visual end, not the actual end, of the text.

That change improves the backup() function, too. The left arrow now backs up from the start of one line to the visual end of the previous line. Before you decide that this is all too easy, check the Backspace key.

When you backspace with the cursor at the left end of a line, you expect that the return at the end of the previous line will be deleted, joining the two lines. This is how we programmed it originally.

Now what happens is that the Backspace key calls backup() and then deletes a character. If the end character on the previous line is nonblank, this still works. On the other hand, if the previous line has trailing blanks, backup() lands just past the last nonblank. The delete process then deletes one of the blanks, not the return character.

(I'm talking about our mental image of the text on the screen, of course. We don't really have return characters at the ends of our lines, but a good text editor should behave as if it had return characters. At least I think it should. If you disagree, go right ahead and do it your way.)

We want a deletion after the end of the visible line to join the next line, as if a return character had been deleted. This change is quite simple, since our code depends on the del_char() function to do these deletions.

You need to change two lines in del_char(). First, it too should use vstrlen(), not strlen(), to check on the length of the current string. If you just make that one change, however, your subsequent call to cat_next_text() will be disastrous. It will create space enough for the current visible string (excluding trailing blanks) plus the next text. Then it will try to write the entire current string (including trailing blanks) and the next text into this space. This action will overwrite memory past the end of the newly allocated string.

To avoid this problem, the simple trick is to stick a trailing null into the current text at the cursor. Then cat_next_text() will copy only the visible portion of the current text into the new string, which is just what you want. Listing 13-8 shows the two changes in del_char() in TEFIL.CPP.

Listing 13-8: TEFIL.CPP

```
void file_win::del_char()
{
    int slen = vstrlen( cur_line->text );
    if ( (lchar + curx) <= slen )
```

```
        {
            char* cp = cur_line->text
                + lchar + curx - 1;
            del_chars( cp ); // deletes one char

            show_line( top+cury, cur_line );
            goto_xy();
        }
        else
        {
            *( cur_line->text + lchar + curx - 1 ) = 0;
            cat_next_text();
            delete cur_line->next;
            show_all();
        }
    }
}
```

While this approach works well, remember that we still have a serious problem here: We are deleting lines without revising our line number data. This will cause problems in the work we've done so far, and it will be a disaster for line groups. Let's highlight our line groups, so we can really see what's happening. At the end of the next section, we'll get after these bugs in a thorough, meticulous way.

MARKING LINE GROUPS

Start by adding three command messages to EDITCMDS.H:

▶ LINE_BEGIN—(1701) begin line group here

▶ LINE_END—(1702) end line group here

▶ LINE_UNMARK—(1703) remove group marks

Be aware of my opinions as you do this work. I'll try to make them explicit, but I'm sure you'll find some of them buried along the way. For example, in TCLite, the WordStar-based *block hide* command (Ctrl+K, H) is available. I prefer actually to unmark the line group—not just to hide the markings. Again, my preferences aren't any better (or worse) than your own.

With these messages in EDITCMDS.H, go ahead and add them to TECMD. I don't copy TCLite (or WordStar) in my choice of keystrokes. I use Ctrl+L followed by a line group command. These are three examples:

▶ Ctrl+L, B—begin line group (place marker)

▶ Ctrl+L, E—end line group (place marker)

▶ Ctrl+L, U—unmark line group

I prefer to have both line groups and rectangular blocks, which is why I'm being careful to use the word *group* in this discussion. For me, line groups are far more important. I'm going to put blocks into my personal editor, too, but they won't appear in this book. (You'll see all the techniques you'll need here in this section, so adding your own won't be too hard, if you want blocks.)

The marked blocks in TCLite, as in many editors, are partly line groups and partly rectangular blocks, which just confuses me. When I mark the start of a line group, for instance, I don't drop the mark in the middle of the current line just because that's where the cursor is. I mark the whole line, regardless of the cursor's location.

I think this approach saves the trouble of moving the cursor to the beginning of the line before you mark the beginning of the group. It sacrifices the ability to fiddle with a partial line, but I almost never find that useful. Again, think about your own habits and do it your way.

If you're following my way (or if you're implementing any other two-keystroke commands) you'll need to add changes to TECMD.CPP similar to mine. Listing 13-9 shows the additions I made.

Listing 13-9: TECMD.CPP

```
        case CTRL_END:
            return GO_EOS;

        case CTRL_L:
            return line_cmd();

        case CTRL_V:
        case INS:
            return TOGGLE_INSERT;

        case F5:
            return TOGGLE_SCREEN;

        case CTRL_F5:
```

```
        {
            in_mode = win_mode;
            return win_cmd();
        }

        default:
            return NOP;
    }
}
```

```
int line_cmd()
{
    int c = user_cmd();

    switch ( c )
    {
        case 'b':
        case 'B':
        case CTRL_B:
            return LINE_BEGIN;

        case 'e':
        case 'E':
        case CTRL_E:
            return LINE_END;

        case 'u':
        case 'U':
        case CTRL_U:
            return LINE_UNMARK;

        default:
            return NOP;
    }
}
```

```
int win_cmd()
```

You can see in line_cmd() that I allow uppercase, lowercase, and control letters for the second letter in a two-keystroke command. The case statement makes this choice simple.

I also added a new case in TEFIL.CPP's file_win::edit_do() to handle each of those messages. This time I didn't neglect to start with a msg() line for each one so that I could be sure I was sending the correct message for each keystroke.

Now let's get on to marking our groups.

Marking Line Group Beginnings

There really isn't any problem in coding a marking capability. We've given our memlines a flag to say if they're marked or not, and we've got our show_line() method using this flag. The only point to think about, before we charge into the code, is what we really want the marking commands to do.

When I place a beginning marker, I actually mark the current line as both the beginning and end of the line group. This means that the LINE_BEGIN command marks a single-line group. I unmark any existing group before I do this.

A sensible alternative is to have the LINE_BEGIN command relocate the beginning of a group, if a group is already marked. My way is more convenient for marking individual lines, but it's a nuisance if all you want to do is add or drop a line or two at the start of a group.

If you really can't make up your mind which approach you like better, add another command and implement both. Have one command start a new group, removing any prior marks, and have the other command move an existing group start marker.

The two functions I added are shown in Listing 13-10. The first function, line_begin(), does the marking. It uses the second one, line_do_unmark(), to remove any existing group.

Listing 13-10: TEFIL.CPP

```
    return ( (lchar < xloc) && (( lchar+lwid ) >= xloc) );
}

void file_win::line_begin()
{
```

```
        if ( group_start_line_no )
        {
            line_do_unmark();
            show_all();
        }

        group_start_line = group_end_line = cur_line;
        group_start_line_no = group_end_line_no = cur_row;

        cur_line->marked = TRUE;
        show_line( top+cury, cur_line );
        goto_xy();
}

void file_win::line_do_unmark()
{
    if ( group_start_line_no )
    {
        memline* ml = group_start_line;
        while ( ml->marked )
        {
            ml->marked = FALSE;
            if ( ml->next )
                ml = ml->next;
        }
    }
}
```

```
void file_win::back_up()
```

The line_begin() function calls the unmarking routine, if there is an existing line group. (The line_do_unmark() method actually does the unmarking. We'll write a line_unmark() method that responds to the LINE_UNMARK message. It will also use line_do_unmark() for the actual work.) Then it sets the new group lines and line numbers.

The line_do_unmark() logic loops from the first marked line, if any, until it comes to the end of the group, turning the marked flag off. Before you continue, assure yourself that it will actually stop, even when the last marked line is also the last line of text.

Add declarations for these new methods to the class definition in TEFIL.H, too. After you replace the msg() in edit_do(), you can run and mark the first line of a group. Next, we'll mark the ends (and the intervening lines).

Marking Line Group Endings

There's a decision to make about marking the ends of groups. I find it easier always to have my start come before the end of a group. So what do you do if the command to mark the end of a group is given before the existing beginning of a group? I simply go ahead and mark it and then internally flip the two marks.

My method lets me do perfectly ridiculous things, such as marking the beginning of a group at line 5 and then moving the cursor up to line 3 and marking the end. The screen will highlight lines 3 through 5 as a line group. Internally, line 3 is marked as the beginning and line 5 is the end, of course. There are lots of other ways that you may want to handle these marks. Many alternatives are more logical than mine. Some alternatives may even be more useful.

You also have to decide what you want to do when there is no group start marked. I mark a group start in that case. Listing 13-11 shows the new file_win::line_end() method I've added to TEFIL.CPP.

Listing 13-11: TEFIL.CPP

```
    goto_xy();
}


void file_win::line_end()
{
/*
    Sets end of line group.
    If current line comes before line group start,
    sets current line as start and resets former
    start as end.
*/
    if ( !group_start_line_no )
    {
        line_begin();
        return;
    }
```

```
        line_do_unmark();

    if ( group_start_line_no <= cur_row )
    {
        group_end_line    = cur_line;
        group_end_line_no = cur_row;
    }
    else
    {
        group_end_line    = group_start_line;
        group_end_line_no = group_start_line_no;

        group_start_line    = cur_line;
        group_start_line_no = cur_row;
    }

    memline* ml = group_start_line;

    do
    {
        ml->marked = TRUE;
        if ( ml == group_end_line )
            break;
        ml = ml->next;
    }
    while ( ml );

    show_all();
}
```

`void file_win::line_do_unmark()`

It takes more lines of code to mark the end, but there's nothing too obscure about the work being done. Don't forget to add a declaration to the class definition in TEFIL.H and replace the appropriate msg() call in file_win::edit_do() with a call to this function.

If you test the line_end() code before you mark a line beginning, you'll find that it may or may not work. To make it robust, you need to add a line to the file_win constructor that says there are no marked groups.

Initialize group_line_start_no to FALSE (or zero) in the constructor and you'll have this problem solved.

Unmarking

The last function to add in this section is one that unmarks a line group. (If you want the equivalent of TCLite's hide command, you're on your own.) Mine is shown in Listing 13-12, from TEFIL.CPP.

Listing 13-12: TEFIL.CPP

```
    show_all();
}

void file_win::line_unmark()
{
    if ( !group_start_line_no )
        return;

    line_do_unmark();
    group_start_line_no = 0;
    show_all();
}

void file_win::line_do_unmark()
```

Again, you need to add a declaration and a call to test this function. Once it more or less works (it should work just fine as long as you stay on one screen page), let's get on to taking some of those lingering bugs out of our code.

Tracking Lines and Numbers

If you've done more than cursory testing, you've seen what happens when you start moving lines around and especially when you start adding and deleting lines. All our code depends on knowing line numbers and having valid pointers. We have to clean up this code so that our Tiny Editor will be robust. (A non-robust text editor won't get much use!)

Deleting Lines

The first problem to eliminate is the line deletion problem. If you delete a line, all the line numbers of lines that come after the deleted one need to be decremented. In the next section you'll see how we depend on our line numbers to adjust the display after, for example, deleting a line group. We need to be sure that our line numbers are continuously maintained.

To do this, I've added a method that finds a line's number, given a pointer to the line. It does this by simply counting down from the line to the beginning of the file. I've also added two new del_line() functions. One version takes a line and its number as inputs. The second version takes a line without a number and handles looking up the number so that it can call the first version.

Once you know a line's number, you can use it to see if you need to decrement any of the other line numbers. For example, if the deleted line's number is greater than top_line_no, you don't need to change top_line_no.

In addition to adjusting the line numbers, you have to handle other adjustments for marked line groups. For example, if the line you are deleting is the top line of a group, you have to adjust group_top_line to point to the next line in the group. If the deleted line is the only line in a group, then you have to cancel the group.

Listing 13-13 shows the file_win::find_no() method, and Listing 13-14 shows the two del_line() methods, all in TEFIL.CPP. (For both, if you need a disk listing use 13-13.CPP.)

Listing 13-13: TEFIL.CPP

```
    cur_line->text = new_str;
}

int file_win::find_no( memline* ml )
{
    int n = 0;

    if ( !(ml->prev) )
        return n;

    while ( ml->prev )
    {
        ml = ml->prev;
        n++;
    }
    return n;
```

```
}
```

```
memline::memline( memline* after_line, char* txt )
```

Listing 13-14: TEFIL.CPP

```
            show_all();
        }
    }
```

```
void file_win::del_line( memline* ml )
{
    del_line( ml, find_no(ml) );
}


void file_win::del_line( memline* ml, int ml_no )
{
// adjust line group, if any:
    if ( group_start_line_no )
    {
        if ( ml_no < group_start_line_no )
        {
            // delete above group
            group_start_line_no--;
            group_end_line_no--;
        }
        else if ( ml_no == group_start_line_no )
        {
            if ( ml_no == group_end_line_no )
            {
                // delete whole group:
                group_start_line_no = 0;
            }
            else
            {
                // delete first line in group:
                group_start_line =
                    group_start_line->next;
                group_end_line_no--;
```

```
            }
        }
        else if ( ml_no < group_end_line_no )
        {
            group_end_line_no--;
        }
        else if ( ml_no == group_end_line_no )
        {
            group_end_line_no--;
            group_end_line = group_end_line->prev;
        }
        // else deletion is after group
    }

// delete line:
    delete ml;
    if ( mem_file->tail_line_no )
        mem_file->tail_line_no--;
}
```

```
void file_win::use_char( int cmd )
```

Are you wondering about top_line_no and bot_line_no? The del_line() method is called for a line that's on screen, so del_line() can't affect top_line_no, except in the special case where the top line of the screen is also the bottom line of the text file. We've already handled that case. After deleting a line, we'll always call show_all(), which sets bot_line and bot_line_no for us.

Of course, these new functions don't do any good if you don't call them. You need to change the four calls to the *delete* operator that delete memlines. Start with the DEL_LINE: case in edit_do(). Each of the three deletions there is for the current row, so you can use cur_row as the number. Change them this way:

```
    delete <some_memline>;                  // old version

        // change that to:

    del_line( <some_memline>, cur_row ); // new version
```

The other call goes into del_char(), where you can't be sure what row number you are deleting. If you press Del when your cursor is over the end of the text, you'll bring the next line's text up onto the current row. On the other hand, if del_char() is called after you have backspaced from the left end of the line back into the previous line, you'll be working one line before the formerly current row. So in del_char(), just change the delete to a call to del_line(), this way:

```
    delete cur_line->next;        // old version

        // change that to:

    del_line( cur_line->next ); // new version
```

With these changes, test again. Your groups should appear solidly planted as you do deletions. Make sure you use PgUp and PgDn to do deletions when the marked group is off the screen.

Inserting Lines

Of course, adding new lines is the other side of the coin to deleting lines. We need to keep all our numbers adjusted after an insertion, too. And just as with deletions, we need to keep the line group adjusted.

That is an interesting problem, however. What actually do you want to do with the line group when a line is inserted? Chances are that insertions outside the group shouldn't change the group itself. But what about insertions when your cursor is at the start or end of the group?

I have a simple rule: If the cursor is in the group, the new line is also in the group. You'll want to test this rule for yourself to see if it matches your expectations.

To get insertions right, I've added an ins_line() method that functions in the same way as del_line(). It's shown in Listing 13-15 in TEFIL.CPP.

Listing 13-15: TEFIL.CPP

```
        show_all();
    }
}

void file_win::ins_line( memline* ml, char* txt )
{
```

```
    memline* new_ml = new memline( ml, txt );
    mem_file->tail_line_no++;

// insert is after cur_row

    if ( group_start_line_no )
    {
        if ( cur_row < group_start_line_no )
        {
            group_start_line_no++;
            group_end_line_no++;
        }
        else if ( cur_row <= group_end_line_no )
        {
            group_end_line_no++;
        }
    }


// mark, or not, new line
    if ( group_start_line_no &&
        cur_row >= group_start_line_no &&
        cur_row <= group_end_line_no )
        new_ml->marked = TRUE;
}
```

```
void file_win::del_line( memline* ml )
```

To use ins_line(), you'll need to add a declaration in the class definition in TEFIL.H. Mine reads this way:

```
void ins_line( memline* current_line, char* new_text );
```

Have you been using parameter names in your declarations? It's completely optional. This declaration would work just as well:

```
void ins_line( memline*, char* );
```

I use names to help make the declaration more readable. The second form could leave you wondering exactly what the memline pointer pointed to, or why a char pointer was needed. Using a name like "current_line" helps explain things.

I didn't use that name in the actual function definition, however. The parameter name in the function definition is the one that matters in your code.

In addition to declaring the function, you'll need to call it. This is a replacement for all existing uses of the *new* operator to create additional memlines. There's only one such use, in the do_enter() method. It's in this line:

```
// create new next line
    memline* ml = new memline( cur_line, cp );
```

Replace it with a call to the new method, like this:

```
// create new next line
    ins_line( cur_line, cp );
```

This change will also remove that annoying compiler warning that tells you that "ml" wasn't actually used. We could have fixed that earlier, but I knew it would go away here, so I ignored it. The *new* operator returns a pointer, but as with any expression, you can use it as a complete statement, ignoring the return value. If there's no use for the pointer, this statement will work perfectly:

```
// create new next line
    new memline( cur_line, cp );
```

Of course, if you don't capture the pointer returned by the *new* operator, you'll need some other way to use the *delete* operator when you are done with your object. Members of a linked list are one example in which you have captured the pointer elsewhere, so you can dispense with the additional copy that the *new* operator returns.

When you run your Tiny Editor now, you should be able to mark groups and have them maintained correctly, however many lines you insert and delete. When you're done testing this code, let's go on to moving, copying, and deleting the line groups.

MOVING LINE GROUPS

Originally, I planned to implement deleting line groups first. It seems sensible to think of moving a group of lines as a two-part process: You delete the group at its current location, and then you insert it at its new location.

As sometimes happens, the code surprised me. Actually moving the line group from here to there turns out to be almost trivial. Our linked-list structure makes it simple. The only complications are in adjusting the display after you've finished the move. It turns out that the display complications after deleting a line group are much more extensive than the ones after a move, and all that code isn't useful in a move, anyway. Let's get to the code.

I've added the messages LINE_MOVE, LINE_COPY, and LINE_DELETE to my EDITCMDS.H. I've added them as 1711 through 1713, keeping the line commands together.

Once you've added these messages to EDITCMDS.H, you'll need to add three more cases to the line_cmd() function in TECMD.CPP. I've used M for Move, C for Copy, and D for Delete. (Actually, I've added nine cases, counting uppercase, lowercase, and Ctrl versions for each letter.)

Then you should go to file_win::edit_do() and add cases that use msg() to report your intended work. When that tests correctly, let's consider an actual line_move() method.

Listing 13-16 shows the file_win::line_move() method that I've added to TEFIL.CPP.

Listing 13-16: TEFIL.CPP

```
    show_all();
}
```

```
void file_win::line_move()
{
// if no line group, quit
    if ( !group_start_line_no )
        return;

// can't move group into itself
    if ( (cur_row >= group_start_line_no) &&
        (cur_row <= group_end_line_no) )
    {
        message( "Move destination must be",
                "outside marked line group" );
        return;
    }
```

```
// values needed later
    int grpsize =
        group_end_line_no - group_start_line_no + 1;


    memline* after = group_end_line->next;

// adjust tail_line, if necessary
    if ( group_end_line == mem_file->tail_line )
        mem_file->tail_line = group_start_line->prev;
    // tail_line_no won't change


// unhook at old loc
    group_start_line->prev->next =
        group_end_line->next;

    if ( group_end_line->next )
        group_end_line->next->prev =
            group_start_line->prev;

// rehook above cur_line
    cur_line->prev->next = group_start_line;
    group_start_line->prev = cur_line->prev;

    cur_line->prev = group_end_line;
    group_end_line->next = cur_line;

// adjust display
    if ( group_end_line_no < top_line_no )
    {   // group ends above screen
        if ( cur_line == top_line )
            top_line = group_start_line;

        top_line_no -= grpsize;

        // cury unchanged
    }
    else if ( group_start_line_no <= top_line_no )
    { // group starts at or above tos (cursor below group)
        cury -= group_end_line_no - top_line_no + 1;
```

```
        top_line = after;
        top_line_no = group_end_line_no - grpsize + 1;
    }
    else if ( (top_line_no+cury-1) < group_start_line_no )
    { // cursor above line group
        if ( cur_line == top_line )
            top_line = group_start_line;
        // top_line_no unchanged

        // cury unchanged
    }
    else // cursor below line group
    {
        // top_line & line_no unchanged
        cury -= grpsize;
    }
    cur_line = group_start_line;

// reset line #s and display
    group_start_line_no = find_no( group_start_line );
    group_end_line_no = group_start_line_no + grpsize - 1;

    show_all();
}
```

void file_win::line_do_unmark()

At first this will probably strike you as a huge routine. It's certainly longer than most that I write. But look closely, and you'll see that it's really quite straight-forward. The real work of moving the lines starts with the group under the "unhook" comment and ends with the next group under the "rehook" comment.

For the rest, it's just one detail at a time. The "adjust display" section assumes that we'll leave lchar (the horizontal scroll) and curx alone, so all it has to do is get the vertical position correct. That means setting top_line, top_line_no, and cury.

I try to make the display adjustments so that the current line (cursor location) doesn't change—I just want the moved lines to appear at the cursor. Of course, this means different adjustments depending on the location of the line group relative to the cursor.

After you enter this routine, be sure it is declared and called as you have been doing for the other routines. When I tested it, I found some bugs.

I traced my bugs to the show_line() function. As you often find, I immediately saw some improvements I could make that would give me a simpler show_all(), so I made them. As a nice side effect, the simplifications made the bugs go away. Listing 13-17 shows my new show_all() code. (If you need a starting point on disk, use 13-16.CPP.)

Listing 13-17: TEFIL.CPP

```cpp
void file_win::show_all()
{
    memline* cl = top_line;

    if ( (!cl->prev) && (cl->next) ) // at head line in
    {                                // non-empty file
        top_line = cl = cl->next;
        top_line_no = 1;
    }

    bot_line_no = top_line_no;

    for ( int row = top+1; row < btm; row++ )
    {
        show_line( row, cl );

        if ( row < (btm-1) )      // not last screen line?
        {
            if ( cl->next )       // not last file line?
            {
                cl = cl->next;
                bot_line_no++;
            }
            else
            {
                while ( ++row < btm )
                    show_line( row, NULL );
                break;
```

```
            }
        }
    }

    bot_line = c1;
    goto_xy();
}
```

How do you debug code like this? I do it with a huge watch window. After contracting the code window and expanding the watch window you can put all the key values on display in the watch window and set a breakpoint at a key location. I used the end of the show_all() routine as the breakpoint. (Almost everything interesting does a show_all() call.)

Then for code such as the display adjustments, I just work slowly from the first case to the last, testing one at a time. When you have your line moves working, let's go on to copy the line groups.

COPYING LINE GROUPS

Copying is like moving without deleting. Although I had planned on reusing some of the move code, I found it easier to write an entirely separate copy routine. Listing 13-18 shows this new method in TEFIL.CPP.

Listing 13-18: TEFIL.CPP

```
    show_all();
}

void file_win::line_copy()
{
// exit if no line group
    if ( !group_start_line_no )
        return;

// value needed later
    int grpsize =
        group_end_line_no - group_start_line_no + 1;

// build new linked list, copying old
    memline* newlist = new memline( NULL, " " );
```

```
    memline* mlnew = newlist;
    memline* mlold = group_start_line;

    while ( TRUE )
    {
        mlnew = new memline( mlnew, mlold->text );
        mlnew->marked = TRUE;
        mlold->marked = FALSE;

        if ( mlold == group_end_line )
            break;
        mlold = mlold->next;
    }

// link in new list
    // newlist->next is first new line
    // mlnew          is last   new line

    cur_line->prev->next = newlist->next;
    newlist->next->prev  = cur_line->prev;

    mlnew->next = cur_line;
    cur_line->prev = mlnew;

// switch to new line group
    group_start_line = newlist->next;

    newlist->next = NULL;
    delete newlist;

    group_end_line = mlnew;

// adjust display
    if ( top_line == cur_line )
        top_line = group_start_line;
    // top_line_no unchanged

    cur_line = group_start_line;
    // cury unchanged
```

```
// adjust line #s and display
   group_start_line_no = find_no( group_start_line );
   group_end_line_no = group_start_line_no + grpsize - 1;
   mem_file->tail_line_no += grpsize;

   show_all();
}
```

```
void file_win::line_do_unmark()
```

There's a much higher ratio of real work to messy bookkeeping details in this routine than we saw in line_move(). It starts the work by building a new linked-list starting line. Then it loops through the existing line group, using the text property to create new memlines in the new linked list. It adjusts the old and new marked properties as it goes along.

When the new linked list is built, it's linked into the existing list, just before the current line. It becomes the new line group. When it is linked into the main list, its starting memline, newlist, is deleted. Before newlist is deleted, its *next* pointer is replaced with NULL so that the destructor doesn't try to rehook newlist->next (the first line in the copied group) when it deletes newlist.

Adjusting the display is very simple, since no lines are being deleted. Additionally, since the insertion is done before the current line, the copy can't possibly change the mem_file->tail_line.

DELETING LINE GROUPS

The last line group command to implement is the deletion. This one has less work and more bookkeeping than any we have seen yet. The display adjustment possibilities are almost endless.

Listing 13-19 shows the new method in TEFIL.CPP.

Listing 13-19: TEFIL.CPP

```
   show_all();
}
```

```
void file_win::line_delete()
{
// if no line group, quit
```

```
    if ( !group_start_line_no )
        return;

// prepare constants
    memline* before = group_start_line->prev;
    int before_no = group_start_line_no - 1;

    memline* after = group_end_line->next; // may be null!
    int after_no = group_end_line_no + 1;

    int grpsize =
        group_end_line_no - group_start_line_no + 1;

// make the old lines history
    memline* ml = group_start_line;
    memline* mln;

    while ( TRUE )
    {
        mln = ml->next;
        delete ml;
        if ( ml == group_end_line )
            break;
        ml = mln;
    }

// fixup the display
    if ( group_start_line_no <= top_line_no )
    {
        if ( group_end_line_no < top_line_no )
        {
            // top_line unchanged
            top_line_no -= grpsize;
            // cur_line unchanged
            // cury unchanged
        }
        else if ( group_end_line_no <= bot_line_no )
        {
```

```
                    int hilit = group_end_line_no - top_line_no + 1;

                if ( after )
                {
                    top_line = cur_line = after;
                    top_line_no = after_no;

                    if ( cury > hilit )
                    {
                        cury -= hilit;
                        for ( int j = 1; j<cury; j++ )
                            cur_line = cur_line->next;
                    }
                    else
                        cury = 1 ;
                }
                else
                {
                    top_line = cur_line = before;
                    top_line_no = before_no;
                    cury = 1;
                }
            }
            else // end below screen
            {
                top_line = cur_line = before;
                top_line_no = before_no;
                cury = 1;
            }
        }
        else if ( group_start_line_no <= bot_line_no )
        {
            // top_line (and top_line_no) unchanged
            if ( cur_row < group_start_line_no )
            {   //cursor above delete
                // cur_line and cury unchanged
            }
            else if ( cur_row <= group_end_line_no )
            {   // cursor in delete
```

```
                cur_line = before;
                cury = before_no - top_line_no + 1;
            }
            else
            {   // cursor below delete
                // cur_line unchanged
                cury -= grpsize;
            }
        }
        // else group is below screen
            // nothing changes

// compute new end line #
    mem_file->tail_line_no -= grpsize;

// set "no line group" flag
    group_start_line_no = 0;

    show_all();
}
```

void file_win::line_do_unmark()

When you get this code working, you'll be able to delete line groups (a trivial job) and to properly update the display regardless of the location of the deletion (a trivial-sounding job that turns out to be nontrivial indeed).

You are now the proud owner of a text editor you've coded yourself that has most of the features of a professional editor. Early in the next chapter we'll teach it to save your work, so you can put it into service.

SUMMARY

In this chapter we learned very little about C++, since the C++ we've already learned is enough for us to do our work. We did stop and consider static variables, which aren't reinitialized each time we enter a function, and we gave a moment's thought to using variable names in function declarations to help document our work. Mostly, though, we concentrated on programming line group manipulators.

We started with preparatory work, adding additional data members and a utility "goto x,y" function. Then we moved on to rewriting our display code, making show_all() and show_line() both faster and simpler.

After we built the base, we paused to add new features. We added top- and end-of-screen commands, and we used the visual end of the string in place of the true end in our screen manipulation.

Then we went on to marking and unmarking line groups. We programmed beginning and end marking code, as well as unmarking code. We carefully went through the existing code to update our lines and line numbers correctly when we did line deletions and insertions.

After we finished marking, we went on to the three main line group functions—moving, copying, and deleting. We added three of the longest functions we'll see, because a seemingly simple task, updating the screen, turned out to be a large collection of simple tasks. Each combination of group and cursor start and end positions seemed to demand its own few lines of logic, and there were lots of these combinations.

But you've made it, and you are ready to march on to the last main programming chapter, where we'll first save our file and quit and then go on to opening and closing multiple files. The next chapter is the last one where you'll code along with me, and I'll leave lots of the work for you to do on your own.

I think you're up to the challenge by now.

In this chapter, you'll see that the stack object is very useful and, in many ways, easier to use than the built-in array capabilities. I'm not going to finish all the multifile programming with you. I'll do some of it with you, as we've been doing all along, and I'll point you in the right direction for you to do some of it on your own.

While we do this work, I'll introduce a number of C++ topics. We'll cover:

► STDIO.H functions fputs() and freopen()

► Using an array of pointers to char data

► Using argc and argv to read command line arguments

► Using the modulus operator

► Using an array of pointers to objects

► Compile-time and run-time data initialization

► The global use of the scope resolution operator

► The continue statement

► Friend functions

► Using pointers to void

► Using pointer casts

► Gaining speed with inline functions

This list almost completes every topic in our C++ language syllabus. There are just a few further advanced topics that we'll glance at in the last chapter, but the features described will give you a pretty thorough working knowledge of C++.

chapter

14

Using Multiple Files

In the last chapter, we added the ability to manipulate groups of lines to our Tiny Editor. Now we've got just about all the features we need to begin real text editing. The one thing that we can't do yet is save our work. That will be the very first thing we do in this chapter.

After we can save a file, we'll show our Tiny Editor how to open several files at once. We'll start with an array of pointers to file_win objects, which should give you a lot of new ideas about what you can do with C++. After we've worked with an array of pointers to objects, we'll toss that structure out and add a new object, a stack of pointers.

Looking ahead, I should warn you that we'll totally restructure all the work we've done so far. The good news is that this will be easy, since I've been planning on doing it from the start. Let's get started.

S A V I N G   F I L E S

As promised, the first item on our agenda is saving our work. I should warn you that I've postponed this for very late for the simple reason that it may let you turn your useful test file into useless hash, at the speed of a modern computer disk.

If your TEST.FIL has survived this far it's been because we haven't given ourselves an opportunity to destroy it. Now we'll change that. Backing up is definitely a good idea, before we get going.

Save and Quit Commands

Begin by adding a selection of save, quit, and done commands to EDITCMDS.H. I use FILE_SAVE (defined as 1601) for saving the file and continuing editing; FILE_QUIT (1602) to stop editing without saving, and FILE_DONE (1603) to save and then quit. Add options that make sense to you.

Continue by adding cases that return these messages from the edit_cmd() function in TECMD. I've added a new function, block_cmd(), that is triggered by Ctrl+K. The second letters S, Q, and D trigger FILE_SAVE, FILE_QUIT, and FILE_DONE, respectively. I've also added F2 (FILE_DONE) and ALT_F3 (FILE_QUIT) as new plain_cmd() cases.

In TEFIL's file_win::edit_do(), add cases stubbed out with a msg() call that tells you what will happen. If you set the variable "done" to TRUE after FILE_QUIT and FILE_DONE, you'll stop, automatically.

Implementing the Save

If you take a look at the memfile constructor in TEFIL.CPP, you'll see the code that reads a file. Writing a file is simpler. Start by closing your project and shutting all your windows. Then enter the test routine, T.CPP, shown in Listing 14-1. (It's all new, so there's no disk listing.)

Listing 14-1: T.CPP

```
#include <STDIO.H>

int main()
{
    FILE* outfile = fopen( "t.t", "wt" );


    fputs( "a", outfile );
```

```
    fputs( "bc", outfile );

    fputs( "def", outfile );

    fclose( outfile );

    return 0;
}
```

After you run this program, use F3 to open T.T. Did you get what you expected? My file has a single line in it: "abcdef." That shows you what fputs() does. It writes strings, excluding the trailing null, to the end of the file.

W A R N I N G

The open mode "wt" is for writing text. This will either create a new file or truncate an existing file to zero bytes, so be careful using it. It will destroy a perfectly good file instantly.

If you want multiple lines in your file, you need to add a newline character explicitly. Listing 14-2 shows a modified T.CPP.

Listing 14-2: T.CPP

```
#include <STDIO.H>

int main()
{
    FILE* outfile = fopen( "t.t", "wt" );

    fputs( "a", outfile );
    fputs( "\n", outfile );

    fputs( "bc", outfile );
    fputs( "\n", outfile );

    fputs( "def", outfile );
    fputs( "\n", outfile );
```

```
    fclose( outfile );

    return 0;
}
```

Close your T.T window in TCLite before you run this version. Then run it and open T.T again. This time you'll have a file with three lines in it. As you can guess, this means that we'll save our file by using fputs() in a loop, going from the first to the last memline, writing the text data member and then a newline character.

H I N T

Writing a newline character is identical to writing a carriage return and linefeed (characters 13 and 10, decimal) in a DOS-based environment. If you use the new-line character, however, the same code will work correctly on a Macintosh or a UNIX-based computer, too.

Now there's one small problem to solve before we can save our file. The existing stream is open for reading, not for writing. Why don't you check help (Shift+F1) for STDIO.H and see if you can find an appropriate function to solve this problem.

Got it? The freopen() function will do the job nicely. However, it needs a file-name as an argument, and we haven't saved the name of the file. We need this name before we can write the file.

Begin by adding a new data member, file_name, to the memfile class definition in TEFIL.H. Then add a parameter to the memfile constructor declaration in the memfile class definition and to the memfile constructor's definition in TEFIL.CPP.

Add the two lines shown in Listing 14-3 that create and fill the file_name in the memfile constructor.

Listing 14-3: TEFIL.CPP

```
    next->prev = prev;
}
```

```
memfile::memfile( FILE* tf, char* name )
{
    file_name = new char[ strlen(name) + 1 ];
    strcpy( file_name, name );

    text_file = tf;
    head_line = new memline( NULL, "" );
```

Next, return to TE.CPP, where we first get the name from our string_dialog
object, sd. The function sd->sval() returns the string (file_name) so this is what
we want to hand to the memfile constructor. Since the memfile constructor is
called from the file_win constructor, you'll have to add a char* parameter to the
file_win constructor (I called mine "name"). Then you'll need to add this as an
argument when you get a new memfile.

You can carefully think through the additions you need to make in TEFIL.H
and TEFIL.CPP, or you can just add something and let the compiler tell you
what it's missing. However you do it, you should have the file's name as a data
member in your memfile when you are done.

I tested my code by putting a hard breakpoint on the line after the memfile was
created, in file_win's constructor. When the code stops there, use Alt+F4 to
inspect your memfile object.

Now that you have a file_name, Listing 14-4 shows a file_win::file_save()
method that you can add to TEFIL.CPP:

Listing 14-4: TEFIL.CPP

```
    return n;
}

void file_win::file_save()
{
    FILE* outfile = freopen(
        mem_file->file_name, "wt", mem_file->text_file );

    if ( outfile )
    {
        memline* cl = mem_file->head_line;

        while ( cl->next )
```

```
    {
        cl = cl->next;
        fputs( cl->text, outfile );
        if ( cl->next )
            fputs( "\n", outfile );
    }
}
else
    message( "Could not open", mem_file->file_name );
}
```

```
memline::memline( memline* after_line, char* txt )
```

Replace the msg() calls in the FILE_SAVE and FILE_DONE cases with calls to file_save(), and you're ready to test. When you test this code, be sure to start with a little, disposable file like T.T. When you run this, you'll have a text editor that you can put to work!

The first problem (or six-legged feature) I noticed about my Tiny Editor was that it writes any trailing blanks that are at the end of its text lines. I wanted it to stop doing that. Since you've got a vstrlen() function, all you need to do is slip a null character into cl->text at vstrlen() before you do the fputs(). Go ahead and try it. (Set a breakpoint at the next line before your first try, and don't use any file you'll want later.)

A much better way to do a save is to rename the existing file to .BAK and then write out the new file. I'll let you try this on your own. Start by looking over STDIO.H for a function that will rename your file. When you find it, you're halfway home. The other part of the job is to pick the extension off a name and replace it with .BAK. You get full credit for doing an excellent job if you can correctly handle these strings:

```
FILENAME
FILENAME.EXT
\DIR\NAME
\DIR\NAME.EXT
DIR.EXT\NAME
DIR.E\N
\DIR.EXT\SUBDIR.E\N.E
```

(The rule is this: An extension follows a period if the period is within four characters of the right end and is not followed by a backslash.)

While you're improving this functionality, there's no reason to leave the file open as you edit it. In a monotasking operating system such as DOS, it really doesn't matter much, but with a multitasking system (even a partial multitasker such as Windows 3.*x*) you may want to use the file in several applications. Even in DOS, you may want to edit the file in two or more windows. Why don't you have the memfile constructor close the file after it has read it and then open another FILE stream when it is time to write it out?

Are you in business? Congratulations. You've got a text editor. I'd suggest that you use your editor, running it for all your editing. This isn't as convenient as using the built-in editor, but it's the way you'll find out what you like and what you want to fix. (If you have a good backup procedure you'll stay out of trouble. Without good backups, Murphy and his Law will come visit you.)

OPENING FILES

Let's get on to opening files, picking up arguments from the command line if they're there. Let's start with a reasonable file open function.

An Open Function

Our mainline code, in TE.CPP, has not gotten much of our attention so far. Object-oriented programming's like that. Now, however, it's time to put some of our objects to use and build a nice front end.

Let's start by picking up the filename from the DOS command line, so you can say:

```
C:>TE whatever.fil
```

Of course, with TCLite, your .EXE will run only from the IDE, but that's not terribly inconvenient when you're already in the IDE working on TE. Ctrl+F9 has been for testing, but now you can use it for editing, too. Later, when you upgrade to Borland's TC++ or another C++ environment, you'll be able to use TE from the DOS prompt just by recompiling and linking.

To set up command line arguments, choose Run|Arguments... from the menus. You'll get the Program Arguments dialog shown in Figure 14-1.

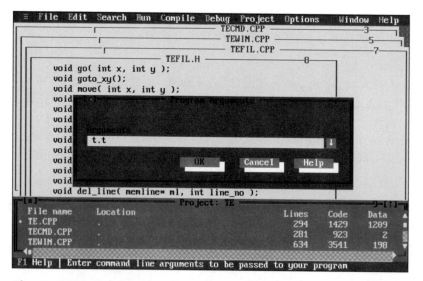

Figure 14-1: Setting a DOS command line with Run I Arguments.

Add the name of your favorite little file (but not TEST.FIL). When you press Ctrl+F9, nothing will have changed—the string_dialog will still default to TEST.FIL.

C's command line handling has been entirely inherited by C++. It might have been better if we had a more object-oriented capability, but we don't. We've got two parameters available within main().

▶ argc—an int, a count of the command line arguments

▶ argv—a vector, or list, of the arguments

The second parameter, argv, is an interesting one. It's a pointer to an array of strings. As you know, a string in C++ (or in C) is really a pointer to an array of characters. So argv is a pointer to list of pointers to char variables.

The most common way to write the parameters in main() is this:

```
int main( int argc, char* argv[] ) ...
```

This form is similar to other declarations using array subscripts. For instance:

```
char border[8]; // border points to an array of 8 chars
```

This usage creates two things. Obviously, it creates a character pointer variable, called "border" in the example. It also allocates eight characters somewhere in memory and initializes border to point to this space. You could also use one of these forms:

```
char border[];   // array size not specified

    // this is the same:

char* border;
```

In either case, border is allocated, but providing something for it to point to is up to you. You can take this process further. Suppose you had four box border types. You could do this:

```
char borders[4][8];   // pointer to 32 character array

    // this is similar:

char* borders[4];     // pointer to 4 pointers to char

    // these are also similar:

char* borders[];      // pointer to ?? pointers to char
char** borders;       // same
```

In the last two examples, you have "borders" pointing to the first of an unspecified number of pointers to char. It's up to you to allocate the space for the array of pointers, as well as to allocate the space for the strings they point to.

As for the command line arguments, the C++ startup code creates one string with the full path and executable filename. In our case, this will be something like:

```
C:\TCLITE\TE.EXE
```

Since this argument is always provided, argc will never be less than 1. The program name is a string pointed to by argv[0].

If you include arguments, separated as DOS specifies, they will be placed in argv[1], argv[2], and so on. Figure 14-2 shows a test file that is examining the contents of argc and argv[ ]. Check how this process works by writing your own T.CPP and using the debugger with watches or inspect in combination with Run|Arguments... to explore the command line.

Some C and C++ programmers delight in the tricky things one can do with pointers to pointers. Figure 14-3 shows some tricky ways to address the argv[ ] data, using dereferencing and pointer arithmetic. These usages make for fun puzzles, but they are horrible abuses of the language if you use them in working code.

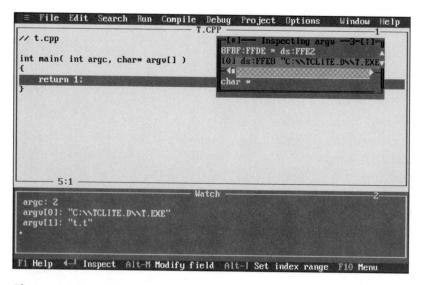

Figure 14-2: Examining argc and argv[] with the debugger.

In the very early days of C programming, some C authorities argued against using the subscript operator since it was less efficient than using pointer dereferencing. Unfortunately, some of the obscure code that results from this old habit is still haunting us today. You should use the subscript operator when it makes your intent clear. Using dereferencing to access the contents of pointers to pointers should be saved for puzzles.

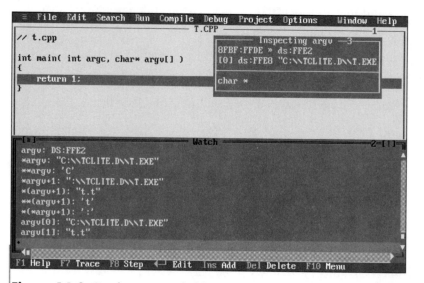

Figure 14-3: Testing unreadable pointer constructions in the debugger.

There is, of course, no reason to not carry this notion further. You can have pointers to pointers to pointers to. . .

To me, this sort of "cleverness" is a sign of a beginner's work. Plain, readable code is likely to work and keep working. Let's go on to use some plain code to open a file whose name we read from the command line.

Listing 14-5 shows TE.CPP's main(), modified to use the first command line argument (presumably, the name of the file you want to edit) if there is one. It pops up the dialog box if you don't provide the command line argument.

Listing 14-5: TE.CPP

```
char inbuf[ MAX_CHARS ];

int main( int argc, char* argv[] )
{
    startup();
    char* name;

    if ( argc > 1 )
        name = argv[1];
    else
    {
        string_dialog* sd = new string_dialog(
        "                                          ",
        " Open File " );
        name = sd->sval();
        delete sd;
    }

    FILE* infile = fopen( name, "rt" );

    if ( !infile )
```

In addition to the code shown, there are two later uses of sd->sval() that need to be changed to "name" for this new code to work. (Don't waste a moment looking for them—your compiler will find them for you. Try to think of it as your meticulous, if none-too-bright, friend.)

This code is much nicer. It's especially nice for us, since we can put TEST.FIL (or whatever we want) in the command line arguments and TCLite will save this value from session to session. But it still does not behave very well when it doesn't find the file that we specify.

We can make the code work better still if we localize the file open logic in a function and use a yes_no dialog object in this function. Looking ahead, the next command I want to implement is FILE_OPEN. You can see that this will be simple to write if we handle the filename dialog nicely at this point.

Listing 14-6 shows a file_open() routine, and Listing 14-7 (from disk, use 14-06.CPP for both) shows the modified main() code that calls it. You'll also need to declare the two new functions near the top of TE.CPP.

Listing 14-6: TE.CPP

```
    return 0;
}


FILE* file_open( char* nm, char* mode )
{
    string_dialog* sd = NULL;
    FILE* retfile;

// use dialog to get nm if not supplied
    if ( is_blank(nm) )
    {
        sd = new string_dialog( nm, " Open File " );
        nm = sd->sval();
        delete sd;
    }


// open
    retfile = fopen( nm, mode );

// keep trying, if not opened
    while ( !retfile )
    {
    // ask
        yes_no* yn = new yes_no(
            "Could not open",
            nm,
            "Try again?" );
```

```
        int ans = yn->ans;
        delete yn;

        if ( !ans )
            break;

    // try again
        sd = new string_dialog( nm, " Open File " );
        nm = sd->sval();
        delete sd;

        retfile = fopen( nm, mode );

    }

    return retfile;
}

int is_blank( char* s )
{
    while( *s )
        if ( *s++ > 32 )
            return FALSE;

    return TRUE;
}
```

```
void startup()
```

Listing 14-7: TE.CPP

```
int main( int argc, char* argv[] )
{
    startup();
    char* name =
        "                                                    ";
    if ( argc > 1 )
        strncpy( name, argv[1], strlen(argv[1]) );
```

```
    FILE* infile = file_open( name, "rt" );

    if ( !infile )
        return 1;

    char* title = new_titleize( name );
```

Can you see the reason for copying argv[1] into the name buffer? It would be simpler not to do this. It would also be simpler to use strcpy() rather than strncpy(), too. Try it without the extra work (and use the online help to check on the string copy functions) to find out why you need this extra bit of work.

The file_open() logic will work for any file we want to open, so it will help make the FILE_OPEN logic very simple. It's a good example of how much work you can do just by creating and using objects from your collection.

When I got tired of using just my test file, I started opening code files, such as TE.CPP. Doing that quickly pointed up another detail that you have to handle to do practical work.

Handling Tabs

One of TCLite's nice edit features is the slick way it handles tabs at the left side of the line. Tabbing gets you to the next tab stop, and the Backspace key deletes a full tab when you use it before the first nonwhite character on a line. You can add your favorite version of those features at your leisure.

One thing you can't ignore, however, is the handling of tabs when you read in the file. As it stands now, our files show the tab character (ASCII 9) instead of expanding it into an appropriate code indentation. Handling a variety of tab stops could be quite tricky, but handling files compatible with TCLite (and Borland's other C++ products) is very simple.

Tabs are expanded to the next tab stop, and tab stops are placed every fourth character, starting with character 5. What we need to do is to read the input file line and to expand the tabs into spaces before we return the memline object. This approach requires a little more smarts in the memfile constructor in TEFIL.CPP.

I've written a somewhat general tab expansion routine, tab_exp(), and used it in the memfile constructor. Specifically, I call the memline constructor with "tab_exp(inbuf)" instead of just "inbuf." You'll need to make that change and to add appropriate declarations in TEFIL.H, before you use the two new routines shown in Listing 14-8, from the end of TEFIL.CPP.

Listing 14-8: TEFIL.CPP

```
memfile::~memfile()
{
    delete file_name;
}
```

```
#define TAB   '\x09'
#define TSET 4

char* tab_exp( char* s )
{
    int n = num_of( TAB, s );
    if ( !n )
        return s;

    char* s2 = new char[ strlen(s) + TSET*n ];
    char* zero = s2 - 1; // char before start of string

    while ( *s && (( *s )!='\n') )
    {
        if ( (*s) != TAB )
            *s2++ = *s++;
        else
        {
            for( int i = ( s2 - zero ) % TSET; i <= TSET;
                i++ )
                *s2++ = ' ';
            s++;
        }
    }

    *s2 = 0;

    return zero+1;
}
```

```
int num_of( char c, char* s )
{
    int n = 0, slen = strlen( s );
    char* cp = s;
    char* ocp;

    while ( TRUE )
    {
        ocp = cp;
        cp = (char*) memchr( cp, c, slen );
        if ( !cp )
            break;


        cp++;
        slen -= cp-ocp;
        n++;
    }


    return n;
}
```

`// end of TEFIL.CPP`

The modulus operator, %, may be new to you. It returns the remainder after integer division. For examples, 4 % 4 returns zero, 5 % 4 returns 1, 6 % 4 returns 2, and so on. Other than that, the code is plain procedural C++. (Note that I use the num_of() function to do an immediate exit if there aren't any tabs to expand. Code that does nothing is very, very fast.)

When you use this new code, you should be able to read in the code files written by TCLite and have them look exactly as they look when you use TCLite's built-in editor.

If you like, you can add parallel tab compression logic to the file save routine, but I'm not sure it's worth the trouble. If your machine has any sort of disk compression, strings of consecutive blanks may be just as short as, or even shorter than, the equivalent set of tabs.

For a simple, if inconclusive, test, make a copy of TEWIN.CPP and save it using your Tiny Editor. This effectively expands the tabs. When I tried this, I expanded

10,743 bytes with tabs to 12,869 bytes with just spaces—just about a 20 percent increase.

Using PKZIP, I compressed both versions. With tabs the result was 3,224 bytes; without tabs it was 3,298 bytes. I'd write a tab compression routine to save 20 percent of my disk space, but there's no such saving available after compression. (Apart from compression, other chores are simplified using spaces, too, such as reading your code into WinWord to document it.)

Opening Multiple Files

A modern text editor should be able to open several files at once—a feature we'll add to our Tiny Editor right now. We can start directly with procedural code, maintaining another array of pointers. This time, we can maintain an array of pointers to file_win objects. In the next section, we'll switch to an object-oriented approach using a generalized pointer stack.

Neither this section nor the next, which is also the last active coding section of this book, will give you the full set of multifile capabilities that you'll want. It will nonetheless show you some possibilities. We'll begin by opening windows and then closing them in the reverse order. You'll see that it will take the stack approach to make it easy to handle a task such as switching to a middle window in a group of windows. Even with the stack, you'll need to add some code to get this capability.

I'll also leave it to you to expand the line-group logic to cross file_win object boundaries, copying from one window to another, for instance. That won't be hard, though. At this point, you should be well equipped to handle that problem.

Let's get on to adding an array of pointers to file_win objects, so that we can open as many files as you like. An array of pointers to objects is declared like any other array:

```
class jar
{
public:
    int shape;
    int volume;
    char* style_name;

    jar( int shape );
    ~jar();
```

```
        pour( int amount );
    };



    jar* set_of_jars[10]; // 10 pointers to jars
```

Once you have an array of pointers to objects, each element of that array can be used just as you would use any other pointer to an object:

```
    set_of_jars[3] = new jar( 10 );


    cprintf( "shape # = %d", set_of_jars[3]->shape );


    set_of_jars[i]->pour(3);
```

With that in mind, let's rewrite our main() so that it opens the first of an array of file_win objects. Listing 14-9 shows the changes to make in TE.CPP.

Listing 14-9: TE.CPP

```
#define MAX_CHARS 1024

char inbuf[ MAX_CHARS ];

#define MAX_FILES 20
file_win* fwins[ MAX_FILES ];
int active_fwin = -1;

int main( int argc, char* argv[] )
{
    startup();
    char* name =
        "
                                                    ";
    if ( argc > 1 )
        strncpy( name, argv[1], strlen(argv[1]) );

    FILE* infile = file_open( name, "rt" );

    if ( !infile )
        return 1;
```

```
    char* title = new_titleize( name );
    fwins[0] = new file_win( title, infile, name );
    active_fwin = 0;
    delete title;

    fclose( infile );

    delete fwins[0];

    return 0;
}
```

You'll need to use your debugger to check your work, since you'll see nothing different when you run this code. If you set a hard breakpoint at the line that assigns zero to active_fwin, you'll be able to use the inspect feature to take a look at your array of file_win objects.

Now that we can open one element of the array, let's go on to opening more. There's some trouble here in assigning default coordinates so that opening successive windows shows a nice cascade. We'll also need to modify our exit logic so that quitting a window doesn't quit from Tiny until we have closed the last window.

Along the way, we'll use the active_fwin variable to keep track of where we are in the array. I'm not going to add any logic that will keep us from overflowing the array, since the array itself is only temporary. Just be sure not to open too many files and you'll be okay. In the next section, we'll use a stack approach that won't have this limit.

Begin by adding a FILE_OPEN message (mine's 1604) to EDITCMDS.H. Then add one or more commands that send that message in TECMD.CPP. I respond to Ctrl+K, E (the old WordStar command) and to F3 (from TCLite).

Then add a FILE_OPEN case in TEFIL.CPP. Mine calls file_open(), a file_win method that just uses msg() to report that it intends to open a file. Get this running and check your keystrokes to be sure you're actually calling your file_open() routine, before you go on.

With that done, we're ready for a first try at a file_open() method. My first try is shown in Listing 14-10. Listing 14-11 shows the extern statements I've added at the top of the TEFIL.CPP file to tell the linker to go looking elsewhere for those variables. Along with the extern statements, you see the declarations of the functions called here that are defined in TE.CPP.

Listing 14-10: TEFIL.CPP

```
void file_win::file_open()
{
    active_fwin++;

    char* name =
        "
                                                        ";

    FILE* infile = ::file_open( name, "rt" );

    if ( !infile )
    {
        active_fwin--;
        return;
    }

    char* title = new_titleize( name );
    fwins[ active_fwin ] =
        new file_win( title, infile, name );
    delete title;

}
```

Listing 14-11: TEFIL.CPP

```
int screen_height = 49;

extern file_win* fwins[];
extern int active_fwin;

FILE* file_open( char* name, char* mode );
char* new_titleize( char* fname );

void msg( char* debug )
```

Before you test this code, note that a common mistake has been made here. See if you can figure out what the contents of "name" will be the second time this routine is called. (There are other bugs too, particularly some that are evident when you try to close a file. We'll get to them in due course.)

While you're thinking about the contents of name, note the use of the scope resolution operator to call ::file_open() when we are in a method called file_open(). That double colon specifies the global function, file_open()—the one in TE.CPP—as opposed to a class method such as file_win::file_open().

Now let's consider that bug. Try using file_win::file_open() twice. The second time, it will reopen the same file as it opened the first time. It won't even stop to ask you for a filename. Consider what this line does:

```
char* s = "initial string";
```

The type, char*, specifies that s is a pointer to char. The string in quotes is placed somewhere in the load module by the compiler. The pointer, s, points to the start of that string. Each time that statement is executed, s will be assigned the address of that string. The assignment of constant values, in this case "initial string," is made before the program is loaded. If you subsequently write different data into that location, s will point to the same place, but with new values.

This is what has happened to our "name" string. The pointer "name" initially points to a string of blanks. During the run of ::file_open() those blanks are overwritten with a real filename. On the second run of file_win::file_open(), the name pointer is reinitialized to point to the location of those blanks, but that location doesn't happen to hold blanks anymore. Our ::file_open() code takes a nonblank string and opens it, if possible. It asks us for a name only if it doesn't have one.

An improved file_win::file_open() that avoids this problem is shown in Listing 14-12.

Listing 14-12: TEFIL.CPP

```
void file_win::file_open()
{
    active_fwin++;

    static char* blanks =
        "                                                    ";
```

```
char name[50]; // sized to fit blanks[]
strcpy( name, blanks );
```

```
FILE* infile = ::file_open( name, "rt" );
```

With that change in place, each call to file_win::file_open() will call ::file_open() with a string of blanks, so the dialog box will pop up, asking us for a filename. By the way, there's no check here to see that we don't open the same file several times. I'm not going to write one, either, because I like to be able to open the same file several times. Of course, there are a lot of possibilities there, and many of them are dangerous. Do what you think best.

Let's get on to properly closing the files that we open.

TOTALLY RESTRUCTURING TINY

We're not handling exits from the file correctly. When we had only one file, exiting from the file exited from the program, so the way we did it didn't matter. Now it matters, and you can see that it doesn't work correctly.

We could modify the exit treatment to properly delete each file_win object given our current structure, but that would be cheating. I'm going to leave it to you to finish writing multifile code, but I don't want to leave you with an unsound structure. Consider how we're working now.

You launch a file_win object. Its constructor calls its edit() procedure. The edit() method calls edit_cmd(), which tells edit() what needs to be done. The edit() code then calls all the other methods needed to perform the editing action. That works.

When you open a second file, edit() calls file_win::file_open(), which will open another file_win if it succeeds in opening a file. The call to the second file_win constructor in turn calls that object's file_win::edit() method. The first copy of file_win::edit() has paused, waiting for a return from file_win::file_open(). The second copy of file_win::edit() will be in control until it completes its work and you close the second file. That will work, too.

You've actually written a recursive set of functions. The edit() method calls file_open(), which calls the constructor, which calls edit(). This process will continue down to as many levels as you have open files. This is a good way to write code if the fundamental operation you're performing is hierarchical.

Unfortunately, that's not the case here! Our operation is fundamentally nonhierarchical. Suppose you have five files open. For perfectly logical reasons, you may want to edit the third, then the fifth, and then the third again. We have no way to get back from the fifth to the third except by closing the intervening files.

What we really want is a master controller that is responsible for opening the different file_win objects and for communicating with the edit_cmd() routine. The controller should decide which file_win object is supposed to receive which commands. It should take care of handing the fifth file_win some commands, then giving some commands to the third file_win, and then going back to the fifth.

The controller can also see to it that the file_win is deleted when you exit from a file_win (via a FILE_QUIT or FILE_DONE). It should be smart enough to close an individual file_win and then close down entirely when the last file_win is shut.

Luckily, our file_win::edit() method doesn't do much except grab commands from edit_cmd() and pass them along to edit_do(). If we replace our edit() routine with a central controller, edit_do() will still be there ready to do all our work. In other words, our structure can be fundamentally changed just by replacing one little routine.

Add the control() routine, along with the associated changes in main(), as shown in Listing 14-13, but don't try to run it just yet. This routine uses a new statement, continue, to handle the FILE_OPEN message.

Listing 14-13: TE.CPP

```
    char* title = new_titleize( name );
    fwins[0] = new file_win( title, infile, name );
    active_fwin = 0;
    delete title;

    control();

    return 0;
}

void control()
{
```

```
    message( "in control" );

    int cmd;
    int done = FALSE;

    fwins[active_fwin]->show_cursor();

    do
    {
        cmd = edit_cmd();
        if ( cmd == FILE_OPEN )
            continue;

        done = fwins[active_fwin]->edit_do( cmd );

    } while ( !done );

    delete fwins[0];

    message( "outta here" );
}
```

```
FILE* file_open( char* nm, char* mode )
```

The continue statement is the opposite of the break statement. While break exits from a loop, continue skips over the rest of the code between itself and the end of the loop. It transfers you immediately to the loop test of the innermost do, while, or for loop. In this case, it is skipping the call to the edit_do() method.

Go to TEFIL.CPP, remove the call to edit() that's in the file_win constructor, and try to run this code. You'll get a complaint from the compiler—it says the edit_do() method isn't accessible in control(). It's correct, as always. The edit_do() method is private.

Just as you can make one class a friend of another, a class can declare a particular function a friend, giving it access to the class's private and protected members. We used the first of these two forms already:

```
class my_class
{
```

```
friend class needs_access;   // class friend

friend int my_func( int p1, char* p2 ); // function friend
...
};
```

You need the full declaration for your function, since you could have several functions of the same name if you use overloading for that function name. The compiler wouldn't know what to do with this:

```
class my_class
{
friend my_func; // Won't work. Confuses the compiler!
...
};
```

So go to your file_win class definition in TEFIL.H and add a line like this:

```
friend void control();
```

Now your code should run. You'll have no idea that anything is at all different, but internally the structure is completely revised.

Now it's time for a little cleanup work. First, those message() calls in the new control() can be thrown out. Second, the msg() calls that are left in the various editing commands can be thrown out. We're not using file_win::edit() anymore, so you can delete that, too. Finally, the msg() function itself is history, so you can get rid of it.

HINT

A good way to delete a function is to enclose it in C-style comment delimiters: /* ... func here ... */. Then you can thoroughly test before you actually delete the code. You can also leave debugging code in the source file if you might need it later. Comments cost nothing in the executable.

Our multiple file capability can be brought back to life, under the watchful eye of the controller, and without recursive functions, with this new structure. Basically, you want to move the logic from file_win::file_open() into the controller, where the continue statement is now short-circuiting the loop.

Begin by moving the file_win::file_open() method, all of it, from TEFIL.CPP to TE.CPP. Then change its name to file_open_ctl(). Add a declaration for file_open_ctl() at the top of TE.CPP and replace the continue statement with a call to file_open_ctl(). When you try to run, your linker will tell you that it can't find file_win::file_open().

Of course it can't find it. It's gone. To fix that problem, remove the entire FILE_OPEN case from the edit_do switch in TEFIL.CPP. To be thorough, get rid of the function declaration in TEFIL.H, too. This job will now be handled in control(), not by the file_win object. Finally, get rid of the two function declarations and two externs that we added at the top of TEFIL.CPP so that we could support file_open().

Now you'll be able to run, opening as many files as you want. (Remember that you're not supposed to want to open more than fit in our file_win pointer array, yet.) The windows don't cascade as nicely as we could want, and the entire collection is closed down when we quit. Let's get that last problem solved and then make a nice cascade.

Listing 14-14 shows just how simple that file_win closing problem is to solve. All you need to do is to delete file_win when you are done with it. Remember that a few levels back in the chain, file_win has inherited from the popup box object, so it knows how to restore the screen (popping down). Enter the changes in TE.CPP's control() function and you'll be able to open and close files gracefully. For now, use Ctrl+F5 and the arrow keys to manually create a multiwindow cascade.

Listing 14-14: TE.CPP

```
void control()
{
    int cmd;
    int done = FALSE;

    fwins[active_fwin]->show_cursor();

    do
    {
        cmd = edit_cmd();
        if ( cmd == FILE_OPEN )
            file_open_ctl();
```

```
        done = fwins[active_fwin]->edit_do( cmd );

      if ( done )
      {
          delete fwins[ active_fwin ];
          active_fwin--;

      }

  } while ( active_fwin > -1 );
}
```

Don't forget to delete the line underneath the while loop that deleted the first file_win object. This task is now handled in the loop. The test in the while portion is now looking for an active_fwin above –1. When you delete the last file_win, decrementing active_fwin reduces its value to –1.

CASCADING OUR FILE WINDOWS

There's nothing particularly hard about launching a window cascade. Each file_win object inherits coordinate properties—lft, top, rgt, and btm—from the underlying box object. To cascade windows you just open each window one space to the left and down from the previous box, provided you have room.

Unfortunately, we didn't carry our coordinate parameters all the way up our object inheritance tree. They are parameters of the box constructor and of the popup, which inherits from box. Similarly, the dialog, which inherits from popup, also has parameters for the box coordinates. It was at the dialog that we assigned default values in the constructor's definition, making the coordinates optional.

The classes that inherited from dialog—message, yes_no, and file_win—take advantage of the fact that the coordinates are optional parameters with default values. This makes their definitions simpler, but it also means that we have to go back and modify the classes when we find that we really need to change the defaults.

Of course, cascading the file_win objects requires modifying the default values of the coordinates, so we'll need optional coordinate parameters in the file_win constructor. As we've seen before, the good news is that adding optional parameters to a constructor can be done without impacting any existing uses of the class.

I began by adding #defines for the default values (which really would have been a good idea to begin with) in TEWIN.H, as shown in Listing 14-15. With these defined, replace the corresponding constants in the declaration of the dialog class constructor in TEWIN.H.

Listing 14-15: TEWIN.H

```
#define DIAG_TIP_CLR 48 // Black on cyan

#define DIAG_DEF_LFT 15 // default dialog box location
#define DIAG_DEF_TOP  8
#define DIAG_DEF_RGT 65
#define DIAG_DEF_BTM 15

#define FILE_WIN_OUT_CLR  126 // Hi yellow on white
```

When you press Ctrl+F9 after these changes, watch the Compiling window. You'll see that changing TEWIN.H triggers a recompile of TE, TEWIN, and TEFIL, since this header is included in all those .CPP files. When your code runs, nothing should have changed.

I added a similar group of #defined constants to position the default file_win. They are FWIN_DEF_LFT, FWIN_DEF_TOP, and so on, in TEFIL.H. These constants are used as arguments to the dialog class constructor, called from the file_win class constructor in TEFIL.CPP. Again, it would have been a good idea to #define these constants initially, but some cleanup now will have us up and running with improved code. Again, when you test there should be no difference in your running code.

Now we're ready to actually add the default constants as optional parameters to the file_win constructor. In TEFIL.H, change the declaration of the file_win constructor, as shown in Listing 14-16. Then revise the definition of the constructor in TEFIL.CPP, as shown in Listing 14-17.

Listing 14-16: TEFIL.H

```
public:
    file_win( char* file_name, FILE* tf, char* name,
        int lf = FWIN_DEF_LFT, int tp = FWIN_DEF_TOP,
        int rt = FWIN_DEF_RGT, int bt = FWIN_DEF_BTM );
    ~file_win();
```

Listing 14-17: TEFIL.CPP

```
file_win::file_win(
    char* file_name, FILE* tf, char* name,
    int lf, int tp, int bt, int rt ) :
    dialog( file_name, lf, tp, bt, rt,
        SING_DOUB, FILE_WIN_OUT_CLR, FILE_WIN_CON_CLR )
```

Again, with these changes your test should run just as before, but the payoff is that we can now change the location of a file_win when we launch it, which is our next job.

Before we go on to the simple but lengthy code we'll want to position our cascade, let's just check that we've done everything correctly so far. Look in file_open_ctl() in TE.CPP. Find the statement that assigns a new file_win. Add one or two extra arguments to the call to the file_win constructor. I added just one:

```
5 + 2*active_fwin
```

That change will move each window you open to the right by two spaces. It's not exactly a cascade, but it's enough to prove that we're on the right track.

The actual cascading looks at the coordinates of the current active window and adds 1, both horizontally and vertically. It doesn't add 1, however, if you've already reached the screen's right or bottom. For the left and top, it doesn't add 1 if you've reached the edge of the screen less our specified minimum window size. Listing 14-18 shows the full code that does this job.

Listing 14-18: TE.CPP

```
    if ( !infile )
    {
        active_fwin--;
        return;
    }

    int lf = fwins[ active_fwin-1 ]->lft;
    int tp = fwins[ active_fwin-1 ]->top;
    int rt = fwins[ active_fwin-1 ]->rgt;
    int bt = fwins[ active_fwin-1 ]->btm;
```

```
lf += lf < ( FULL_RGT - FILE_WIN_MIN_WIDTH  ) ? 1 : 0;
tp += tp < ( FULL_BTM - FILE_WIN_MIN_HEIGHT ) ? 1 : 0;
rt += rt < ( FULL_RGT - 1 ) ? 1 : 0;
bt += bt < ( FULL_BTM - 1 ) ? 1 : 0;

    char* title = new_titleize( name );
    fwins[ active_fwin ] =
        new file_win( title, infile, name,
        lf, tp, rt, bt );
    delete title;


}


FILE* file_open( char* nm, char* mode )
```

Enter this new code and, at the top of the file, add:

```
extern int screen_width;
extern int screen_height;
```

Give file_open_ctl() friend access in the file_win class in TEWIN.H, and our FILE_OPEN commands should now create a neat cascade of open files. When you test, use Ctrl+F5 to shrink the first window and then to move it to the bottom-right corner of the screen. Continue by opening more files, and your cascade should respect the minimums we've set.

Got it? Congratulations. You've written a multifile, multiwindowing text editor.

A STACK OF FILE WINDOW OBJECTS

It would be nice if we could do something other than closing windows 4 and 5 if we want to go back to window 3, wouldn't it? That's the last job where I'll actually present you with finished code. In fact, I'll only help you build the foundation. For the actual file changes, you'll have to write your own code.

As I mentioned, an array of object pointers isn't really the best way to structure our data. What you want is a stack that makes it easy to push things onto the top. In addition to the regular pushing and popping that you expect from a stack, we'll add a new operation, pull, that will let us pull something out of the middle of the stack.

There are several ways you can approach this job. You can write a class that handles a stack of file_win pointers, or you can write an entirely generalized stack class. I'll take a middle approach, writing a class that handles pointers to anything but just handles pointers.

To do this, we'll use pointers to void. Void isn't a data type. What it tells the compiler is that we haven't made up our mind about type, but that it should accept pointer operations on these variables. You declare pointers to void like any other pointer:

```
void* pv; // pointer to void

void* pva[]; // array of pointers to void
```

You use pointers to void like other pointers:

```
void* pv;

... *pv ... // item pointed to by pv
... pv++ ... // increment the pointer
```

The compiler will not accept, however, assignments of possibly conflicting pointer types:

```
char* pc;
int*  pi;
void* pv;

pi = pc; // Error!
pc = pv; // Error!
```

With a pointer to void, you can use a cast to tell the compiler how you want it to use the pointer:

```
char* pc;
void* pv;

pc = (char*) pv; // OK -- casts pv as char*
```

A cast does not change the data value of the item being cast. It just tells the compiler that you are deliberately using the value in a different way. There are lots of ways to abuse this privilege, of course. On the other hand, this freedom lets you write very useful, maintainable code, as the pstack class will show.

The pstack class manipulates a stack of pointers to void. It will be up to you to cast pointers from each stack when you use them. Begin with T.CPP (all new, so it's not on disk) as shown in Listing 14-19.

Listing 14-19: T.CPP

```
// t.cpp

#define TRUE   1
#define FALSE  0
#define NULL   0

class pstack
{
protected:
    int stack_size;
    int top;

    void** stack;

public:
    pstack( int size );
    ~pstack();

    int push( void* );
    void* pop();
    void* pull( int item_no );
    void* look();
    int size(){ return top+1; }
};

int main() // pstack test routine
{
    pstack* ps = new pstack( 3 );
    char* ptr = new char[5];

    char* p1 = ptr+1, * p2 = ptr+2, *p3 = ptr+3;

    ps->push( ptr );
    ps->push( p1 );
```

```
    ps->push( p2 );

    void* p = ps->pull( 1 );
    p = ps->pull( 0 );
    p = ps->look();
}

pstack::pstack( int size )
{
    stack = new void*[size];

    stack_size = size;
    top = -1;
}

pstack::~pstack()
{
    delete stack;
}

int pstack::push( void* ptr )
{
    if ( top < stack_size-1 )
    {
        stack[++top] = ptr;
        return TRUE;
    }
    else
        return FALSE;
}

void* pstack::pop()
{
    if ( top == -1 )
        return NULL;
    else
    {
        return stack[top--];
    }
```

```
}

void* pstack::pull( int item_no )
{
    if ( item_no > top )
        return NULL;

    void* ret = stack[item_no];

    for ( int i = item_no; i < top; i++ )
        stack[i] = stack[i+1];

    top--;

    return ret;
}

void* pstack::look()
{
    if ( top == -1 )
        return NULL;
    else
        return stack[top];
}

// end of t.cpp
```

There is a new item here. In the size() method, the function definition is included in the class's definition. This arrangement tells the compiler that this is an "inline" function. The inline designation tells the compiler that you want the actual function code inserted instead of a call to the function. This will give you a faster system, since it saves some overhead. It will also lead to code bloat unless you save it for very tiny functions, such as this one.

You can declare and define a nonmember inline function as long as you do so before it is used:

```
inline int foo(){ return 1; }

int main()
{
    return foo();    // probably doesn't do
                     // a function call

}
```

H I N T

If you use inline functions, remember that the compiler is not under orders to put the code inline—it is just your suggestion. The compiler will actually use whatever implementation it thinks is best, and this may change from one compiler version to another and between one compiler and another.

Enter this pstack code slowly, thinking about each function. When you get it running, use a combination of inspect windows and the watch window to step through it slowly. The test routine I've left is checking pull() operations. Also change main() to test pop() operations.

If you build a watch window with ps->stack[0], ps->stack[1], and ps->stack[2], all your testing will be easier. As you test, you'll be looking at pointers to addresses such as DS:1234. The actual values of these addresses aren't important. What is important is that the pop operation, for example, gets the value that was the top of the stack.

You'll find that this code is extremely useful in many systems, so take your time testing. Get to know it thoroughly. When you're happy with it, let's go on to integrate it into our Tiny Editor.

Begin by creating a header file, TE.H, and copying the existing declarations and #defines from the top of TE.CPP into it. (Leave the global variables in TE.CPP.)

Next, copy the pstack class definition from T.CPP into TE.H. Then copy the definitions of the pstack methods from T.CPP into TE.CPP. (I've put them near the bottom of my file. You can choose to put them into another source file that you add to the project, too.) Finally, #include the new header at the top of TE.CPP, and you should be back in business, running just as you were before. Now we're ready to drop our array of pointers and replace it with a stack.

Begin by changing the array of pointers and the active_win index variable into a pointer stack and a file_win pointer variable. These are the global variables, above main(). Mine read this way:

```
pstack* fwins = new pstack( MAX_FILES );
file_win* active_fwin;
```

What we're doing here is making a stack to hold file_win pointers. I'm going to use the active_fwin variable to hold a copy of the pointer that's on the top of the stack. You'll see that this will make all the code that uses these pointers very simple.

By the way, you can't call a function before main() in C++, can you? Actually, you certainly can. By assigning an object to a global variable, as you see here, you call that object's constructor function. This is another chance to do real violence to the intent of the designers, or to use the language constructively. It's up to you.

With that done, take a look at the modified code in Listing 14-20, showing the changes to control() and to open_file_ctl() in TE.CPP. These functions both are simpler, now that we've thrown away the array of pointers. For example, all the uses of fwins[active_fwin] are replaced by active_fwin uses.

Listing 14-20: TE.CPP

```
void control()
{
    int cmd;
    int done = FALSE;

    active_fwin->show_cursor();

    do
    {
```

```
        cmd = edit_cmd();
        if ( cmd == FILE_OPEN )
            file_open_ctl();


        done = active_fwin->edit_do( cmd );

        if ( done )
        {
            delete active_fwin;

            fwins->pop();
            if ( fwins->size() > 0 )
                active_fwin = (file_win*) fwins->look();
            else
                active_fwin = NULL;
        }

    } while ( active_fwin );
}


void file_open_ctl()
{
    if ( !fwins->push(NULL) )
    {
        message( "Out of file space." );
        return;
    }
    else
        fwins->pop(); // get rid of the test NULL

    static char* blanks =
        "                                             ";

    char name[50]; // sized to fit blanks[]
    strcpy( name, blanks );

    FILE* infile = ::file_open( name, "rt" );

    if ( !infile )
        return;
```

```
    int lf = active_fwin->lft;
    int tp = active_fwin->top;
    int rt = active_fwin->rgt;
    int bt = active_fwin->btm;

    lf += lf < ( FULL_RGT - FILE_WIN_MIN_WIDTH  ) ? 1 : 0;
    tp += tp < ( FULL_BTM - FILE_WIN_MIN_HEIGHT ) ? 1 : 0;
    rt += rt < ( FULL_RGT - 1 ) ? 1 : 0;
    bt += bt < ( FULL_BTM - 1 ) ? 1 : 0;

    char* title = new_titleize( name );
    active_fwin =
        new file_win( title, infile, name,
        lf, tp, rt, bt );
    delete title;


    fwins->push( active_fwin );
}
```

The only part of this code that is the least bit tricky is the opening test in file_open_ctl(). I push a NULL pointer onto fwins, just to see if there's space enough for a real pointer. If this push fails, there's no more space, so I use the message() dialog and give up. If the test succeeds, I pop the NULL off, immediately, and continue with the real work of the function.

When you run this code, you'll have a new, pstack-based structure for your file_win objects and for your flow. It should look the same, but internally, of course, it's quite different. From here on, I'm leaving the job in your hands. If you haven't tested the limits, yet, that's a good place to start. Change MAX_FILES (in TE.H) to something smaller than 20 and try again.

If you haven't tested the limits, yet, that's a good place to start. Change MAX_FILES (in TE.H) to something smaller than 20 and try again.

For your next job, try implementing an ALL_DONE message. That would be an Alt+X keystroke to parallel TCLite, or Ctrl+K, X for you WordStar afficionados. I've added both. Just save and exit from every open file for starters. Later on you can come back and add a logical flag that you set when a file's been modified. The only part of this code that is the least bit tricky is the opening test in file_open_ctl(). I push a NULL pointer onto fwins, just to see if there's space enough for a real pointer. If this push fails, there's no more space, so I use the message() dialog and give up. If the test succeeds, I pop the NULL off, immediately, and continue with the real work of the function.

SUMMARY

If you've come this far, you're entitled to call yourself a C++ programmer. In the next chapter I'll collect all the loose ends. We'll talk about the bits of C++ that you haven't seen in this project, and we'll talk about the bits of this project that I'm sure you'll want to add on your own, such as mouse control and a search and replace capability.

What you've got now is a solid base for your own text editor, along with a solid grounding in using the C++ language. While we've worked through this final project chapter, we've used freopen() and fputs() for file output.

We considered pointer arrays. We read command line arguments with argc and the pointer array, argv. We went on to implement our own array of pointers to objects, as a first cut at controlling multiple file_win objects.

We touched on a number of minor topics, such as the modulus operator, the difference between runtime and compile-time data initialization, the use of the scope resolution operator to select nonmember functions, break's companion the continue statement, and friend functions.

In our last section, we replaced our array of pointers to objects with a stack of pointers to void. You used pointers to void as a generic pointer type, and you used a pointer cast to tell the compiler about a specific pointer use. In the pointer stack we also used an inline member function to eliminate (possibly!) function call overhead.

Anyone that has written a stack object and used it for maintaining a stack of pointers to objects is entitled to call themselves a C++ programmer. That means you. Congratulations!

In the last chapter, I'll touch on some of the work you'll want to do on your own to add to your Tiny Editor, and I'll mention some of the C++ topics that didn't fit into this project. You can dive right in, or you can take a break and use what you've learned to improve your Tiny Editor.

Your Tiny Editor is in your hands now. I'm not going to guide you through any more programming. In this chapter we'll conclude with a look at some features of C++ that you'll want to explore on your own.

► Multiple inheritance

► Operator overloading

► Virtual base classes and functions

► References

► Static member variables

► Templates and exception handling

► Bit fields

► Memory management and models

► Floating-point math

► Const-type variables

► Pointers to functions

► Multidimensional arrays

► The comma operator

► The goto statement and program labels

chapter

15

Wrapping Up

You really know more than enough about C++ to do your own work, now. Unless your job is developing C++ compilers, you'll never get to know 100 percent of the language, and you're already someplace over 90 percent. Don't worry about the few features you haven't used, and don't try to memorize the contents of this chapter. We'll discuss:

Learn about what's available so that you can recognize a match between language features and your program's needs as you work on your C++ projects. When you need a feature, it's enough to know that it's there. You can look up the details when you have a reason to use it.

I'll also make some suggestions in this chapter about features that you'll probably want to include in your Tiny Editor. For example, you'll need search and replace, which shouldn't be a problem. You'll also probably want to integrate the mouse, which goes beyond C++ into the gray area where language, operating system, and hardware meet.

I'll show you enough code that you can get started on your own mouse work, although strictly speaking the code won't be C++.

Finally, I'll conclude with some remarks about the world of GUI interfaces, and where you may want to go next. Let's begin with multiple inheritance.

MULTIPLE INHERITANCE

C++ originally supported single inheritance—the kind we've been using. Some people argued that this was theoretically sufficient and that anything more invited poor programming practices.

Others argued that although single inheritance was theoretically sufficient, the convenience of direct language support for multiple inheritance in some situations far outweighed its potential for abuse. As has always been the case with C and C++, the programmers who wanted more power won the argument.

Our file_win object is one that I would have built using multiple inheritance, were it not for the fact that this would have simplified the code too much! I confess that the single-inheritance structure was chosen because the complications it forced on us allowed me to show you a lot more features of the language, not because it was the best design.

We should have built the file_win object by inheriting from both the memfile object and the dialog object. If you say that the "has a" relationship implies including a data member, while "is a" means that you inherit, the file_win "is a" dialog box, and it "is a" memfile, in many ways. The acid test comes by asking yourself if you couldn't model file_win as a memfile with an attached dialog box as easily as you could model it as a dialog box with an attached memfile. The fact that neither seems obviously right means that file_win is both a memfile and a dialog, and that it should be built with multiple inheritance.

Figure 15-1 shows a simple T.CPP that creates two classes, a and b, and then creates a third class, ab, that inherits from both a and b.

You can see in the Inspect window and in the Watch window that x, an object in the ab class, has inherited the properties of both class a and class b. If you look at the code for class ab, you see that multiple inheritance was no more complicated than listing the inherited classes—separating them with commas—where we had been listing just one class.

When you inherit from two (or more) classes, you run the constructors of those classes when you construct the inheriting object, and you run the destructors when you delete the object. As with single inheritance, you can't put your own code into the inherited class constructor and have it run before the base class constructors. If you use an object pointer member, you can explicitly use *new* to

```
≡ File Edit Search Run Compile Debug Project Options Window Help
┌──────────────────────── T.CPP ─────────────────────1─┐
│ // t.cpp                    ┌──── Inspecting x ──2─┐   │
│                             │ Register (SI) » ds:04CC│ │
│ struct a { int a1; };       │ a::a1         11 (0x000B)│
│                             │ b::b1         22 (0x0016)│
│ struct b { int b1; };       │                        │ │
│                             │ struct ab *            │ │
│ struct ab : a, b {};        └────────────────────────┘ │
│                                                        │
│ int main()                                             │
│ {                                                      │
│     ab* x = new ab();                                  │
│     x->a1 = 11; x->b1 = 22;                            │
│     return 1;                                          │
│ }                                                      │
├─[■]──────────────────── Watch ──────────────────3─[↑]─┤
│ x->a1: 11                                              │
│ x->b1: 22                                              │
└────────────────────────────────────────────────────────┘
 F1 Help  F7 Trace  F8 Step  ⏎ Edit  Ins Add  Del Delete  F10 Menu
```

Figure 15-1: Class ab inherits from a and from b.

create the object whenever your constructor finds it appropriate. Programming is full of tradeoffs, and C++ is rich in choices.

OPERATOR OVERLOADING

One of the richest possibilities of the C++ languages is the ability to overload operators, as well as functions. This was one of the first things that attracted me to the language. It wasn't just that you could define your own data types in a rich variety of ways, but you could also tell the language what operators such as + and * meant when you applied them to those types.

In most languages, the + operator is overloaded to some degree. In C++, for example, it will add two ints, or any combination of the integer types (such as long + char). It can also add floating-point numbers or add integers to floating-point numbers or to pointers. It can't do nonsensical things, such as add two pointers.

There are many other sorts of things that you might want to add. For example, if your accounting application featured invoice objects, the + operator might return the sum of the amounts due when applied to two invoices. Consider this little program:

```
// t.cpp
#include <stdio.h>
```

```
struct invoice {
    char* cust_name[40];
    float due;

    invoice( float amt ){ due = amt; }
    float operator+(invoice inv2){ return due + inv2.due; }
};

int main()
{
    invoice x = *new invoice( 10.0 );
    invoice y = *new invoice( 20.0 );

    printf( "\ntotal is %5.2f", x+y );

    return 0;
}
```

As you see in the printf() statement, this capability can lead to very handy nota-tion. As you see in the definition of operator+(), the function definition is con-fusing at first.

Operators are either unary or binary in C++. (Actually, there is a ternary opera-tor, the conditional ?:, but you can't redefine it.) You can replace any binary operator, such as a + b, with a two-argument function call, such as add(a,b). Similarly, you can replace unary operators, such as i++, with one-argument function calls, such as incr(i).

With a binary operator, the function definition has the object as one implicit argument, so it needs only the second argument. You might think of it this way:

```
some_obj x, y;

...

... x+y ... ; // same as x->operator+(y)
```

Here you call x's operator+() method with the argument y. That's why our invoice operator+() returns "due + inv2.due"—the first "due" is the data mem-ber of the object on the left side of the plus sign.

If all this has your head in a tangle, maybe you'll enjoy the following explana-tion of a good reason not to use operator overloading.

We could define a subscript operator for our linked-list class. We could define it so that:

```
... llist[5] ... ; // the fifth item in the list
```

(I'll let you decide whether that's the fifth from the start, or whether the first is numbered zero so that it's really the sixth.) For a linked list, the subscript function would just start at the head of the list and follow the next pointer the appropriate number of times, something like this:

```
member = ... ; //set to head of list

for ( int i = 0; i < subscript; i++ )
    member = member->next;


return member;
```

That would make certain linked-list operations incredibly convenient to code. Consider a show_all() capability:

```
for ( int row = start; row < stop; row++ )
    show_line( row, list[row] );
```

But now consider what will happen if we start this show_all() with, for example, row 2000 in a 3000-line file. To find list[2000], it will march forward from zero (or one) 2000 times. Then to find line 2001, it will do the same thing 2001 times. Then 2002 times, and so on.

If we write show_all() the hard way, each extra row will follow the next pointer exactly once, to get to the next list item. Clearly, the subscript operator can be a remarkable aid to coding linked-list operations, but if you aren't careful, it can result in a remarkable loss of efficiency.

So should you use overloaded operator functions? I do. But I don't do it very often anymore. I used to do it a lot, but it can cost you in efficiency, and it can mean that you need to study the operator functions before you can read the code, too. On the other hand, used judiciously they can be both readable and efficient.

Keep operator functions in the back of your mind until the time comes when you really think one could be helpful. Then you'll find it worth the trouble of wading through the syntax of the function for the convenience of the code you can write when you've defined the operator.

OTHER C++ FEATURES

In this section, I'll list and briefly explain some of the features of C++ that haven't made it into our project. Since our Tiny Editor is a fairly typical project, you can rest assured that these are not the features you'll meet commonly in your other work.

Virtual Base Classes and Functions

With multiple inheritance, you can think of the inherited classes at one level as siblings. For instance, if we had programmed our file_win as a class inheriting from dialogs and from memfiles, we could consider dialogs and memfiles to be siblings in the inheritance tree.

There are situations in which you want to have siblings that both inherit from a single base (directly, or at whatever depth). In these situations, some interesting problems appear.

Assume that class C inherits from classes B1 and B2. Assume that both B1 and B2 inherit from A. What happens when you call the C class constructor?

Without some other mechanism, C's constructor would call B1's constructor first and B2's constructor second. B1's constructor and B2's constructor would both call A's constructor, running it twice. This could be harmless, or it could double-allocate storage or do considerable damage, depending on the details of A's constructor.

Chances are pretty good that what you would really want to happen is to have A's constructor run once, and then have B1's constructor and B2's constructor run. Last, C's additional constructor code should run.

Virtual base classes and virtual functions come into play when you run into this situation. Through the use of these tools you can control exactly what happens, and when. You'll need to look into them when your inheritance trees stop looking like simple trees and start looking like complex inheritance networks.

References

C is a simple language. One of its simplicities is that all arguments are passed by value. When you call foo(x), you don't pass the address of x, you pass its value to whatever parameter foo() declares. When foo() modifies its parameter, it won't impact the argument x. The parameter inside foo() is local to foo().

Of course, in C and in C++, many times you'll pass an argument that is the address of a string. By using the address, the function can modify the value of the string directly. So although you always pass values, there really isn't any limit to what can be done. If you want to pass an address, you can always use the & operator to take the address of an argument.

C++ lets you pass references, which are neither values nor addresses. They have enough benefits that I'll recommend you study them someday, and they have enough quirks that I'll recommend you don't start that study until you consider yourself a near-total C++ expert.

Static Member Variables

Static member variables really overload the keyword static. In other contexts, something is static when it is unchanging. Static variables are not created and destroyed with each run of a function, for example.

Classes can have static data members, too, but don't let the keyword fool you. A static data member has one instance for the entire class, as opposed to a non-static data member, which has a separate instance for each object of that class.

You can use static members to keep track of classwide values. For example, in a linked-list class each member might be an item in the list while static values kept track of the size of the list. This works if you only have one list, since static class members occur just once for each class.

Templates and Exception Handling

The C++ standards committees, of which CBEMA's X3J16 is the most important in the U.S., are busily working on new features. As I write this, templates and exception handling are two features that are being refined.

Templates allow you to create a general structure for a class from which you can derive specific classes. Exception handling allows elegant treatment of otherwise messy events, such as attempting a disk write when the computer might run out of disk space.

Bit Fields

C++ provides an elegant mechanism for dealing with hardware-oriented code that assigns meanings to bit fields within a char or word. If you want to interface to a device that specifies that bits 2 and 3 at port 1 mean one thing and bits 4 through 6 mean another, look into bit fields.

Memory Management

One of the things we've done that we definitely should fix pertains to memory management. We've just assumed that when we call the *new* operator it will find the space it needs. Of course, sooner or later you'll call *new,* and it won't find the space you want. It will return a null pointer, telling you that it failed.

To be error-free, our code really should have checked each return value and provided a sensible alternative (such as closing down after saving open files) in an out-of-memory situation.

I didn't do that because C++ provides a much better mechanism. You can write your own *new* handler. In its more sophisticated form, a custom *new* handler could actually take care of memory allocation. The more common case, however, is to provide a general mechanism for failing more or less gracefully when you simply run out of memory.

TCLite doesn't let you create your own *new* handler, unfortunately, or we would have done so before you got here. In fact, I would have made it one of our first orders of business. When you move your Tiny Editor code from TCLite to Borland's TC++ or whatever C++ you use next, make checking your documentation for the *new* handler in STDLIB.H one of your first orders of business.

By the way, you'll be happy to find that you can create a global *new* handler in a very few minutes.

Outside TCLite, you'll also need to pick the "memory model." TCLite limits you to the "small" model, which allows up to 64K for data and 64K for code. This is fine for learning, but you'll want more space for some of your work.

In other C++ environments you can choose memory models ranging from "tiny" (64K total for both code and data) to "huge" (up to 4G for each). The tiny model lets you generate .COM files, which are fine for little utilities. The huge model lets you write the biggest, most complex systems.

Pick the smallest model that fits your needs. Larger models take more space on disk and in RAM and are slower.

OTHER C-BASED FEATURES

C++ is almost a superset of the C language. There are a number of features of C that we have not touched on. You'll find them handy sooner or later.

Floating-Point Math

If your work involves floating-point math, as most science and engineering does, you'll know it already. C++ lets you declare and use floating-point values with no trouble. (The invoice example in the operator overloading section above used floating-point numbers.)

If you don't routinely use floating point, I've some advice: Don't start now! Most people look at currencies such as the American or British that use fractional parts and begin writing accounting or bookkeeping applications that use floating-point numbers to handle, for example, dollars and cents. Then they have no end of problems with the rounding errors that floating point brings with it.

Using long integers, you can correctly model almost all transactions in dollars, pounds, marks, or francs. The indivisible currency unit in each of those cases is the cent or other hundredth part. If you do your counting in cents, you'll only need to convert to a pseudo-fractional representation when you read values or report them, and your applications will never have rounding problems. Three-thirds of a dollar will be exactly 99 cents, every time.

Const-Type Variables

The "const" qualifier appeared in C and was specified robustly in C++. It tells the compiler that the following value is not to be changed. Any attempt to change it is an error.

```
const float pi = 3.14159;

pi = pi+1; // Error!  Can't assign to a const!
```

For single-word values, the const qualifier is probably not as sensible as using a #define constant. For multiple-word tables, however, it makes sense to use a const. Consider an application that does date arithmetic. It needs to know how many days there are in each month. This stub program illustrates a const:

```
const int moends[12] = { 31, 28, 31, 30, 31, 30,
                         31, 31, 30, 31, 30, 31 };

moends[3] = 14; // Error! Can't assign to a const!
```

This feature lets you, in effect, ask the compiler to yell at you if you do something stupid. I like features like this, since I often do stupid things.

Pointers to Functions

A function name is a pointer to the code in the function. Exploiting this fact can lead to all sorts of very complex code, and occasionally it can lead to some marvelously simple, direct code. You'll see one typical use when you create a new handler to trap out-of-memory conditions. Here's another one that lives in the gray area between fast code and tricky code.

When you create a long switch, such as the one in our edit_do() code for the file_win object, your compiler writes code that tests one condition at a time. Consider this code and the accompanying pseudo-machine output:

```
switch ( exp )
{
    case 'a':
        do_a();

    case 'b':
        do_b();

    ... // etc.
}
```

Your compiler writes output code, something like this:

```
Evaluate the expression (exp) and store the result.

If result == 'a'
    then call do_a;

If result == 'b'
    then call do_b;

... // etc.
```

This is fine, provided that the list of cases in the switch isn't too long, and that the most common cases are found near the top of the switch. If you have a very long list of cases, it can be faster to create an array of addresses of functions and use a subscript to call the appropriate function.

To do this, you'll not be able to use messages picked for your convenience, as we did in EDITCMDS.H. You'll need to use messages that start with 0 and continue with 1, 2, and so on. An enum would be a better choice than #defines.

If you create an array of pointers to functions, called, for example, actions[], then this statement will call the first function in that array:

```
actions[0]();
```

The trailing parentheses tell the compiler that this is a function call. (You could put parameters inside the parentheses, of course.)

If you want to experiment with building and calling an array of pointers to functions, try something like this:

```
#include <stdio.H>

void a(){ printf( "\n in a" ); }
void b(){ printf( "\n in b" ); }
void c(){ printf( "\n in c" ); }

void(* actions[3])() = {a,b,c};

int main()
{
    for ( int i = 0; i < 3; i++ )
        actions[i]();

    return 0;
}
```

In the following list, I'll use the variable name to help explain itself. For instance, pv_v is a pointer to a void function with void arguments. It goes like this:

```
void(* pv_v)(); // pointer to void function void args

int(* pi_v)();  // pointer to int func, void args

int(* pi_i)(int); // ptr to int func, int arg

int(* api_i[3])(int); // array, 3 ptrs to int funcs, int arg
```

If you work your way through this syntactic maze, you can actually write lucid code this way. Suppose you named your array of function pointers call[] and used descriptive names in your enum, such as LineDelete. Then you could write code like this:

```
call[LineDelete](); // calls line_delete()
```

If you do this, please be verbose in your comments!

Multidimensional Arrays

Let's drop back into the comfortable zone of simple, regular concepts. C doesn't support multidimensional arrays, but it does support arrays of arrays, which allow you to do the same thing. Consider this:

```
int ai[3][4];
```

This statement creates an array, ai, of type integer. The array ai has three elements. Each of those elements is itself an array of four elements. You can address:

```
int ai[3][4];
```

```
... ai[0]     ... // The first array, 4 ints long
... ai[0][1] ... // The second int in a[0]
... ai[1][0] ... // The first int in a[1]
```

Or consider this code:

```
int a[3][4];
int* ip = ( int* )a; // cast a as pointer to int
for ( int i = 0; i < 12; i++ )
    *(ip++) = i;

/* Run this and you get:
    a[0] = { 0, 1, 2, 3}
    a[1] = { 4, 5, 6, 7}
    a[2] = { 8, 9,10,11} */
```

As always, don't use arrays of arrays when some other construct is better suited to the problem. (Programmers from other languages can sometimes overdo multidimensional arrays.) But use them when they fit the problem. Don't use pointers to pointers just to write more "C-style" code.

The Comma Operator

You can use commas to separate multiple expressions. Except as we've seen in argument lists, I never use the comma operator. Someday you'll meet it—probably in the code of a young programmer proud of how tricky his or her code is.

If you separate expressions with commas, they will be evaluated from left to right. The value returned is the value of the rightmost expression.

```
int a, b, c;

a = ( b = 1, c = 2 );
```

If you figured out what was assigned to a in the above example, you get one point. If you decided that you'd rewrite that screwball code, you get two points.

The goto Statement and Program Labels

There is a goto statement in C++ that works much like the goto statement in BASIC. I've never used it. Like the goto statement in BASIC, it lets you branch to a statement label directly from any point in a function.

The goto statement is a good way to write unmaintainable code. Don't even look it up. If you are used to programming with goto in BASIC or another language, break the habit. It will only hold you back.

It's been theoretically proven that the goto is not needed. I've never seen an example in practice where rewriting code to eliminate a goto didn't help clarify the code.

That ends your introduction to the C++ features that we haven't put to use in our Tiny Editor. Before I close, I'll spend a short while discussing some of the features that you'll want to add immediately.

SEARCHING AND REPLACING

You can't really have a text editor if you don't have a search-and-replace capability. Professional editors vie with each other to see who's gotten the most flexibility in their search procedures. In the fullest procedures, regular expression searching lets you find, for example, every "foo(" that is within two lines of a closing brace. Or anything else!

On the other hand, as is often the case, 20 percent of the features satisfy 80 percent of the requirements. Start by programming a simple search capability.

Inherit a "search" class from the dialog class. Drop in a string_dialog object and launch the search object in response to a SEARCH message. Don't do anything at first with the response except pop up a message() box telling yourself what you'll look for. (Remember, msg() is gone!)

Next, write a simple search function. Start by using memchr() (check the online help) to find the first character of the search string. Then use strcmp() to compare the string you're looking for with the text you're searching in. If you find it, your search is done. If not, advance a pointer and try memchr() again, checking the additional occurrences of the first character until you find the string or memchr() reports that you're out of luck.

Use a T.CPP to debug your search logic using test strings. When it works, build it into your program in a loop. Test the current memline's text member. If you don't find what you're looking for, go to the next memline. Keep going until you find it, or until you find the end of your text file.

The memchr() and strcmp() built-ins are fast assembly language routines. Your search will be very fast, even in a big file. Your biggest problem (where'd you see this before?) will be repositioning the display after you've found an occurrence.

Don't worry about searching the whole file, or from the current location backward. You can always add those features later.

Once you've got search working, go for replace. Add a new message, and create a replace object that inherits from search. This one will be simple. Your del_chars() and ins_chars() routines are there just waiting to help you out with a replace.

When you add features, think through the object that gets them. For example, if you were adding an option to go backward, you'd add it to the search object so that replace would inherit the capability. If you were adding a "replace all" option, of course, it would go into the replace object only.

Good luck!

USING THE MOUSE

In contrast to searching and replacing, which you know how to do, using the mouse leads you out of the familiar into relatively uncharted territory.

To begin with, TCLite doesn't have any built-in mouse-support functions. To add them, you'll have to directly call the Microsoft Mouse Extension Routines (an extension to DOS) that provide mouse information.

To continue, the Microsoft Mouse Extension Routines don't do very much. You might reasonably hope that they'd handle common actions, such as double-clicks and drags, but they don't. They just tell you where the mouse is and what's happened to the buttons since the last time you asked.

The good news is that our TECMD.CPP was built from the start with the thought that eventually we'd add mouse support.

In this section I'll tell you about the things you need to know to get access to the mouse. It will be up to you to put this knowledge to use. Let's start with interrupts.

Interrupts

Back in the earliest days of computers we discovered that there had to be a way for the computer to tell us that something important was going on. It wasn't enough for our code to try to direct everything.

For example, an interrupt could tell us that the data we had requested from disk were ready, or that the operator had pressed the Halt button. Since the hardware had no way to know what we would do with this information, two-way communication was needed.

The 80*x*86 architecture has a typical interrupt setup. The hardware can trigger interrupts, or software can trigger interrupts. When the hardware triggers an interrupt, it actually calls a subroutine through the interrupt table. The interrupt table is simply a list of pointers to subroutines. In the *x*86, it occupies the lowest physical addresses in RAM. (It starts at physical location 0.)

```
void(* intrpts[???])() = { ... }
```

```
...
```

```
// got interrupt 10?
    intrpts[9]();
```

This code will call the tenth subroutine listed in the interrupt table.

Our code won't write these interrupt handlers (which are the subject of several good books), but it will call the ones DOS provides. Interrupts are almost always called by their hexadecimal numbers. The common convention is to write about them with assembler-style notation:

```
10h == hexadecimal 10, or decimal 16
21h == hexadecimal 21, or decimal 33
```

The two interrupts above are famous ones. INT 10h is the BIOS video interrupt, through which you can manipulate the cursor, video modes, and so on. INT 21h is DOS itself, through which almost all file I/O, among other things, is performed. The mouse functions are found at INT 33h.

As you've probably guessed, you need to provide additional data when you call, for instance, INT 33h. You may want to turn the mouse cursor on, to find out where the mouse cursor is, to check the mouse button status, or whatever. This range of choices would imply a variety of parameters if we had a single mouse subroutine in C++.

Instead of parameters, the *x*86 registers are used to pass the data that the mouse interrupt (subroutine) needs. A register is a named location inside the CPU itself. C++ has no syntax for manipulating registers, since every computer is different in its registers and register names. So here we're going to walk right out of C++ into *x*86-specific extensions that Borland provides. Of course, these extensions are Borland-specific; other compiler vendors have their own way of doing these operations. You should place all of this hardware-specific code in a single source file so that you know what needs translating when you change compilers or port to new hardware.

Beginning with the original 8086 chip, Intel provided four general-purpose registers, called AX, BX, CX, and DX. These are 16-bit registers. Subsequent generations of Intel processors have added to this set. For example, the 80286 processor added registers EAX, EBX, ECX, and EDX, which are 32 bits wide. DOS has always used the four originals since even the Pentiums (and, it seems safe to assume, later processors) have these registers.

The E*xx* registers actually include AX, BX, CX, and DX as their right halves. (I'm going to speak as if the registers were laid out with the most significant bit on the left, for our convenience. That has absolutely nothing to do with CPU design, of course.) AX is the right side of the EAX register, so writing data to AX also writes to EAX.

Similarly, each of the general-purpose registers could be addressed by byte. The most significant (left) byte of AX is called AH, and the right byte is called AL. (Think of High and Low.) Similarly, you can address BX as BH and BL, CX as CH and CL, and DX as DH and DL.

Borland provides several ways to actually use the *x*86 registers. One is the union REGS, defined in DOS.H. REGS is a union of two structures, WORDREGS and BYTEREGS. The part that interests us looks like this:

```
union REGS {
  struct   WORDREGS   x;
  struct   BYTEREGS   h;
};
```

```
struct  BYTEREGS  {
  unsigned char   al, ah, bl, bh;
  unsigned char   cl, ch, dl, dh;
};


struct  WORDREGS  {
  unsigned int   ax, bx, cx, dx;
};
```

(There are other registers defined in WORDREGS, but they don't have any immediate use for us. See the online help for a complete list.)

The union lets you place an int in AX or two chars in AL and AH. Either member addresses the same location in memory.

REGS is used in the general-purpose interrupt call, int86(). It is called with an interrupt number and two REGS unions, for input and output. You assign any necessary register values to the first REGS. It runs the interrupt code and then copies the register values into the second REGS, which you can examine and act on.

Let's begin with a simple program to find the location of the cursor on the screen. The video mode is returned by video service 0xF. You request a service by putting its number in the AH register. A video service is one of the INT 10h services.

This program requests service 15:

```
#include <dos.h>

#define VIDEO 0x10 // for interrupt 10h

int main()
{
    REGS in, out;

    in.h.ah = 0x0f; // service 15 -- get video mode

    // service 15 returns mode in AL, width in AH
```

```
int86( VIDEO, &in, &out );

return 0;  // set a breakpoint here to look at output
}
```

Figure 15-2 shows me using the Watch window to look at my results. I've used a cast to int on the results. Without that cast you'll find out that the width of your screen is "P" characters. (I suppose "P" is a perfectly correct answer to the question, "What's in the AH register?" but it doesn't really tell me what I want to know.)

If you're thinking that this approach unlocks all the secrets to direct control of the PC, you're almost right. You'll need to buy a good reference book that lists all the PC interrupts, including their inputs and outputs. With that in hand, really getting down to the lowest level of control is just a matter of setting up register values in your "in" REGS and reading results via the "out" regs.

If you remember that we didn't really do a good job setting screen_height, you'll be disappointed to find out that there is no BIOS call that tells you how many rows are on your screen. You can check the video mode for a guess. In video mode 3 there are 25 lines. Otherwise, 50's a pretty good guess.

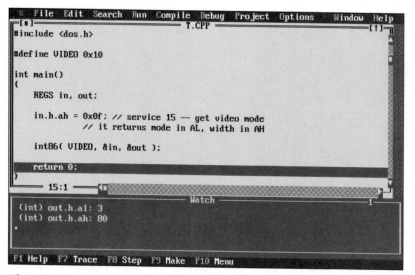

Figure 15-2: Watching the result of a call to video service 15.

Mouse Interrupts

With a general-purpose way of calling the BIOS interrupts, what you need now is the rundown on the mouse. Mouse services are found at interrupt 33h. Unlike most BIOS interrupts, mouse services demand that you set register AX (not AH) with the service number.

Let's begin looking at mouse interrupts from the beginning.

Mouse Service 0, Reset and Status

Mouse service 0 resets the mouse to a sensible default status (cursor in the middle of the screen, but turned off, for example) and returns either −1 or zero. The −1 indicates an available mouse. The zero value is returned when there is no mouse, or there's a hardware or software problem the keeps you from using it.

You should call for service 0 in your startup() routine. If AX returns −1, set a flag that says there's a mouse present and always put your mouse code under that flag, like this:

```
// in startup():

    ... // call service 0
    has_mouse = out.x.ax;


// everywhere else:
    if ( has_mouse )
    {
        ... use the mouse here
    }
```

Test service 0 by stepping through a program like this one:

```
#include <dos.h>

#define MOUSE 0x33

int main()
{
    REGS in, out;

    in.x.ax = 0x00; // service 0 -- reset and get status
            // it returns status in AX
```

```
    int86( MOUSE, &in, &out );

    return 0;
}
```

Mouse Service 1, Show Cursor

Calling mouse service 1 turns the mouse cursor on. You should do this in startup() as soon as you find out that there is a mouse.

To test the routines from here on, you'll need to place a getch() in your test code. You won't see the mouse if you halt at a breakpoint and use Alt+F5 to toggle to the user screen.

Mouse Service 2, Hide Cursor

Calling mouse service 2 turns the mouse cursor off. See the later section, Mouse Droppings, to find out why you need this service.

Mouse Service 3, Button Status and Position

Calling mouse service 3 returns the button status in BL. If BL is zero, neither button is pressed. The value 1 specifies that the left button is pressed; 2, that the right button is pressed; and 3, that both are pressed.

The x location is returned in CX, and the y location, in DX. Both these values specify a pixel-based location. Dividing by 8 converts the location to characters.

Mouse Service 4, Set Cursor Position

Calling mouse service 4 sets the mouse location to the coordinates specified in CX (x) and DX (y). Multiply your character coordinates by 8 to set these values.

This code uses service 4:

```
#include <conio.h>
#include <dos.h>

#define MOUSE 0x33

int main()
{
    REGS in, out;
```

```
    in.x.ax = 0x00; // service 0--reset and get status
              // it returns status in AX


    int86( MOUSE, &in, &out );


    in.x.ax = 1; // service 1--turn mouse on
    int86( MOUSE, &in, &out);
    getch();


    // set loc 40, 13:
    in.x.ax = 4; in.x.cx = 40*8; in.x.dx = 13*8;
    int86( MOUSE, &in, &out );


    getch();


    return 0;
}
```

Mouse Service 5, Get Button Press Information

Calling mouse service 5 gets the number of times the left or right button has been pressed since you last called this service and the location of the last button press. If called with BX equal to zero, the service reports on the left button. If called with BX equal to 1, it reports on the right button.

BX returns the number of times the button was pressed since you last called this service. CX and DX report the x and y coordinates.

For a simple use, just check the left button for a click. Any nonzero number in BX indicates that the button was clicked. Once you know you have a click, your software then can look at the location and decide what to do. (A click in the current edit window, for instance, positions the text cursor.)

For sophisticated uses you can combine the count data with timing information to check for double-clicks. You can check the time with gettime() (declaration in DOS.H). By combining this service with service 5, you can write a nice double-click detector. Try this algorithm:

```
// was button clicked more than once?
    // assume it's a double-click


// was button clicked once?
```

```
// wait a bit (start at about 0.25 secs)
// got another click?
   // it's a double click

// else it's a single click
```

Microsoft's double-click in Windows seems to be defined as two clicks within the defined time that are *not* separated by any mouse movement. I think an algorithm that ignores mouse movement does a much friendlier job.

Other Mouse Services

There are many more mouse services. Some are specific to graphics cursors, and some are applicable to text cursors. You can, for instance, change the default cursor and set regions within which the mouse operates.

You'll want a complete reference book if you want to dive into this area. The six services listed here, however, are all that you'll need to build mouse support into your Tiny Editor.

Mouse Droppings

Mouse droppings (the on-screen kind) are the worst problem in mouse programming. This is because the mouse cursor is created by software that manipulates video RAM. (The text cursor doesn't have this problem since it is created and maintained by your hardware.)

Mouse droppings happen this way: The mouse cursor is on-screen when a dialog box pops up. That popup saves the screen (including the image of the mouse cursor) just before it pops up. Clicking with the mouse, the user dispenses with the dialog box, and it pops down (restoring the screen).

You now have a second mouse cursor on your screen. One is the real mouse cursor, and the other is the cursor image that got caught when the screen under the popup was saved. Other combinations of mousing around with saving and restoring the screen can create other sorts of mouse droppings, too.

You avoid mouse droppings by turning the mouse cursor off before you do any screen saves or restores. You can protect your work by writing covers for puttext() and gettext(), like this:

```
mcc_puttext( ... ) // mcc == Mouse Compatible Cover
{
    if ( has_mouse )
        mouse_off();
```

```
    puttext( ... );

  if ( has_mouse )
      mouse_on();
}
```

Call the mcc version instead of calling puttext() or gettext() directly. You'll need to write your own mouse_off() and other mouse handling functions. They should isolate you from all the details of the direct interface to the *x*86-specific BIOS calls you need to make to work with a mouse.

Don't approach your mouse work as a grand design problem. Get your feet wet with a few simple cover functions. Then add nice big clickable "Yes" and "No" buttons to our yes_no object. (We left enough space.) That's a good first project.

Positioning the cursor in the active file_win is a good second project. Selecting a file_win is a good third project, but only after you've added a keyboard method for doing this. Have fun!

G O I N G   G U I

Everyone wants to write Windows programs, or Presentation Manager, Macintosh, or X-windows programs, or whatever. Text mode is definitely on its way out.

I'm sorry to see it go, speaking personally. Text-mode programs have incredible speed on today's hardware. And text mode is still the best mode for working with text. The manuscript for this book, for example, was written in text mode.

But that's not the way the world is going. The world is going toward graphical interfaces in everything, appropriate or not. I want to make two observations to help you on your way.

Porting the Tiny Editor to a GUI

Our Tiny Editor does all its screen I/O through only a handful of routines. At the bottom level, we use gotoxy(), cprintf(), and textattr() for all our text work. If you can find equivalent routines in your GUI environment, you'll find that all the internal logic in your Tiny Editor is still completely sound (or at least as sound as it ever was).

For a complete port, you'll find that we've used putch() in our box::draw() code, but you'll probably replace that entirely with whatever calls create a window.

All things considered, you've just about written all of a perfectly good, GUI-based text editor.

MFC, OWL, and Class Libraries

For Windows programming and for cross-platform programming, a serious class library is a must. Microsoft Foundation Classes (MFC) and Borland's Object Windows Library (OWL) are two of the most common. Third-party vendors have the edge when it comes to libraries that allow you to code once and port instantly across multiple platforms, such as Windows, UNIX, and Macintosh.

None of these libraries are, however, the next step in your education. You can go on to additional work in C++ in text mode, concentrating on C++ itself, or you can go on to a graphical platform. If you want to learn Windows programming, for example, start right out on Windows.

If you start with OWL or MFC, you'll save yourself some of the pain of learning Windows—a project that is at least as challenging as learning C++. But you'll also be limited to writing very large applications. MFC and OWL both are far too big for writing simple utilities.

Eventually, you'll find that you have to back down to the level of Windows programming that you passed over, either because you want to handle smaller utilities or because you need to break out of the standard interface paradigm. (These remarks also apply to Macintosh, UNIX, and other GUI environments.)

You started with this book so you could master C++, free from worrying about the complexities of Resource Editors and Foundation Classes. You made the right choice. Stick with that philosophy.

SUMMARY

I hope you've enjoyed this book as much as I have. I hope you've worked up a Tiny Editor that you're proud to claim as your own. If you've taken this book one step at a time, you're entitled to make that claim.

In this chapter we've wrapped up some of the final details. We started with a look at two major C++ topics, multiple inheritance and operator overloading. Then we proceeded to consider a grab bag of lesser topics in C++ and in the predecessor C language.

We discussed using virtual base classes and functions when sibling bases inherit from a common base. We noted that references provide an alternative to passing addresses and values. We discussed class statics, which are variables that occur once for the class, not once for each object in the class. We went through other C++ topics, finishing with a consideration of writing a new handler to trap out-of-memory conditions.

From the C language, we mentioned floating-point math, which didn't appear in our Tiny Editor. We talked about using the const qualifier to have the compiler help catch your errors. We saw how pointers to functions (and arrays of pointers to functions) can be created and can speed up some portions of a program. We also looked briefly at multidimensional arrays and some other C-based topics.

Then we went back to our Tiny Editor. I started with some suggestions for getting a search-and-replace capability up and running quickly.

We continued with a long (or perhaps much too brief) discussion of the mouse. Talking to the mouse means using the x86 registers and directly interfacing with the operating system. We looked at the routines you need to do this and at the half dozen most important mouse services.

I offered some advice on how you can implement a mouse capability and briefly pointed out the problem of "mouse droppings," concentrating on how to avoid them.

Finally we finished with a few concluding remarks on GUI programming.

Remember where you were when you started this book? You wanted to write C++ and you were willing to do some real work to achieve that goal.

Now you've written a serious text editor in C++. Objects, inheritance, and overloading were vague concepts, but now they're part of your everyday working tools. You'll need some more practice to become a total C++ expert, but you've certainly learned how to write working code in this language.

It's certainly been fun writing this book, and I hope you've had some fun working your way through our project. Remember, programming should be more play than work. Code slowly and you'll get done quickly.

Enjoy your C++ programming!

IDG BOOKS WORLDWIDE LICENSE AGREEMENT

Important — read carefully before opening the software packet(s). This is a legal agreement between you (either an individual or an entity) and IDG Books Worldwide, Inc. (IDG). By opening the accompanying sealed packet(s) containing the software disk(s), you acknowledge that you have read and accept the following IDG License Agreement. If you do not agree and do not want to be bound by the terms of this Agreement, promptly return the book and the unopened software packet(s) to the place you obtained them for a full refund.

1. License. This License Agreement (Agreement) permits you to use one copy of the enclosed Software program(s) on a single computer. The Software is in "use" on a computer when it is loaded into temporary memory (i.e., RAM) or installed into permanent memory (e.g., hard disk, CD ROM, or other storage device) of that computer.

2. Copyright. The entire contents of this disk(s) and the compilation of the Software are copyrighted and protected by both United States copyright laws and international treaty provisions. The individual programs on the disk(s) are copyrighted by the authors of each program respectively. Each program has its own use permissions and limitations. You may only (a) make one copy of the Software for backup or archival purposes, or (b) transfer the Software to a single hard disk, provided that you keep the original for backup or archival purposes. To use each program, you must follow the individual requirements and restrictions detailed for each in Chapter 1 of this book. Do not use a program if you do not want to follow its Licensing Agreement. None of the material on this disk(s) or listed in this Book may ever be distributed, in original or modified form, for commercial purposes.

3. Other Restrictions. You may not rent or lease the Software. You may transfer the Software and user documentation on a permanent basis provided you retain no copies and the recipient agrees to the terms of this Agreement. You may not reverse engineer, decompile, or disassemble the Software except to the extent that the foregoing restriction is expressly prohibited by applicable law. If the Software is an update or has been updated, any transfer must include the most recent update and all prior versions. Each shareware program has its own use permissions and limitations. These limitations are contained in the individual license agreements that are on the software disks. The restrictions include a requirement that after using the program for a period of time specified in its text, the user must pay a registration fee or discontinue use. By opening the package which contains the software disk, you will be agreeing to abide by the licenses and restrictions for these programs. Do not open the software package unless you agree to be bound by the license agreements.

4. Limited Warranty. IDG Warrants that the Software and disk(s) are free from defects in materials and workmanship for a period of sixty (60) days from the date of purchase of this Book. If IDG receives notification within the warranty period of defects in material or workmanship, IDG will replace the defective disk(s). IDG's entire liability and your exclusive remedy shall be limited to replacement of the Software, which is returned to IDG with a copy of your receipt. This Limited Warranty is void if failure of the Software has resulted from accident, abuse, or misapplication. Any replacement Software will be warranted for the remainder of the original warranty period or thirty (30) days, whichever is longer.

5. No Other Warranties. To the maximum extent permitted by applicable law, IDG and the author disclaim all other warranties, express or implied, including but not limited to implied warranties of merchantability and fitness for a particular purpose, with respect to the Software, the programs, the source code contained therein and/or the techniques described in this Book. This limited warranty gives you specific legal rights. You may have others which vary from state/jurisdiction to state/jurisdiction.

6. No Liability For Consequential Damages. To the extent permitted by applicable law, in no event shall IDG or the author be liable for any damages whatsoever (including without limitation, damages for loss of business profits, business interruption, loss of business information, or any other pecuniary loss) arising out of the use of or inability to use the Book or the Software, even if IDG has been advised of the possibility of such damages. Because some states/jurisdictions do not allow the exclusion or limitation of liability for consequential or incidental damages, the above limitation may not apply to you.

7. U.S. Government Restricted Rights. Use, duplication, or disclosure of the Software by the U.S. Government is subject to restrictions stated in paragraph (c) (1) (ii) of the Rights in Technical Data and Computer Software clause of DFARS 252.227-7013, and in subparagraphs (a) through (d) of the Commercial Computer—Restricted Rights clause at FAR 52.227-19, and in similar clauses in the NASA FAR supplement, when applicable.

Index:
Quick Reference

Index

logical expressions, 112, 203–209
logical not operators, 204, 252
logical operators, 205
loop(s), 496, 504, 530, 550–552

breaking out of, 206, 208, 242, 345,
    472–473, 550
building single-line editors and, 220–
    221, 242, 275
counters, 472–473
debugging and, 129–130
do while loops, 220–221
infinite, 208
for loops, 204, 206, 496
moving by whole words and, 275
top-tested/bottom-tested, 220–221
while loops, 73, 122, 206, 275
lowercase/uppercase letters, 32, 193
lvalue, 368, 375, 421

M

Macintosh, 530, 591, 592–593
macros, 184, 203, 249, 304
    GOHOME macro, 235, 236–237, 238,
        264
    switch statements and, 244
    user command management and, 193–
        196
main(), 20–24, 42, 100–101
    building single-line editors and, 234,
        240–241, 247, 255, 277
    drawing boxes and, 60–65, 68–71, 80,
        89, 92
    file windows and, 340
    inheritance and, 147, 154, 156, 161,
        169–170, 181, 185–186
    member access privileges and, 107
    multiple files and, 534, 537, 538–539,
        543–544, 561–562
    popup boxes and, 161
    project files and, 197–198, 212, 215–
        216
    reading text files and, 289, 292–293,
        296, 328
    return statements and, 26–27
    startup() and, 60–65
mainline files, adding, 196–199
MAX_ANIMALS, 315
MAX_FILES, 564

IDG BOOKS WORLDWIDE

Order Center: **(800) 762-2974** *(8 a.m.–6 p.m., EST, weekdays)*

Quantity	ISBN	Title	Price	Total

Shipping & Handling Charges

	Description	First book	Each additional book	Total
Domestic	Normal	$4.50	$1.50	$
	Two Day Air	$8.50	$2.50	$
	Overnight	$18.00	$3.00	$
International	Surface	$8.00	$8.00	$
	Airmail	$16.00	$16.00	$
	DHL Air	$17.00	$17.00	$

*For large quantities call for shipping & handling charges.
**Prices are subject to change without notice.

Ship to:

Name _____

Company _____

Address _____

City/State/Zip _____

Daytime Phone _____

Payment: □ Check to IDG Books (US Funds Only)

□ VISA   □ MasterCard   □ American Express

Card # _____ Expires _____

Signature _____

Subtotal _____

CA residents add applicable sales tax _____

IN, MA, and MD residents add 5% sales tax _____

IL residents add 6.25% sales tax _____

RI residents add 7% sales tax _____

TX residents add 8.25% sales tax _____

Shipping _____

Total _____

Please send this order form to:

IDG Books Worldwide
7260 Shadeland Station, Suite 100
Indianapolis, IN 46256

*Allow up to 3 weeks for delivery.
Thank you!*

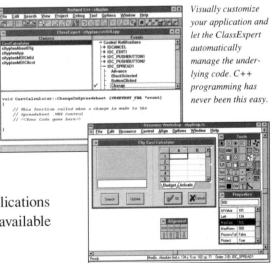

- **NEW!** 16-bit optimizing linker and profiler help speed up your 16-bit Windows applications.
- **NEW!** Faster 32-bit compilation is 50% faster and code runs up to 25% faster!

Turbo C++ 3.0 for DOS

Turbo C++ is a full-featured compiler that makes programming in C and C++ easy. With context-sensitive help, color syntax highlighting, and the Programmer's Platform IDE, you can create great applications quickly. A complete tutorial helps you quickly navigate the development environment and gain insight into C and C++ languages. Novices and professionals alike will appreciate the intuitive help system that answers your questions instantly. There's even sample code that you can paste into your own applications.

Turbo C++ 3.0 for DOS features:

- Easy-to-use Programmer's Platform IDE with color syntax highlighting
- Macro-based editor that supports full undo and redo, and editing of large files
- Integrated debugger with data and Object Inspectors,® and conditional breakpoints
- 100% ANSI C–compatible runtime libraries
- Turbo Librarian™ for creating and managing .LIB files
- On-line, context-sensitive help system
- Hands-on tutorials on C and C++ programming

This offer good in the U.S. and Canada only. International customers please contact your local Borland office for the offer in your country. Corporate Headquarters: 100 Borland Way, Scotts Valley, California 95066-3249, 408-431-1000. Internet: http://www.borland.com/ CompuServe: GO BORLAND. Offices in: Australia (61-2-911-1000), Canada (416-229-6000), France (33-1-41-23-11-00), Germany (49-6103-9790), Hong Kong (852-2572-3238), Japan (81-3-5350-9380), Latin American Headquarters in U.S.A. (408-431-1074), Mexico (52-5-687-7582), The Netherlands (+31 [0] 20 540 5472), Taiwan (886-2-718-6627), and United Kingdom ([0800] 973139).

Name _____

Address _____

City _____

State/Province _____ Zip/Postal code _____

Phone (_____) _____ Fax (_____) _____

To redeem this coupon, mail the original coupon (no photocopies, please) along with payment and shipping information to:

Borland International, Inc.
Order Processing
P.O. Box 660005
Scotts Valley, CA 95067-0005

Select one:

❏ Borland® C++ 4.5 for DOS, Windows, and Win32 (regularly $499)	CD-ROM	**$199.95**
❏ Turbo C++ 3.0 for DOS (regularly $99.95)	3.5″ disks	**$69.95**

Method of payment: ❏ Check enclosed†
❏ VISA ❏ MasterCard ❏ American Express

__ __ __ __ - __ __ __ __ - __ __ __ - __ __ __ __
card number

Expiration date: __ __ / __ __

Z1221

Subtotal	$ _____
State sales tax*	$ _____
Freight ($10.00 per item)	$ _____
Total order	$ _____

Limited to one per customer. Offer expires April 30, 1996.
*Residents of AZ, CA, CT, DC, FL, GA, IL, MA, MD, MN, MO, NC, NJ, OH, TN, UT, and VA, please add appropriate sales tax.
CO, MI, NY, PA, TX, and WA residents, please calculate tax based on product **and** freight charges. †Make checks payable to Borland International, Inc. Offer good in U.S. and Canada only. Purchase orders accepted upon approval—$500 minimum. Terms: Net 30 days. Borland reserves the right to modify or cancel this offer at any time. Copyright © 1995 Borland • BOR 8613

Borland

IDG BOOKS WORLDWIDE REGISTRATION CARD

RETURN THIS REGISTRATION CARD FOR FREE CATALOG

Title of this book: Learn C++ Today

My overall rating of this book: ❏ Very good [1] ❏ Good [2] ❏ Satisfactory [3] ❏ Fair [4] ❏ Poor [5]

How I first heard about this book:

❏ Found in bookstore; name: [6] ❏ Book review: [7]

❏ Advertisement: [8] ❏ Catalog: [9]

❏ Word of mouth; heard about book from friend, co-worker, etc.: [10] ❏ Other: [11]

What I liked most about this book:

What I would change, add, delete, etc., in future editions of this book:

Other comments:

Number of computer books I purchase in a year: ❏ 1 [12] ❏ 2-5 [13] ❏ 6-10 [14] ❏ More than 10 [15]

I would characterize my computer skills as: ❏ Beginner [16] ❏ Intermediate [17] ❏ Advanced [18] ❏ Professional [19]

I use ❏ DOS [20] ❏ Windows [21] ❏ OS/2 [22] ❏ Unix [23] ❏ Macintosh [24] ❏ Other: [25]_____
(please specify)

I would be interested in new books on the following subjects:
(please check all that apply, and use the spaces provided to identify specific software)

❏ Word processing: [26] ❏ Spreadsheets: [27]

❏ Data bases: [28] ❏ Desktop publishing: [29]

❏ File Utilities: [30] ❏ Money management: [31]

❏ Networking: [32] ❏ Programming languages: [33]

❏ Other: [34]

I use a PC at (please check all that apply): ❏ home [35] ❏ work [36] ❏ school [37] ❏ other: [38] _____

The disks I prefer to use are ❏ 5.25 [39] ❏ 3.5 [40] ❏ other: [41]_____

I have a CD ROM: ❏ yes [42] ❏ no [43]

I plan to buy or upgrade computer hardware this year: ❏ yes [44] ❏ no [45]

I plan to buy or upgrade computer software this year: ❏ yes [46] ❏ no [47]

Name: _____ Business title: [48] _____ Type of Business: [49] _____

Address (❏ home [50] ❏ work [51] /Company name: _____)

Street/Suite# _____

City [52]/State [53]/Zipcode [54]: _____ Country [55] _____

❏ **I liked this book!** You may quote me by name in future
IDG Books Worldwide promotional materials.

My daytime phone number is _____

IDG BOOKS
THE WORLD OF COMPUTER KNOWLEDGE

❏ YES!

Please keep me informed about IDG's World of Computer Knowledge.
Send me the latest IDG Books catalog.